HEMINGWAY'S ART
OF REVISION

HEMINGWAY'S ART OF REVISION

THE MAKING OF THE SHORT FICTION

JOHN BEALL

Louisiana State University Press ▐▐ Baton Rouge

Published by Louisiana State University Press
lsupress.org

Designer: Michelle A. Neustrom
Typefaces: Sentinel, text; Metropolis, display

Jacket photograph: Ernest Hemingway at his desk in Sun Valley, Idaho, 1940. Robert Capa © International Center of Photography / Magnum. The Robert Capa and Cornell Capa Archive, Gift of Cornell and Edith Capa, 1992.

Excerpts of Ezra Pound's unpublished "Inquest Sketch," "Essay on Inquest," and unpublished correspondence are used with the permission of New Directions, Mary de Rachewiltz, and the Estate of Omar S. Pound.

Portions of chapters 3, 4, 5, 6, and 8 were originally published, in somewhat different form, as follows: "Hemingway's Formation of *In Our Time*," *Hemingway Review*, vol. 35, no. 1, fall 2015, pp. 63–77, copyright © 2015 The Ernest Hemingway Foundation; "Hemingway as Craftsman: Revising 'Big Two-Hearted River,'" *Hemingway Review*, vol. 36, no. 2, spring 2017, pp. 79–94, copyright © 2017 The Ernest Hemingway Foundation; "Bugs and Sam: Nick Adams's Guides in 'The Battler' and 'The Killers,'" *Hemingway Review*, vol. 38, no. 2, spring 2019, pp. 42–58, copyright © 2019 The Ernest Hemingway Foundation; "Hemingway's and Perkins's Formation of *Men Without Women*," *Hemingway Review*, vol. 36, no. 1, fall 2016, pp. 94–102, copyright © 2016 The Ernest Hemingway Foundation; "Nick Adams's Interior Monologues in 'A Way You'll Never Be,'" *Hemingway Review*, vol. 40, no. 2, spring 2021, pp. 94–115, copyright © 2021 The Ernest Hemingway Foundation. All Rights Reserved.

Chapter 1 is a revised version of "Pound, Hemingway, and the Inquest Series," *Paideuma*, vol. 44, 2017. Chapter 3 is a revised version of "Hemingway's 'Cat in the Rain': The Presence of Stein and Joyce," *MidAmerica*, vol. 42, 2015. Chapter 6 is a revised version of "Hemingway's 'Now I Lay Me': Rivers, Writing, and Prayers," *MidAmerica*, vol. 44, 2017. Chapter 8 is a revised version of "The Dark Humor of Hemingway's 'A Way You'll Never Be," *Midwestern Miscellany*, vol. 47, spring/fall 2019. Chapter 10 is a revised version of "Hemingway as Craftsman: Revising 'Fathers and Sons,' *MidAmerica*, vol. 43, 2016.

Library of Congress Cataloging-in-Publication Data

Names: Beall, John, author.
Title: Hemingway's art of revision : the making of the short fiction / John Beall.
Description: Baton Rouge : Louisiana State University Press, [2024] | Includes bibliographical references and index.
Identifiers: LCCN 2023045162 (print) | LCCN 2023045163 (ebook) | ISBN 978-0-8071-8115-7 (cloth) | ISBN 978-0-8071-8224-6 (pdf) | ISBN 978-0-8071-8223-9 (epub)
Subjects: LCSH: Hemingway, Ernest, 1899–1961—Criticism, Textual. | Fiction—Editing. | Short stories, American—History and criticism.
Classification: LCC PS3515.E37 Z582343 2024 (print) | LCC PS3515.E37 (ebook) | DDC 813/.52—dc23/eng/20240213
LC record available at https://lccn.loc.gov/2023045162
LC ebook record available at https://lccn.loc.gov/2023045163

for
Sandy, James, William, and Elizabeth

CONTENTS

LIST OF ABBREVIATIONS ix

ACKNOWLEDGMENTS xi

Introduction 1

1   Pound's Influence on Hemingway's Revision of *in our time* 8

2   Joyce's "The Sisters" and Hemingway's Revision of
    "Indian Camp" 22

3   Stein, Joyce, and Hemingway's Rewriting "Cat in the Rain" 44

4   Revising "Big Two-Hearted River" 66

5   Revising "The Battler" and "The Killers" 95

6   Revising "Now I Lay Me" 113

7   Revising "Hills Like White Elephants" 133

8   Revising "A Way You'll Never Be" 153

9   Revising "The Gambler, the Nun, and the Radio" 187

10 From "Tomb of My Grandfather" to "Fathers and Sons" 209

    Conclusion 240

NOTES 251

WORKS CITED 269

INDEX 281

ABBREVIATIONS

I will refer to the Ernest Hemingway Collection at the John F. Kennedy Presidential Library and Museum as KL/EH.

In the abbreviations below, I follow the practice of Suzanne del Gizzo, editor of the *Hemingway Review,* and Sandra Spanier, general editor of the Cambridge Edition of *The Letters of Ernest Hemingway.* I am grateful to their editorial teams for creating and sharing this tool.

BL	*By-Line Ernest Hemingway: Selected Articles and Dispatches of Four Decades.* Edited by William White, Scribner's, 1967.
CSS	*The Complete Short Stories of Ernest Hemingway: The Finca Vigía Edition.* Scribner's, 1987.
DLT	*Dateline, Toronto: The Complete* Toronto Star *Dispatches, 1920–1924.* Edited by William White, Scribner's, 1985.
Letters vol. 1	*The Letters of Ernest Hemingway: Volume 1 (1907–1922).* Edited by Sandra Spanier and Robert W. Trogdon, Cambridge UP, 2011.
Letters vol. 2	*The Letters of Ernest Hemingway: Volume 2 (1923–1925).* Edited by Sandra Spanier, Albert J. DeFazio III, and Robert W. Trogdon, Cambridge UP, 2013.
Letters vol. 3	*The Letters of Ernest Hemingway: Volume 3 (1926–1929).* Edited by Rena Sanderson, Sandra Spanier, and Robert W. Trogdon, Cambridge UP, 2015.

Letters vol. 4	*The Letters of Ernest Hemingway: Volume 4 (1929–1931)*. Edited by Sandra Spanier and Miriam Mandel, Cambridge UP, 2017.
Letters vol. 5	*The Letters of Ernest Hemingway: Volume 5 (1932–1934)*. Edited by Sandra Spanier and Miriam Mandel, Cambridge UP, 2020.
MF	*A Moveable Feast.* Scribner's, 1964.
Poems	*Complete Poems.* Edited, with an introduction and notes, by Nicholas Gerogiannis, rev. ed., U of Nebraska P, 1992.
SAR-HLE	*The Sun Also Rises: The Hemingway Library Edition.* Edited by Seán Hemingway, Scribner's, 2014.
SL	*Ernest Hemingway: Selected Letters, 1917–1961.* Edited by Carlos Baker, Scribner's, 1981.
SS-HLE	*The Short Stories of Ernest Hemingway: The Hemingway Library Edition.* Edited by Seán Hemingway, Scribner's, 2017.

ACKNOWLEDGMENTS

I remain grateful to Don Daiker, who introduced me to Hemingway's work when I was his student at Miami University (Ohio). My favorite professor at Miami University, my mentor, and my lifelong friend, Don has offered me his unstinting encouragement since I first began writing what became the chapters on "Indian Camp" and "Cat in the Rain." I began that work in Sligo, Ireland, where I was studying in 2013 with Helen Vendler at the Yeats International Summer School. Somehow, in ways I cannot explain, my study of Yeats's process of composing poems like "The Wild Swans at Coole," so well presented in the Cornell series of Yeats's manuscripts and typescripts, led me back to Hemingway, then to the Hemingway Collection at the John F. Kennedy Presidential Library and Museum, and then to the archives at the Berg and Astor Collections of the New York Public Library, the Joyce Collection at the University of Buffalo, the Sylvia Beach and Scribner's Archives at the Firestone Library of Princeton University, and the Ezra Pound and Bill Bird archives at the Beinecke Library of Yale University. To the curators and archivists at those libraries, I owe my thanks. I owe a special word of thanks to Stacey Chandler, an archivist at the Kennedy Library. Early in my research, Stacey was kind enough to show me Hemingway's unbound press copy of James Joyce's *Ulysses*. Our examination of the cut and uncut pages of Hemingway's copy led to one of my first scholarly essays, "Ernest Hemingway's Reading of James Joyce's *Ulysses*." Late in my research for this book, Stacey was immensely helpful in answering a specific question about a passage in a manuscript of the short story "Hills Like White Elephants." Especially during the days of COVID-19, Stacey provided me with a long-distance lifeline to the Hemingway Collection at the Kennedy Library.

I am also deeply grateful to Abigail Malangone, an archivist at the Kennedy Library, for her support during a research visit to the Kennedy Library's Hemingway Collection in October 2023, my first visit since the onset of COVID-19.

Several of these chapters originated as presentations at biannual conferences of the Hemingway Society in Venice, Italy; Oak Park, Illinois; Paris, France; and Sheridan, Wyoming. Other presentations took place at the annual conferences of the Society for the Study of Midwestern Literature at Michigan State University. I want to thank three of my fellow panelists at those conferences for their ongoing and extremely helpful advice: Elizabeth Lloyd-Kimbrel, Ai Ogasawara, and Michael Kim Roos. I am grateful to the Van Horne Foundation led by Roger Murray Jr. Grants from the Van Horne Foundation enabled me to travel to those conferences, as well as to Boston for research in the Hemingway Collection. I have appreciated the support of the recent and current presidents of the Hemingway Society—the late H. R. ("Stoney") Stoneback, Joseph Flora, and Carl Eby. There is a long list of Hemingway scholars I would like to thank for their exemplary dedication to this work. Here I will simply single out Susan F. Beegel, who was kind enough to send me a copy of her book *Hemingway's Craft of Omission* when I had a hard time locating a copy. Susan's example of careful, independent scholarship remains a model I strive to follow. I am grateful as well to the late Peter Hays, who was kind enough to share his thoughts about the nature of Nick's wound in "A Way You'll Never Be." In addition, I am extremely grateful to J. Gerald Kennedy, Boyd Professor of English at Louisiana State University, for encouraging and supporting me as I have worked to complete this book.

I am deeply grateful to Helen Vendler and Teodolinda Barolini, two scholars who have taught me by example how to read lyric poetry and bring that poetry to life for my students. Helen's seminar on lyric poetry, sponsored by the National Endowment for the Humanities, remains an inspiration to me, as does Helen herself. Likewise, Teo's yearlong seminar on Dante's *Commedia* at Columbia University led me to teach dozens of students at Collegiate School about the comedy of Dante's poem. Those two classes remain high points in my career as a secondary school English teacher, ever striving to remain a student.

I want to pay tribute to my hundreds of students whose questions and insights into Hemingway's stories have inspired me. The students in the final class I taught at Collegiate School in New York City contributed substantially to my reading of "A Way You'll Never Be." My students helped me hear the crazed humor and appreciate the divergent narrative strands of this story. Our discussion of "A Way" began in March 2020 in a seminar room on the sixth floor of the school at 301 Freedom Place South in Manhattan. After spring break, we resumed our discussion online in April via ZOOM, as the spread of COVID-19 forced the school to shift to distance learning. In addition to the ZOOM discussions, my students carried on a lively, asynchronous exchange via an online forum. I remain in their debt for not only sustaining, but sharpening, their edge in probing the depths of this challenging, powerful story.

I want to express my particular gratitude to two exceptionally meticulous and supportive editors, Suzanne del Gizzo, editor of the *Hemingway Review,* and Marcia Noe, editor of *MidAmerica.* To Suzanne I am particularly grateful for taking the time to explain to me the copyright restrictions on extensive quotations from the manuscripts and typescripts that I transcribed and studied at the Hemingway Collection at the Kennedy Library. Moreover, I am thankful to her for her patience in bearing with me through sometimes lengthy and complicated revisions of my essays. To Marcia I remain grateful for her editing and publishing my first essay devoted to a Hemingway story, "Cat in the Rain," and for her support in carefully editing subsequent essays. In addition, I want to express my appreciation to the anonymous readers and reviewers of my submissions to these journals. These readers' feedback contributed mightily to my revising my submissions for the better. So, too, I owe a large debt of gratitude to the readers of my manuscript of this book for LSU Press. Their feedback was encouraging, constructive, and meticulous. I want to thank James W. Long, acquisitions editor at LSU Press, for his encouragement, support, and extensive guidance during the process of preparing my manuscript for publication. Furthermore, I am grateful to Susan Murray, freelance copyeditor, and Ashley Gilly, editorial assistant at LSU Press, for their careful work with the manuscript for this book.

I thank my wife, Sandra; two sons, James and William; and daughter, Elizabeth, to whom this book is dedicated. Their emotional support during my years of work in between teaching my classes at Collegiate School sustained me in ways I lack the words to express, except to say, "Thank you."

*
* *

Several of these chapters appeared in a different and earlier form in *Paideuma, MidAmerica, Midwestern Miscellany,* and the *Hemingway Review.* I want to thank the editors of these journals for granting permission to publish revised versions of those essays as chapters in this book. Specifically, I thank Betsy G. Rose, publications specialist, National Poetry Foundation, University of Maine, for permission to use material that originally appeared in my essay in *Paideuma.* I thank Marcia Noe, editor of *MidAmerica* and chair of the editorial committee for the Society for the Study of Midwestern Literature, for permission to use material that originally appeared in my essays in *MidAmerica* and *Midwestern Miscellany.* I thank Suzanne del Gizzo, editor of the *Hemingway Review,* for permission to use material that originally appeared in my essays in the *Hemingway Review.*

HEMINGWAY'S ART
OF REVISION

INTRODUCTION

In his column "Old Newsman Writes: A Letter from Cuba" (1934), Ernest Hemingway included a word of advice to young writers: "When you are excited about something is when the first draft is done. But no one can see it until you have gone over it again and again until you have communicated the emotion, the sights and the sounds to the reader" (*BL* 185). This book will offer new, close readings of major Hemingway stories based on manuscript studies of his revisions. The scholarly books in the *Reading Hemingway* series published by Kent State University Press have offered excellent commentaries about Hemingway's process of revising his novels: Mark Cirino on *Across the River and into the Trees;* Kirk Curnutt on *To Have and Have Not;* Carl P. Eby on *The Garden of Eden;* Robert W. Lewis and Michael Kim Roos on *A Farewell to Arms;* H. R. Stoneback on *The Sun Also Rises;* and Bickford Sylvester, Larry Grimes, and Peter L. Hays on *The Old Man and the Sea.* Frederic J. Svoboda's *Hemingway's* The Sun Also Rises: *The Crafting of a Style,* was a major early work focused on Hemingway's process of revising that novel. However, this book concentrates on Hemingway's short fiction. The major manuscript studies of Hemingway's short stories by Susan F. Beegel, Kathryn Derounian, Scott Donaldson, Bernard Oldsey, and Paul Smith are now decades old. Hilary Justice's more recent discussion of stories such as "A Canary for One" and "Hills Like White Elephants" offers perceptive observations about Hemingway's revision of his drafts. The even more recent publication of the Hemingway Library Edition of some of the stories makes possible the examination and direct quotation from Hemingway's drafts previously protected by copyright.

Most of the research for this book came during days of poring over and transcribing manuscripts and typescripts, with Hemingway's handwritten revisions, as preserved in the Hemingway Collection at the John F. Kennedy Presidential Library and Museum. Since the mid-1980s, copyright restraints have proscribed any extensive quotations from those drafts. However, many of those manuscripts and typescripts now are published in the Hemingway Library Edition of the stories—and therefore can be quoted and discussed. These stories include "Indian Camp," "Cat in the Rain," "Big Two-Hearted River," "The Killers," "Hills Like White Elephants," "A Way You'll Never Be," "The Gambler, the Nun, and the Radio," and "Fathers and Sons." In addition, the publication by Cambridge University Press of Hemingway's *Letters* provides new insight into his three major collections of stories: *In Our Time, Men Without Women,* and *Winner Take Nothing.*

The value of manuscript study is to trace the writer's creation of his work of art—to "reconstruct an author's process of composition" (Beegel, *Hemingway's Craft* 9). Viewers of the PBS series on Hemingway by Ken Burns and Lynn Novick saw glimpses of this process of composition in the projection of pages of manuscripts in Hemingway's own handwriting. Careful study of manuscripts to trace a writer's process of revision has been a key aspect of major studies of Shakespeare and Yeats—to cite just two examples. In his chapter "Second Thoughts" in *A Year in the Life of William Shakespeare: 1599,* James Shapiro examines Shakespeare's extensive revisions while writing *Hamlet.* As a result of his careful study of the quarto and folio editions of the play, Shapiro concludes, "The revisions also tell a story of Shakespeare's decision to alter the trajectory of the play and shore up the resolve of its hero" (305). Aside from exploring such a major element of Shakespeare's revisions, Shapiro also examines the significance of his smaller alterations in the text. Observing that "Shakespeare tinkered excessively—far more than his reputation for never blotting a line would suggest," Shapiro demonstrates how "the smallest of changes complicate Hamlet's character" (305–6). His careful study of the various texts for *Hamlet* enabled Shapiro to shed light not just on Shakespeare's compositional process but on his artistic decisions about portraying Hamlet.

Likewise, Helen Vendler in *Our Secret Discipline* draws continuously from the manuscripts of Yeats's poems collected in the multivolume series published by Cornell University Press. To refer to just one of the examples in her book, Vendler discusses Yeats's revision of the couplet that ends "Among School Children." Quoting the original couplet preserved in the manuscript materials of *The Tower*, the volume in which Yeats published the poem, Vendler discusses the "radical revision" the poet made. In the early draft Yeats ended the poem with this couplet:

> O dancing couple, glance that mirrors glance,
> How can we know the dancer from the dance?

Vendler then explains the limits of this couplet's ending the poem with an "immemorial sexual image of a dancing couple moving in perfect synchrony and gazing into each other's eyes" (285). Thus, with access to the earlier draft, she discusses Yeats's couplet as it appeared in *The Tower*:

> O body swayed to music, O brightening glance,
> How can we know the dancer from the dance?

By tracing Yeats's evolution of the closing couplet in "Among School Children," Vendler unfolds how the poem's music "leaves open an infinite number of possibilities for self-choreography," not limited to the mutual sexual gaze of a dancing couple (285). In studying Yeats's composition of "Among School Children," Vendler makes fruitful use of the manuscript materials that the Cornell Yeats series has made available to readers.

  With the partial publication of manuscript materials related to several of Hemingway's major stories in the Hemingway Library Edition, a renewed attention to his revisions can explore his developing from a young craftsman learning from his mentors Gertrude Stein, Ezra Pound, and James Joyce to a master craftsman revising major stories like "Big Two-Hearted River," "A Way You'll Never Be," and "Fathers and Sons." Whereas Susan F. Beegel's emphasis is on Hemingway's revision by omission, a major focus of this book will be on his revision by replacement and addition. In that regard I follow Scott Donaldson's lead in his 1978 essay on the story "A Canary for One." In that essay Donaldson discusses the significance of "several additions to the final draft of his story" ("Preparing for the End" 264). Donaldson argues persuasively that these additions "make the climax seem less abrupt" (267). He concludes that Hemingway's revisions to "Canary" show the work of "a masterly craftsman in command of difficult and sensitive subject matter" (268). This book will explore Hemingway's craftsmanship from small touches to major revisions of his short stories.

As an editor of Ford Madox Ford's *Transatlantic Review,* Hemingway observed firsthand James Joyce's revision by addition in the "Work in Progress" that would become *Finnegans Wake.* As Hemingway wrote to Ezra Pound about the excerpt of Joyce's "Work" that appeared in the April 1924 *Transatlantic Review* (along with his own story "Indian Camp"), "His manuscript started at 7 pages (printed) but by additions to the manuscript in microscopic handwriting eventually reached about 9 pages" (*Letters* vol. 2, 103). Furthermore, a principal influence on Hemingway's revision by addition was Joyce's *Ulysses,* as illustrated so vividly in a recent exhibition at the Morgan Library and Museum in New York, *One Hundred Years of James Joyce's* Ulysses (Tóibín). Understandably, scholars have focused on the influence of Pound and Imagism on Hemingway's spare style, but in fact he also learned from his mentors about revision as expansion. Indeed, in Hemingway's novel *The Garden of Eden,* the character David Bourne reflects on his process of revising his African stories: "He read it over and saw the gaps he must fill in to make it so that whoever read it would feel it was truly happening as it was read and he marked the gaps in the margin" (201). In this regard, David Bourne's plan to revise, in part, by filling in the gaps seems to reflect Hemingway's own process of revision by addition in his fiction.

The first chapter of this book examines the process of Hemingway's revising drafts from the initial publication of six vignettes in the *Little Review,* followed by the eighteen chapters of *in our time* (1924), and finally appearing in print as the interchapters of *In Our Time* (1925). In the case of *in our time,* the drafts of "Nick sat against the wall" have already been published and discussed (Derounian), and the composition of *in our time* as a whole has been thoroughly examined by Milton Cohen in *Hemingway's Laboratory.* However, this chapter focuses more completely on the impact of Ezra Pound, Hemingway's first editor, who deeply influenced his art of revision. The second chapter explores the manuscripts and typescripts, now accessible with the publication of the Hemingway Library Edition of the stories, that show the development of "Indian Camp." The chapter discusses James Joyce's revisions of "The Sisters" and Hemingway's revisions of "Indian Camp" as stories opening *Dubliners* and *In Our Time* with narratives of boys encountering death. Specifically, the chapter traces Hemingway's revising "Indian Camp" to focus on young Nick Adams's viewpoint at the moment he discovers that the Ojibway father has slit his throat with a razor. In so doing, Hemingway follows Joyce's "The Sisters," with its focus on a young acolyte's viewpoint as he peers at the face of his dead priest lying in his coffin on his bed.

The third chapter examines "Cat in the Rain," a story Hemingway started during a visit to Pound in Rapallo, Italy—and then substantially rewrote several times. Hemingway's revisions reflect the influence of Gertrude Stein and James Joyce in the story's hypnotic repetitions, clipped dialogue, and juxtaposition of marriage stories with vignettes of bullfighting. The fourth chapter explores three directions of Hemingway's revisions to his initial drafts of "Big Two-Hearted River"—his efforts to capture a vernacular American voice, to keep the focal viewpoint inside Nick Adams's perspective, and to evoke a tactile sensation of Nick's fishing, losing, and catching trout. Considering Hemingway's revision by expansion, this chapter examines in detail three pages Hemingway added by hand to the draft describing the flight of a kingfisher and swimming of a trout that Nick observes carefully when he first arrives at the river. In addition, the chapter examines two distinct areas of his revision by omission: first, his deleting or altering virtually every single reference to war. Second, in one of his most well-known omissions, he followed the strong advice of Gertrude Stein and cut the original ending full of digressive, metafictional self-reflection. With his process of massively revising "River," Hemingway both responded to the critical feedback of Gertrude Stein and forged his own path in this masterful work of fiction.

The fifth chapter explores Hemingway's revision of "The Battler" and "The Killers" to develop two African American characters as guides for the white boy, Nick Adams. For example, Hemingway revised "The Killers" to relocate the setting from Petoskey, Michigan, to Summit, Illinois, a suburb of Chicago. Hemingway shifted to a location where his portrait of Sam, an African American character, would present racial conflict as an important dimension of the story. Although Sam is not as central to "The Killers" as Bugs is to "The Battler," Hemingway's portrait of this character is subtle and complex. The sixth chapter explores the extensive process of revision that Hemingway undertook from the initial drafts of "Now I Lay Me" to its publication as the final story in *Men Without Women*. The chapter focuses on the multiple drafts of the story, with Hemingway presenting Nick Adams as a soldier near the Italian front, keeping himself awake by remembering both actual and imagined rivers. Thus, Hemingway portrays Nick's real and imagined fishing as evoking the therapeutic effect of his writing stories like "Big Two-Hearted River." The seventh chapter offers a close reading of "Hills Like White Elephants," based on a comparison of a manuscript Hemingway drafted in 1925; a completely different manuscript he wrote by hand in 1927 (likely the basis for the version he sent to the editors of the journal *transition,* published in its August 1927 issue); and the final version of the story published that same year in *Men Without Women,* his second collection of stories.

The eighth chapter examines the complex process of revisions Hemingway undertook in transforming "A Way You'll Never Be" into a haunting portrait of postwar trauma. This chapter explores how Hemingway revised the story to include the relatively late addition of complex interior monologues with stream-of-consciousness shifts of setting and time. Bearing the influence of Joyce's *Ulysses,* these monologues depict Nick Adams's struggle to cope with his traumatic memories of being wounded while fighting on the Italian front. Furthermore, in the process of massively revising the story, Hemingway shifted from an extended, serious lecture by an Italian lieutenant to a comical, manic monologue by Nick Adams about his role as an advanced guard of American soldiers coming to join the Allied forces in the war. Added to the story as Hemingway revised it, these monologues, both interior and spoken, are pivotal to the story's portrait of Nick's recovery of balance. The end result is one of Hemingway's most powerful narratives of trauma and endurance.

The ninth chapter examines Hemingway's process of revision in composing a story that began as a sketch of patients on the same floor of a hospital where he was recuperating from a badly broken arm after a car accident. In a letter to Archibald MacLeish, Hemingway offered a portrait of a Mexican gambler, a nun, and a radio that became the central characters in that story. Focusing on the multiple manuscript and typescript drafts published in the Hemingway Library Edition of the short stories, this chapter includes a study of Hemingway's various additions to the story's ending—additions even after its initial publication with the title "Give Us a Prescription, Doctor" in *Scribner's Magazine.* Furthermore, the chapter considers how Hemingway's story, ultimately titled "The Gambler, the Nun, and the Radio," subverts conventions of the Western, as reflected in both Owen Wister's *The Virginian* and the 1929 film adaptation of the novel.

The tenth chapter concludes this study of Hemingway's art of revision in his short fiction with "Fathers and Sons," the final story in *Winner Take*

Nothing, the final collection of new stories Hemingway assembled. In his *Reader's Guide to the Short Stories of Ernest Hemingway,* Paul Smith observes that "No other manuscripts show more extensive and detailed revisions through so many versions than do those of 'Fathers and Sons'" (310). This chapter takes advantage of the recent publication of drafts, including the full-length "The Tomb of My Grandfather," in the Hemingway Library Edition. In "Fathers and Sons," Hemingway's late additions and revisions show his striving to strike a balance between elegiac memories of his father, starkly ironic comments about the cosmetic art of a mortician, and a candidly critical portrait of a teenage Nick as a truculent racist defending his sister. Thus, in the last Nick Adams story published in a collection Hemingway assembled during his life, he explores Nick both as son and as father of a boy whose curiosity echoes the young Nick's inquisitiveness in "Indian Camp" about birth, death, and suicide. The book's conclusion offers reflections about the future of manuscript study as a means of exploring Hemingway's art. Taking "The Snows of Kilimanjaro" as a case study, the conclusion considers both the challenges and the opportunities facing readers of Hemingway wishing to understand his process of composition and revision.

The ultimate aim of this book is twofold: First, to document and underscore the deep extent to which Hemingway was persistently committed to the art of revision. As he preached in his advice to young writers in "Old Newsman Writes," Hemingway wrote and rewrote his best stories "over and over again." This book takes advantage of the recent publication of the Hemingway Library Edition of most of the stories discussed in the chapters below. ("The Battler" and "Now I Lay Me" are the two exceptions.) Thus, I hope to follow in the footsteps of the masterful manuscript studies by Susan F. Beegel, Kathryn Derounian, Scott Donaldson, Paul Smith, Hilary Justice, and others. Second, my aim is to offer a series of close readings that explore the artistic craftsmanship of some of Hemingway's finest stories. In that regard, I strive to follow the lead of Joseph Flora and Robert Paul Lamb, two scholars whose books about the stories have deeply influenced my own readings and teaching.

1

POUND'S INFLUENCE ON HEMINGWAY'S REVISION OF *IN OUR TIME*

As a writer in the avant-garde Paris scene of the early 1920s, Ernest Hemingway came under the tutelage and guidance of Ezra Pound. Recently having been central to the editing and revision of James Joyce's *Ulysses* and T. S. Eliot's *The Waste Land,* Pound was Hemingway's principal sponsor and editor for the "Exiles" issue of the *Little Review* in 1923, published by Margaret Anderson and Jane Heap. Despite losing an obscenity court case after publishing the "Nausicaa" chapter of *Ulysses* in its April 1920 issue, the publishers Anderson and Heap remained active, with Ezra Pound listed alongside them as "Administration" on the title page of the "Exiles" issue. As they explained in a "Comments" section at the end, "This number is called an Exiles number because all of the contributors are at present pleasantly exiled in Europe. Although it was Ezra Pound's idea, we have nothing in the issue to represent him" (Anderson and Heap 25). Although Pound included none of his own work in the issue, as its first entry he included six prose pieces by Ernest Hemingway, entitled in bold caps **IN OUR TIME**.

These six vignettes opened an issue that included works by Gertrude Stein, H.D., E. E. Cummings, an essay by Fernand Léger dedicated to Pound, a musical score of "Airplane Sonata" by George Antheil, artwork by Léger (including an abstract cover of a strange upright figure with a hole in its belly), and Joan Miró's *The Farm,* a painting Hemingway would later purchase. Nicholas Joost argues that the placement of Hemingway's "Imagist vignettes" so prominently at the opening of the "Exiles" issue "is evidence enough of the impression he made on Margaret Anderson and Jane Heap" (53). The placement of Hemingway's six sketches is more likely to reflect Pound's idea, as editor of the issue. In short, probably due to Pound, Hemingway made his first appearance in the "Exiles" issue that was a showcase of modernist French, British, and American artists living in Paris at the time. Hemingway's six vignettes provide a baseline with which to observe his work with Ezra Pound as his first editor. In this case Pound encouraged and guided Hemingway in reusing and recasting these vignettes as part of the Paris *in our time*. Thus, this study of Hemingway's art of revision begins with his collaboration with Pound in contributing to the *Little Review* and to the "Inquest" series of which Hemingway's *in our time* was the concluding work.

The complicated story began in early 1922, when Hemingway met Pound, probably at Sylvia Beach's bookstore in Paris, Shakespeare and Company (Hurwitz 470; Reck 40–41). In a letter to his mother on 15 February 1922, Hemingway mentioned that "Friday we are going to tea at the Ezra Pounds. He has asked me to do an article on the present literary state of America for the Little Review" (*Letters* vol. 1, 329). Even though no such article was published, Hemingway wrote Sherwood Anderson on 9 March that Pound "took a story for the Little Review" (*Letters* vol. 1, 331). In the same letter, he wrote Anderson that he was teaching Pound how to box "wit [*sic*] little success." However, less than two weeks later, Hemingway wrote that he was "boxing regular" with Pound, who "has developed a terrific wallop" (*Letters* vol. 1, 335). In April 1922 Hemingway, a special staff correspondent for the *Toronto Daily Star,* met Bill Bird, the European manager of the Consolidated Press Association, when they were both covering the Genoa Economic Conference in Italy (Ford 95; Reynolds, *Paris Years* 41–47). The story continued later that year in July, when Bill Bird purchased an old hand press and founded Three Mountains Press. Hemingway suggested that Bird should contact Pound about potential manuscripts (Reynolds, *Paris Years* 80). Meanwhile, the young American artist Henry Strater met both Hemingway and Pound. By Christmas 1922 Strater had begun work on the illustrations for the capitals of Pound's *A Draft of Sixteen Cantos* (Culver 448–49).

Thus, the foundation was laid for the remarkable story of Pound's eliciting and editing Hemingway's short prose chapters, six of which were first published in the "Exiles" 1923 issue of the *Little Review* that Pound directed. Unnumbered, and separated by three asterisks on the center of the page, those six vignettes include a monologue narrated by a former kitchen colonel who recalls a drunken battery of soldiers marching toward Champagne, where a bloody battle would take place. The second vignette is of a bullfight before Hemingway had ever witnessed one firsthand (Cohen 133–34). The third is of a Greek retreat, a reprise of two journalistic pieces, "A Silent, Ghastly Procession" and "Refugees from Thrace," reports that Hemingway had written for the 20 October and 14 November 1922 issues of the *Toronto Daily Star* (*DLT* 232, 249–52). Then follow two vignettes narrated in a British voice about fighting at Mons, site of a battle between British and German soldiers in August 1914 (Cohen 144). The final vignette is an imaginative revision of newspaper accounts of the execution of six Greek ministers by firing squad on 28 November 1922 (Cohen 148). Below the final line of these six vignettes, in all caps, is the author's name, ERNEST HEMINGWAY.

Pound's role in sending Hemingway's poems to Harriet Monroe for *Poetry Magazine* and to Scofield Thayer for the *Dial,* and including him so prominently in the "Exiles" issue of the *Little Review,* must have encouraged the young writer, probably known more for his reporting on postwar conferences at Genoa and Lausanne than as a writer of fiction (Reynolds, *Paris Years* 26–28). In a letter written during the winter of 1922–23 to the editors of the *Little Review,* Pound offered to "arrange a number" of the *Review* including "possibly Cocteau, B. M. G. Adams, Hemingway," and others. As a price for his services, Pound stipulated that the publishers should include in the *Little Review* a "full page ad, of THREE MOUNTAINS PRESS"—that is, of the six volumes in the "Inquest" series (*Pound/*The Little Review 297). As Pound insisted, the publishers of the *Little Review* included at the back of the "Exiles" issue dated April 1923 (but published later) a full-page ad for the "Inquest" series. The final title listed was "blank" by Ernest Hemingway, who did not yet have a title. Pound's inclusion of Hemingway in the "Exiles" issue as the first author in an avant-garde ensemble including Gertrude Stein, George Antheil, E. E. Cummings, H.D., and Fernand Léger was an important, early step in his mentoring the younger writer.

Readers who wish to explore marks of Hemingway's revising these pieces published in the *Little Review* should consult especially the "drafts" sections of Milton Cohen's comprehensive study *Hemingway's Laboratory: The Paris* in our time (132–33, 136, 142–43, 146, 152–53). For example, Cohen discusses the substantial revisions in the narrative of the Greek retreat published in the *Little Review* from his journalistic versions that had appeared earlier in the *Toronto Star.* He concludes by emphasizing Hemingway's revision by excision: "The cutting of colorful details demonstrates Hemingway's art of compression, of letting the single image stand for the plethora" (139). Without naming Pound in his discussion of Hemingway's revision, Cohen's analysis suggests the impact of Pound's "Imagism." As Pound recalled his role in shaping the principles of Imagism, he emphasized the importance of "direct treatment, economy of words. . . . Use no superfluous word, no adjective which does not reveal something" (*Literary Essays* 4). Also worth noting is that the pieces in the *Little Review* reflect a substantial step in Hemingway's development from a writer of journalism to a writer of fiction. Even the vignettes based on events he witnessed firsthand, like the retreat of the Greeks, are shaped, altered, and reshaped, as Hemingway practiced his craft.

Those six vignettes were then published as chapters, with a dozen additional chapters, in the 1924 publication by Three Mountains Press of *in our time*, edited by Ezra Pound as part of the "Inquest" series that began with Pound's *Indiscretions* (Ford 95–116; Moody 78–79; Reynolds, *Paris Years* 4, 22, 26–27, 80). Bird's plans for publishing Hemingway's *in our time* were preparatory to his publication of what he called, in a letter to Hemingway dated 4 September 1923, "the great folio edition of the modern divina commedia"—that is, Pound's *Draft of XVI Cantos*.[1] Hemingway's letter to Pound dated 5 August 1923 is a direct testament to Pound's editing of specific chapters ("Have redone the death of Maera altogether") and to his defending the unity of the collection. In response to Pound's apparent challenge, Hemingway wrote that the chapters "all hook up" and explained why (*Letters* vol. 2, 41–42). Hemingway attested directly to the influence of Pound as his editor who encouraged him to revise "altogether"—that is, completely recast—his earlier draft of the Maera chapter. Thus, Pound's collaboration with Hemingway on *in our time* was significant in his shepherding the younger writer at the beginning of his vocation.

Central to this story of Pound's guiding the development of Hemingway's *in our time* is his role in overseeing the "Inquest" series. In an unpublished essay that Pound wrote, probably in 1926, he gave a clear account of the inception of this series. According to Pound, in 1922 Bill Bird approached him, initially asking him to write a series of pieces to be published by Three Mountains Press: "That is to say I was to write it all, and he was to print it all, with pomp and no circumstance. I declined. I also declined to publish a small series of books by myself in favour of the series now labled [*sic*] 'The Inquest'" (Pound, "Essay on Inquest").[2] As he continued, Pound explained that the focus of the inquest was on the possibilities for fiction after *Ulysses:* "In 1922 the world groaned under the weight of Ulysses: was there anything else to be written? Had not the eminent J.J. killed off ALL imbeciles, cleared the air of ALL the crapule . . . could anyone write anything in prose that wouldn't be simply a come-down?" ("Essay on Inquest"). Pound seems to ask that question rhetorically with the implied answer as "no," but his oversight of the "Inquest" series, during years when he was completing his *Draft of XVI Cantos,* suggests his personal involvement in the question of the room left for writers after *Ulysses.* Perhaps he was asking himself such questions as a poet who was composing his first cantos before and after helping Joyce finish *Ulysses* and Eliot complete *The Waste Land* (Bush 239; Read 125–44). The only part of his "Essay on Inquest" that Pound published was a note at the end of the version of *Indiscretions* reprinted in *Pavannes and Divagations.* Pound listed the six works that were part of the series exploring "the state of prose after *Ulysses.*" Looking back, he concluded, "The series constituted a critical act" (51). That is, Pound regarded the series as "critical" in exploring whether writers like William Carlos Williams and Hemingway could "tell the truth . . . without fake, melodrama, conventional ending" (50–51). Thus, Pound's work on Hemingway's *in our time,* which followed his editing of Joyce's *Ulysses* and Eliot's *The Waste Land,* was part of his oversight of a series explicitly designed to reflect the state of English prose after Joyce's novel.

Hemingway himself was not so certain about his role in the Three Mountains Press series. On 8 November 1922, he wrote to Pound expressing his reservations, commenting that "I know what I'm after in prose" and adding, "I hope to give you a couple of samples of it at the end of six months." Hemingway added that he appreciated "that you stuck me on the Three Mountains dodger out of friendship." Continuing in this colloquial vein, Hemingway pledged not to "crab the act, bust up the show or detonate in any other way if you now regret having backed some one who you realize has nothing worth printing and want to yank me out of the sextette" (*Letters* vol. 1, 364). Hemingway's hesitation may have reflected his having written more journalism than fiction in the preceding months. Indeed, on 16 November 1922, Hemingway wrote Harriet Monroe, editor of *Poetry,* asking if she would give him permission to use the poems she had accepted for her journal in the volume that Ezra Pound was editing for Three Mountains Press (*Letters* vol. 1, 366–67). His letters suggest his lack of confidence about how well his fictional prose would contribute to the "Inquest" series.

In a letter to his father dated 19 May 1923, Pound wrote: "Hem coming on. Prose hopes. Some of D's designs for Elimus very good" (*Pound to His Parents* 512). By connecting Hemingway's "prose hopes" with Dorothy Shakespeare's designs for another work in the "Inquest" series, Pound clearly had *in our time* in mind in his positive comment about Hemingway. After all, by May 1923, Hemingway already had his first six chapters coming out in the *Little Review,* and he was probably already at work on the next chapters, starting with "Nick sat against the wall" (Cohen 40–42). The first chapter Hemingway wrote after the six that appeared in the *Little Review* was probably the first reference in Hemingway's published work to his character Nick Adams. Under Pound's supervision, Hemingway's revision of this chapter also reflects his learning to substantially improve his writing by reworking his initial drafts.

Hemingway's extensive and meticulous revisions in the drafts for this chapter have been transcribed and analyzed by Kathryn Derounian. There are basically three types of revisions: (1) deletions reflecting what Susan F. Beegel has called Hemingway's "craft of omission," (2) replacements indicating his rewriting words or phrases, and (3) additions expanding on the earlier drafts. All told, the drafts published in Derounian's essay amount to dozens of revisions, large and small. These revisions contribute in two major ways to the power of the chapter. First, Hemingway's revisions replace earlier, explicit references to humor—for instance, explicit references to Nick's bemused laughter—with the implied irony in Nick's pledging a "separate peace" while speaking to an Italian soldier who may already be unconscious or dead. Furthermore, the revisions focus more on the wounded Nick's point of view, as he lies against the wall of a church, waiting for stretcher bearers to carry him away from the battle. As Kathryn Derounian concludes, Hemingway's revisions "conveyed Nick's shocked reaction" to his being wounded (75).

Hemingway initially planned an explicitly comical version of Nick's wounding, as suggested by the titles of earlier drafts as "Humor" and "Humorist" (Derounian 66, 68, 71). In the course of revising his drafts, Hemingway deleted each explicit reference to Nick's laughter at a joke—laughter that would seem incongruous with a soldier seriously wounded. In the draft Derounian labeled "B," Hemingway struck "laughed" from the sentence that became "Nick turned his head" (Derounian 69; *CSS* 105). Hemingway ended this draft with the sentence, "It was a good joke," as if Nick is laughing off his comrade's "breathing with difficulty" as part of a cosmic comedy. By draft "C," Hemingway has cut the last line with its reference to "a good joke." He struck out the clause "but the joke was good" (Derounian 73). The final typescript version tones down the explicit reference to a "joke" and instead implies Nick's sense of a failed performance in speaking to Rinaldi about "a separate peace." Hemingway ends the chapter with an understatement: "Rinaldi was a disappointing audience" (*CSS* 105). Thus, the grim joke becomes more implicit and less obvious: the dark humor is that Nick is speaking either to himself, as Rinaldi may be unconscious and perhaps fatally wounded, or to Rinaldi, who, though conscious, is struggling and cannot respond. These revisions suggest the mark of Pound's editing—or of Hemingway's internalizing Pound's teaching him to cut the fat from his writing. The stark comedy of this chapter is strengthened by Hemingway's letting the joke—Nick's assuring a possibly unconscious man about a separate peace—stand for itself. Hemingway's simple, direct prose would seem to fit the prescriptions Pound implied in his praise of H.D.'s poems in a letter to Harriett Monroe as "no slither, direct" (*Letters of Ezra Pound* 11) and of Joyce's fiction as "hard, clear-cut, with no waste of words" (Pound and Reed 90). By leaving out any sense of Nick's macho laughter, Hemingway in this chapter of *in our time* essentially revised tales he had told and poems he had written earlier about the Italian front.

In his letter to John Quinn dated 10 August 1922, Pound wrote: "Hemingway is a good chap. Was with Italian Arditi, buried alive, or rather dead for five days, with no special reason for coming to. Nonsense knocked out of him, if there ever was any in him" (*Letters to Quinn* 216–17).[3] Hemingway's story to Pound about being buried alive while fighting with the Arditi was almost certainly a fiction (Reynolds, *Young Hemingway* 18). Hemingway honed the story when he was recuperating in Milan from his war wound (Reynolds, *Young Hemingway* 32). When he returned home to Oak Park, he spoke at his high school and was featured in newspaper stories (Reynolds, *Young Hemingway* 56; L. Hemingway 54–56). He wrote "The Woppian Way," an unpublished short story about an ex-boxer turned fighter with the Arditi (KL/EH folder 844; Reynolds, *Young Hemingway* 58–59). The Arditi again appeared in Hemingway's "Riparto d'Assalto"—a poem Pound helped Hemingway publish in *Poetry Magazine*—as the shock troops who swept to Mount Grappa in "camion" trucks (*Poems* 46; Reynolds, *Young Hemingway*

56). That Pound believed Hemingway's tale suggests the latter's ability to recount war stories with a compelling air of truthfulness.

Aside from revision by deletion, Hemingway also revised by replacing his initial phrasing with less melodramatic and more vivid language. In Hemingway's earliest draft, the chapter began with what Pound described in "Hugh Selwyn Mauberley" as "hysterias, trench confessions" (*New Selected Poems* 113). In the initial draft, Nick is positioned in a trench, actively trying to stanch his wound: "Nick was sitting in the trench twisting a tourniquet around his ankle" (Derounian 66).[4] In revising this draft Hemingway presented Nick as more passive—not in a trench but propped "against the wall of the church," seemingly benumbed and dazed (*CSS* 105). Hemingway shifted from Nick in the setting for a "trench confession" to Nick's leaning against the exterior of a church, perhaps poised for a more religious confession (Nickel 41). Thus, Hemingway revised the opening of this chapter from a melodramatic scene of Nick in a trench frantically improvising a tourniquet to the more understated setting of Nick's lying, immobile, against a wall.

Other replacements clarify and specify what Nick observes in the battle scene around him. Initially, Hemingway wrote simply that "they had dragged him from what was going forward." Instead of that vague explanation for why Nick had been dragged to the church, Hemingway replaced "what was going forward" with the more specific "to be clear of machine gun fire in the street" (Derounian 66–68). At times Hemingway replaced and altered initial words or phrases several times. For instance, in Draft A, Nick observed "two *cadavre* crumpled looking" before turning his attention to the Italian soldier who "lay still" next to him (Derounian 66). In Draft B, he added "Austrian" before "cadavre" but retained the French word out of keeping with the rest of the scene. By Draft C, Hemingway changed "two Austrian *cadavre*" to "corpses." He then deleted "corpses" and replaced it simply with "Two Austrian dead." Likewise, Hemingway revised his description of Nick's final physical movement—turning his head to look at the Italian soldier beside him. In Draft A, Nick "laughed twist" [*sic*] his head carefully" (Derounian 66). Hemingway fixed the phrasing error in Draft B; he deleted "laughed" and wrote, "Nick turned his head" (Derounian 69). In Draft C, Hemingway at first wrote: "Nick turned his head away smiling brilliantly." By hand he then added "carefully" in pencil after "head"; in ink he struck out "brilliantly" and replaced it with "sweatily." While these may seem slight changes, they present Nick as an alert observer perspiring (not smiling "brilliantly") under the hot sun. Thus, Hemingway replaced fancier references to the dead and to Nick with simpler, more concrete language.

In the course of revising his drafts for this chapter, Hemingway also added several details that render Nick's observations more vividly. For instance, at the bottom of Draft A, Hemingway typed a sentence that remains in the print version, "The pink wall of the house opposite had fallen out from the roof and an iron bedstead hung twisted toward the street" (Derounian 66–68; *CSS* 105). This addition evokes the signs of battle that Nick can see, even if he is immobilized, with the twisted iron bedstead a vivid suggestion of his own body's damage. Likewise, in the initial Draft A, Hemingway wrote in pencil beneath the typed text more sentences that remain in the print version: "Things were getting forward in the town. It was going well. Stretcher bearers would be along any time now" (Derounian 69; *CSS* 105). These added sentences offer a bridge between Nick's visual observations of the battle rubble and his spoken words to the Italian soldier next to him. In particular, the sentences move from Nick's vague optimism ("It was going well") to his anxious hope that stretcher bearers would arrive soon to remove him from the line of fire. Only then does Nick turn his attention from the shattered roof and bed frame before him to the soldier at his side. Hemingway's revisions slow down the scene so that the reader is, as Derounian suggests, "looking at separate frames of a film and seeing . . . from Nick's restricted viewpoint" (64).

Pound probably edited Hemingway's drafts of chapter 7 during the spring and early summer of 1923, when he was working on that chapter (Cohen 40–42). Hemingway's letter to Pound of 5 August 1923 reported that he had redone the chapter on Maera's death (now "altogether different") and "fixed the others" (*Letters* vol. 2, 41). There is little reason to doubt Pound's editing of Hemingway's chapters for *in our time,* despite the absence of Pound's handwritten editing, such as is preserved in Valerie Eliot's edition of her husband's *Waste Land.* Besides his letter in which he wrote of having revised the chapter with the fictionalized death of Maera and having "fixed the others," Hemingway also wrote by hand a personal note to "Dearest Old Izz" at the top of a typescript draft for chapter 14, the chapter about the celebrated bullfighter Villalta, after whom Hemingway and his wife gave their son his middle name.[5] The closest to certain evidence of Pound's editing is with Hemingway's fictional chapter of the bullfighter Maera's death, chapter 16 of *in our time.* Hemingway would narrate the scene of Maera's actual death from tuberculosis in "A Banal Story," the penultimate story of his collection *Men Without Women* (*CSS* 275). Among Hemingway's papers at the John F. Kennedy Presidential Library and Museum are two manuscript drafts of Maera's fictional death that give a clear picture of the chapter before Pound's editing. The first line of these drafts is "Maera was in bed with" (cited by Cohen 192).[6]

Milton Cohen has speculated about what these manuscript drafts suggest concerning Pound's advice to Hemingway. While admitting that "Pound's specific advice to Hemingway is unknown," he focuses on two major changes from the rough drafts to the final draft as the chapter appeared in print: First, as he points out, Hemingway shifted the setting from the infirmary that initially "occupied the whole chapter" to the bullfight arena. Second, Hemingway abandoned the first-person viewpoint from the narrator who witnessed Maera's lying wounded on his deathbed to a third-person narration from within Maera's consciousness (Cohen 192–93). In the initial draft, quoted by Cohen, Maera recounts in the first person his being gored: "he got me three times in my belly with the horn" (Cohen 192). These changes amount to a complete recasting of the chapter—shifting its setting and its narrative point of view.

Three other major changes in the earlier drafts of chapter 16 resulted in a radical recasting of the scene. These revisions are more substantial than the deletions, replacements, and additions of chapter 7, with Nick leaning against the wall of a church. In revising the chapter of Maera's fictional death scene, Hemingway stripped the chapter of any dialogue. While conversations between Maera, another bullfighter, and a doctor dominate the earlier draft, in the final draft not a single word is spoken. Thus, Hemingway struck out the repetition of Maera's hyperbolic and sentimental complaints and replaced them with the third-person narrator's matter-of-fact understatements. The manuscript fragment in folder 564, the typescript fragments in folder 564a, and the full typescript draft in folder 564a are all dominated by dialogue. The *previous* chapter in its print version of *in our time* is also dominated by spoken words, as Maera urges the narrator to retrieve his fellow bullfighter Luis from a drunken spree, and then scoffs at the narrator when he fails. However, whereas in chapter 15 Maera speaks with force, in the earlier drafts of chapter 16 his speech is maudlin and self-pitying. In all three drafts of chapter 16, Maera bemoans repeatedly that he is going to die. In the first fragment, Maera asks the narrator to tell Luis, the bullfighter he scorned in chapter 15, that he is going to die. In the full rough draft, he complains that, after the bull gored him, he kept waiting for Luis to intervene and distract the bull. Either way, Pound would have been justified in pointing out to Hemingway that the lines he gave Maera in each draft were melodramatic. In the final draft, chapter 16 gains much of its power from the absence of the spoken word—from the story's focusing almost completely on a fictional version of Maera's dying thoughts.

Whereas the repetitions in the earlier drafts of the chapter come mainly in Maera's self-pitying lamentations, in the revised version the repetitions evoke his consciousness of his surroundings as he lies dying. First is the simple repetition of "he felt" that connects his feeling "warm and sticky from the bleeding" on the hospital bed to his feeling "the horn coming" and his memory of having "felt it go into the sand"—the latter a gruesome sign of how Maera sensed the horn penetrating his body from his front through his back (*CSS* 161). Then, near the end of the chapter, "Maera felt" again, with the repetition of "felt" leading to the most dramatic repetition not present in any of the earlier drafts: "Maera felt everything getting larger and larger and larger and then smaller and smaller. Then it got larger and larger and larger and then smaller and smaller" (*CSS* 161). This repetition was a late revision by Hemingway not present in the first typescript of the chapter preserved in folder 94a at the Kennedy Library, but present in the second typescript and in the print version.

Likewise, Hemingway's narrator compared Maera's final moments of consciousness to the fast-forwarding in a "cinematographic film," a reference that was not present in the earlier drafts—another example of revision by addition (*CSS* 161). Thus, Hemingway's revisions in response to Pound's editing shifted the repetitions from Maera's self-pitying, spoken words to his blurry consciousness of moving shapes in his vision, like images on a cinema screen. Finally, the remarkable comparison of Maera's sense of quickening time to a fast-motion film comes in Hemingway's late revisions of the "Maera was in bed" drafts. None of the manuscript or early typescript drafts has any reference to film. In contrast, both typescripts in folder 94a end with the final sentences as published in chapter 16 of *in our time:* "Then everything commenced to run faster and faster as when they speed up a cinematograph film. Then he was dead" (*CSS* 161). The reference to a fast-motion film is the narrator's representation of Meera's thoughts accelerating. That reference prepares for the simple return to the narrator in the terse final words: "Then he was dead." From the exaggerated references in the rough drafts with Maera's saying that an hour seemed to pass between each goring (Cohen 192), Hemingway shifted to the subtler suggestion that, at the end of his life, time accelerated. This chapter is the only appearance in Hemingway's *Complete Short Stories* of the word "cinematographic" and the first of just a few uses of the word "film" in the context of movies, though Hemingway is clearly aware of the role of film in journalism, as his references to his friend Shorty, "a film service movie operator," in his reports for the *Toronto Star* of November 1922 and September 1923 make clear (*DLT* 249–50, 295). In chapter 16 of *in our time*, Hemingway's reference to film— especially to the sense of quickened time, like a fast-forward scene in a silent movie—adds power to his fictionalized narrative of Maera's death.

In looking back on the "Inquest" series, Pound praised Hemingway's *in our time* as reflecting an "Eye disillusioned by war, or shall we say first sign of new generation, that had got rid of all the buncomb, I personally had been dynamiting for years. Or trying to dynamite. Relief to find that old idiocies had lost hold. Again the hard clear statement" ("Inquest Sketch"). Striking about Pound's praise is his focusing on the war chapters of *in our time* in terms that sound akin to his own indictment of "buncomb" about the war in "Hugh Selwyn Mauberley" and in the "Hell" and "Purgatory" cantos of *A Draft of XVI Cantos*. Pound explicitly personalizes his praise as "[r]elief" in finding a writer who has portrayed war without the "old idiocies." Pound's praise for *in our time* seems as enthusiastic as his reflections about any of the six books published in the "Inquest" series. Conversely, Hemingway remembered Pound in *A Moveable Feast* as the man whom he "trusted the most as a critic . . . the man who had taught me to distrust adjectives" (*MF* 134). Such praise implies lessons Hemingway learned from Pound while working on the Three Mountains Press publication of *in our time*.

Before Hemingway's tribute to Pound in *A Moveable Feast,* the poet had already signaled his enduring, high regard for *in our time*. From St. Elizabeth's Hospital, Pound dictated a letter to Robert M. MacGregor, for delivery to James Laughlin, his publisher at New Directions. In the letter (not dated), Pound suggested a reprint of the "Inquest" series, "following Ulysses, Inquest into state of prose, indicating the main track (in contrast to monstrosities)" (*Pound and Laughlin* 230–31). He included *in our time,* the only work in the series for which he names the author's current publisher, Scribner's. Pound later dictated a letter to send to Hemingway about his proposal to reprint the "Inquest" series. In the letter, Pound acknowledged that Hemingway might not profit very much from the sales of the reprint, but presented it as "E.P.'s affirmation of the permanent value of some parts of your work" (*Pound and Laughlin* 232). While it is not clear what Pound leaves out of "some," he explicitly included *in our time* as of "permanent value."[7] Pound offered to write an anonymous preface for Hemingway explaining "that you were responsible for the 3 mts press doing anything of interest, and for getting some of the best stuff into Ford's transatlantic" (232). Pound ended his letter with the compliment that *in our time* stood as the "norm and canon of eng/prose, reasserted after the sport or gargoyle" (233). For whatever reason, Pound's late attempt to revive *in our time*, as published in 1924 by Three Mountains Press, was not successful.

Nonetheless, Hemingway publicly praised Pound's influence on his development as a young artist. In his "Homage to Ezra" in the first issue of *This Quarter*, his correspondence, and his chapter "Ezra Pound and the Bel Esprit" in *A Moveable Feast*, Hemingway acknowledged his debt to the poet. There are several facets of that enduring influence on Hemingway's short fiction. First, Pound influenced Hemingway's short fiction through his involvement with Imagism. One can imagine Pound's giving Hemingway the advice he gave William Carlos Williams in a letter dated 13 June 1928: "comb also the rest of it for stray bits of *slag*" (*Pound/Williams* 84). In looking back on Hemingway's chapters for *in our time*, Pound praised them as containing "hard, spare prose . . . almost as good as poetry" ("Essay on Inquest"). In praising *in our time*, Pound hearkened back to his Imagist aesthetic. Furthermore, under Pound's tutelage, Hemingway learned the importance of research and revision as central to an artist's working on his craft. During his conversations and travel in February 1923 with Pound, as he was working on the Malatesta cantos, Hemingway probably absorbed how much research and revision are a crucial part of a writer's craftsmanship (Reynolds, *Paris Years* 113; Moody 46–47). He likely observed how assiduously Pound revised his own poetry, as his work composing *A Draft of XVI Cantos* coincided with his work editing Hemingway's *in our time*.[8] In a letter dated 17 March 1924, Hemingway wrote Pound that he was "writing some damn good stories. I wish you were here to tell me so, so I would believe it or else what is the matter with them. You are the only guy that knows a god damn thing about writing" (*Letters* vol. 2, 103).

In short, although one can only speculate on what, specifically, Pound advised Hemingway as the young writer of the chapters in *in our time,* it is clear that Hemingway learned from Pound how to revise his work as a craftsman would. Pound's encouragement continued as Hemingway began to write the short stories that would accompany his chapters in *In Our Time.* In May 1924, he wrote his father about "Indian Camp": "Hem has good story in April Transatlantic" (*Pound to His Parents* 527). That was a sentiment he echoed in his anonymous letter to the *Transatlantic,* dated 17 May 1924, complimenting the April number, "Especially Hem and Djuna" (*Pound/Ford* 77). Given Hemingway's active role editing the *Transatlantic* at the time, he surely read the compliment about "Indian Camp," his first story in *In Our Time.* Furthermore, Hemingway clearly valued Pound's editing his chapters of *in our time.* In a letter to Pound dated mid-November 1924, Hemingway praised him as "the only guy who can say, as a technician, this is wrong and this is the way to make it right.... [Y]ou tell me what is wrong and how it can be fixed" (*Letters* vol. 2, 414). Pound was Hemingway's first important mentor in his learning the art of revision "to make it right."

2

JOYCE'S "THE SISTERS" AND HEMINGWAY'S REVISION OF "INDIAN CAMP"

Looking ahead to the publication of *Three Stories and Ten Poems,* Hemingway wrote to his friend Bill Horne on 18 July 1923, "I have one book being published this month" by "[t]he same gang that published Ulysses" (*Letters* vol. 2, 37). He was referring to Contact Press, run by Robert McAlmon, who used the same printer, Maurice Darantière, that Sylvia Beach employed to print *Ulysses.* Copies of *Three Stories and Ten Poems* arrived at Beach's Shakespeare and Company bookstore on 13 August 1923 (*Letters* vol. 2, 38n11). The stories included "Up in Michigan," "My Old Man," and "Out of Season." According to Paul Smith, the manuscripts of "Up in Michigan" show the author as "indecisive, inconsistent, and at times, I think, dead wrong" (*Guide* 287). As for "My Old Man," Smith notes that the manuscripts "show little revision" (1983, 286). "Out of Season," a story Hemingway apparently based on an argument Hadley and he had while skiing in the Italian Alps, "was written with an anger that would not allow him to punctuate, much less revise" (*Guide* 16; "Early Manuscripts" 287). Hemingway's earliest stories suggest that he had not yet learned the importance of revision.

In the same July 1923 letter to Bill Horne, Hemingway wrote that "another" book was due out in the fall, published by Three Mountains Press—that is, *in our time.* About both books, Hemingway expressed the hope that his hard work would be evident: "I think you'll like some of the yarns. I've worked like hell on them" (*Letters* vol. 2, 37). Hemingway wrote this letter a month *before* his letter to Pound telling his editor that he had "redone the death of Maera altogether different and fixed the others" and pledging that he "will do the hanging"—that is, the penultimate chapter of *in our time,* the hanging of Sam Cardinella. Taken together, these letters imply that, under

Pound's guidance, Hemingway was learning the craft of writing and rewriting. As discussed in chapter 1, Hemingway clearly worked hard at revising chapters like "Nick sat against the wall" and the death of Maera. Between the appearance of *Three Stories and Ten Poems* at Sylvia Beach's Shakespeare and Company Bookstore on 13 August 1923 and the publication of *in our time* in mid-March 1924, Hemingway and Hadley sailed on 26 August 1923 to Canada, so Hadley could give birth at a hospital in Toronto (Chamberlin 53, 57). The move to Toronto was for Hemingway a reversion from writing fiction to journalism—and, thus, a suspension of his practicing the art of revision. The one notable exception was Hemingway's "earliest draft of 'Indian Camp,'" a story he probably began in Toronto during the fall of 1923 (*Letters* vol. 2, 64n).[1]

That reversion would not last more than a few months. By mid-December he apparently had already decided to "chuck journalism," as he wrote to Gertrude Stein and Alice B. Toklas in a letter begun on 9 November 1923 and continued the following month. In the same letter he confided: "I have been invited today in a letter by Pound to come home and direct its policy etc" (*Letters* vol. 2, 91). He is referring to Pound's role in having Hemingway serve as subeditor of Ford Maddox Ford's new *Transatlantic Review*.[2] At the end of this letter, Hemingway explicitly connected his decision to leave journalism at the *Toronto Daily Star* and his return to writing stories: "I'm quitting on January 1. I have some good stories to write—will try not to be turgid—" (*Letters* vol. 2, 91). By mid-January, the Hemingways left Toronto by train for New York; when they sailed for France on the *Antonia* on 13–14 January 1924, their fellow passengers included Jane Heap and Margaret Anderson, publishers of the *Little Review*. Within a month they were settled into an apartment at 113, rue Notre Dame de Champs (Chamberlin 56–57). In a letter to Ezra Pound on 10 February, Hemingway wrote, "I am going to try and write something for the Trans etc"—perhaps a reference to "Indian Camp," the story he would publish in the April 1924 issue of the *Transatlantic*. In the same letter, he sounded both ambitious about his plans and frustrated with not knowing when he would have the time and a quiet place to work: "I have about 7 stories to write. Don't know when or where able to write" (*Letters* vol. 2, 97). According to Michael Reynolds, by the early morning of 20 February, Hemingway was at work on "Indian Camp," a story he began writing "in his head on the morning bus ride to work" in Toronto (*Paris Years* 165). Based on Hadley's reference to "two dandy stories" he wrote that week in a letter on 20 February to Hemingway's mother, Paul Smith suggests that Hemingway had completed "Indian Camp," a story that Ford Madox Ford accepted for the *Transatlantic Review,* as Hemingway wrote Pound on 17 March (Smith, *Guide* 34; *Letters* vol. 2, 102).

Probably the first story Hemingway completed when he returned with Hadley and their son, Jack, to Paris in the winter of 1924, "Indian Camp" is perhaps the earliest story to show Hemingway's return to the art of revision under the influence of James Joyce. Hemingway first met Joyce, likely at Sylvia Beach's Shakespeare and Company bookstore, in February or March 1922 (Chamberlin 39). On 9 March 1922, already in the throes of reading *Ulysses,* Hemingway wrote to Sherwood Anderson that "Joyce has a most goddamned wonderful book" (*Letters* vol. 1, 331). In the same letter he referred to Pound's sending six of his poems to the editor of the *Dial* magazine and taking "a story for the Little Review"—likely one of the stories that would become part of the "Exiles" issue (*Letters* vol. 1, 331). Although it is unclear when Hemingway read the stories in *Dubliners,* Michael Reynolds concludes that he probably read them "by 1924" (*Hemingway's Reading* 143). In discussing "Indian Camp," Reynolds argues that Hemingway's decision to delete the opening pages—the most salient revision in the story—reflected his learning "from the way Joyce began his stories" (*Paris Years* 166). Paul Smith conjectures that Hemingway could have learned from Joyce's "Araby" how to end his story "with a simple dialogue" (*Guide* 37–38). Both Reynolds and Smith saw the influence of Joyce's stories on "Indian Camp."

As Robert Gajdusek recognized, "Indian Camp" bears a strong resemblance to the first story in Joyce's *Dubliners,* "The Sisters." Even though Hemingway did not initially plan to place "Indian Camp" first in his collection, its placement makes much more sense than his original choice, "Up in Michigan" (Beall, "Formation" 64–66). Instead of a story about a young man's sexual assault on a girl, Hemingway begins his collection with an innocent boy who faces death for the first time. In that regard, the first stories in *Dubliners* and *In Our Time* bear "a close thematic parallel" in that, in both stories, a boy encounters decay and death (Gajdusek, *Hemingway in His Own Country* 209). This chapter will focus not only on such close thematic parallels but on how Hemingway revised the turning point of his story—when Nick sees that the Ojibway father slashed his throat—so that he keeps the reader within Nick's viewpoint. Thus, despite the differences between Joyce's first-person narrator and Hemingway's third-person limited point of view through the eyes of a young Nick Adams, Hemingway's revisions suggest that he learned from Joyce how to keep the boy's eyes as the focus of the narrative camera. This chapter will show that Hemingway learned more from Joyce than just to cut the initial opening. He learned how to maintain the narrative point of view focused on what a young boy sees in his first encounter with the shock of witnessing a suicidal death.

Paul Smith explains why it is unclear exactly when Hemingway decided to cut the opening pages of his initial draft before the story was published in the April 1924 issue of the *Transatlantic Review*. He suggests that Hemingway may have made the decision to cut the first pages "a week or two before 17 March" (*Guide* 35). On the other hand, Smith conjectures that Hemingway might have retained the initial opening when he constructed "Indian Camp" as a two-part story, just as "Big Two-Hearted River" ends *In Our Time* with a two-part story. As Smith concludes, Hemingway's decision to delete the first pages of the story provides "the earliest example of what came to be known as his 'theory of omission'"—in this case, where he deleted a substantial part of the original story, as he would later do with the original ending of "Big Two-Hearted River" (*Guide* 34–35). Robert Paul Lamb is even more blunt in his extensive analysis of the original beginning of the story as "unfocused, mistake-ridden, and verbose" (*Short Story* 11).

Hemingway's decision to cut the first pages strengthened the story by focusing on Nick's character as a rather innocent young boy. As Joseph Flora points out, "Nick should be an attractive character, and Hemingway, rightly, chose to emphasize Nick's innocence rather than his cowardice" (*Hemingway's Nick Adams* 31). Hemingway revised the story to begin with the predawn arrival of a canoe from the Indian camp: "At the lake shore there was another rowboat drawn up. The two Indians stood standing" (*CSS* 67). As revised, the story puts us in the mind of young Nick, who might be wondering why the Indians have rowed across the lake before dawn. Instead, in the original opening, Nick is "undressing in the tent. He saw the shadows of his father and Uncle George cast by the fire on the wall" (KL/EH folder 493; *SS-HLE* 60). These opening sentences imply that Nick feels exposed and wary of his father's and uncle's shadows. Rather than suggest Nick's wondering why the Indians have rowed across the lake, as in the revised version of the story, readers immediately are told, "He was ashamed because undressing reminded him of the night before" (*SS-HLE* 60). That is, Hemingway gives the backstory at the front—Nick's undressing, his feeling ashamed because undressing reminds him of how he exposed his fears by shooting three times the night before, and his remembering how hearing the church hymn "Some day the silver chord will break" instilled in him his fear of death (*SS-HLE* 60–61). In this initial draft, the words "frightened," "afraid," and "fear" recur at least ten times. In the initial draft, his hearing a church hymn was the first time Nick "ever realized that he himself would have to die sometime" (*SS-HLE* 61).[3] A sentence Hemingway added by hand and continued along the right margin of the manuscript repeats the emphasis on Nick's fear: "But it was always on the edge of fear and became fear very quick when it started" (*SS-HLE* 61). The original draft emphasizes Nick's cowardice more than his innocence.

Furthermore, the original draft connects Nick's fears with his lying to cover those fears—his improbable story that the noise he heard "sounded like a cross between a fox and a wolf" (*SS-HLE* 62). By revising the story to begin with Nick's watching two Indians draw up their rowboat on the shore, Hemingway begins at the predawn of the morning story. Thus, the story does not dwell on Nick's fears at shadows and sounds but instead more subtly portrays a young boy whose first spoken words are a simple, understandable question: "Where are we going, Dad?" (*CSS* 67). In the earliest draft, that simple question does not come until four pages into the story, when we have already heard about Nick's fears and lies. In the initial draft, as Nick's father and uncle talk on the way back to their camp after hearing the three gunshots, his uncle remarks, "He's such an awful liar" (*SS-HLE* 61). In that version of the story, Uncle George's cutting comment turns out to be prophetic. Rather than covering up his fears, Nick's lying about what he heard makes his fears of wild animals at night seem even more childish.

In the original version of the story, Uncle George's calling Nick a "liar," while strictly accurate, presents a caricature of a cruel uncle. By cutting the original opening when he revised the story, Hemingway offered a more subtle portrait of Uncle George as an unsympathetic character, about whom Nick cares enough to notice he had disappeared after the Caesarean section and to ask his father where he went. In the original beginning, Nick fired three shots, following his father's instructions that, "if any emergency came up while they were gone," he needed to alert them (*SS-HLE* 60). Uncle George's first words, not heard by Nick, are "Damn that kid." He contemptuously ridicules Nick as a coward who "got the Heebie-Jeebies," and he says out loud: "I can't stand him. He's such an awful liar" (*SS-HLE* 61). When

Nick explains that he heard a sound like a cross between a fox and a wolf, Uncle George comments derisively, "He probably heard a screech-owl" (*SS-HLE* 62). In short, in the original opening Uncle George is a caricature of an uncle who misses no chance to demean Nick's masculinity and maturity.

A third improvement in Hemingway's revision by omission comes in maintaining the focus of the story on Nick's point of view. This steady focus reflects one of the lessons Hemingway may well have learned from Joyce's "The Sisters," where Joyce filtered the reader's understanding of what happens through the young narrator's first-person point of view. Nick is both asleep and out of earshot when his father and uncle "put out their jack light on the other side of the lake" (*SS-HLE* 61). There is no indication whatsoever that Nick awakens to overhear his father and uncle when they are rowing back to camp after hearing the gunshots. Joseph Flora rightly points out that, in the original draft of the story, Hemingway allows us to hear that conversation—possible only if the story has shifted to a third-person omniscient point of view. By cutting that part of the story, Hemingway keeps us within Nick's point of view. As Flora explains, in the revised story, "nothing occurs that we do not experience with the young boy" (*Hemingway's Nick Adams* 32). Thus, the story does not dwell on Nick's fears of shadows and nocturnal sounds but instead more subtly portrays a young boy who experiences the traumas of watching a Caesarean section and then viewing the dead Indian father who slit his own throat. As revised, the story keeps our focus on Nick's ingenuous inquisitiveness. Near the beginning of "Indian Camp," Nick asks a rather simple, innocent question about where they are going at predawn. By the end, Nick asks his father a series of seemingly innocent, but profound, questions about life and death.

By excising the first pages of the initial draft, Hemingway followed Joyce's lead in "Sisters" by gradually unfolding a boy's pondering the mysteries of a man's death as affecting his own sense of self. Joyce began "The Sisters" with two simple, declarative clauses connected by a colon: "There was no hope for him this time: it was the third stroke" (*Dubliners* 9). Thus, Joyce began in the middle of the story about the young narrator's reaction to the priest's death—after his meetings where he studied with Father Flynn, and before his visiting the coffin where the priest's corpse was laid. Likewise, once he revised the story, Hemingway also began "Indian Camp," as Joyce did, *in medias res*—no backstory about Nick's prior fears, his firing a set of shots out of panic, or his lying about what he heard outside the tent.

Like "The Sisters," "Indian Camp" began with two simple, declarative sentences presenting Nick's first sight in the dark that morning: "At the lake shore there was another rowboat drawn up. The two Indians stood waiting" (*CSS* 67). As shown in a comparison of the draft reproduced in the Library Edition and the published version, Hemingway improved that second sentence by revising the original version, "Two Indians ~~standing~~ stood beside it" (*SS-HLE* 62). By changing "standing" to "stand" and then to "stood waiting," Hemingway leaves the reader to wonder, along with Nick, what are they waiting for? He also added a more vivid verb phrase to emphasize the actions of the Indian who boarded the camp rowboat with Uncle George. Instead of simply "The other Indian got in with him" (*SS-HLE* 62), Hemingway rewrote the sentence to stress the youth and vigor of the rower: "The young Indian shoved the camp boat off and got in to row Uncle George" (*CSS* 67). This added detail suggests the force of the Indian's desire for departure, which might lead Nick to ask himself about the reason for such urgency. These minor revisions evoke Nick's attentive observations that leave him with questions as to the purpose of the visit and journey across the lake.

As the stories unfold, both Joyce and Hemingway emphasize the boys' attempts to see in the dark. Joyce and Hemingway both set their opening stories in midsummer or late summer: Father Flynn's death occurs on 1 July, as the card pinned on a "crape bouquet . . . tied to the door-knocker with ribbon" announces (*Dubliners* 12). "Indian Camp" presumably occurs during the summer, making the hour of Nick's departure in the dark with his father and uncle quite early. After hearing of Father Flynn's death, the narrator of "The Sisters" tries to puzzle out the meaning of old Cotter's insinuations about the Father. While he lies "[i]n the dark of my room," the boy imagines seeing "again the heavy grey face of the paralytic" (*Dubliners* 11). When he reads the death notice, the narrator thinks of the routine he would have followed if Father Flynn were still alive: "I would have gone into the little dark room behind the shop to find him sitting in his arm-chair by the fire" (12). Likewise, Hemingway repeats the signs that Nick is looking through darkness: the two boats left the Adams camp "in the dark" (*CSS* 67), his Uncle George is smoking a cigar "in the dark" (*CSS* 67), and the Indian men had moved away from the hut "to sit in the dark" (*CSS* 68). Particularly in "Indian Camp," Hemingway's repeating the phrase "in the dark" from Nick's viewpoint sets up a central irony of the story: Nick looks to his Uncle George and to his father to shed light on what is happening, but as the story unfolds his uncle is more in the dark than is Nick. The point is made even more sharply when Hemingway adds "in the dark" to the sentence in the draft: "Uncle George was smoking a cigar" (*SS-HLE* 63)—there is no reference to his doing so "in the dark" in the initial draft. Thus, both Joyce and Hemingway carefully begin their stories so that the central viewpoint of the story comes through a boy's eyes trying to see in shades of darkness.

Joyce and Hemingway present each boy's avuncular figures as unreliable guides. The first words of old Cotter, a friend of the narrator's uncle, seem to answer a question asked offstage: "No, I wouldn't say he was exactly . . . but there was something queer . . ." (*Dubliners* 9–10). He continues offering insinuations that the priest is not to be trusted around a young boy. When the narrator's aunt asks the first two of ten questions that an adult poses in "The Sisters," Cotter replies, in both cases, with an unsavory innuendo, the second time letting his statement trail off: "When children see things like that, you know, it has an effect . . . ." (11). The narrator's actual uncle is too passive to be of any comfort. With a mildly casual tone, he earlier had said, "Well, so your old friend is gone, you'll be sorry to hear" (10). The uncle *did* earlier explain that Father Flynn taught the narrator "a great deal" (10), but to Cotter's insinuations he offers no defense or explanation and does not figure in the second half of the story, when the narrator and his aunt go to visit the priest's sisters. If old Cotter is an irritating surrogate uncle, the narrator's uncle in "The Sisters" is an ineffectual surrogate father.

Likewise, the only light from Nick's Uncle George comes from the cigar that he rather vainly is smoking "in the dark" (*CSS* 67). Furthermore, the young Indian's practical way of securing the boat by pulling it "way up on the beach" (*CSS* 67) contrasts with Uncle George's empty gestures of celebratory cigars. In the initial draft of the story, the young Indian with the lantern accepted Uncle George's offer of a cigar. In the handwritten manuscript, when Uncle George "had given one to the young Indian," the Indian "cut it in half and was chewing it." By hand, Hemingway crossed out "was chewing it" and wrote instead "lit it as they came up" (*SS-HLE* 63). For the print version, he wrote, "Uncle George gave both the Indians cigars" (*CSS* 67), but he mentions nothing about what the Indians did. Given the young Indian's laughter later over the pregnant woman's biting Uncle George, his silence here about the gift implies his rejection of the uncle's usurping the role of the Indian father. Hemingway's revision implies that the young Indian resisted Uncle George's gift. However, because we are viewing the scene through Nick's eyes, Hemingway does not have Nick form an inference about what the young Indian did with the cigar—just that in the revised version the Indian did not chew on it or light it up.

Hemingway presents the sequence of landing, walking on the beach through a meadow, and following a trail leading to a logging road completely through Nick's point of view. He particularly focuses on the young Indian's carrying a lantern, and then, when they reach the logging road where it is "much lighter" because of the trees cut away for the road, Nick observes the Indian stopping and blowing out the lantern. At this point, the one significant revision is Hemingway's cutting a comment that the group was "walking toward the camp where the Indian bark peelers lived" (*SS-HLE* 63). By deleting those words, Hemingway leaves readers (with Nick) more in the dark as to where they are headed and what the Indians who live there do. In the print edition, only in the next paragraph, after Nick hears a dog barking and sees "the light of the shanties," does he know that he has arrived at the camp "where the Indian bark-peelers live" (*CSS* 67). As Robert Paul Lamb observes, Hemingway presents the approach to the Indian camp entirely through Nick's innocent point of view (*Short Story* 29–35).[4] Unlike Joyce's first-person narrator, who forms mature, skeptical judgments during the story, Hemingway depicts young Nick making observations, not inferences or judgmental responses.

Aside from following Joyce in keeping the reader's view of the story through a young boy's perspective, Hemingway learned from Joyce about developing his story around a series of unspoken and spoken questions. Near the beginning of the revised "Indian Camp," Nick's father answers both Nick's spoken and unspoken questions: where are we going ("Over to the Indian camp") and why are we going there so early in the morning ("There is an Indian lady very sick" [*CSS* 67]). By cutting the initial opening of the story, Hemingway has Nick's questions and his father's responses drive the beginning. This exchange also sets the stage for the story's ending full of Nick's questions and the best answers his father can give. Indeed, in "Indian Camp" young Nick's questions form the arc of the story. In contrast, Joyce's narrator has no father present, and the only direct questions he asks out loud are the disingenuous "Who?" and "Is he dead?" in response to his uncle's "your old friend is gone" (*Dubliners* 10). However, over the course of the story, he asks himself many rather sophisticated questions, often presented in interior monologue, starting with the implied questions he asks himself at the beginning of the story: whether his teacher has died; what the words "paralysis," "gnomon," and "simony" mean; and why the words sound "maleficent and sinful"—sophisticated questions for a boy to ask himself (*Dubliners* 9). Later in the story, the narrator continues to ask himself questions: what old Cotter's "unfinished sentences" imply (11), why the priest (in the narrator's apparent dream) "desired to confess something" (a role reversal of priest and acolyte), why the priest "smiled continually," and "why the lips were so moist with spittle" (11)—as if he, too, is picking up some of old Cotter's innuendoes about the priest's interest in him. In his initial, angry response to Cotter, the narrator speaks only to himself in a terse interior monologue: "Tiresome old red-nose imbecile!" (11). At this point, the narrator's reference to old Cotter as "red-nose" seems dismissive of a drunkard's gossip. In contrast, Nick never dismisses his father or uncle so assertively, even in his thoughts. Rather, Hemingway portrays Nick as anxious, uncertain, reserved, but not caustic.

Perhaps the most surprising question that Joyce's narrator asks himself is when he wonders why he feels such a sense of release after Father Flynn's death. In "The Sisters," walking by the dead priest's home, the narrator asks himself why he felt "a sensation of freedom . . . by his death" (*Dubliners* 12). In an extended interior monologue, Joyce's narrator remembers when Father Flynn "amused himself by putting difficult questions to me," a memory not present in an earlier draft of the story (compare *Dubliners* 13 with 241–42). Joyce suggests that the narrator is beginning to suspect his priest may have had ulterior motives in asking him such difficult questions and by teaching him "that the fathers of the Church had written books as thick as the *Post Office Directory*" (*Dubliners* 13). Near the end of this interior monologue, the narrator remembers: "When he smiled he used to uncover his big discoloured teeth and let his tongue lie upon his lower lip—a habit which made me uneasy in the beginning of our acquaintance before I knew him well" (13). Set just before the narrator's reference to remembering "old Cotter's words," this memory implies that the narrator is now connecting the priest's habit that made him uneasy with Cotter's recent insinuations, making him *more* uneasy the more he remembers the priest's puzzling movements with his teeth and tongue.

At the end of the story, the narrator's aunt asks the spoken questions, at first mostly to do with social decorum and the last rites, only at the end to inquire about the role her nephew may have had in the priest's breaking a chalice and then in his mental breakdown: "'And was that it?' said my aunt. 'I heard something…" (*Dubliners* 17). In revising his draft to the story, Joyce added the aunt's spoken question about the narrator's contributing to the priest's breakdown. Missing from the earlier draft was her question, "And was that it?" (compare *Dubliners* 17 with 245).[5] Once again, the narrator listens closely as his aunt's voice, like old Cotter's earlier in the story, now trails off. Joyce implies that the first-person narrator is asking himself the deeper questions: Why was the priest's breaking the chalice "the boy's fault" (*Dubliners* 17)—that is, my fault? Why was "James," his priest's Christian name, "so nervous"? (17). Why was his mentor "in his confession-box, wide-awake and laughing-like softly to himself?" (18). Eliza, one of the priest's sisters, gives the final spoken question in the story, a rather rhetorical one: "And what do you think but there he was, sitting up by himself in the dark … laughing-like softly to himself" (18). That is, Eliza's spoken question seems less a genuine question asking for an answer but rather a way of reporting what she heard that the clerk, Father O'Rourke, and another priest saw in the chapel. In revising his earlier draft of "The Sisters," Joyce changed Eliza's statement about her brother "laughing like—softly to himself" into a question with a hyphenated "laughing-like" rather than a dash (compare *Dubliners* 18 and 246). Eliza also suggests the implicit, unspoken, and final question an adult raises in the story: why was "something gone wrong with him . . . ." (18). To which the narrator might silently ask himself, what was my role in that "something gone wrong"? Instead of presenting these questions in a monologue the narrator speaks to himself—or even thinks— Joyce deftly leaves those questions between the lines, or after ellipses. Joyce presents these questions as overheard or thought silently by the alert, wary boy; thus, he keeps the reader within the boy's first-person point of view.

Whereas Joyce's introverted narrator does not speak most of the questions in "Three Sisters," Nick gives voice to numerous questions in "Indian Camp." Hemingway builds toward the ending of "Indian Camp" with a series of Nick's voiced questions that convey his deep unsettlement about what he has witnessed: a bloody Caesarean section and a bloody suicide. Thus, the ending of the story unfolds with dialogue that Robert Paul Lamb describes as "a marvel of indirection, miscommunication, suggestiveness, and compression" (*Art Matters* 181–82, repeated in *Short Story* 69). Whereas Joyce implies his narrator's unvoiced questions in his interior monologues, Hemingway depicts Nick's in clipped dialogue that makes the ending so poignant and memorable. His first voiced question early in the story—"Where are we going, Dad?" (*CSS* 67)—implies an unasked question: why are we going there this early in the morning? To his father's answer, Nick's "Oh" suggests his initially docile response to his father's explanation as to *why* they are going there so early in the morning—before a summer's dawn.

In the original opening of the story, Nick loudly announces his fears by firing three gunshots. In contrast, and closer to the narrator of "The Sisters," Nick keeps his anxieties mostly to himself, at first. Upon entering the "shanty," Nick sees that a young pregnant woman lies on a "wooden bunk" (a harder surface than what Hemingway initially wrote, "bed" [*SS-HLE* 63; *CSS* 67]). His second voiced question in the story expresses his discomfort at hearing the woman scream: "Oh, Daddy, can't you give her something to make her stop screaming?" (*CSS* 68). His father's response seems clinical and detached—not just in the factual "I haven't any anaesthetic" but also in the emotionally distant reference to the screams: "I don't hear them because they are not important" (*CSS* 68).[6] Ironically, after his father's "I don't hear them," Nick may have heard the sound the husband made when he "rolled over against the wall." As is the case in the manuscript of the story, Hemingway presented the sentence about the Indian's rolling over against the wall in a separate, one-sentence paragraph, just as it appears in the print version (*SS-HLE* 64; *CSS* 68). Although Hemingway does not *explicitly* state that Nick heard the body hit the wall, that seems as likely as his actually seeing the husband roll against the wall. In what retrospectively is a turning point of the story, Nick notices (perhaps hears) but does not understand the significance of the Indian's body's hitting the wall. By the end of the story, Nick asks, "Do many men kill themselves, Daddy?" and "Do many women?" (*CSS* 69). Nick's questions reveal his anxious vulnerability about what he has observed—both the Caesarean section and the suicide.

As is the case with Joyce's "Sisters," Hemingway's first story in *In Our Time* focuses on the reaction of a young boy to seeing a dead man. Before seeing the priest's dead face or the Indian's slit throat, Joyce's narrator and Nick are acutely conscious of the smell in what Joyce calls "the dead-room" (*Dubliners* 14). After seeing the dead priest's "truculent, grey, and massive face" in the coffin, the narrator of "The Sisters" smells "a heavy odor in the room—the flowers" (14), as if the flowers serve as incense around his priest's corpse. Joyce's dash implies the narrator's sensing that the flowers may be a natural cover for the corpse's smell. His narrator makes inferences about the emotional state of the priest at his moment of death, reading the face as suffused with the priest's "truculence." It is as if the young narrator sees in the priest's face a mirror image of his own bitter disillusionment. Hemingway is more explicit about what Nick smells: the odor from the husband's "very badly" cut foot (perhaps gangrenous if badly cut three days before) and the odor from his pipe (a kind of incense to cover the gangrenous odor). To Nick, "The room smelled very bad" (*CSS* 68). Hemingway is also explicit about what Nick hears: the woman's screams, his uncle swearing at the Indian woman, and the young Indian laughing at his uncle (*CSS* 68). At the same time, Nick does not form conjectures about what the smells and sounds mean. He hears his father's musing ("Ought to have a look at the proud father") without Nick's speculating about what his father's "look" will bring. Thus, besides smelling "very bad" air without knowing the precise significance of the odor, Nick hears a cacophony of voices—without fully understanding what he hears.

The climax of both "The Sisters" and "Indian Camp" comes when each boy views a dead man, but with an important difference. Whereas Joyce's narrator studies the posture, body, hands, and face of the priest, Nick does not see the dead man's face, turned to the wall, but rather sees his cut throat (*CSS* 69). Besides focusing on his "truculent" face (a sign of the priest's discontentment), Joyce's narrator focuses on the hands "loosely retaining a chalice" (*Dubliners* 14)—a revision from the "cross" the priest holds in the earlier draft (243). By replacing "cross" with "chalice," Joyce implies that Father Flynn's body was arranged in the coffin to present him as if on a spiritual quest, like the chalice the narrator of "Araby" imagines himself carrying: "I imagined that I bore my chalice safely through a throng of foes" (*Dubliners* 31). This initial reference to the narrator's seeing Father Flynn's corpse holding a chalice leads to the gossipy conversation among the sisters about a "chalice he broke" that reportedly "was the boy's fault" (*Dubliners* 17). Even then, Joyce keeps from the reader a definite knowledge of the narrator's responses to the innuendoes that he may have contributed to the priest's disorder, culminating in the scene where he was heard laughing to himself in his confession box. Thus, the narrator's viewing his priest's corpse and hearing his aunts' gossip about Father Flynn's odd laughter suggest an unspoken question: what, the narrator might ask himself, does the priest's "laughing-like to himself" have to do with me?

Although with less sophistication than Joyce's narrator, Nick's shocked response to the Indian husband's suicide likewise leaves him pondering mysteries, first silently, but eventually in questions he asks aloud to his father. Considered in comparison with Joyce's narrator, Nick seems younger, more innocent, more inquisitive than skeptical. Hemingway worked and reworked the narration of the turning point of the story: the moment when Nick discovers that the Indian father had slit his throat "from ear to ear" (*CSS* 69). His revisions show his concern to make clear how Nick had a direct view of his father's uncovering the blanket from the Indian's head. Here is Hemingway's initial, handwritten draft, before cross-outs and replacements:

> ~~He stood on the edge of the lower bunk and~~
> He pulled back the blanket from over the Indian's head. His hand came away wet. He mounted on the edge of the lower bunk with the lamp in one hand and looked in.
> ~~An open razor lay under the man's~~
> The Indian lay with his face toward the wall. His throat had been cut from ear to ear. The blood had flowed down into a pool where his body sagged the bunk. His head rested on his left arm and the open razor lay just beyond his fingers. (KL/EH folder 493; *SS-HLE* 65–66)

The final version reads: "He pulled back the blanket from the Indian's head. His hand came away wet. He mounted on the edge of the lower bunk with the lamp in one hand and looked in. The Indian lay with his face toward the wall. His throat had been cut from ear to ear. The blood had flowed down into a pool where his body sagged the bunk. His head rested on his left arm. The open razor lay, edge up, in the blankets" (*CSS* 69). Hemingway's revisions keep us carefully inside Nick's point of view throughout the grisly scene.

In the final draft, Hemingway shows us the scene as Nick would have seen it: his father pulled back the blanket, and Nick saw his father's hand come away wet. In the initial draft, Hemingway wrote that Nick watched as his father "stood on the edge of the lower bunk" and looked in—presumably, seeing the dead Indian before Nick did, and seeing the open razor with which he killed himself. In the manuscript draft, Hemingway crossed out the words that suggest Nick's father climbed on the edge of the lower bunk *before* he pulled back the blanket to reveal the dead man: "He stood on the edge of the lower bunk" (*SS-HLE* 65). In the manuscript Hemingway replaced these words with language that suggests Nick saw the blood at roughly the same time as his father did: "He pulled back the blanket from over the Indian's head. His hand came away wet" (SS-HLE 65; CSS 69). In seeing his father's wet hand, Nick does not seem to know, at first, what had made his hand wet. Then, Nick's eyes seem to follow his father as he "mounted" the bunk. His father looked in, unwittingly enabling Nick to see the throat cut "from ear to ear." In watching his father make the discovery of the Indian father's slashed throat, without necessarily understanding that he has killed himself, Nick makes his own discovery.

In the initial manuscript version, the doctor might indeed have blocked Nick's view if he had climbed up the bunk before he drew back the blanket. In his revision, Hemingway suggests Nick's view of what the drawn blanket, his father's wet hand, and the lamp revealed: "The blood had flowed down into a pool where his body sagged the bunk" (CSS 69). Thus, Nick saw his father's wet hand before his father mounted to look directly at the top bunk. Nick's father may *feel* the blood first, but Hemingway largely keeps us within Nick's viewpoint: Nick sees his father pull back the blanket, sees his father's wet hand, and then sees his father mount to the top bunk. The reader sees what Nick sees when his father pulled the blanket from the Indian's head and brought his wet hands back into view. The sequence of short, declarative, interconnected sentences conveys what Nick saw in simple words such as a young boy might use. As Robert Paul Lamb notes, "The words selected would all be found in the vocabulary of a small child" (*Short Story* 63).[7]

Hemingway's revision of the final sentences of this paragraph—with references to the Indian's head resting on his arm and the razor—also records Nick's observations. In the initial version, Hemingway first mentioned the razor immediately after Nick sees that his father "stood on the edge of the lower bunk and" (crossed out). In the manuscript he also crossed out the following sentence: "An open razor lay under the man's" (SS-HLE 65). Thus, Hemingway deleted the sentence that gives readers the impression that Dr. Adams "stood on the edge" and immediately saw the marks of the Indian's suicide: "His head rested on his left arm and the open razor lay just beyond his fingers" (SS-HLE 66). In this initial draft, the sight of the razor appears to come to the father, not to Nick. In revising this passage, Hemingway delayed a reference to the open razor until after evoking sights Nick could have seen once his father pulled back the blanket and shone a lamp—the Indian's cut throat, the pool of blood, and *then* the open razor (SS-HLE

66; *CSS* 69). Nick has already seen his father roll back the blanket and has seen his father's bloody hand, so he could also now see the Indian's bloody neck and fingers, with the open razor dropped.

A typescript draft of "Indian Camp," completed apparently after its publication in the April 1924 issue of *Transatlantic Review,* further suggests Hemingway's efforts in revising the story for *In Our Time* to maintain the focus during the discovery scene as Nick's point of view. The Hemingway Library Edition reproduces the first few paragraphs of this draft of "Indian Camp," but nothing further (KL/EH folder 449; *SS-HLE* 67). In the climactic paragraph beginning "He pulled back the blanket," the first sentences are the same in this typescript as they are in the final version printed in *In Our Time* (KL/EH folder 494; *CSS* 69). Then, in the typescript, Hemingway initially had the following sentence: "His head rested on his left arm and the open razor lay beyond his fingers." At the end of this sentence, he added by hand and then crossed out by hand the phrase "in the blanket." For the version printed in *In Our Time,* Hemingway restored the phrase "in the blanket," but with an emphasis on how the razor "lay, edge up, in the blankets." In the final version, he cut the phrase "beyond his fingers" to place more emphasis on the position of the razor, "edge up," rather than on whether the razor had fallen out of the Indian's grasp. Likewise, in the typescript he added by hand (and did not cross out) the sentence: "He had pulled the blanket over his head before he did it" (KL/EH 494). In both cases, Hemingway's revisions present the grisly sight of the Indian's open razor and his slashed throat as Nick would have seen it. In particular, by cutting the sentence he had initially added to the typescript to indicate that the Indian father covered his head with the blanket before slashing his throat, Hemingway made clearer how Nick could have seen that the Indian had cut his throat "from ear to ear" (*CSS* 69). In the final version, Hemingway divided the sentence in two, so that Nick's focus on the razor is its own, terse sentence: "The open razor lay, edge up, on the blankets" (*CSS* 69). With the pauses around "edge up" (the pauses not present even in a later typescript, KL/EH folder 495), Hemingway implies the numbed shock of Nick's recognition: not only does he see the slit throat and the fingers that held the knife; he sees that the razor remains "edge up" for him to see, with the blood it shed.

A reader of "Indian Camp" might well wonder whether Hemingway could have made clearer where Nick was standing so that he could see not only the blood on his father's hand but also the Indian's throat "cut from ear to ear" and the pool of blood where the Indian's body "sagged the bunk" (*CSS* 69). How did Nick move to where he could see the Indian father's neck, slit, once his father pulled back the blanket? Hemingway does not tell us at first but only indicates Nick's perspective after the doctor orders his brother to take Nick outside: "Take Nick out of the shanty, George" (*CSS* 69). Again, Hemingway's process of revision shows his carefully keeping readers inside Nick's point of view. After Nick's father tells his brother to "Take Nick out," the narrative initially follows with, "But it was too late." By hand, Hemingway crossed out "But it was too late" and replaced the sentence with "There was no need of that" (*SS-HLE* 66). In the original draft, Hemingway initially crossed out and then restored the key phrase "had a good view of" to describe Nick's vantage point when "his father tipped the Indian's head back" (*SS-HLE* 66). For the final, printed draft, he slowed down the sentence with commas that provide telling pauses and added a key phrase not in the manuscript: "Nick, standing in the door of the kitchen, had a good view of the upper bunk when his father, the lamp in one hand, tipped the Indian's head back" (*CSS* 69). Aside from capitalizing "Indian" (consistently lowercase in the original manuscript), Hemingway emphasized, by adding two pauses, Nick's view from the kitchen door of his father's tipping back the Indian's head. In the final version, Hemingway added the phrase "the lamp in one hand" to emphasize that not only was Nick in a position to see the slit throat but his father unintentionally shone a light on the scene. As Lamb notes, Hemingway "repeats exactly a phrase from the discovery paragraph ('the lamp in one hand')" in the next paragraph to suggest that "the upper bunk was well lit" and thus to enable Nick to see the Indian's slit throat (*Short Story* 66).

Robert Paul Lamb has criticized this passage—particularly the sentence "There was no need of that" (*CSS* 69)—as what he judged to be "an unnecessary authorial intrusion" (*Art Matters* 93). Subsequently, in *The Hemingway Short Story*, Lamb speculates that Hemingway might have allowed this "authorial intrusion" as a way of "giving way, for just a moment, to self-pity" (65). In my view, the short statement "There was no need of that" conveys Nick's terse recognition that there is no need for his father to tell his uncle to remove him from a view of the suicide's throat and razor. Nick has already seen the suicide from the kitchen doorway—ironically, "a good view," words Hemingway crossed out of the original manuscript and then restored (*SS-HLE* 66; *CSS* 69). Hemingway presents Nick's recognition as twofold:

first, that the Indian's throat has been slit; second, that his father not only could not prevent his seeing what he saw but "tipped the Indian's head back" (*CSS* 69). By tipping the Indian's head back, he inadvertently gave Nick a full view of the grisly scene. In contrast to Nick's simple, spoken response early in the story to his father's explanation as to where they are going, "Oh" (*CSS* 67), his interior reflection here marks his dramatic growth after seeing the blood, the throat, and the knife. Nick's thought—"There was no need"— quietly registers his temporarily distancing himself from his father's effort to reassert control over what he can see. Instead of constituting an authorial intrusion into the story, the statement "There was no need of that" seems to be Nick's brief, interior reflection. Although Nick is not as confident or in-dependent in his judgments as Joyce's narrator in "The Sisters," he is begin-ning to draw his own conclusions about what he sees and thinks.

In short, at the climax of the story, Nick continues to see and know more than his father knows he does. Particularly upon rereading the story, one can see that Nick knew more than might appear to be the case. As he ap-proaches the Indian camp, he seems to know what the Indians do with the wood ("bark peelers" [*CSS* 67]). He seems to sense that the dogs' rushing toward them signals that the Indians do not regard the doctor as welcome, even if they came to seek his help. During the operation, the details of which a reader does not see because Nick intentionally does not watch, his father's directions ("These must boil") imply a command in an operating room (*CSS* 68). Furthermore, Nick's father does not know that, to Nick, the operation seemed to take a long time. Presumably responding to his father's direction, "Nick held the basin for his father" (*CSS* 68). To the manuscript in folder 493, Hemingway added the next sentence by hand: "It all took a long time" (*CSS* 68). Another irony is Nick's two-word response to his father's an-nouncement that the baby is a boy. His father seems to care that the baby is a boy; Nick does not. His response, "All right," belies his physical action of "looking away so as not to see what his father was doing" (*CSS* 68). Nick knows why he is turning his head away; his father appears not to notice. Hemingway gives Nick's father the role of a methodical, certain, authori-tative father, similar to the role in which Joyce depicts an offstage Father O'Rourke, who took care of arrangements after the priest's death (*Dubliners* 16). But, like Joyce's narrator with his aunts and uncle, Nick moves past his father's effort to cast him as "interne" (*CSS* 68), an assistant attending an operation by his doctor-father. The narrator of "The Sisters" and Nick Adams of "Indian Camp" both see a corpse, and, like Joyce, particularly after he revised the manuscript draft, Hemingway maintains the narrative perspective within the independent eyes of a young boy. Hemingway's revision of that pivotal scene when Nick sees the slit throat, blood, and open razor suggests his learning from Joyce about focusing the story on the young boy's point of view—and about the importance of revision.

Joyce and Hemingway both end their stories with a series of questions. In "The Sisters," adults—mainly the narrator's aunt—ask ten questions during the course of the story, initially the aunt's questions about the arrangements for the funeral, but eventually questions that lead to the sisters' innuendoes about the narrator's possible role in their brother's mental crackup. In "Indian Camp," Nick asks ten questions—mainly probing his father for assurance. In "The Sisters," the adults ask the final questions: "And was that it" (the aunt is referring to the broken chalice). The narrator's aunt then refers to a rumor about Eliza's brother, Father Flynn: "I heard something." Eliza responds first with a statement ("That affected his mind") and then with a rhetorical question about how the priest was found laughing to himself in his confessional box: "And what do you think but there he was" (*Dubliners* 17–18). Neither of these spoken questions is present in the earlier draft; Joyce added the questions during his process of revision (compare *Dubliners* 17–18 with 245–46). Eliza is asking a rhetorical question about how, one night, Father O'Rourke found her brother in the confessional box "laughing-like softly to himself." Joyce ends his story with Eliza's answering her own question: "that made them think there was something wrong with him . . . ." (18). However, the ellipses with which Joyce ends the story— ellipses not present in the earlier draft—suggest that the young narrator still has his own questions (compare *Dubliners* 18 with 246).

Hemingway is more explicit in giving voice to Nick's questions. Near the end of "Indian Camp," Hemingway presents Nick's rapid-fire questions to his father. The ending of the story is little changed between the manuscript draft and the version that appeared in *In Our Time*. Nick's first question in the final sequence ironically echoes his father's courtly reference to the mother as "This lady" (*CSS* 68), but Nick asks more generally, "Do ladies always have such a hard time having babies?" (*CSS* 69). Nick's next question about the Indian's suicide ("Why did he?") is much harder for his father to answer. Indeed, Nick's question leads to his father's first admission of unknowing: "I don't know, Nick. He couldn't stand things, I guess" (*CSS*

69). That is, to Nick's "Why did he?" question, for the first time his father responds that he has only a speculative guess, not an answer. In a question ending with the second time when he calls his father "Daddy," Nick asks his father whether "many men" kill themselves. To the father's "not very many" response, Nick's next question ("Do many women?") seems a sign that he is still pondering questions about suicide while shifting from men to women. To his father's next response, "Hardly ever," Nick seems to probe further. Nick's next question about suicide and death implies his unsettlement with his father's response that women "Hardly ever" kill themselves: "Don't they ever?" (*CSS* 69–70). His eighth question of the story is one word: "Daddy?" This question implies Nick's uncertainty as he shifts from questions about suicide to his inquiry about Uncle George. His ninth question—"Where did Uncle George go?"—implies his concern or puzzlement as to why Uncle George has disappeared. Nick's tenth question shifts from his questions directly about suicide, as he asks a child's question about death: "Is dying hard, Daddy?" This question ends with the fifth time "Daddy" appears as a word in the story. In "Indian Camp," Hemingway centers the ending on Nick's spoken questions that neither his father nor he can answer easily. Hemingway deftly ends this clipped dialogue with the father's understandably vague, "It all depends" (*CSS* 70). Like the silence of Joyce's narrator in response to adults' conversations, the silences between Nick's questions and his father's answers are resounding.

Near the end of "The Sisters," Joyce provides the reader with a final glimpse into the young narrator's thoughts via a brief interior monologue that he added when revising the story. After Eliza's rhetorical question about the priest's crazed laughter in his confession booth, Joyce focuses on the narrator's final interior recognitions: "I knew that the old priest was lying still, as we had seen him" (18). Based on his earlier look at the dead face, the narrator judges that the priest died in a "solemn and truculent" mood (*Dubliners* 18)—repeating his earlier interpretation of the corpse's face as "solemn" and "truculent" (14). That Joyce repeats the same words suggests that, whatever the narrator has heard from his aunts about the priest's being "in his confession box, wide-awake and laughing-like softly to himself" (18), he retains his own internal register of the priest's last state of mind. No longer face-to-face with the priest's corpse in the coffin, the boy's vision of the dead priest is nonetheless presented as conclusive.

His final impression about the chalice shows a slight, but important, adjustment in his reaction to its lying in the priest's hands. Whereas at first glance, the narrator focused on the physical sight, "his large hands loosely retaining a chalice" (14), his final judgment is more intellectual and judgmental: "an idle chalice on his breast" (18). He views the chalice on the priest's breast, not held "loosely" in his hands. The slight shift suggests that the narrator now suspects that someone placed the chalice, then in his hands, now lying on the priest's "breast" as an "idle" symbol of blessed piety. Joyce added this brief, interior monologue about the "idle chalice" to the earlier draft of the story (compare *Dubliners* 18 with 245–46). In the last interior monologue in "The Sisters," Joyce focuses on the narrator's final, unspoken response to the priest's death and to the conversation he hears. The narrator's silence suggests his inner detachment from the "idle" parlor gossip about the priest's "laughing-like" in a manner that may be hysterical, but is not funny.

Like Joyce, after the questions and answers end during the canoe trip back from the Indian camp to the Adams camp, Hemingway focuses in an interior monologue on what young Nick touches and feels and thinks. After seeing a bass "making a circle in the water," Nick "trailed his hand in the water" (*CSS* 70). He is not fishing; he is trying to feel the cool water, perhaps in order to feel his hand. Near the beginning of the story, the water felt "cold," despite his father's arm circling around him (*CSS* 67). Now, although his father's arms are "rowing," Nick feels the water as "warm in the sharp chill of the morning" (*CSS* 70). Since it "was just beginning to be daylight" when Nick and his father left the Indian camp, the warm feeling does not seem to come just from the sun's heat (*CSS* 69). Perhaps that sense of warmth comes from his sense of still being alive, with his father in the front of the rowboat. The handwritten draft of the final sentence was: "Sitting in the stern of the boat with his father rowing, he felt quite sure he would never die." Hemingway crossed out "Sitting . . . boat with" and added, in small cursive script above the crossed-out line, "In the early morning on the lake sitting in the stern of the boat with his father rowing, he felt quite sure he would never die" (KL/EH folder 493; *SS-HLE* 66–67; *CSS* 70). Thus, Hemingway slows the ending down by adding two conditional phrases that qualify Nick's absolute self-assurance: "In the early morning" (no longer dark), "on the lake" (no longer in the Indian camp), "he felt quite sure he would never die." Although Nick's final certitude sounds absolute and idealistic, in his mind he has qualified that faith as dependent on the permanence of time and place. In revising the final line, Hemingway suggests that Nick would not be so sure if he were not sitting in the stern behind his father in a boat in the morning on the lake.

As different as they are, both "The Sisters" and "Indian Camp" portray young boys encountering death for the first time in the company of adults who can (at best) partly comfort a child's discovery of mortality. Both writers end their stories focusing on what the boys reflect upon after facing death. In "The Sisters," Eliza and the narrator's aunt, if anything, contribute unwittingly to the boy's disillusionment about the priest's "idle chalice." In "Indian Camp," Nick's father cannot shelter him either from the trauma of witnessing a birth and a death on the same chilly morning or from posing questions he cannot answer, such as why the Indian father killed himself.[8] Following the lead of Joyce's "The Sisters" as the opening story of *Dubliners,* particularly as he revised "Indian Camp," Hemingway composed a poignant story of the shock of a child's first encounter with mortality.

3

STEIN, JOYCE, AND HEMINGWAY'S REWRITING "CAT IN THE RAIN"

And all were connected in some way to Stein or Joyce, sometimes to both.

—VIRGIL THOMSON, *Virgil Thomson*

The story of the genesis of Hemingway's small gem "Cat in the Rain" leads back to Ezra Pound. In early February 1923, roughly nine months before he started "Indian Camp," Hemingway and Hadley were visiting Pound and his wife, Dorothy Shakespeare, at their home in Rapallo, Italy (Reynolds, *Paris Years* 100–104). Of Ernest Hemingway's short stories set in Italy, "Cat in the Rain" is the first story he began—in February 1923, even before he wrote "Out of Season" in April 1923 (Smith, *Guide* 17, 43). During this visit Pound apparently gave Hemingway a copy of T. S. Eliot's *The Waste Land* to read. The earliest version of the story, titled "Rapallo," includes allusions to cats mating, Ezra Pound, Eliot's *Waste Land,* and his happiness in bed with his wife Hadley: "Cats love in the garden. On green tea tables to be exact. The big cat gets on the small cat. Sweeney gets on Mrs. Porter. Ezra gets nowhere except artistically of course" (KL/EH folder 670.4, quoted in Smith, *Guide* 43). The second draft, a "possible Fascisto story," sets a couple's romantic train ride from Genoa to Portofino to Rapallo—an Italian travelogue—against the hostility of a hotelkeeper's fascist son. By hand, Hemingway described this second draft as a "False Start Rapallo Story possible Fascisto Story" (*SS-HLE* 73). Paul Smith dates this "false start" as late February 1923 "or soon after" he wrote the earliest notes for "Cat" (*Guide* 43). Then, a year after he sketched his first notes for the story and wrote his "False Start" draft, Hemingway labeled his next version as "First Draft Original Manuscript/March,

1924/E.M.H." (*SS-HLE* 74). These drafts record what is one of the longest and most substantial pieces of revision Hemingway undertook for one of his stories. As revised, "Cat in the Rain" reflects the presence of both Gertrude Stein and James Joyce as mentors for Hemingway.

The "False Start Rapallo Story" was not promising. Its beginning sets the stage for a conflict between the hotel owner's son, "a fascisto," and the "two Americans stopping at the hotel" (*SS-HLE* 73). The first paragraph is laced with material one might find in a travel guide: "The Riviera Splendide only served breakfast. The coffee and rolls were good. . . . The rooms were cheap and all faced the sea" (*SS-HLE* 73). The second paragraph includes notes about the American couple's room facing the sea, the public garden, and the war monument that "Italians came from a long way off" to see (*SS-HLE* 73). At the end of this paragraph Hemingway adds a cautionary note to potential tourists: "Even in February there were a few mosquitoes" (*SS-HLE* 73). Nowhere in these paragraphs does the story develop a conflict between the *fascisto* son and the Americans, nor even hint at any tension between the couple.

Hemingway circled the next paragraph, as if signaling himself to revise it or move it to the story's beginning. In this paragraph, he describes the approach by train from Genoa, passing landscapes of cypresses, orange trees, grey rocks, and glimpses of the sea. After this circled paragraph, Hemingway continued with a paragraph that appears to be a revision and expansion of the paragraph describing the approach to Rapallo. In this version of the approach, the narrator focuses on the ebullience of the wife, who could "almost touch the oranges in the trees outside the window" (*SS-HLE* 74). Hers is the narrative point of view, as when the train comes out of tunnels "she saw hillsides with grey olive trees and out of the other window the sea, very blue, with a line of white surf along the rocks" (*SS-HLE* 74). That romantic image of the fertile landscape and the beautiful, "very blue" sea is matched by gushing conversation. The American wife asks, "Why didn't you tell me about this before?" Lest readers mistake her question as hostile, the narrator explains, "She was very happy." Underscoring the marital harmony reflected in the idyllic landscape, the husband responds, "Aren't we happy Kitty?" To which she replies, "I'm so *happy*" (*SS-HLE* 74). This "false start" contains not a whiff of the tense, terse dialogue in "Cat in the Rain."

Thus, the genesis of "Cat in the Rain" involves a cluster of Hemingway's modernist teachers. He began the initial draft while he was with Ezra Pound in Rapallo, Italy, where he first read Eliot's *The Waste Land,* and sent Gertrude Stein his review of her collection *Geography and Plays* (Hemingway, *Letters* vol. 2, 11).[1] The second draft ("False Start") recounts elements of Hemingway and Hadley's travel by train from Milan to Rapallo, where the Pounds lived on the Italian coast. They stayed at the Hotel Splendide (identified in that draft of "Cat in the Rain") overlooking the harbor on the Italian coast (Smith, *Guide* 43; Chamberlin 48). Aside from loaning Hemingway a copy of Eliot's *The Waste Land,* Pound probably also discussed Joyce's *Ulysses,* an unbound press copy of which Sylvia Beach had sent to Hemingway earlier that winter.[2] A year would pass before he returned to the story in the draft labeled "First Draft Original Manuscript/March, 1924/E.M.H."

By the time Hemingway rewrote the story extensively in March 1924, he stripped personal and local references to Pound, Hadley, fascists, and cities on the Italian Riviera in order to portray two Americans in an unnamed hotel in an unnamed town in Italy with a war monument. As signaled by Hemingway's revisions to "Cat in the Rain," the story that once had a clear narrative of a husband and wife vacationing in an identifiable coastal city in Italy became an enigmatic, minimalist story with more mysteries than clues. Having initially titled his story "Rapallo," Hemingway replaced the specific place-name with the puzzling title "Cat in the Rain." Taking his cue particularly from Stein's *Geography and Plays* and Joyce's *Ulysses,* both published in 1922, Hemingway composed a story whose charm lies in its rhythmic repetitions, barbed dialogue, comically ambiguous ending, and ironic juxtapositions with the bullfighting chapters that surround the story.

"Cat in the Rain" makes sense as a puzzling story framed by two seemingly unrelated bullfighting chapters in the spirit of Picasso's placing the inscription "La Jolie" on top of a military helmet in *The Architect's Table,* a painting Hemingway probably saw every time he visited Gertrude Stein's salon (Bishop et al., 242, 374).[3] The presence of Stein and Joyce in Hemingway's "Cat in the Rain" is felt in his boldly staking a claim for American fiction away from the naturalists like Dreiser to follow his modernist teachers like Stein, Joyce, and Pound in presenting jagged narratives instead of linear stories. Although Hemingway's falling out with Stein is well known, in the mid-1920s they collaborated closely on the publication of her novel *The Making of Americans.* In the winter of 1924, Hemingway was already working in the editorial office of *Transatlantic Review,* spending "precious hours retyping and copyediting the manuscript for serialization in Ford's little magazine" (Kennedy and Curnutt 3). Moreover, she was a major influence on his revising "Big Two-Hearted River" (Kennedy, Introduction, *Letters* vol. 2, liii). At least as strong an influence on the young Hemingway was James Joyce. Aside from Ezra Pound, Joyce may be the only writer Hemingway consistently praised. As he wrote to Arthur Mizener on 1 June 1950: "Jim Joyce was the only alive writer that I ever respected. He had his problems but he could write better than anyone I knew" (*SL* 696). Eight years later, in an interview for the *Paris Review* by George Plimpton, Hemingway identified "Joyce, Pound, the good of Stein" as the "few writers" whom he "respected" (Hemingway, Interview by Plimpton 225–26). In answer to the question as to whether he found himself influenced by what he is reading, Hemingway responded, "Not since Joyce was writing *Ulysses* (Hemingway, Interview by Plimpton 226).[4] Pound himself wrote about how Joyce's "clean and hard" writing "influenced let us say the early Hemingway" (Pound and Read 252).

At about the same time that Hemingway returned to "Cat in the Rain" in March 1924, he was anticipating the publication of the Paris *in our time* in mid-March (Chamberlin 57). The April 1924 issue of the *Transatlantic Review* contained reviews of *Three Stories and Ten Poems,* along with *in our time* (Stephens 1); the first installment of Stein's *The Making of Americans;* an installment of what later became Joyce's *Finnegans Wake;* and (in a section titled "From Work in Progress") an untitled story by Hemingway that became "Indian Camp." Thus, Hemingway began and revised "Cat in the Rain" and assembled *In Our Time* at a time when he saw the cubist art in Gertrude Stein's salon, read and reviewed her *Geography and Plays,* listened to Pound's discussion of Eliot's and Joyce's work, and read Stein's and Joyce's work published in the same issue of *Transatlantic* as "Indian Camp." Both Stein and Joyce, writing during virtually the same span of time from 1905 to 1922, contributed to Hemingway's architectural design for the center of *In Our Time,* where he interlocked tales of marriage with chapters about bullfighting in a complex suite.[5]

The presence of Stein and Joyce in Hemingway's "Cat in the Rain" can be seen in the story's first paragraph, as revised from the "False Start Rapallo Story" of 1923. In the "First Draft Original Manuscript" of March 1924, Hemingway began with exactly the same first sentence as in the print version: "There were only two Americans stopping at the hotel" (*SS-HLE* 75; *CSS* 129). In revising this manuscript draft, Hemingway moved his introduction of the cat from the end of the first paragraph to the second (*SS-HLE* 75; *CSS* 129). Thus, the first paragraph in the final draft begins with concatenated repetitions casting a hypnotic spell before the next paragraphs introduce the central characters as "the American wife," "a cat," and "her husband." Several of the early reviewers of *In Our Time,* like Paul Rosenfeld, noted the influence of Stein's "steady reiterations" on Hemingway (in Stephens 9). More recently, scholars have focused on the influence of her repetitions on such stories as "Up in Michigan," "Soldier's Home," "Mr. and Mrs. Elliot," "Cat in the Rain," and "Big Two-Hearted River."[6] Less often has attention been paid to the influence of Joyce's repetitions on Hemingway (O'Connor 151–64). Whereas Stein's and Joyce's rhythmic repetitions convey an erotic energy, those of Hemingway in the opening paragraph of "Cat in the Rain" are a prelude to the absence of eroticism between the American couple in his story.

The final paragraph of Stein's "Ada" (composed 1910, published 1922) gains its incantatory power from echoing chants. In a 175-word paragraph, she repeats "living" eight times, "loving" seven times, and "listening" six times. Here is the first half of that paragraph in "Ada" from *Geography and Plays:* "She came to be happier than anybody else who was living then. It is easy to believe this thing. She was telling some one, who was loving every story that was charming. Some one who was living was almost always listening. Some one who was loving was almost always listening. That one who was loving was almost always listening. That one who was loving was telling about being one then listening. That one being loving was then telling stories having a beginning a middle and an ending" (16). In a climactic moment of this portrait, Stein interweaves a teller and a listener of stories in a refrain that unites them. First Stein begins with a tribute to the "loving" listener to her "stories." Then she implicitly refers to herself as "one who was loving was telling"—Stein as the author of pieces that Alice B. Toklas heard and typed. Then she unites the two: "That one who was loving was telling about being one then listening." Stein's repetitions seem part of an inventive marriage vow: the listener and the teller seem to be "one." Later in the final paragraph Stein evokes sensual pleasure in the union of the pair: "Trembling was all living, living was all loving, some one was then the other one" (16). The gerunds of arousal link together in a chiasmic ring of "trembling," "living," and "loving," as if in climactic fusion. The triple repetitions—"that one," "some one," and "the other one"—sound a note of unison, of the couple as "one." Stein's repetitions inscribe into her sketch the union with "Ada" (Alice) as her sexual partner. Hemingway's repetitions evoke no such sexual intimacy. Several scholars, such as Robert Paul Lamb and Marjorie Perloff, have previously noted that Stein's repetitions influenced Hemingway. That said, Lamb devotes an entire chapter in *Art Matters* to explore how dramatically different Hemingway's repetitions are from Stein's (chapter 5, 113–35). His repetitions here in "Cat in the Rain" are far different in effect, inserting a numbing distance between a couple rather than arousal and sexual union.

While less incessant, Joyce's repetitions evoke an inspired poet in his portrait of Stephen Dedalus as a young artist. In a prelude to the villanelle Stephen composes in *A Portrait of the Artist as a Young Man,* Joyce presents Stephen's ecstatic awakening in a pulsating rhythm:

> Towards dawn he awoke. O what sweet music! His soul was all dewy wet. Over his limbs in sleep pale cool waves of light had passed. He lay still, as if his soul lay amid cool waters, conscious of faint sweet music. His mind was waking slowly to a tremulous morning knowledge, a morning inspiration. A spirit filled him, pure as the purest water, sweet as dew, moving as music. But how faintly it was inbreathed, how passionlessly, as if the seraphim themselves were breathing upon him! His soul was waking slowly, fearing to awake wholly. It was that windless hour of dawn when madness wakes and strange plants open to the light and the moth flies forth silently. (*Portrait* 235)

In this passage, one hears the linked repetitions. For instance, the repetition of "a tremulous morning knowledge, a morning inspiration" sounds notes of a chanted *aubade,* Joyce's invocation to seraphic muses. In the final sentence, "the light" to which the plants open echoes the "cool waves of light" that "passed" over Stephen's limbs. In Joyce's evocation of Stephen's reverie, his repetitions build a sense of inspiration, as a young poet quickens to a mothlike flight that points forward to his final flight as an artist.[7] Or, as Colin Gillis has argued, Joyce's repetitions convey "an autoerotic experience" in Stephen Dedalus's conception of his villanelle in *Portrait* (622). In both Stein's closing paragraph to "Ada," and in Joyce's passage leading to Stephen's composing a villanelle in *Portrait,* repetitions serve to build a sense of sexual climax, whether between a teller and a listener as a loving couple, or within a solitary writer awakening in a mood to compose a poem formed of interlocking rhymes. Hemingway's concatenated repetitions, in contrast, convey an absence of the erotic intimacy present in Stein and Joyce.

Hemingway's repetitions at the beginning of "Cat in the Rain" in *In Our Time* evoke a dull emptiness of disconnection between Italians and Americans, a statue and a garden, the sea and the hotel, and the "two Americans," distant from each other:

> There were only two Americans stopping at the hotel. They did not know any of the people they passed on the stairs on their way to and from their room. Their room was on the second floor facing the sea. It also faced the public garden and the war monument. There were big palms and green benches in the public garden. In the good weather there was always an artist with his easel. Artists liked the way the palms grew and the bright colors of the hotels facing the gardens and the sea. Italians came from a long way off to look at the war monument. It was made of bronze and glistened in the rain. It was raining. The rain dripped from the palm trees. Water stood in pools on the gravel paths. The sea broke in a long line in the rain and slipped back down the beach to come up and break again in a long line in the rain. The motor cars were gone from the square by the war monument. Across the square in the doorway of the café a waiter stood looking out at the empty square. (*CSS* 129)[8]

In this 193-word paragraph, at least sixteen words are repeated. The repetition is not as constant as in Stein's closing paragraph for "Ada" (the most frequent recurrence in the opening paragraph of "Cat in the Rain" is "rain," repeated five times) and more closely resembles Joyce's linked repetitions. That is, "their room" leads to "[t]heir room was," just as "facing the sea" leads to "faced the public garden," which leads to "in the public garden," which leads to "hotels facing the gardens and the sea." The repetitions link the separate images of garden, monument, and sea into one composition of place.

This opening paragraph of "Cat in the Rain" illustrates Hemingway's revision by adding details to the earlier draft. Up through the references to the palm trees in the public garden, the manuscript draft and the published story are virtually the same (*SS-HLE* 75; *CSS* 129). However, in late additions to the draft of this first paragraph, Hemingway refers to a single "artist with his easel" and then to "artists" facing the hotel to sketch "the bright colors of the hotels facing the gardens and the sea," as followers of the impressionists might have done (*CSS* 129). As late as the draft that Hemingway labeled "First Draft Original Manuscript," dated March 1924, and signed E.M.H, there are no references to artists in the first paragraph (KL/EH folder 319; *SS-HLE* 75). Hemingway added these references in a manuscript of the story titled "Cat in the Rain" (Hemingway crossed out the title "The Poor Kitty") and signed the draft with his address as "113 Rue Notre Dame des Champs" (KL/EH folder 320).

Furthermore, as Hemingway revised this paragraph, he made the repetition of "rain" even more incessant in setting the mood. After the sentences about the war monument, the "First Draft original manuscript" reads: "It was made of bronze and glistened in the rain that had been falling since daylight" (*SS-HLE* 75). As he revised that sentence, he divided it into two shorter sentences and added another repetition about the rain: "It was made of bronze and glistened in the rain. It was raining" (*CSS* 129). With this revision, Hemingway emphasized that the rain was falling in the continuous past. He cut the part of the sentence cast in the past perfect, "rain that *had been falling* since daylight" (my emphasis). By doing so, Hemingway rendered the rain as persisting into the moment the American wife was looking out the hotel window.

Linking together the separate elements of the scene, the repetitions of "public garden" and "sea" lead to the repeated phrase "in a long line in the rain." This repetition of "long line" is not in the manuscript draft and came only when Hemingway added the reference to artists and added a second "line in the rain" phrase at the end of the sentence that begins "The sea broke" (*SS-HLE* 75; *CSS* 129). As Massimo Bacigalupo writes about the repetitions in this passage, "each phrase repeats the last word of the preceding phrase, suggesting perhaps the spent rhythm of the waves that appear at the end" (120).[9] Hemingway follows Stein and Joyce in linking repetitions, but in the case of his opening to "Cat in the Rain" the repetitions evoke solitude and dull emptiness. The American wife looking out the window notices that cars are "gone from the square by the war monument"—an absence of mobility. In a sentence Hemingway added to the draft, she observes that across the square a solitary waiter stood regarding an "empty square"—empty of cars, empty of people (*SS-HLE* 75; *CSS* 129). The American wife and the waiter mirror each other in their solitude.

Hemingway learned from both Stein and Joyce the value of repetition but then made their rhythms convey his own vacuums. That is, whereas the repetitions in Stein and Joyce evoke erotic arousal, the repetitions in Hemingway's opening paragraph evoke an erotic absence—a striking change from the earliest draft of the story. In what Paul Smith has identified as Hemingway's "earliest notes" for the story sketched in Rapallo in February 1923, Hemingway's repetitions, internal rhymes, and sexual puns resemble Stein's: "Hadley and I are happy sometimes. Her friends call her Hadley. We are happiest in bed. In bed we are well fed. There are no problems in bed. Now I lay me down to sleep in bed. There are no prayers in bed. Beds need only be wide enough. If the beds wide enough we will be bride enough" (KL/EH folder 670.4, quoted in Reynolds, *Paris Years* 103–4).[10] As Reynolds observes, in the earliest draft of "Cat" Hemingway was "in the lighthearted world of Stein songs" (*Paris Years* 104). Indeed, as Carl Eby points out, in that draft of "Cat," one finds that "the story is *not* so devoid of erotic investment" (*Hemingway's Fetishism* 135). By the time he revised "Cat in the Rain" a year after his first sketch, Hemingway had developed his own variation on Stein's and Joyce's repetitions—moving from their erotic pulsations to his own arid rhythms.[11]

The spare conversations Hemingway weaves into "Cat in the Rain" reflect his most significant departure from Gertrude Stein's fiction. In his use of dialogue, Hemingway follows Joyce more than Stein, whose "Melanctha," for example, is laced with extremely long monologues between Melanctha and Dr. Jeff Campbell. In contrast, the conversations in "Cat in the Rain" are terse—more like the clipped dialogue in *Dubliners, Portrait,* and *Ulysses.*[12] Furthermore, the mixture of spoken English and Italian sets this story apart from most of the other stories in *In Our Time.* Marjorie leaves Nick with a sharp farewell ("You don't need to . . ." [*CSS* 82]), and Bugs sends Nick away with a simple message ("Good-bye and good luck!" [*CSS* 103]). In both cases, communication in English is clear. In contrast, "Cat in the Rain" evokes tension in part by an American couple's trying to speak in Italian as well as in English.[13] The mixture of Italian and English in the dialogue evokes two types of tension—one benign between the maid and the wife, the other a more hostile tension between the wife and her husband.

The more hostile tension in the mixture of English and Italian comes in the three-way exchange between the husband, wife, and maid at the end of the story. After the wife concludes her list of desires, spoken in English to her husband, the maid knocks on their door. His one spoken word in Italian, "*Avanti,*" seems to welcome the maid as an interruption of his wife's spoken desires, to which he "was not listening" (*CSS* 131). Thus, "*Avanti,*" or "come in," seems the husband's assertion of control. Ironically, the wife understands better than her husband that the maid's entry, presenting the cat (presumably in Italian), reasserts the connection between the Italian host and the wife as guest. In "Cat in the Rain," Hemingway presents a husband and wife communicating with one another, but with more coldness and distance than the wife, at least, shows in conversing with the hotelkeeper and maid. In the earliest draft of the story, dated February 1923 by Paul Smith, there is no dialogue at all (*Guide* 43). In the second draft, dated late February 1923 by Smith, the only brief dialogue is between the husband and the wife. That dialogue in the "False Start" evoked romantic harmony, not marital tension. A year or so later, when he returned to completely rewrite the story, Hemingway's dialogue between the American wife and her husband was a far distance from such smarmy language. Rather, Hemingway sharpened his use of dialogue as a central means of suggesting discord. In the final draft of the story, Hemingway interweaves spoken English and Italian as a means of evoking mild tension between the wife and the deferential maid and more severe conflict between the American wife and her husband.

The Italian hotel owner seems conversant in basic English; the maid does not. The husband utters one word of Italian in the story; his American wife seems, if not fluent, at least working on a basic conversational ability to speak the language. Ironically, the American husband and the Italian maid both seem limited in communicating across their language barrier, whereas the hotelkeeper and the wife show an ability to speak at least the rudiments of each other's language. The American wife's "*Il piove*" is the first Italian spoken, a simple clause from the wife to the hotelkeeper. He responds in Italian that he translates into English: "*Sí, sí, Signora, brutto tempo*. It's very bad weather" (*CSS* 129–30). His translation into English suggests his uncertainty as to how much Italian the "Signora" understands. After the wife is unable to find the "kitty," the maid asks: "*Ha perduto qualque cosa, Signora?*" (*CSS* 130). In revising, Hemingway corrected a mistake in the draft, where he wrote "qualque causa" (*SS-HLE* 76). Unlike the hotelkeeper, she does not translate, probably because she does not speak English. When the maid does not seem to understand the wife's response ("There was a cat"), the "American girl" responds in Italian that she is looking for a cat: "*Sí, il gatto.*" The wife's explanation in Italian is curious as, earlier from her point of view, she referred to a female cat: "The cat was trying to make herself so compact that she would not be dripped on" (*CSS* 129). The shifts in the gender of references to the cat are present in the 1924 draft, and the dialogue is virtually the same from that draft to the final version (*SS-HLE* 75–76; *CSS* 129–130).

Thus, although her response implies that the wife understood the maid's question about what she has lost, her shifting genders from a female cat to a male cat seems part of a comical confusion over genders. Is the cat male or female? Is her search for "*il gatto*" a significant slip: she saw a female "kitty" earlier, but she wants a male "*il gatto*"? Or is she simply confused as she speaks in rudimentary Italian? After the wife's reference to "*il gatto,*" the maid laughs and responds (in Italian but reported as English): "A cat in the rain?" (*CSS* 130). The maid's question suggests her puzzlement over why the male "*il gatto*" would be out in the rain—in Italian, the feminine "*la pioggia.*" Her laughter suggests that much is comical in this story. The maid seems to ask, rhetorically, "What would a cat be doing in the rain?" Then the wife's response to the maid's question seems to fluster the maid: "When she talked English the maid's face tightened" (*CSS* 130). When the American wife speaks English, the Italian maid's laughter fades. Therefore, the maid is probably speaking Italian when she encourages the wife to go back inside. The wife seems to have understood the maid, since she says, "I suppose so," in response to the maid's simple warning in Italian: "You will be wet." The wife understands the maid better than the maid understands her, and she converses in Italian better than does her husband. The blend of languages in the story not only contributes to its comedy of errors but also conveys a subtle hierarchy from the hotelkeeper, whose fluency in both languages establishes him as more adept at bilingual conversations, to the least conversant, the husband and the maid.

In contrast to the maid's laughing question about a "cat in the rain," the exchange in English between the husband and wife in the hotel room is a tense part of the story. When the wife returns from hunting for the cat, she sees George "on the bed, reading" (*CSS* 130). The narrative comment implies that her husband has been immobile on the bed while his wife has been searching for the cat outside. His question ("Did you get the cat?") implies an interest in his wife's search. That question prompts what might be the most intimate movement of the story: "She sat down on the bed" (*CSS* 130). Hemingway added this sentence when he revised the manuscript draft (compare *SS-HLE* 76 with *CSS* 130). This addition suggests the wife's movement toward physical intimacy, to which her husband responds by "reading again" (*CSS* 130). Her sitting on the bed might lead to physical contact but instead results in the wife's repeated refrain of desire: "wanted it so much," "wanted it so much" (*CSS* 130). Again, Hemingway added a simple sentence to the manuscript draft: "I wanted that poor kitty" (compare *SS-HLE* 76 and *CSS* 130). This added sentence not only evokes a rising intensity in the wife's repeated efforts to convey her desires to her husband but suggests *why* she wanted the "poor kitty"—out of possibly maternal empathy for the "kitty" (now apparently younger in her mind than the "cat") exposed to the rain. Her expressions of desire—sitting on the bed, repeating what she "wanted"—suggest *eros* frozen.

In response to George's absorption in his book, the wife turns to a mirror to look at herself as a prelude to the conversation about whether she should grow her hair out. As shown by comparing the manuscript draft with the published version, Hemingway rewrote this part of the conversation more than any other piece of dialogue in the story. In the manuscript the wife wants to "pile my hair up high" (a phrase crossed out twice). She wants to "wear a Spanish comb and have an Yteb gown and a cat to sit in my lap and purr in front of the fire while I waited for someone to come home" (*SS-HLE* 77). This version of the wife's longest monologue portrays her as rather spoiled and trendy, as she wants to wear not only a Spanish comb in her hair but also a stylish evening gown in fashion during the 1920s. In this earlier version she wants a cat to "purr in front of the fire" and keep her company while she awaits her "someone" to return to her. Her husband's response is little short of contemptuous: "You're a swell mixture." To that "swell" response, the wife sounds even more desperate to be sheltered from distress: "and I don't want to know what's going to happen" (*SS-HLE* 77). In this draft, the American wife concludes her list of "wants" with a desire to be oblivious—presumably, to the bad things that are going to happen in her marriage.

In revising this exchange, Hemingway toned down the wife's expressions of desire and more deftly suggested the tension between her voicing her desires and her husband's command for silence. As the conversation continues, the wife's expressions of desire mount but seem less extravagant than in the manuscript: she wants to let her hair grow out, pull her hair back tight, stroke a kitty on her lap, have her own silver and candles, brush her hair out in front of a mirror, and have new clothes (*CSS* 131).[14] She expresses a desire for owning her possessions and for touching a cat's fur and her own hair. Her husband, tersely, wants only quiet: "Oh shut up, and get something to read" (*CSS* 131). He commands her to join him in the silent act of reading. He does not seem to care what she reads, as "get something" implies. Her response, a climax of repeated desire ("I want a cat" three times), is insistent, as if resistant to command. Thus, Hemingway's blend of the wife's monologue about what she wants, along with a terse dialogue between the couple, drives the story's rising tension. Whereas in the first draft of the story, the repetitious, rhymed language sounded like Gertrude Stein's, Hemingway's final draft portrays the couple's conflict through clipped dialogue that sounds more like Joyce's.

In their earlier stories, both Gertrude Stein and James Joyce offer conclusions that provide an unyielding sense of closure. Each story in Stein's *Three Lives* ends with the death of the title character: Anna dies in a hospital a few days after surgery, Melanctha dies in "a home for poor consumptives," and Lena dies (like Catherine in *A Farewell to Arms*) after a stillborn delivery (Stein, *Writings* 123, 239, 270). Near the end of "The Gentle Lena," Stein suggests that from the outset of her marriage to Herman Kreder, Lena has lost any independence or vitality of spirit she may have had. In the penultimate appearance of the word "married" (110 appearances in *Three Lives*), the narrator contrasts Herman's energy as a new father with her passivity as a mother: "He always did all the active new things in the house and for the baby. . . . Lena never got any better in herself of this way of being that she had had ever since she had been married" (Stein, *Writings* 268–69). The narrator's language suggests that marriage itself was, for Lena, an illness from which she "never" recovered. The repetition of adverbs hammers a sense of finality into the portrait of this American wife: she "never" was herself, "ever" since her marriage to Herman. Marriage brought a final seal to her life, as Stein brings her story to a close.

Similarly, in the stories from "The Boarding House" through "A Painful Case," Joyce's narratives end with a bleak sense of cyclical abuse and dislocation. In *Dubliners* Joyce's portraits of marriage are perhaps even darker than Stein's—laced with trickery, coercion, alcoholism, child abuse, and suicide. At the end of "Counterparts," an alcoholic father beats his son mercilessly. The stark ending portrays Farrington as a father whose cycle of abuse is suggested even in the repetitions of the boy's futile litany: "And I'll . . . I'll say a *Hail Mary* for you, pa, if you don't beat me . . . . I'll say a *Hail Mary*. . . ." (*Dubliners* 98). That Joyce ends the story with an incomplete supplication suggests the father's blows stop the boy from repeating "if you don't beat me . . ." Although the middle stories of *Dubliners* do not end in the deaths of the main characters, as do Stein's *Three Lives,* they conclude as portraits of enclosed, fractured, empty lives.

Both the sketches of *Geography and Plays* and the chapters of *Ulysses* offered Hemingway models for a different type of ending. Rather than the closed endings of Stein's *Three Lives* and Joyce's marriage tales in *Dubliners,* the endings of the later works are more open, comical, and indeterminate. Stein concludes "Ada" (1910), her portrait of Alice B. Toklas, with a repetitive proclamation far different from the closure of each story in *Three Lives:* "Certainly this one was loving Ada then. And certainly Ada all her living then was happier in living than anyone else who ever could, who was, who is, who ever will be living" (*Geography and Plays* 16). Whereas the repetition of adverbs at the end of "Gentle Lena" signals a finality of closure, here the repetitions present an opening of possibilities for union and enduring pleasure. At the end of "Lena," adverbial time markers spell an end; in "Ada," time markers ("then" and the repeated "ever") celebrate a lasting union of lovers. Beloved, Ada loves and lives in past, present, and future time.

In contrast to the rapturous conclusion of "Ada," in the open-ended conclusion of "I Must Try to Write the History of Belmonte" in *Geography and Plays,* Stein mocks male bravado and leaves uncertain what will happen after her portrait of the lame bullfighter. In "Belmonte" (written 1916, published 1922), Stein sets her portrait of the bullfighter in the context of her comical asides about marriage: "It is said that the Queen hit the King. Not here. In Greece" (*Geography and Plays* 70). She follows the deadpan portrait of a Greek queen's hitting a king (but not here in cultured Paris) with a slapstick scene of wives who scurry to see their husbands as they disembark from ships: "In places they go to see their husbands. They wait until he is off the boat. Then they rush" (71). Stein presents her portrait of a star bullfighter (hobbled by bronchitis and a hurt foot) alongside scenes of a Greek queen beating her king and of American wives rushing to greet their husbands. Stein continues the comedy by invoking a love song to Fanny: "I love you Fanny Fanny is your name isn't it" (71). This last question seems a case of jocular whimsy, perhaps of sexual innuendo.

In this sequence, Stein mocks the worlds of Spanish bullfighting, Greek patriarchy, and American couples abroad while affirming her own love for Fanny/Alice. However different "Ada" and "Belmonte" are, in both cases Stein's profiles leave open multiple possibilities in their endings. In so doing, Stein provides Hemingway with comic models for intertwining marriage tales and bullfighting chapters as narratives for exploring gender roles. Moreover, she concludes the portrait of Belmonte on a peremptory note of three terse, declarative sentences: "I choose Gallo. He is a cock. He moves plainly." At the end of her sketch, Stein's final pun on the bullfighter Gallo's name as Spanish for "rooster" or "cock" seems a tongue-in-cheek echo of her earlier mockery of heroic chronicles: "This is not the history of Belmonte because there are so many mounted men." Is Stein's reference to "mounted men" an *aficionada*'s tribute to picadors, or a wry pun at the expense of machismo? Both "Ada" and "Belmonte" offered Hemingway models for concluding narratives with comical puns and open-ended ambiguities.[15]

Likewise, in the chapters of *Ulysses,* Joyce left the bleak closures of the stories in *Dubliners* for more indeterminate endings. Take, for example, the mock-heroic conclusion of "Cyclops." Having taunted the antisemitic, Gaelic champion "Citizen" with the Jewishness of Mendelssohn, Marx, and Jesus, Leopold Bloom soars off in a carriage that the narrator likens to Elijah's chariot. In a mock epiphany, the narrator of "Cyclops" presents Bloom's departure as an ascent to a cloudy paradise approached at a comically precise angle: "And they beheld Him even Him, ben Bloom Elijah, amid clouds of angels ascend . . . at an angle of fortyfive degrees over Donohue's in Little Green street like a shot off a shovel" (*Ulysses* 283). Where Bloom is heading is unclear, and only in the next chapter, "Nausicaa," does Joyce suggest an ironic connection between the Citizen of "Cyclops" and his granddaughter, Gerty MacDowell (*Ulysses* 289). However, Bloom's ascent at a forty-five-degree angle—the conclusion of "Cyclops"—is a comical foreshadowing of the "shot" of his masturbatory response to the exhibitionist Gerty's erotic display of her legs. Such punning and ambiguity seem influential in Hemingway's ending his story with a mysterious "big tortoise-shell cat" that the maid holds "tight against her" before offering the cat as a gift from "the padrone," as physically intimate as any contact in the story (*CSS* 131). That is, in "Cat in the Rain," Hemingway chose to follow the open endings and comical puns of Stein's sketches in *Geography and Plays* and Joyce's chapters in *Ulysses* rather than the closed conclusions of their earlier stories.

Hemingway ends the story with the maid's presentation of an enigmatic cat. Whatever one makes of the wife's desire to "have a kitty sit on my lap and purr when I stroke her," the "kitty" (a word she repeats seven times in the story) seems to figure as a substitute for a warmth of touch her marriage is not bringing her. Hemingway added this "when I stroke her" sentence to the manuscript draft, where the wife simply wants "a cat to sit on my lap and purr" (compare *SS-HLE* 77 with *CSS* 131). In the earlier draft, the wife does not express a desire to "stroke" the cat. In the revision with the added sentence, the American wife is imagining herself in physical contact with a feline "her" she wants to "stroke." Hemingway's earlier use of the verb "stroked," near the end of "Up in Michigan," was clearly sexual (*CSS* 62). In "Cat in the Rain," the wife's desire to "stroke" a cat seems a wishful replacement for erotic touch, such as Havelock Ellis discussed in "the cases in which the contact of animals, stroking, etc., produces sexual excitement or gratification" (Ellis 71).[16] In the case of the wife in "Cat," the desire to "stroke" seems a substitute for sexual touching, as in the mirroring scenes in *The Sun Also Rises* when Brett "stroked" Jake's head (*SAR-HLE* 45) and when Jake later "stroked her hair" (196)—in both cases, gestures of attempted comfort short of sexual fulfillment. At the end of her list of desires, the wife in "Cat" presents the cat she wants as an explicit replacement for growing her hair out and having "fun": "If I can't have long hair or any fun, I can have a cat" (*CSS* 131). The word "fun" here echoes Marjorie's question at "The End of Something": "Isn't love any fun?" (*CSS* 81). The word recurs in Nick Adams's "It's more fun," as he encourages Kate to undress in the sexually explicit story "Summer People" (*CSS* 502). Having "fun" seems Hemingway's coded pun for sex—his version of Stein's "press juice from a button" (*Geography and Plays* 39), or her "A Persian kitten is a purring kitten" (*Geography and Plays* 152), or of Joyce's fireworks in "Nausicaa" (*Ulysses* 300). For the American wife, stroking a kitten seems as much "fun" as she can have—a substitute for sexual intimacy with her husband.

At the end of "Cat in the Rain," the maid knocks, George speaks his one word of Italian and beckons her to enter, and she does, bearing a large tortoiseshell cat. Strikingly, Hemingway altered the one word of Italian that the husband speaks. In the manuscript, the husband says, "Vengo," or "I am coming" (*SS-HLE* 77). That simple response implies that he is going to get up from the bed on which he is reading for the first time in the story. While revising the draft, Hemingway changed his one-word response to the maid's knock on the door to "Avanti," a command or invitation for the maid to enter (*CSS* 131). Thus, in the revision, Hemingway leaves George inert on the bed for the entire story, and leaves readers guessing about his response to the maid's entry holding a cat "pressed tight against her" (*CSS* 131). Hemingway only tells us that he "looked up from his book" (*CSS* 131). He also leaves undetermined to whom the maid speaks her final line. To the manuscript draft, Hemingway added the deferential phrase, "Excuse me," before the maid speaks her final words, presumably in Italian (compare *SS-HLE* 77 with *CSS* 131). Is she saying "Scusi" to the husband, the wife, or both? After most of the story in which the American girl is referred to simply as "she" and "her," the maid uses the formal address, "Signora," as part of a presentation of a gift from "the padrone." What that gift represents is teasingly ambiguous. Is the gift the same cat in the rain the American wife sought or different? Is the gift a sign of pregnancy, as the large cat swung against the maid's body seems a picture of a swollen womb? Is the tortoiseshell cat male or female?[17] A sign of a sterile male? A sign of a female's replacing a detached husband as bed partner, lightly echoing the final paragraph of "Mr. and Mrs. Elliot"? While Hemingway's ending of "Cat in the Rain" may provoke such questions, answers are prolific and inconclusive. Rather, as David Lodge argues, "It would be a mistake, therefore, to look for a single clue, whether pregnancy or barrenness, to the meaning of 'Cat in the Rain.'" What Lodge phrases as "the story's indeterminacy" seems the right note about the ending (17). In "Cat in the Rain," Hemingway chose to follow Stein's lead in *Geography and Plays* and Joyce's in *Ulysses* by ending the story with ambiguities and enigmas.

Hemingway concluded "Cat in the Rain" by leaving open to question whether the American wife is entrapped in a cold marriage.[18] Rather, he portrayed her as deftly, tersely navigating her husband's attempts to control her: to keep her hair short, or to insist that she "shut up, and get something to read" (*CSS* 131). In this regard, the wife in "Cat in the Rain" seems among Hemingway's female characters who independently assert their identity: Tiny in "Out of Season," Marjorie in "The End of Something" (the next story Hemingway wrote after "Cat"), Kate in "Summer People," Brett in *The Sun Also Rises,* Jig in "Hills Like White Elephants," the unnamed woman in "Sea Change," Pilar in *For Whom the Bell Tolls,* and Catherine in *The Garden of Eden.*[19] Against his portrait of George as an immobile American husband in an Italian hotel room, Hemingway sets the "American girl" as having more empathy, adaptability, and force. Hemingway does not tell his readers, for certain, whether she keeps her hair cut short, but she does not "shut up," she shows no sign of responding to her husband's command to "get something to read," and she *does* get the cat—whatever that gift suggests. With the padrone's gift of a big cat, Hemingway deftly parodies the husband's order for silence.

Several Hemingway scholars have noted how his sequence of stories from childhood to adulthood follows that of Joyce's *Dubliners*.[20] After his four stories of young boys and a girl, and after two stories about young gallants gallivanting about Dublin, Joyce includes five tales that revolve around marriages: "The Boarding House," "A Little Cloud," "Counterparts," "Clay," and "A Painful Case." Likewise, after four stories of Nick Adams growing up, and after four stories of adolescents and young adults, Hemingway presents four tales that focus on couples: "Mr. and Mrs. Elliot," "Cat in the Rain," "Out of Season," and "Cross-Country Snow." Michael Reynolds groups these stories as Hemingway's "marriage tales," although he does not connect the group to Joyce's stories (*Paris Years* 188). To my knowledge, only one scholar has connected several of Joyce's marriage tales in *Dubliners* with Hemingway's in *In Our Time* (Gajdusek, *Hemingway in His Own Country* 209–13). And no one, so far as I know, has discussed the significance of Hemingway's interweaving his marriage tales with the bullfighting chapters. Following Stein and Joyce in their jarring transitions in *Geography and Plays* and *Ulysses,* Hemingway connects the art of bullfighting with the travails of marriages and affairs in ironic juxtapositions that point ahead to *The Sun Also Rises.*

Hemingway's decision to use the chapters in the 1924 Paris *in our time* as interludes between the stories of *In Our Time* is the most striking development in his shaping the latter collection. This grouping of marriage tales and bullfighting chapters was Hemingway's plan when he wrote, by hand, on several sheets of Câblogramme Western Union paper, his early blueprint for structuring *In Our Time.* Hemingway clearly took pains to shape his collection—even to the extent of listing word counts for each story.[21] When Hemingway drafted this plan for *In Our Time,* he placed the four stories and the four bullfighting chapters in the same order in which they appear in the first edition. At the center of *In Our Time,* Hemingway intertwined the marriage tales and bullfighting stories tightly together once he decided to move the first bullfighting vignette from chapter 2 of the 1924 Paris *in our time* to chapter 9 of the 1925 *In Our Time.* Hemingway framed the stories of married couples with the bloody, farcical chapters of bulls and bullfighters.

In the 1924 *in our time,* most of the bullfighting chapters directly followed one another—the gored horse (chapter 12), the bad bullfighter (chap-

ter 13), Villalta (chapter 14), the drunken bullfighter (chapter 15), and Maera's fictional death (chapter 16). In *in our time,* only the chapter Hemingway
wrote before ever seeing a bullfight is separate, sandwiched as chapter 2 between "Everyone was drunk" (the march toward Champagne) and "Mina-
rets stuck up" (the Greek retreat). As arranged for *in our time,* these bullfighting chapters seemed to form juxtaposed pairs. Thus, the vignette of the
bad bullfighter and of the virtuoso Villalta face each other on the same page,
as if directly inviting a reader to contrast them. The chapter in *in our time*
of the drunken bullfighter ends with Maera's mockingly anticipating his
needing to risk his own death by replacing the bullfighter too drunk to enter
the ring. That single page of chapter 15 faces the single page of chapter 16,
Hemingway's fictional narrative of Maera's death, as if his anticipation of
his death and his consciousness of dying mirror one another.[22]

Whereas the bullfighting chapters of *in our time* form a relatively self-
contained unit, Hemingway arranged them in the 1925 *In Our Time* to frame
the stories of tense relationships. The chapter preceding "Cat in the Rain,"
about a gored horse, seems an ironic comment on the lack of physical contact between George and his wife. The "whack whack" the *monos* give the
horse—the *monos* forcing a gored horse to stand on its legs—enacts a theater
of cruelty. The frantic efforts of the *monos* to prop up a white horse on its
legs, while its "entrails hung down in a blue bunch," seem more cruel, but no
less absurd, than the picador who "shook his lance at the bull" while "Blood
pumped" from between the horse's legs (*CSS* 127). Such horrific, slapstick
bravado builds an ironic bridge between two stories portraying frigid marriages. The standoff between a bull and a picador at the end of chapter 10
("The bull could not make up his mind to charge" [*CSS* 127]) seems a comical echo of the marriage at the end of "Mr. and Mrs. Elliot" and a prelude to
the marriage portrayed in "Cat in the Rain." That is, there seems no charge
left either in Mr. Elliot, who spends the night writing poems while his wife
makes "conversation" with her friend, or in George, whose reading shields
him from physical contact with his wife. The ambiguities that Milton Cohen
observed about this chapter serve to connect "Mr. and Mrs. Elliot" and "Cat
in the Rain" as narratives of irresolution—husbands and wives, and then a
picador and a bull, all pausing.[23]

Though there is a considerable distance between the Italian hotel of
"Cat in the Rain" and the Spanish bullfighting ring of chapter 11, Heming-

way's pairing contrasts the appreciative audience the wife finds in the hotel's owner and maid with the jeering crowd at the arena. Following the gift from the Italian padrone of a cat, chapter 11 presents the sardonic trophies—insults rather than compliments—of a Spanish crowd. The maid's polite offering from "the padrone" to "the Signora" honors the American wife as not merely an ordinary guest but as a favored patroness. How the wife—or her husband—responds to the gift is left to the reader's imagination. In contrast, in chapter 11, the pieces of bread spectators were eating, cushions on which they were sitting, and leather wine bottles from which they were drinking all become projectiles as forms of derision (CSS 133). The bad bullfighter is the direct object of the crowd's hoots and jeers. Furthermore, an anonymous "some one" has cut off the bullfighter's pigtail, an emasculating insult (CSS 113). That "a kid" ran off with the pigtail seems to deepen the ironic indignity, as the bullfighter's hair has become a toy for boys to mock—a harsh echo of the conversation in "Cat" about George's desire to keep his wife's hair short.

Moreover, the effusive confession of the bad bullfighter at the end of chapter 11 contrasts with the monosyllabic comments of the husband in "Cat": "I'll do it" (then George doesn't fetch the cat [CSS 129]), "Don't get wet" (CSS 129), "Did you get the cat?" (130), "Yeah?" (131), and "Avanti" (131). In contrast to the husband's terse declarations, questions, and commands in "Cat," Hemingway places no quotation marks around the bullfighter's confession in chapter 11, as if to suggest his spoken words flow without interruption (CSS 133). This hapless man, who ends the chapter by admitting, "I am not really a good bullfighter" (CSS 133), seems an ironic comment on the laconic husband of "Cat in the Rain," who feigns concern for what happened to the cat his wife sought, but who seems unresponsive to her needs. Ironically, the gendered references in the final paragraphs of "Cat in the Rain" suggest the power of the maid and the wife: "She held . . . she said . . . for the Signora" (CSS 131). The gendered references in chapter 11, in contrast, suggest the powerlessness of both the male bull ("his knees") and the male bullfighter ("grabbed him and held him" [CSS 133]). Hemingway's setting chapter 11 after "Cat in the Rain" seems to connect the bullfighter with Mr. Elliot and George as inert males, akin to the inept husband in "Out of Season."

The downward trajectory in chapters 10 and 11—from a bullfighting chapter without a matador (just the picador and the monos) to a chapter focused on a bad bullfighter—mirrors a decline in the fragile marriages Hemingway portrays. The compensations for a lack of marital intimacy diminish from "Mr. and Mrs. Elliot" to "Out of Season"—from a "girlfriend" with whom Mrs. Elliot sleeps, to a "tortoise-shell cat" presented to the American wife in "Cat," to no compensation at all for the woman in "Out of Season." Hemingway's framing of "Cat in the Rain" with the bullfighting stories underscores the comic ironies of the sequence: the picador's farcically shaking his lance at the bull that gored the horse, the maid's presenting an ambiguous gift to a wife who wanted a "kitty" and receives a large cat, and the spectators' mockery of the bullfighter in chapter 11. The entire suite of marriage tales and bullfighting chapters hearkens back to the mock-heroic parodies of machismo in Stein's "History of Belmonte" and in the "Cyclops" chapter of Joyce's *Ulysses*—Belmonte is lame, the Citizen can barely walk, George seems bound to his bed, and the bullfighter is sitting "quite drunk" in a café (*CSS* 133). In effect, Hemingway revised the bullfighting chapters when he placed them between the sequence of short stories. The ironic juxtaposition of bullfighting and marital sparring places the *correra* and hotel bedrooms as images set jaggedly against one another. As Linda Wagner-Martin observes, "this practice of essentially omitting transition, of placing one concrete image against another, edge on edge, was also an outgrowth of Joyce's *Ulysses* and Pound's *Cantos*" (226).

Hemingway learned from Stein, Joyce, Pound, and Picasso about ironic juxtapositions in collages. Stein placed "Ada" right before "Miss Furr and Miss Skeene" (a celebration of her relationship with Alice B. Toklas next to a portrait of a lesbian couple who splits up). Joyce placed "Cyclops" before "Nausicaa" (the Irish "Citizen" chasing Bloom out of a pub, and his granddaughter bringing Bloom on). In Canto 16, Pound juxtaposed without transitions eyewitness voices, in various dialects, speaking about the Franco-Prussian War, the Battle of Verdun in World War I, and a scene from the Russian Revolution (*Cantos* 70–75). Picasso placed a headline "La Jolie" as if printed on a military helmet in *The Architect's Table,* a painting in Stein's collection until her death. In what seems an act of whimsical homage, Picasso drew a rough rendition of Stein's signed calling card in the bottom right of the painting. Hemingway's ending "Cat in the Rain" with the padrone's gift of a cat to the American wife seems attuned to such ironic pairings, as if a "big tortoise-shell cat" is imprinted over an "Oh, shut up": the prospect of the American wife's and the Italian cat's remaining silent as humorously unlikely. Even as Hemingway leaves readers wondering at the couple's reaction to the gift of the cat, the maid has the last word, "Signora." In designing *In Our Time* by putting "Cat in the Rain" between chapters of a gored horse and an unmanned bullfighter, Hemingway created a comical collage of savage sport and fraught marriage.[24]

4

REVISING "BIG TWO-HEARTED RIVER"

Two months passed in the spring of 1924 between Hemingway's completing the revision of "Cat in the Rain" in March and his beginning "Big Two-Hearted River" in May. Both stories share the distinction of having a long duration and involving extensive revision during the process of composition (Smith, *Guide* 43, 85). From earliest sketch to final draft, "Cat" took roughly a year, and "River" took over half a year to complete. In between writing these two stories, Hemingway composed six more of the stories that would form part of *In Our Time:* "The End of Something," "The Three-Day Blow," "The Doctor and the Doctor's Wife," "Soldier's Home," "Mr. and Mrs. Elliot," and "Cross-Country Snow." These six stories came in rather quick succession in the two months of March and April during that miraculous spring in Paris. During that same spring, Hemingway saw his *in our time* published in mid-March by Bill Bird's Three Mountains Press. He saw his "Work in Progress" (later titled "Indian Camp") appear next to Joyce's "Work in Progress" in the April issue of the *Transatlantic Review,* where as an editor he was responsible for the serial publication of parts of Gertrude Stein's massive novel *The Making of Americans* (Chamberlin 57). For a young writer in his early twenties, this must have been a heady time.

In little more than another six months, Hemingway submitted his story "Big Two-Hearted River" to the avant-garde journal *This Quarter,* where it appeared in the first issue of spring 1925 alongside works by Gertrude Stein, Kay Boyle, H.D., Bryher, and William Carlos Williams. In a letter to its editors, Ernest Walsh and Ethel Moorhead, dated 12 January 1925, Hemingway wrote that "The Big Two Hearted River . . . is the best thing I've done by a long shot" (*Letters* vol. 2, 202). On 20 March 1925, he wrote to his father that he had "written a number of stories about the country—the country is always true"—singling out his "Big Two Hearted River" as "a story I think you will like" (*Letters*, vol. 2, 285). Hemingway even explained the geographical location of the story as if his father would recognize the fiction of a two-hearted river: "The river in it is really the Fox about Seney" (285). This pride, expressed to the first publishers of "River" in the first issue of *This Quarter*, and to his father, suggests the importance of the story to Hemingway. He placed "Big Two-Hearted River" as the capstone of *In Our Time*, as Joyce had put "The Dead" at the end of *Dubliners*.

A wide array of scholars has discussed the influence of Joyce's "The Dead" as a source and model for "Big Two-Hearted River." Paul Smith sees Hemingway's final and longest story in *In Our Time* as his "attempt to match 'The Dead'" ("1924" 42). Michael S. Reynolds notes that Hemingway placed "Big Two-Hearted River" at the end of *In Our Time* to follow the model of Joyce, who used "'The Dead' to weld *Dubliners'* themes together, placing it last to anchor the collection. Ernest needed such a story to end his book, a story bringing together everything he had learned" (*Paris Years* 202). Robert Gajdusek connects "The Dead" and "Big Two-Hearted River" as stories about "psychic therapy" to reconcile "the dichotomized self" with "despised or feared darkness" (*Hemingway in His Own Country* 213–15). Robert Paul Lamb compares the "float-off" ending of "The Dead" with the ending of "Big Two-Hearted River" (*Art Matters* 150–51).

To be sure, "Big Two-Hearted River" is in many ways a vastly different story from "The Dead." Set in the woods and rivers of the Upper Peninsula in Michigan, Hemingway's story is far from Joyce's Dublin—no family gathering (not a single reference to a family member), no servants, no music, no port or wine, no carving, no goose, no arguments, no women, no banquet, no long speech or formal toast, no rival lover, no falling snow. However, just as Joyce's "The Dead" circles back to the death of Father Flynn in "The Sisters," with its emphasis on ritual at a family gathering and its blend of dialogue and inward meditation by the young narrator, so "Big Two-Hearted River" circles back to "Indian Camp"—its young Nick Adams now grown, its father Dr. Adams out of the picture, its bass mentioned at the end of "Camp" becoming the trout for which Nick fishes. However, in "Big Two-Hearted River" there is no dialogue. The only spoken words are Nick's to himself and to a grasshopper. His inward meditations, on the other hand, are far more complex and more sustained than those in "Indian Camp." One focus of this chapter will be on Hemingway's blend, especially as he revised the story, of narrative action and interior monologues—a blend that Hemingway found in Joyce's "The Dead."

Most of the critical attention to Hemingway's revision of "Big Two-Hearted River" has focused, understandably, on his replacing the original ending of part 2, posthumously published as "On Writing" in *The Nick Adams Stories*, with his final ending published in *In Our Time*. Not fully discussed is that Hemingway went through several stages of substantially revising his "best thing"—from an original draft with at least two companions joining Nick, to a handwritten three-page addition to the story, to a projected ending that involves Nick and his camp rained out in a flood.[1] Hemingway's revisions show a young writer rising to the height of his artistry—beginning a beautiful tale, becoming derailed, sticking at first to his original ending, and then letting go and rewriting his fishing story as a narrative of accommodation, persistence, and renewal.

In the Hemingway papers at the Kennedy Library is an intriguing manuscript where Hemingway sketched out his initial idea for "Big Two-Hearted River." In this draft, written in Hemingway's hand on four pages, the story begins initially in the first-person plural ("We") and then shifts to the third person "They." Two characters named Jack and Al join Nick getting off the train in Seney. "This was the toughest town in Michigan," Al says, framing the story as a trip near a domestic war zone, akin to the diner with hired killers named Al and Max in Hemingway's later story "The Killers." In these first pages, the extent of Hemingway's cross-outs and additions (at least ten, by my count) suggests that he had started this story intently. In evoking a scene of ruin resembling the opening of "The End of Something," Hemingway described the dilapidated Mansion Hotel as a battlefield of "twisted iron work, melted too hard to rust. Thrown together were four gun barrels, pitted and twisted by the heat in one the cartridges had melted into the magazine and formed a bulge of lead and copper" (KL/EH folder 279; *SS-HLE* 126).[2] In some ways, this draft points ahead to the story Hemingway wrote: the blasted foundations of the Mansion House Hotel, for instance. However, a comparison of the draft with the published story shows that Hemingway decided to excise any explicit references to munitions or guns or bullets. Initially, he also composed the scene as if a shell had exploded. Perhaps at one point Hemingway thought of echoing his description of the barricade in chapter 4 of *In Our Time*. If so, the "big old wrought-iron grating" (*CSS*

83) at Mons becomes the "twisted iron work" of the early draft of "Big Two-Hearted River." In his revision, Hemingway erased virtually all signs of a war zone from his evocation of the landscape as Nick approaches the river: no twisted ironwork, no gun-barrels, no cartridges. Instead, in the final version, Seney is an abandoned town whose foundations "had been burned off the ground," not by bombardment in warfare but by the fires of "burnt timber" surrounding the ruins (*CSS* 163).

Moreover, as he started the story anew, he decided to portray Nick in solitude on his fishing trip. On the fourth page of the manuscript is a single sentence that Hemingway crossed out by hand with a big *X,* referring to a plural "they" who looked around after leaving the train. On the back of the tenth page of the manuscript are the same sentences referring to "they" in Hemingway's hand (KL/EH folder 274; cited in Oldsey 219). Thus, on two separate pages of the initial manuscript are identical beginnings involving companions who accompany Nick on his fishing trip. At some point, the manuscript evidence shows that Hemingway decided to focus the story on Nick, alone with the trees, river, fish, swamp, and his own camp—no encounters with anyone. In folder 274 are forty-seven pages of handwritten manuscript of part 1, labeled simply "Big Two Hearted River." These forty-seven pages contain most of the first part: Nick's dropping off from a train, hiking to his campsite, setting up camp, cooking dinner, and falling asleep. Then come pages forty-eight to ninety-seven, a section Hemingway originally labeled "Chapter Two" (crossed out and then labeled "Part Two"): cooking breakfast the next morning, fishing that second day, and cleaning the fish he caught. This shift from a party of fishermen to a story with Nick, alone, is the first of two fundamental changes in Hemingway's fashioning his story. The second is his decision to revise the original ending, when the story veers off into a digression about Hadley (renamed Helen), bullfighters, Joyce, Pound, Cézanne, and friends from Horton's Bay (reprinted with Hemingway's revisions in *SS-HLE* 129–35).

Hemingway substantially revised the story's opening to shift from a first- to a third-person narration, to place Nick alone on his fishing journey, and to eliminate any explicit references to a war scene. In addition, there are several types of changes from the dozens of revisions evident in the manuscript and typescript. First, Hemingway renders the language with which he evokes Nick's thoughts in a more colloquial, midwestern American idiom. Second, in one notable case, by adding three handwritten pages to part 1 of the original manuscript, he slows down the narrative to build a portrait of Nick's deliberative observations, reflections, and feelings while preparing to fish. Third, Hemingway revises the scenes of Nick's fishing to present his working to land the trout by evoking his visual and tactile sensations from his point of view. Even though the Nick of this story is much older than the boy in "Indian Camp," Hemingway's revisions again demonstrate his carefully showing the actions of the story through Nick's perspective—his voice, his vision, and his sense of touch. Fourth, Hemingway cut the original ending and replaced it by resuming Nick's fishing story with his observations and reflections about fishing in the river, not digressions about writing, art, friends, and himself. Finally, the focus of Hemingway's late changes, even to the revised ending, is his careful blend of narrative accounts of Nick's actions and interior monologues revealing his inner thoughts and feelings. These changes show Hemingway's painstaking work as a craftsman whose manuscripts and typescripts reflect a constant process of revision to convey Nick's voice, vision, touch, and consciousness as the focus of the story.

Several of Hemingway's handwritten alterations, with cross-outs and additions, evoke Nick's vernacular voice in "Big-Two Hearted River." The first time in the story that Nick speaks aloud, he addresses a grasshopper, after examining its blackened belly: "'Go on, hopper,' Nick said, speaking out loud for the first time. 'Fly away somewhere'" (*CSS* 165). Nick's voice in speaking to the grasshopper is friendly, informal, and affectionate. The next time Nick speaks is to himself, after he has made his camp and begun to cook the store-bought cans of pork and beans and of spaghetti. As if responding to a criticism that he is preparing to eat food he did not catch himself, Nick says in simple idiom, "I've got a right to eat this kind of stuff if I'm willing to carry it" (*CSS* 167). Noteworthy is that Hemingway struck out a sentence where Nick speaks to himself in self-defense using words like "justify" that seem out of place with a phrase like "this kind of stuff" (KL/EH folder 274). After giving the words that Nick spoke to himself, Hemingway added his brief, inward reflection upon hearing his voice: "His voice sounded strange in the darkening woods. He did not speak again" (*CSS* 167). With utmost brevity, Hemingway gives readers a quick insight into Nick's reflection about hearing his voice and his resolution to be silent from here on. However, after another paragraph in which the narrative of his eating dinner gives way to his vision of the mist rising across the river, he *does* speak in a vernacular voice of wonder: "Chrise."

In his initial manuscript version, Hemingway had Nick exclaiming, almost childishly, "oh Boy," a phrase he later cut when he completed a typescript of part 1 (KL/EH folder 275). In the manuscript, he followed "oh Boy" with "Jesus Christ," twice (KL/EH folder 274). By hand, Hemingway struck out the entire sentence, cutting both exclamations that some readers might regard as sacrilegious. By the time Hemingway completed the typescript, he wrote what is close to the print version, where he simply added commas: "'Chrise,' Nick said, 'Geezus Chrise,' he said happily" (*CSS* 168). In his revision, Hemingway not only cut the original "oh Boy" but found a folksy version of Nick's oath. Hemingway's revisions capture Nick's exhilaration at seeing what, in other contexts, might seem threatening: a mist rising from a darkening swamp. For instance, in "The Battler," Hemingway depicts Nick's seeing "the swamp ghostly in the rising mist" (*CSS* 98)—an eerie moment after he was tossed off a train that contrasts with Nick's exhilarating response to the mist rising in "River." Looking at the mist with his self-made tent and camp in sight, Nick swears with words in an American idiom affirming the comfort of solitude in a home he has made for himself in the woods. As Nick responds to the sight of the mist, Hemingway completes a pattern in part 1 of hearing Nick's occasional spoken words interspersed among narrative accounts of his actions and interior monologues reflecting his thoughts.

The breakfast scene near the beginning of part 2 provides another example of Hemingway's revisions to capture an American vernacular. In the manuscript, Hemingway added "buckwheat" before "cake" to the paragraph about Nick's cooking his pancakes for breakfast (*CSS* 174). He used "buckwheat" two other times in that cooking scene; the triple repetition of the word drives home Nick's sense that, while the dinner he cooked the night before came from store-bought cans, these "buckwheat" cakes have a more native aroma (*CSS* 174). Likewise, slightly later, Hemingway crossed out "cake" and replaced it with "flapjack," for the simple clause of the print edition, "It made another big flapjack and one smaller one" (*CSS* 174). He repeated the change in the very next sentence: "Nick ate a big [crossed out, "cake"] flapjack and a smaller one" (*CSS* 174). Hemingway's replacement of "cake" with "flapjack" presents Nick's thoughts in his colloquial voice as he cooks. So too does Hemingway present Nick's voice in his simple thought about cooking the flapjack: "I won't try to flop it" (*CSS* 174). By that thought Nick meant that he would not try to "flop" the pancake by flipping it over with the skillet. In the very next sentence, Hemingway shifts smoothly from

Nick's action of flopping the flapjack with a wood chip to his observation: "He slid the chip of clean wood all the way under the cake, and flopped it over onto its face. It sputtered in the pan" (*CSS* 174). By revising the passage so that Nick is flopping flapjacks, Hemingway evokes a folksy sound.

After breakfast, and after Nick has gathered his fly rod, fly line, and leader box, Hemingway describes Nick's feelings as he heads to the river: "Nick felt awkward and professionally happy with all his equipment hanging from him" (*CSS* 175). The simpler word "equipment" replaced the earlier word "paraphernalia," which Hemingway crossed out in the manuscript. Thus, Hemingway's revisions evoke Nick's American vernacular as he prepares to fish. Robert Paul Lamb sees "equipment" as part of "a figurative description of young Ernest sitting down to write" (*Short Story* 181). Hemingway's revision suggests both a fisherman's and a writer's practical tools, as the "equipment" Nick carries includes a "hook book" and "fly book" (*CSS* 175). The repetition of "book" lightly suggests a parallel between Nick's fishing and his writing, but does so in his simple vernacular.

In addition to helping readers hear Nick's American voice, Hemingway revised his story to dramatize Nick's initial vision of the river, a kingfisher, and the trout. The most substantial revision in part 1 comes when Hemingway inserted three additional pages between the third and fourth pages of the manuscript (KL/EH folder 274; *SS-HLE* 128). In the original version, which he crossed out, the movement of the trout that Nick sees comes mainly in one complex sentence (beginning, "As he watched") where Hemingway subordinates his watching the trout to the action of its shooting out of the stream and reentering: "He watched them hold themselves steady where the It had been years since he had seen trout. As he watched a big trout shot up stream in a long angle burst through the surface of the water and curved in the air to re-enter the water and then under the surface in the fast water again then seemed to float back down stream with the current to its post under the bridge. Nick's heart tightened as the trout moved. He felt all the old thrill" (KL/EH folder 274; *SS-HLE* 127–28). In this original version, Hemingway fused two sentences into one. He apparently did not finish the first sentence, ending in midthought, "where the . . ." He then started the second sentence at "It had been years" but then crossed out "It had been years" and began the three-page insert with "He watched them hold themselves." Thus, in this initial draft, just a couple of sentences in a relatively short, rapid paragraph evoke Nick's initial sight of the trout before his physical and emotional reactions: "Nick's heart tightened," followed by, "He felt all the old thrill" (*SS-HLE* 128). Thus, Hemingway's draft moves Nick quickly from his sight of the first "big trout" to his sensations connecting this fishing trip to his past trips. The earlier draft is simpler, more focused on the actions of the trout without the presence of a kingfisher flying overhead.

In the three pages that Hemingway inserted, he slowed down the process of Nick's watching a kingfisher and many trout and refined his lyrical language to convey Nick's excitement. He considerably delayed Nick's seeing the trout leap above the surface of the stream. Instead, he replaced "a big trout shot up stream" with a paragraph focused on Nick's watching: first, "many trout" swimming; then, the stream's rapid current; and then the "big trout" swimming at the bottom. Below is the first paragraph of the three inserted, handwritten pages, as printed in *In Our Time:*

> He watched them holding themselves with their noses into the current, many trout in deep, fast moving water, slightly distorted as he watched far down through the glassy convex surface of the pool, its surface pushing and swelling smooth against the resistance of the log-driven piles of the bridge. At the bottom of the pool were the big trout. Nick did not see them at first. Then he saw them at the bottom of the pool, big trout looking to hold themselves on the gravel bottom in a varying mist of gravel and sand, raised in spurts by the current (*CSS* 163).

This final print version closely resembles the manuscript paragraph, with Hemingway's adding a hyphen for "log-driven," and commas for pauses before "big trout looking" and "raised in spurts" (*SS-HLE* 127–28; *CSS* 163). These pauses contribute to the mimetic effect of slowing down the sentence to reflect Nick's savoring his seeing "the big trout" visible through the "mist." The triple repetition of "bottom" emphasizes Nick's seeing the big trout by peering deeply into the stream. First the narrator declares simply, "At the bottom were the big trout." Then, the narrative turns back to focus on Nick's process of vision: "Nick did not see them at first." Implying that Nick persisted in looking, despite not initially seeing the trout, the narrator continues, "Then he saw them at the bottom of the pool, the big trout looking to hold themselves steady on the gravel bottom." Only then does the narrator indicate what was screening Nick from seeing the big trout at first—the "mist of gravel and sand." In the three pages Hemingway added to the manuscript, the narrator suggests that Nick's persistence of vision enabled him to see the trout at the bottom of the stream beneath the underwater mist.

Furthermore, the revised, expanded version replaces the past-tense active verbs of the original manuscript ("shot up stream . . . and curved") with mostly present participles ("holding," "fast moving," "pushing and swelling," and "looking"). In this added section the trout are much more active. Nick sees them as if they are moving in the present rather than simply remembered in the past. Hemingway's shift to present participles may reflect the influence of Gertrude Stein's concept of "a continuous present." Discussing her story "Melanchtha," Stein commented about her use of "a prolonged present" in "Composition as Explanation," an address she gave in 1926 (*Writings* 524). To be sure, Hemingway repeatedly employs the past tense to evoke Nick's perceptions, but even with the past-tense verbs the passage reflects a progression from when Nick "did not see" the trout at first to when he "saw them" (*CSS* 163). In the revision, Hemingway also replaces "a big trout" that "shot up stream" (*SS-HLE* 127) with many "big trout": "He watched them" and "Then he saw them . . . looking to hold themselves" (*CSS* 163). The first new paragraph in the three pages that Hemingway added to the story portrays Nick as looking at a stream with many fish rather than with a single trout. This revision contributes a sense of excitement as Nick anticipates fishing in a stream full of trout. Hemingway also suggests a connection between the trout "looking to hold themselves" steady in the current and Nick's trying to hold himself steady while pausing his journey in order to stand on the bank and watch the trout swimming in the river.

The next substantial change in these three added pages comes with the second paragraph introducing a kingfisher. The print version of this paragraph is virtually identical to the handwritten page Hemingway added. Once he brought the kingfisher into this scene, he left that paragraph intact, beginning with two quick sentences, as Nick's and the kingfisher's eyes move in seemingly opposite directions: "Nick looked down into the pool from the bridge. It was a hot day. A kingfisher flew up the stream" (*SS-HLE* 128; *CSS* 163). Subtly shifting Nick's point of view, Hemingway implies that he has moved from the side of the stream where, in the previous paragraph, he watched the current, the piles of the bridge, the bottom of the pool, and its trout. Having climbed up onto the bridge, Nick looks down, apparently for a closer view of the fishing pool. Only now does Nick look backward in time: "It was a long time since Nick had looked into a stream and seen trout" (*CSS*

163). As if to mirror the kingfisher's flying upstream, Nick's thoughts turn to the past, to the "long time" since he had seen any trout in *any* stream. That is, Nick's generalizing of "a stream" (not "this stream") suggests that this is his first fishing in many years—eliding over the war chapters of *In Our Time* and circling back to the trout fishing in "The End of Something."

Within this second added paragraph, with just slight changes in reaching his final version, Hemingway composed one of the longest, most lyrical, and most complex sentences of *In Our Time*. The paragraph begins with five short sentences about Nick's looking down into the pool of water, feeling the heat of the day, watching the flight of the kingfisher, and reflecting back on the "long time" since he had seen trout in a stream. Then, on the second and third pages that Hemingway added to his manuscript, comes an intricate sentence about Nick's watching the kingfisher, the trout, and their shadows: "As the shadow of the kingfisher moved up the stream, a big trout shot upstream in a long angle, only his shadow marking the angle, then lost his shadow as he came through the surface of the water, caught the sun, and then, as he went back into the stream under the surface, his shadow seemed to float down the stream with the current, unresisting, to his post under the bridge when he tightened facing up into the current" (*SS-HLE* 128; *CSS* 163–64). The syntax and exact phrasing bear close study, as does the fact that readers are viewing the scene through Nick's eyes. First, Nick watches as "the shadow of the kingfisher moved up the stream" (*CSS* 163). Nick sees the "shadow," not the kingfisher; he is watching its reflection on the surface of the stream, not the bird itself. As he follows this shadow, he sees that "a big trout shot upstream in a long angle, only his shadow marking the angle" (*CSS* 163–64). Although one might possibly read the trout as casting its shadow after it leaps through the surface of the stream, more likely in this context is that "shadow" is the word describing the angle of the trout moving quickly underwater and waiting for the kingfisher to fly away before leaping out of the stream (Smith, "Early Manuscripts" 281). Thus, Nick traces the shadow of a kingfisher, not the bird itself, and the shadow of the trout before it leapt out of the stream. In both cases, Hemingway keeps the reader inside Nick's range of sight.

In the case of the kingfisher, Nick sees his shadow as he flies *above* the surface of the stream. With the trout, however, Nick follows his shadow on the surface with the trout *below* the surface. Looking at the river, Nick initially could not find the shadow when the trout "came through the surface of the water" (*CSS* 164). In the earlier, shorter version, the "long angle" Nick sees is the actual trout, as it "burst through the surface of the water" (*SS-HLE* 127). In the earlier version, Nick sees the trout having leapt *above* the surface of the stream. In the revised version with the three added pages, Hemingway keeps Nick's eyes focused on the stream's surface and the moving shadow of the trout rising *toward* the surface from below. The revision affords readers a slow-motion version as Nick's eyes follow the trout before it is about to leap out of the stream. In a subtle elision, Hemingway does not specify Nick as the viewer who "lost" the trout's "shadow" as it broke through the "surface," but no other reading seems plausible. Missing is the subject, Nick himself, as he watches the trout leap from the water. Why not simply include Nick in the clause "then [Nick] lost his shadow"? Perhaps in this case Hemingway decided to elide Nick's presence as the observer so that the sentence would focus on the process of his seeing through the reflections of shadows without calling attention to Nick himself. After suggesting what Nick's vision "lost" (his view of the trout's shadow as it leapt from the stream), Hemingway shows what his eyes followed (the trout itself). Here Nick loses the shadow but gains sight of the trout, as it luminously "caught the sun" (*CSS* 164). That is, his vision has shifted from the shadow to the actual trout's breaking the surface and then reentering the stream. Once the trout returned "into the stream, under the surface," its "shadow" (*CSS* 164) again seems to be an underwater image of the trout that looks like the shadow Nick earlier observed under the surface of the stream. The sibilant repetition of "surface," "shadow," and "stream" link the separate frames in Nick's vision into a continuous flow of watching the trout swim underwater and then shoot through the river's surface.

In these inserted pages, Hemingway focuses us on Nick's viewpoint, as he keenly watches the shadows cast by the kingfisher and the trout, while he prepares to fish. As Paul Smith puts it, Nick's vision connects "the shadow of the moving fish until it broke the surface" with the shadow of the kingfisher, and with Nick himself, in a "triangular relationship" of fish, bird, and fisherman ("Early Manuscripts" 281). Thus, Hemingway's revisions center the drama less on what Nick sees than on *how* he sees via its reflections and shadows. He continues watching the trout as it reverses course and seems to retreat under the force of the stream's current. Once Nick picks the shadow back up, he notes that, having earlier "shot upstream," the trout's "shadow seemed to float down the stream with the current, unresisting" (*CSS* 164).

The kingfisher that Nick watched never changed direction as it flew up-stream. In contrast, Nick observes that the trout's shadow, once the trout re-entered the stream, turned downstream "to his post under the bridge where he tightened facing up into the current" (*CSS* 164). This lyrical, winding, seventy-nine-word sentence comes to a close with the trout's return to its "post," as if Nick's metaphor retains a very faint hint of what Hemingway re-jected in cutting the wartime images in his first draft of the story. Just as the trout has found its "post," so has Nick. Only now, repeating the same verb ("tightened") as he gave for the fish, does Hemingway give us, in the three pages he added by hand to his manuscript, Nick's first emotional turning point in the story: "Nick's heart tightened as the trout moved. He felt all the old feeling" (*CSS* 164). Even so small a change from "He felt all the old thrill" to "He felt all the old feeling" presents this moment as an uncertain revival (*SS-HLE* 128; *CSS* 164). Hemingway's slight replacement of "thrill" in the manuscript with "feeling" in the revised and published version shifts from a slightly melodramatic noun to a more neutral word. As John N. Maclean observes about the "lingering lyric" of this passage, "The revised version raises the possibility that Nick has regained a lost ability to feel as he once did" (xxix–xxx). These three pages added to the manuscript of "Big Two-Hearted River" present Nick Adams as carefully watching the trout amid moving currents, solid bridge piles, and shadowy reflections.

After these three inserted pages that present the opening sight of the river from Nick's watchful eye, Hemingway picks up his narrative on the bottom of page four in the manuscript. His revisions for the next several paragraphs stress Nick's gradual walk along the river, as he explores possible sites for his camp: "He adjusted the pack harness around the bundle, pulling straps tight, slung the pack on his back" (*CSS* 164). The participial phrase "pulling straps tight" is a handwritten addition to the original sentence in the manuscript. The slight addition of "pulling" shows Nick's adjusting the straps so that the backpack is tightly in place. Similarly, Hemingway added by hand, "The road climbed steadily" before the simple sentence, "It was hard work walking up hill" (*CSS* 164). Thus, the reader shares Nick's feel-ing as he climbs up the ascending road before hearing Nick's thought about his "hard work" walking up it. Then, in one of the most significant revisions in part 1, Hemingway initially wrote that Nick "was happy. He felt he had left everything behind, the ~~necessity~~ need for thinking, the ~~necessity~~ need to write, ~~the need to talk~~, other needs" (*SS-HLE* 129). In the manuscript, Hemingway crossed out "was" and replaced it with "felt" for "felt happy" (*SS-HLE* 129). He also crossed out "necessity" three times and replaced it with "the need" and crossed out "the need to talk" (*SS-HLE* 129; *CSS* 164). By replacing a fated external "necessity" with "the need," Hemingway focuses on Nick's inner needs. Moreover, by crossing out "the need to talk," Hemingway presents "the need to write" as Nick's last specific thought of an inner need. Such a change suggests that fishing is, for Nick, a rest from his work as a writer. This change is the clearest indication in "Big Two-Hearted River" that Nick considers himself a writer.

This paragraph began with the third-person narrator's describing Nick's actions—his walking with his heavy pack up the road. Hemingway then subtly shifted from the narrative action to Nick's brief, interior monologue. He signaled that shift from Nick's "feeling the ache" in his shoulder to inward, emotional phrases: "felt happy" and "felt he had left everything behind" (*CSS* 164). Just as Joyce in "The Dead" interwove narrative descriptions of Gabriel Conroy's actions along with interior monologues of his thoughts and feelings, so too does Hemingway in "Big Two-Hearted River." Once Hemingway has Nick locating his spot to set up camp, he deftly blends a narrative account of his step-by-step actions to pitch his tent. He follows that narrative account with an interior monologue of his reflections about what he has done: built himself a shelter as the equivalent of a work of art.

Hemingway shows, from Nick's viewpoint, his actions: finding his campsite on the high ground by the river, leveling the ground, and pitching a tent. In both the manuscript and the published version of the story, Hemingway repeats "ground." Indeed, the repetition of "ground" serves to bind together the separate steps of Nick's finding and clearing the place for his campsite: "The ground rose . . .," "Nick . . . looked for a level piece of ground," and "the ground was quite level." That is, the repetition first emphasizes Nick's finding the right location to pitch his tent. Then, Nick's chopping out roots "leveled a piece of ground large enough to sleep on," and "When he had the ground smooth, he spread his three blankets." The second set of repetitions emphasizes Nick's actions to smooth out the ground. The final "ground" in this paragraph reflects Nick's preparing one of his blankets to sleep on: "One he folded double, next to the ground" (*CSS* 166). Three of those six repetitions of "ground" are in Hemingway's manuscript. In revising this paragraph, the two most striking additions are the sentences referring to his blankets in connection to the ground: "When he had the ground smooth, he spread his three blankets. One he folded double, next to the ground" (*CSS* 166–67). Those additional repetitions strengthen the emphasis on Nick's contact with the ground on which he will rest. That concatenated repetition, reminiscent of the opening paragraph in "Cat in the Rain," evokes both the literal sense of Nick's leveling the ground on which he will sleep and the figurative sense of Nick's finding his ground.

In the next paragraph of Nick's building his campsite, Hemingway focuses on his pitching his tent. This is the first reference in *In Our Time* to a tent as a private shelter—not like the Adamses' summer camp in "Indian Camp," but a tent he carried and fastened and secured himself. In these two paragraphs, Hemingway lays alliterative stress on Nick's interconnected physical actions: he "dropped his pack," "took the ax out of the pack," "slit off a bright slab of pine," "tied the rope that served the tent," "poked a pole," and "pegged the sides out taut" (*CSS* 167). These are all actions of building, with simple syntax and quick verb phrases. This passage of pitching the tent is virtually intact from the manuscript to the print version of the story. Hemingway did add, by hand, one step in the process: "Nick poked a pole he had cut upright under the back peak of the canvas and then" (*CSS* 167). This addition suggests that Hemingway, in reading over what he had written, realized that Nick needed to place a pole to support the back end of the tent.

The transition from Nick's building to sitting comes with his final action in pitching his tent. That final action includes his pounding the pegs into the ground, as he "drove the pegs deep, hitting them down into the ground with the flat of the ax until the rope loops were buried and the canvas was drum tight" (*CSS* 167). In completing his task of pitching his tent, Nick acts as an artist hiding the signs of his raw materials and early residue. In this paragraph the key word is "tent" (repeated five times), and the key metaphor is "drum tight." The tent is the shelter Nick nails to the ground to give himself a roof under which to lie. Like the ground earlier, the tent is mostly the object of actions: Nick pitched the tent, he pulled the rope that "served the tent for a ridge-pole" to tie it to a pine tree, and then he "made it a tent" by "pegging out" the sides of the canvas and nailing the "pegs for the tent" into the ground. The tent is a piece of canvas that Nick draped, stretched, and nailed so that its taut surface will cover him. The paragraph concludes with a powerful metaphor connecting Nick to the Ojibway at whose camp he had his first encounter with death in "Indian Camp." Here, the canvas Nick stretched "was drum tight," as if the tent were, for him, an approximation of an Ojibway ceremonial instrument, such as Louise Erdrich would later make the central figure in her novel *The Painted Drum.*

Hemingway's only revision to this passage, besides the addition about the pole under the back end of the canvas, might seem slight. He originally wrote that "the canvas was drum like tight." By striking "like," Hemingway left the phrase as a pure metaphor, "drum tight." The metaphor also suggests a slight shift from Nick's actions to his thought about the tent he had just made. Like an artist surveying his work, Nick views his tent and his camp as "drum tight"—well-made, functional, austere.[3] Hemingway expands from Nick's metaphor to his reflections about the shelter he has made for himself: "Already there was something mysterious and homelike. Nick was happy as he crawled inside the tent. He had not been unhappy all day. This was different though. Now things were done. There had been this to do. Now it was done. It had been a hard trip. He was very tired. That was done. He had made his camp. He was settled. Nothing could touch him. It was a good place to camp. He was there, in the good place. He was in his home where he had made it. Now he was hungry" (*CSS* 167). In these seventeen short, simple sentences, Hemingway portrays Nick's thinking methodically, like the step-by-step process by which he had constructed his tent. Beginning with a sense of the camp as an uncanny creation, both mysterious and homelike, Nick's interior monologue repeats past-perfect and past-tense verbs that evoke his completion of a well-wrought piece of work: "There had been this to do" and "That was done." That is, Nick re-creates in his reflections both the time when his work lay ahead and the time when he could look upon the work and see that "He was in his home where he had made it." Given the campsites and homes that Nick had *not* made in stories like "Indian Camp," "The Doctor and the Doctor's Wife," "The Three-Day Blow," and "The Battler," Nick's meditation on his tent stands out. Hemingway concluded part 1 of "Big Two-Hearted River" with three simple sentences that show how well Nick took to his creation: "He was sleepy. He felt sleep coming. He curled up under the blanket and went to sleep" (*CSS* 169).

Hemingway's revisions to part 1 slow down his story and keep us inside Nick's watchful mind as he studies the terrain, the stream, the kingfisher, and the trout. Most of the revisions to part 2 tend to intensify the dramatic, tactile tension between Nick as a fisherman and the trout he is trying to catch. At the point of Nick's first strike, Hemingway wrote: "Holding the now living rod across the current, he brought in the line with his left hand"

(*CSS* 175). In the manuscript, by hand Hemingway added "now living" and crossed out "the pull of" before "the current," so that the emphasis is on what Nick feels as a trout tugs on the line: the fishing line is "now living" because the trout has taken the bait; the pull is now from the trout, not from the current. Likewise, once he has pulled in this smaller trout, Nick "held the trout, never still, with his moist right hand" (*CSS* 175). To the original draft, Hemingway added "never still," stressing how Nick felt in his right hand the rapid movement of the trout, just before he unhooked the fish and released it to the stream. Especially with this slight revision, Hemingway suggests how Nick's precaution of moistening his hands before touching the fish kept it alive and active before he returned it to the water.

Even more dramatic are Hemingway's revisions to the scene where Nick tries to reel in one of the biggest trout he has ever seen. Hemingway's numerous cross-outs and insertions in the manuscript revisions of this passage show his work to evoke Nick's fishing as tactile. Here is the final version of this passage, a separate, distinct paragraph in the story: "There was a long tug. Nick struck and the rod came alive and dangerous, bent double, the line tightening, coming out of the water, tightening, all in a heavy, dangerous, steady pull. Nick felt the moment when the leader would break if the strain increased and let the line go" (*CSS* 176). In the initial draft in the manuscript, Hemingway repeated "tightening" three times, heightening both the tension of the fishing line and the tension of Nick's fight with the fish. He might well have left that original draft alone. Instead, his revisions intensify the drama. For instance, the phrase "alive and dangerous" is a later addition by hand to the manuscript as if the possibility of the line's breaking poses a physical threat. At the same time, originally Hemingway had a fourth adjective, "irresistible," after "heavy, dangerous, steady." By eliminating "irresistible," Hemingway suggests that Nick's struggle with the trout continues until he decides to "let the line go." After letting go, Nick hears and feels the sensations of the trout's rushing away: "The reel ratcheted into a mechanical shriek as the line went out in a rush" (*CSS* 176). Hemingway worked for the alliterative, shrill sound that accompanies the tactile sensation of the fishing line. To the draft in the manuscript, he added by hand the phrase "ratcheted into a." Not only does the addition of "ratcheted" strengthen the shrill alliteration of "r" sounds, but "ratcheted" as a verb evokes the rapidly clicking sounds Nick heard as the big trout was rushing out. With a poet's ear, Hemingway depicts Nick's hearing the clicking reel as a single, slightly ominous "shriek."

At this point, Hemingway shows that Nick has a change of heart as he decides to fight the trout rather than let it go. In the paragraph that begins, "With the core of the reel visible," Hemingway crossed out three phrases in the original draft in the manuscript referring to his heart's shaking and pounding with excitement. The cross-outs suggest Hemingway's careful work at this pivotal point of the story. In the print version, Hemingway replaced the more tremulous and hesitant "felt shaky" with the firmer "his heart feeling stopped with the excitement" (*CSS* 176). Hemingway's revisions convey Nick as arrested in the thrill of the moment, not shaky but resolute and fixed in the tension of the battle. Hemingway's phrasing here of Nick's *action* stays firm with identical language from the manuscript to the final print version: "Nick thumbed the reel hard with his left hand" (*CSS* 176). While Hemingway struggled to find the right phrase to evoke Nick's inner change of heart, his phrasing remains steady about Nick's physical action—he thumbs the reel in one last attempt to pull in the trout.

Then, Hemingway revised this dramatic sequence to evoke what Nick felt just at the point before the trout broke free. One of the turning points of the story, this passage reflects Nick's tactile sensations as he tries to land the trout: "As he put on pressure the line tightened into sudden hardness and beyond the logs a huge trout went high out of water. As he jumped, Nick lowered the tip of the rod. But he felt, as he dropped the tip to ease the strain, the moment when the strain was too great; the hardness too tight. Of course, the leader had broken" (*CSS* 176). Hemingway's revisions, including cross-outs and additions, are close to the final version. His changes may seem slight, but they are important. To his original sentence about how the fishing line "tightened," Hemingway added by hand the phrase "into sudden hardness," as he suggests that Nick feels the quick, hard tug of the trout's pulling away. As he shifts to convey Nick's final sense of the trout on the line, Hemingway evokes the more dramatic downward motion of the reel with "dropped the tip," which he wrote by hand above the crossed-out phrase "lowered to take." Hemingway slows down and stretches out, ever so slightly, Nick's resignation: he lowered, and then dropped, the tip of the line. By hand, Hemingway added the phrase "the hardness too tight" to reinforce that not only was the "strain" of the trout's pull "too great" for Nick himself to overcome, but also the "hardness" of the line was the last sensation he felt before he realized that he had lost the fish: "Of course, the leader had broken." Hemingway presents first Nick's recognition about the broken leader and only then his memory of his tactile sensation as the leader broke: "There was no mistaking the feeling when the spring left the line and it became dry and hard" (*CSS* 176–77). With these repetitions of "hardness" and "hard" more emphatic in Hemingway's revisions, he conveys the sensation Nick felt in his hands just before the line broke—and the disappointment of temporary failure. In this paragraph full of action as Nick fights to land the trout, Hemingway interweaves Nick's physical sensations ("he felt" and "the feeling") with his conclusions ("Of course" and "There was no mistaking"). Hemingway closely connects Nick's sense of tactile strain with his recognition that he has lost the big fish.

Moreover, Hemingway divided a long, monolithic paragraph from the manuscript into shorter paragraphs that break down Nick's fishing for this "huge trout" into distinct steps. In the manuscript, the sequence from when Nick first feels the tug of the big trout to when he feels dizzy from losing it is one long paragraph, from "Nick leaned back against the current" all the way to "It would be better to sit down" (*CSS* 176–77). In his revision, Hemingway broke that monolithic paragraph into seven paragraphs: (1) Nick baits the line and lets it run; (2) Nick feels the "long tug" of the big trout and at first lets the line go; (3) the reel runs out too fast; (4) Nick "thumbed the reel hard" as he tries to regain control of the trout; (5) he sees the "huge trout" leap out of the water and feels the line break; (6) he reflects upon how this trout was the biggest he has ever seen; and (7) Nick, feeling "shaky" and "a little sick" as he pulls in his broken line, decides to sit down. In revising this section, Hemingway shaped one of the turning points of the story into a careful sequence of seven paragraphs evoking Nick's mounting excitement, heightened struggle, and shaken disappointment.

With slight brushstrokes, Hemingway recorded Nick's reflections on losing the trout. In the paragraph starting, "The leader had broken," Hemingway made two seemingly minor changes to present Nick's interior monologue about the trout that got away. First, as Nick imagines the trout "holding himself over the gravel," Hemingway marked with an arrow the insertion of "steady" between "holding himself" and "over the gravel" (*CSS* 177). This addition of "steady" emphasizes Nick's recognition of the power and control of the big trout in the current. The addition also echoes the repetition of "steady" in Nick Adams's first watching the previous day as the trout were "keeping themselves steady" and working to "hold steady" in the current of the stream (*CSS* 163). Second, the two sentences—"Anything that size would be angry. That was a trout"—were added by hand to the original draft in the manuscript (*CSS* 177). Here—in Nick's interior voice—Hemingway conveys Nick's empathy and respect for the trout.

Between Nick's losing the "big trout" and his catching the first trout he keeps is a sixty-one-word sentence evoking his thoughts when he resolves to continue fishing. Initially, Hemingway broke the long sentence beginning with "He sat on the logs" into at least two separate sentences. After "the logs warm in the sun," Hemingway in the manuscript started with a capitalized "Nick," as if he initially planned to start a new sentence there. Then, crossing out "Nick," he continued the sentence with "smooth to sit on," as Nick gathers himself while feeling the smooth support of the logs. Here is the winding sentence whose pauses and turns suggest Nick's unwinding after the disappointment of losing the biggest trout he had ever seen: "He sat on the logs, smoking, drying in the sun, the sun warm on his back, the river shallow ahead entering the woods, curving into the woods, shallows, light glittering, big water-smooth rocks, cedars along the bank and white birches, the logs warm in the sun, smooth to sit on, without bark, gray to the touch; slowly the feeling of disappointment left him" (*CSS* 177). This long sentence is an example of Hemingway's winding, curving, amplified style in presenting Nick's interior monologue. This passage is a monologue dominated not by memories and reflections, but by physical sensations. The present participles in the monologue evoke Nick's sensations, as he pauses, slows down, and collects himself. The repetition of "warm" suggests both Nick's literally feeling the warmth of the sun after the chill of the water and his emotionally warming up. He felt warmth while he "sat on the logs, smoking, drying in the sun," with the "light glittering" (*CSS* 177). Nick's physical sensations, interconnected through the light repetition of "woods" and "warm" and "smooth," build to the turning point in the sentence. After the phrase "gray to the touch" and a semicolon, Hemingway ended the sentence by simply stating Nick's gradual recovery: "slowly the feeling of disappointment left him" (*CSS* 177). Echoing the long sentence Hemingway added earlier in the story that traces Nick's observations of the kingfisher and trout, this sentence ends with Nick's reflection on his "feeling"—in this case, his disappointment after losing the big trout.

In the next sentence, Hemingway repeated much of the same language, as if to emphasize the gradual change in Nick by dwelling on its slow pace: "It went away slowly, the feeling of disappointment that came sharply after the thrill that made his shoulders ache" (*CSS* 177). Furthermore, he changed the language evoking Nick's feelings after he sits on logs to warm himself in the sun. Instead of indicating that Nick's "hands shake," as in the manuscript, Hemingway wrote that Nick was coping with the disappointment of losing the trout "after the thrill that made his shoulders ache" (*CSS* 177). That "ache" recalls "the ache from the pull of the heavy pack" as Nick climbed the road earlier in the story (*CSS* 164). Having referred four paragraphs earlier to Nick's "shaky" hand, Hemingway's revision suggests that Nick's fishing left him physically aching but emotionally calm. Hemingway shifted the emphasis from a phrase that would suggest Nick's uncontrollable spasms to language that suggests his persevering past his shoulders' pain. "It was all right now," Nick thinks, as Hemingway concluded the paragraph with a simple statement that leads from the disappointment of losing one fish to rousing himself to resume fishing. Hemingway's sentence evokes in its fluidity Nick's settling himself and taking his time before acting: "Nick tied a new hook" and "He baited up, then picked up the rod" (*CSS* 177). Then Nick renews his fishing, with very few changes in the manuscript—not a single word changed between "A trout struck" and "Nick led the trout over the net then lifted" (*CSS* 177–78). Indeed, the only changes in this passage from the manuscript to the print edition are Hemingway's decision to start a new paragraph at "Holding the rod far out" and his addition of commas to signal pauses and slow the pace. At this point of evoking Nick's resilience after loss, Hemingway seemed settled on his development of the fishing story.

Then comes the original ending of "River," with its shift from Nick's fishing in northern Michigan to his living and writing in the Left Bank of Paris. In the manuscript, after referring to "the trees of the left bank" ("of the left bank" added by hand), Hemingway completed his picture of Nick's sizing up the fishing possibilities: "Nick knew there were trout in each shadow" (*CSS* 178). At this point in the manuscript, Hemingway diverged into the digressive, original ending of "Big Two-Hearted River" with the transitional reference to Bill Smith as having shared his discovery: "He and Bill Smith had discovered that on the Black River one hot day" (*SS-HLE* 130). They discovered that when the sun went down, the trout "all moved into the current" from the "cool shadows" near the riverbank (*SS-HLE* 130). For whatever reason, his reference to a previous fishing trip with Bill Smith took Hemingway away from his fictional fishing trip to his position as a writer in Paris in self-imposed exile from "the halcyon world of northern Michigan"

(Kennedy, *Imagining Paris* 94).[4] Then the manuscript of part 2 continues with a discussion referring to Ezra Pound, Bill Bird, Bill Smith, Nick, Hadley, Eric Dorman-Smith, bullfighters, James Joyce, E. E. Cummings, Gertrude Stein, and Cézanne as Nick's ideal artist: "He wanted to write like Cezanne painted.... He was the greatest" (*SS-HLE* 134). Hemingway crossed out gratuitous insults leveled at Pound and Joyce: "Ezra didn't know anything . . . Joyce didn't know anything either" (*SS-HLE* 131).

Some scholars, such as Michael Reynolds, J. Gerald Kennedy, and Robert Paul Lamb, have either admired Hemingway's attempt in this original version of the ending, even if concluding that this version failed, or else they have discussed the deleted ending to shed light on the final version of the story. In his essay "Hemingway's *In Our Time:* Biography of a Book," Reynolds argues that the original ending to "Big Two-Hearted River" was "a pre-Borgesian tour de force that, had it worked, would have turned the collection back on itself endlessly" (200). However, Reynolds's reservation, "had it worked," is telling. "Big Two-Hearted River" is not a Borgesian "Garden of Forking Paths," nor a Chinese box of metafictional involutions and jokes like James Joyce's *Finnegans Wake*. More recently, in his introduction to the Norton Critical Edition of *In Our Time*, J. Gerald Kennedy cites Joyce's *Portrait of an Artist* as a "radically innovative" work such as Hemingway longed to do with the original ending (xvi). In a chapter on "Big Two-Hearted River" in *The Hemingway Short Story*, Robert Paul Lamb makes an excellent case for the parallels between fishing and writing in the story, where "the trout stand as metaphors for stories themselves. In effect what he figuratively asks is this: how does a writer capture stories from the river of memory?" (*Short Story* 174–75). Without the original ending, one can still read the story as a metaphorical tale of fishing for fiction, through subtle hints like the reference to Nick's being able to "choke" his mind from working too hard on "a good ending to the story" about Hopkins's method for making coffee (*CSS* 169). Such intimations of Nick's vocation as a writer work more effectively within the story. Thus, Lamb concludes that "Hemingway wisely removed the original ending" (*Short Story* 172). The original ending is full of what Lamb aptly described as "desultory musings" (*Short Story* 188). The digressions are also self-absorbed, blurring the line between Nick and Hemingway. The shift from Nick's vision of the Michigan landscape to the Paris scene, and from his fishing to his adulation of Cézanne's landscapes, is jarring.[5]

For some time, Hemingway clung to this version of part 2 of "Big Two-Hearted River." Hemingway included the original ending of part 2 in a titled typescript of "Big Two Hearted River" (still no hyphen in the title [KL/EH folder 275]). In this typescript, Hemingway slightly revised part 1 and part 2, the second part more substantially. However, he kept the final section of part 2 mainly intact, changing "Hadley" to "Helen" (KL/EH folder 275; cited in Oldsey 220). Thus, after taking out Hadley's name, Hemingway paired Nick in the original ending of "Big Two-Hearted River" with Helen, presumably the same Helen as Nick's pregnant partner in "Cross-Country Snow." In a second typescript, with very few ink corrections, he retained the original ending (KL/EH folder 276; cited by Oldsey 220). This second typescript was, for Hemingway, "often the publishing stage" (Oldsey 220). Not until a ten-page manuscript, which Hemingway wrote in an upper-right slant, as if he were writing at an angle, does the gorgeous ending begin to appear with "Nick moved along through the shallow stretch watching the bank for deep holes" (KL/EH folder 277; *SS-HLE* 135; *CSS* 178). Once he undertook this new ending, Hemingway seemed to gather steam quickly. There are just a few corrections and revisions in this handwritten draft, as preserved in the typescript of his manuscript version of the revised ending (KL/EH folder 278; Smith, *Guide* 86). His decision to complete "Two-Hearted River" as Nick's fishing story is a response, it now seems clear, to Gertrude Stein's strong advice.[6]

Of the few late changes Hemingway made in the revised ending, preserved in folder 277 of the Hemingway Collection at the Kennedy Library, several are worth discussing. In the paragraph beginning "Nick did not want to go there now," Hemingway's alterations are particularly significant toward the end of the paragraph. The handwritten manuscript of the revised ending, as now printed in the Hemingway Library Edition of the short stories, includes: "Nick did not want to go in there now. He felt a reaction against deep wading with the water deepening up under his armpits, hooking big trout in impossible places to land them. In the swamp ~~with~~ the naked banks, the big cedars coming together over head, the sun hardly ever coming through, the fast deep water, the fishing would be tragic. In the swamp it was a tragic adventure. Nick did not want it. He did not want to go down the stream any further today" (*SS-HLE* 137). Hemingway revised this paragraph so that the published version of *In Our Time* reads: "Nick did not want to go in there now. He felt a reaction against deep wading with the water deepening up under his armpits, to hook big trout in places impossible to land them.

In the swamp the banks were bare, the big cedars came together overhead, the sun did not come through, except in patches; in the fast deep water, in the half light, the fishing would be tragic. In the swamp fishing was a tragic adventure. Nick did not want it. He did not want to go down the stream any further today" (*CSS* 180). In revising the manuscript of the new ending, Hemingway polished his representation of the swamp, as seen through Nick's eyes. Instead of "the naked banks" of the manuscript, he stated that sentence simply, "In the swamp the banks were bare." In rewriting the paragraph, he sharpened Nick's vision of the swamp as a kind of bower he chooses not to enter. In the manuscript, Hemingway presented Nick's view of a canopy of cedars over the dark swamp: "the big cedars coming together over head, the sun hardly ever coming through, the fast deep water" (*SS-HLE* 137). In the print version Hemingway revised that part of the sentence to emphasize Nick's looking back on the past: "the big cedars came together overhead, the sun did not come through, except in patches" (*CSS* 180). The switch from participial phrases to past-tense verbs sets Nick's view of the swamp as a place of darkness more clearly in the definite past, as if he has already distanced himself from the place where he chose not to go.

Furthermore, Hemingway's revisions lead more smoothly to Nick's decision that the swamp would be a stage for "a tragic adventure." In the manuscript version, Hemingway approached the end of Nick's interior monologue rather abruptly; the "fishing would be tragic" is a pronouncement immediately after his viewing the "fast deep water." In the final version, Hemingway led more smoothly to a fusion of conditional prediction ("would be") and definite past tense ("was"). After the phrase "the fast deep water," Hemingway added the phrase "in the half light," as if Nick foresees that the time for a "tragic" fishing would be in a limbo between darkness and daylight. Moreover, in the final draft Hemingway led more clearly from the conditions of the swamp (bare banks, big cedars forming a canopy overhead, a mostly blocked sun, and fast water) to Nick's conclusion based on his observations: "In the swamp fishing was a tragic adventure." By placing a semicolon strategically between Nick's observations and his conclusion, and by replacing the pronoun "it" with "fishing," Hemingway repeated Nick's emphasis on fishing in the swamp as potentially "tragic" were he to continue rather than resolve to return to his self-made camp.

Finally, after the paragraph explaining why Nick decided to cease fishing for the day, Hemingway revised the penultimate paragraph of the story to focus on Nick's knife as a tool for cleaning the fish. In each version, after washing the trout and his hands in the stream, he laid the trout on a sack before putting them in a landing net. Much of the language in this penultimate paragraph is in the manuscript draft of the story. The most telling change is how Hemingway continued refining the penultimate paragraph. After a couple of cross-outs, that paragraph ended: "Then he laid the trout on the sack, rolled them up in it, tied the bundle and put it in the landing net" (KL/EH folder 277; *SS-HLE* 138). In the final, published version, the ending of that paragraph was: "Then he laid the trout on the sack, spread out on the log, rolled them up in it, tied the bundle and put it in the landing net. His knife was still standing, blade stuck in the log. He cleaned it on the wood and put it in his pocket" (*CSS* 180). Aside from including the visual detail that the sack was "spread out on the log," most notable is that Hemingway added two sentences about Nick's knife with which he cleaned the fish. Thus, in the final version Hemingway ended the paragraph not by narrating how Nick moved the washed dead trout to the landing net but rather by focusing on the knife with which he cleaned them.

Hemingway had already described Nick's cleaning both fish and identifying them as male with their "strips of milt," consistent in the manuscript, typescript, and print versions. Then he showed Nick's cleaning his knife—the tool with which he had cleaned the trout. In the print version, the sentences Hemingway added to the manuscript present Nick's knife as a figure for Nick himself: "His knife was still standing, blade stuck in the log" (*CSS* 180). Hemingway's addition of the knife's "still standing" foreshadows Nick's final upward motion: "Nick stood up on the log, holding his rod" (*CSS* 180). Now that his knife has completed its work of "slitting" the trout open and removing "the insides," Nick completes his work by wiping the knife that he used to clean the fish: "He cleaned it on the wood and put it in his pocket" (*CSS* 180). This sentence is one of Hemingway's additions to the manuscript version of the revised ending (compare *SS-HLE* 138 with *CSS* 180). Presumably Nick wiped the knife on the wood of the log on which he had already stuck the knife, twice. He "stuck it in the log" (*CSS* 180) first to free his hands to pull the trout out of his sack; he probably stuck the knife in the log a second time after cleaning the fish, so that his hands were free to wash both the trout and his hands in the stream.

Hemingway includes the first time Nick stuck his knife in the log in the manuscript draft of the revised ending: "He took out the knife, opened it and stuck it in the log" (*SS-HLE* 137). He does not refer in that draft to a second time Nick stuck his knife in the log. Only in the print version does the narrator indicate that Nick's knife was "still standing, blade stuck in the log" (*CSS* 180). That repeated focus on the knife Nick used to clean the fish reflects Hemingway's care in portraying Nick's entire fishing experience as a catharsis, culminating in Nick's final act of cleansing himself ashore. After cutting out the milt from the male trout and removing the rest of their insides "clean and compact," almost like works of art, Nick washed the trout and then cleaned the knife and washed himself: "He washed his hands and dried them on the log" (*CSS* 180). Nick's self-cleansing in the natural water of the river points ahead to Jake Barnes's fishing at Burguette and to his bathing at San Sebastián in the final chapter of *The Sun Also Rises* (238, 242).[7]

Thus, in a massive process of revision, Hemingway began by eliminating virtually any reference to war in the story. He continued by shaping Nick's voice into an American folk idiom. Adding three pages to the original manuscript, Hemingway portrayed Nick as a watcher of currents, shadows, and a trout's turning downstream and settling under the bridge. He presented Nick's fishing as involving one who feels trout as having heft in fighting against his struggles to reel them in. He broke up a monolithic paragraph into seven shorter paragraphs to slow down the pace of Nick's fishing into a methodical process of his physical sensations while pulling in, releasing the line, jamming his thumb inside the reel frame, watching a huge trout break the surface in a beautiful arc, and feeling the line break before feeling his need to sit and rest and think. Throughout the story Hemingway blended narrative accounts of Nick's actions with interior monologues of his feelings and thoughts. Begrudgingly, after retaining the original ending through at least two typescript versions of part 2, Hemingway listened to Gertrude Stein and relinquished the initial ending of "Big Two-Hearted River." Instead, he presented Nick as a fisherman more than as a young artist.[8]

At some point during his process of writing and revising, Hemingway thought about an entirely new ending to the story. After writing by hand "Big two hearted," at the top of a page, with the word "continuation" to the left of the title, Hemingway scribbled notes to himself about where Nick might be heading: "He thinks, gets uncomfortable, restless, tries to stop thinking, more uncomfortable and restless, the thinking goes on, speeds up, can't shake it—comes home to camp—hot before storm—storm—in morning creek flooded, hikes to the railroad."[9] This sketch sounds like an early draft of "Now I Lay Me," a story Hemingway wrote two years later. This draft of a different ending circles back to the rather apocalyptic first draft of the beginning—with its "twisted ironwork," "twisted" gun barrels, and cartridges melted in the heat. Here Hemingway envisions not an apocalypse of fire but perhaps one of flood, with Nick's mind "restless." Following his inner turmoil is a storm that turns the fishing stream into a floodplain. Nick "hikes to the railroad," appearing to end his fishing trip after just two nights. On the bottom of this same page, facing upside down, Hemingway wrote in two lines by hand, "Black River Manuscript."

Rather than pursue this nightmarish scene as the ending of his story, Hemingway instead gives us Nick at the end of a day, his legs freezing in the cold water, his shoulders sore from the weight of his pack and from the pull of the trout. In the final sentence of each version of the story, from the manuscript of the revised ending to the print version, Hemingway indicates that Nick will remain at his camp for "plenty of days" (*SS-HLE* 138; *CSS* 180). The only significant change Hemingway made in the manuscript of the final paragraph was deleting a reference to Nick's "going back to camp to read" (*SS-HLE* 138). Instead, in the print version, Hemingway simply notes: "He was going back to camp" (*CSS* 180). As he heads back to his camp, he both "looked back" at the river where he had fished and looks ahead to a plenitude of "days coming when he could fish the swamp" (*SS-HLE* 138; *CSS* 180). Hemingway ended the story by smoothly blending a narrative of what Nick does ("Nick stood up" and "Nick looked back") with his final inner reflections explaining why he decided to end his fishing for the day. Having excised virtually any reference, direct or oblique, to reading, sleeplessness, storms, and war, Hemingway concludes his fishing story by focusing on Nick's balance and resilience and resolution.

As it was first published in the first issue of *This Quarter*, "Big Two-Hearted River" comes to an end with the words, "when he could fish the swamp" (*CSS* 180). Thus, the story ends with an emphasis on Nick's open-ended sense of possibilities in his future fishing days. However, in the context of its placement in *In Our Time*, the final words of "River" lead to "L'Envoi," the final chapter of the collection. That sequence of chapters flanking the two parts of "River" in itself reflects Hemingway's revisions in forming the final section of *In Our Time*. Hemingway's drafts of the sequence of stories and chapters are preserved in folder 97a in the Hemingway Collection at the Kennedy Library. In several pages of notes on Câblogramme stationery, Hemingway wrote out a "Table of Contents" for *In Our Time* (KL/EH folder 97a). In these notes, one can see him revising his plans for the end of the collection.

On the third of three undated sheets of Câblogramme Western Union stationery, Hemingway wrote out by hand his plan for the end of *In Our Time.* He originally placed chapter 14, the chapter of Maera's death, before "Summer People" or "My Old Man." (At this point of his plans for *In Our Time,* Hemingway intended to include "Summer People.") With a handwritten arrow, Hemingway moved chapter 14—the fictional death of the bullfighter Maera—to a position *after* "Summer People" (or "My Old Man") and before the first part of "Big Two-Hearted River." Likewise, again with an arrow, Hemingway moved chapter 15—about the hanging of Sam Cardinella—from before "Big Two-Hearted River" to between its two parts. In both cases, Hemingway's moving chapters 14 and 15 placed two powerful death scenes—the bullfighter's and the convict's—before and between the two parts of Nick's fishing story. The arrows signaling Hemingway's decisions to move chapter 14 before "Part One" and to move chapter 15 before "Part Two" suggest the author's continuously shaping and reshaping the "rythm [*sic*] of the in our time chapters" between the stories, as he wrote in September 1924 (*Letters* vol. 2, 154).

The ironic juxtaposition of Hemingway's final order adds power to the collection, as the death scenes frame part 1 of "Big Two-Hearted River" with portraits of civilly sanctioned, brutal deaths. The changes also produce more jarring transitions in the settings of the chapters and the story. Instead of moving from the Chicago of Cardinella's execution to the northern Michigan of "Big Two-Hearted River," Hemingway shifts readers from the far more distant bullfighting arena of Spain. Furthermore, in the rearranged sequence, Hemingway shifts from Nick, having made his camp and falling asleep, to Sam Cardinella, waiting in a jail cell in the early morning for his hanging. Then the scene shifts back to Upper Michigan, to Nick's next morning, when "the sun was up and the tent was starting to get hot" (*CSS* 173). During the previous night, Nick's tent and blanket had sheltered him as he "curled up under the blanket and fell asleep" (*CSS* 169). In contrast, one of the prisoners on death row, probably Sam Cardinella, lay in his cot "with a blanket wrapped around his head" in what appears to be a futile gesture to hide himself from the execution to come (*CSS* 171). Nick is alone; Cardinella has two priests and two guards, none of whom offers much comfort. Nick built his tent of natural pine pegs and canvas and rope; Cardinella's cell is of "oak and steel," as if industrial elements of a cage (*CSS* 171). In the Paris *in our time,* Hemingway had placed the vignette of Cardinella's execution between the chapters of Maera's death and the Greek king and queen in their garden, perhaps awaiting their own execution. In *In Our Time* Hemingway revised its placement so that, instead of preceding the first part of "Big Two-Hearted River," the execution inside a jail comes between the two parts of Nick's fishing trip in the outdoors of Upper Michigan. The narrative of Sam Cardinella's execution, placed between the two parts of "Big Two-Hearted River," portrays a failure of nerve, as the convict loses "control of his sphincter muscle" (*CSS* 171). Cardinella's failure to heed the priest's pious injunction to "Be a man, my son" serves as an ironic counterpoint to Nick's maintaining his composure after the loss of the biggest trout he "ever heard of" (*CSS* 177). In short, the vignette of Cardinella's execution suggests how Nick has fashioned for himself a camp—in effect, a sanctuary, a far distance from scaffolding constructed in a county jail for a hanging.

Once Hemingway decided to place "Big Two-Hearted River" as the final story of *In Our Time,* he placed the story before "L'Envoi," as he renamed chapter 18, the last chapter of *in our time.* That arrangement set the story of Nick's resilience alongside a comical scene of a Greek king and queen working in a garden, ordering whiskeys and sodas to share with the narrator, and engaging in gallows humor about their precarious position as prisoners. The king muses that "If Kerensky had shot a few men things might have been altogether different" (*CSS* 181). His contrary-to-fact subjunctive verbs suggest his wishful thinking in hindsight that, had things been different, he might be the ruler of Greece instead of a prisoner. In their present state, the king concedes, "Of course the great thing is not to be shot oneself" (*CSS* 181). Apparently picking up on the king's strained humor, the narrator comments, "It was very jolly," as if to treat the garden as a comic stage rather than a prison. The narrator's final comment is enigmatic but seems given with a touch of irony: "Like all Greeks he wanted to go to America" (*CSS* 181). Thus, instead of ending *In Our Time* with Nick's assuring himself that he could always fish the swamp another day, the narrator of "L'Envoi" ends the collection with a generalization about "all Greeks" and a reference to the American dream. The narrator suggests that the king and queen desire to escape from the type of execution that befell the six Greek ministers in chapter 5 and Sam Cardinella in chapter 15. The last word of "Big Two-Hearted River" is "swamp," the body of water Nick chooses not to fish. The last word of *In Our Time*, however, is "America," the country where "all Greeks" wish to go.

5

REVISING "THE BATTLER" AND "THE KILLERS"

Absent from his draft for a table of contents in the notes of folder 97A, and from the typescript drafts in folders 97 and 96, is "The Battler," a story Hemingway probably wrote between December 1924 and March 1925 (Smith, *Guide* 115–16). He inserted the story between chapter 5 ("They shot the six cabinet ministers") and chapter 6 ("Nick sat against the wall of the church"). Hemingway's use of "The Battler" as a replacement for "Up in Michigan" places a powerful story of Nick Adams's journeying away from his home between the first stories set in Michigan and the stories and chapters set in Italy, Spain, and France. In his letter to Horace Liveright of 31 March 1925, he wrote: "The new story makes the book a good deal better. It's about the best I've ever written and gives additional unity to the book as a whole" (*Letters* vol. 2, 295). In his letter to John Dos Passos dated 22 April 1925, Hemingway conceded that "The Battler" is "better than Up in Mich." (*Letters* vol. 2, 323). By including "The Battler" between "Three-Day Blow" and chapter 6 (with Nick wounded in Italy), Hemingway provided a bridge between the worlds of Walloon Lake and Fossalta, Italy, and gave the sequence from Nick Adams's childhood, adolescence, and adult war experiences more continuity.

Hemingway's "Battler" depicts Nick Adams encountering, for the first time in the stories, an African American. Thus, Hemingway followed two of his most important mentors as a writer, Gertrude Stein and James Joyce, in portraying characters outside the dominant white culture in which he grew up in Oak Park, Illinois. In "Melanctha," a story Hemingway praised in his 1922 review of Stein's *Geography and Plays* as one of the three best stories written in English, Stein focused on a woman whose "wanderings" challenged both the dominant white culture and the expectations of the Black culture in which she grew up (Reynolds, "Hemingway's Stein" 432; Stein, *Writings* 124–239). In *Ulysses,* Joyce portrayed Leopold Bloom as a feisty, resourceful, comical Jewish protagonist navigating his way through the antisemitic, Catholic culture of Dublin. Hemingway drew on these models in composing "The Battler" as the first story of Nick Adams's journey away from Dr. Adams and his childhood home.

Compared to his composition of stories like "Indian Camp," "Cat in the Rain," and "Big Two-Hearted River," Hemingway did not revise "The Battler" as extensively. Between the drafts in folders 269 and 270 at the Kennedy Library, and the print version of the story published by Boni and Liveright, there are no excisions of substantial material at the beginning (as in "Indian Camp") or at the end (as in the original ending of "Big Two-Hearted River"). For example, the conversation between Bugs and Nick Adams at the end of the story is virtually intact from initial to final draft. The most obvious revision is in Hemingway's cutting the use of the racial epithet (the N-word) from sixteen times in the draft to four times in the print version. One effect of the revisions is to portray Nick as more resilient and resolute; another is to reduce Ad's stature in Nick's eyes from "prizefighter" to "little man" (a phrase Hemingway uses twelve times in the story). A third is to strengthen the portrait of Bugs so that he seems more in control, both in terms of the blackjack he uses to knock out Ad, and in terms of the firmer voice with which he speaks to Nick. In the earlier drafts of "The Battler," Bugs appears to be more of a stereotypical "Sambo"—and not just because of the frequent use of the racial epithet. In the earlier drafts, Bugs appears to speak and act more like what Toni Morrison criticized as one of Hemingway's stereotypical Tontos, nursemen, or (citing Kenneth Lynn), "another of Hemingway's dark mother figures" (Morrison 82–83; Lynn 272). In the published story, Hemingway portrayed Bugs as neither nurse nor mother figure but as the first male guide to succeed Nick's father in providing him with protection and direction, both by what he says and by what he does.

The boxing world was Hemingway's initial sphere of confronting racial identities as early as his junior year of high school. In the April 1916 issue of *Tabula,* his school's literary magazine, Hemingway published "A Matter of Colour," a story featuring an unintentional double-cross by a "Big Swede" in a match between the Black boxer Joe Gans and the white boxer Montana Dan Morgan.[1] The narrator, Bob Armstrong, bets a large sum of money on Dan Morgan. When Morgan turns up shortly before the fight with an injured right hand, the two decide to hire the "Big Swede" to knock Joe Gans out with a baseball bat. In the fight that the Black boxer Gans is clearly winning, the Swede knocks out Morgan, not Gans, with a baseball bat. His excuse, "I bane color blind," enables Hemingway to reveal indirectly that Gans is Black. At one point in the story, after noting, "Joe Gans, he's champion now," Armstrong says: "Joe's black, you know." The narrator of the story conveys admiration for Gans as a boxer. As Norman Marcus notes, "Gans was the first African American to hold a modern world boxing title" (n.p.). Brown Elmore, Hemingway's fellow student and the illustrator for the story, must have been aware of Gans's race, since the cover art shows a Black boxer fighting a white man and landing what appears to be a punishing right hook. Although a piece of juvenilia, "A Matter of Colour" shows that, even in suburban Oak Park, the young Hemingway saw the boxing ring as a locus of racial combat—and a place where a Black man could hit a white man without being assaulted, arrested, or lynched.[2]

A few relatively slight revisions Hemingway makes at the story's beginning portray Nick as more resilient and resolute, after he has been knocked off a train by the brakeman, and before he meets either Ad or Bugs. When Nick feels a bump on his head and surmises that he will have a black eye, Hemingway places him as surrounded by darkness. Nick concludes that "he was a long way off from anywhere" (CSS 97). Then, at the bottom of the page, Hemingway added by hand the sentence: "He wiped his hands on his trousers and stood up, then climbed the embankment to the rails" (CSS 97). Just after suggesting that Nick finds himself lost in the darkness, Hemingway emphasizes his wiping his hands clean, standing up, and climbing up so that he can continue his journey on foot. Rather than dwell on his injuries and humiliation, Nick shows resiliency. As he starts up the railroad track after being sucker-punched, Hemingway initially described Nick as "hopping" on the ties of the track—more childlike and playful than would seem likely. In the revised, print version, Nick started up a "well ballasted" track, with "sand and gravel packed between the ties, solid walking" (CSS 97). No longer is he hopping. Thus, Hemingway revised his description of Nick's walking on the track, so that he is striding firmly on solid ground.

Spotting a fire after he crosses a bridge, Nick approaches a man with one ear and a misshapen face. Asked if he wants something to eat, in the earlier draft Nick says, "Yeah" and "Sure" (KL/EH folder 269). Hemingway revised Nick's response so that he seems less acquiescent and more independent: "Don't bother. . . . I'm going on to the town" (*CSS* 99). Instead of quickly agreeing to the man's offer of food, Nick sounds more assertive in the revision. Later in the story, when Bugs appears, Ad asks Nick again if he would like to share their food. This time, having given his full name, "Nick Adams," in response to a question from Bugs, Nick accepts the offer of food, emphatically admitting that he is "[h]ungry as hell" (*CSS* 100). Now that Bugs has joined Ad, Nick seems less reluctant to join in. Soon follows a pivotal conversation—a turning point in the story—when Bugs intervenes assertively to keep Nick from giving Ad his knife. Even in the rough draft, Nick does not resort to a racial slur at this point when he refers to Bugs's race: "'No you don't,' the negro said, 'Hang onto your knife, Mister Adams'" (KL/ EH folder 269; *CSS* 100). Immediately following Bugs's "No you don't" command, Hemingway slightly altered the next sentence in revising the story. Instead of "Ad sat back," as in the typescript draft, Hemingway wrote "The prizefighter sat back" (*CSS* 100). By changing the reference to Ad as "the prizefighter" (one of only two times he refers to Ad as such), Hemingway suggests that the campfire has become, in effect, a boxing ring where a Black man, Bugs, is counterpunching verbally with the white "prizefighter," Ad. As Nick notes later in the story, "The little man whom Nick knew by name as a former champion fighter was silent. He had said nothing since the negro had spoken about the knife" (*CSS* 101). Aside from correcting "who" in the draft to "whom," Hemingway left that sentence completely intact in the print version. By observing the silence of the "little man," Nick seems to sense (but not defer to) Ad's anger in response to Bugs's warning to keep his knife. As he revised the story, Hemingway made just a few slight changes to suggest a shift in Nick toward Bugs in firmly declining Ad's invitations or requests, as well as a shift in Bugs from deferential to assertive.

Although in the print version Bugs addresses Nick formally as "Mister Adams," he sounds more formal and less stereotypical than in the earlier draft. What initially are contractions ("till") and informal ("end") become slightly more formal: "Perhaps we'd better wait until the finish of the meal" (*CSS* 101). However, Hemingway also revised the language so that Bugs's speech sounds more down-to-earth. For instance, instead of offering Nick a piece of bread "impregnated" with ham fat, Bugs asks: "May I offer you a slice of bread dipped right in the hot ham fat?" (*CSS* 101). In contrast to the polite voice of Bugs, Ad speaks with increasingly acid vitriol, calling Nick a "hot sketch" and "yellow-livered Chicago bastard" (*CSS* 101). Again, Hemingway left the spoken words of the initial draft virtually intact. Whereas Ad becomes more and more vociferous, less and less in control of himself, Bugs sounds suave, cool, and plainspoken under pressure.

A second climactic turning point comes when Bugs intervenes to knock Ad out before Ad can attack Nick. Hemingway's revisions of this scene place more stress on the carefulness with which Bugs acts. In the earlier draft, Bugs "struck" Ad across the head with a bare blackjack. As printed in *In Our Time,* Bugs "tapped him across the base of the skull" and then "dropped the cloth-wrapped blackjack on the grass" (*CSS* 102). Not only has Bugs "tapped" Ad lower on his head, but he has done so with a blackjack that is "cloth-wrapped," words Hemingway added by hand to the earlier draft. Furthermore, revisions to the draft highlight Nick's deferential gesture of respect for Bugs and his blackjack. In the earlier draft Bugs put the blackjack back in his pocket after knocking out Ad. In the print version, Hemingway emphasizes that Nick sees the blackjack lying on the grass, bends over, picks it up, and feels its "worn black leather with a handkerchief wrapped around the heavy end"—language added to the earlier draft (*CSS* 102).

In "A Matter of Colour," the young Hemingway refers to a baseball bat as the weapon to deliver a knockout blow to a boxer. In "The Battler," the knockout punch is delivered more deftly: his weapon is a blackjack "with a flexible handle" that Nick feels, when he picks it up, as "limber in his hand"—again, language added in the final draft (*CSS* 102). This quiet moment of Bugs's dropping the blackjack in the grass and Nick's picking it up seems significant. Perhaps sensing that Bugs just saved him from receiving another blow like the one the "crut of a brakeman" struck him on the train, Nick picks up the blackjack and hands it to Bugs rather than waiting for him to retrieve it himself. In doing so, Nick is able to feel what makes this blackjack so soft on the outside and hard on the inside, like Bugs. At this moment, Bugs seems like Melville's Queequeg to Hemingway's Nick as Ishmael. As if detecting Nick's admiration for his weapon, Bugs responds in a manner that treats his blackjack as an artifact: "That's a whalebone handle." Then Bugs smiles, as if assured and satisfied with his work well done with a craftsman's handmade tool. He comments about his blackjack, as if it were a collector's item, "They don't make them any more" (*CSS* 102). Hemingway added this entire exchange about the blackjack to the earlier draft, so that the emphasis is on Bugs's skillful self-control. After flattering Nick with the suggestion that he did not want Nick to "mark him [Ad] up," Bugs smiles again, commenting, "I know how to do it." Furthermore, Bugs makes clear that he has had to knock Ad out often in the past to check his violence: "I seen him like this plenty of times before" (*CSS* 102). In his role as handler of a roving ex-boxer, Bugs exudes self-confidence, grace under pressure, and professionalism.[3]

Aside from Bugs's deft use of his blackjack to control Ad, Hemingway offers several signs that he combines self-assurance with caring immediately after he knocks out Ad. First, from Nick's point of view, Hemingway describes Bugs carefully picking the unconscious Ad up and carrying him closer to the fire. Then he asks Nick to serve in a role similar to that Dr. Adams asked a younger Nick to serve in "Indian Camp," where the narrator indicates that Nick held a basin of boiled water for his father (*CSS* 68). Similarly, Bugs asks Nick (this time in a spoken direction), "Will you bring me the water in the bucket, Mister Adams" (*CSS* 102). Although Bugs continues to address Nick deferentially, with the polite "Mister Adams," he is the caretaker directing Nick to serve in the role of "interne," the word Dr. Adams uses in "Indian Camp" for his son's role in assisting him. That is, Bugs asks Nick to bring him the water that he splashes on Ad's face as he begins to rouse him. Hemingway repeats "gently" to describe how Bugs laid Ad on the ground and, after splashing him with water, pulled his ears. When the water over Ad's face does not restore him to consciousness, the narrator tells us that "Bugs stood up" (*CSS* 102). As he did in the typescript draft, Hemingway presents this taut sentence as a single paragraph, emphasizing Bugs's action and mirroring the first sentence of the story: "Nick stood up." Just as Nick's standing up is a sign of resilience after being sucker-punched by the brakeman on the train, so Bugs's standing seems a sign of determination to stay in control of the scene after knocking out the ex-boxer Ad. Moreover, Hemingway revised Bugs's speech so that he sounds less like a stereotypical Black man. In the earlier draft, using the racial slur, Nick hears Bugs apologize submissively with an "Ah'm sorry Mistah Adams." Hemingway crossed out that line and replaced it with the language that appears in the print version, without the racial slur: "I'm sorry, Mister Adams" (*CSS* 102). To the rough draft, he also adds the detail about Bugs putting some more wood on the fire (*CSS* 102). In short, Bugs seems in charge, literally, of keeping the fire going to shed light and warmth.

After the narrative comment about Bugs's standing up, Hemingway lets us hear Bugs in a monologue soothing Nick and assuring him that "There's nothing to worry about"—a comment that, again, seems to echo the comforting words of Dr. Adams at the end of "Indian Camp" (*CSS* 102). Whereas at the end of "Indian Camp" Dr. Adams speaks with Nick in a two-way conversation presented as dialogue, at this point in "The Battler" Bugs speaks in a monologue, with just a few brief comments by Nick, including Nick's asking, "What made him crazy?" (*CSS* 102). In response, Bugs tells an ambiguous story of Ad and his "sister" being married in New York and then run out of town. With just a slight pause after his story about Ad and his sister, Bugs continues by explaining how he met Ad in jail. Hemingway deleted a line in the earlier draft, where Nick explicitly asks Bugs where he met Ad. In the print version, unprompted by Nick's question, Bugs simply tells Nick about meeting Ad in jail, why they were there, and why he stayed with Ad once they were released (*CSS* 103). Instead of presenting Bugs's explanations as a response to Nick's question, Hemingway presents Bugs as more in charge of the story. Nick's part in the conversation is limited to simple statements ("I remember about it" and "Thanks") and a simple question, "What do you all do?" (*CSS* 103). In his modest revisions to this conversation, Hemingway presents Bugs's voice as dominant, as the dialogue is nearly his monologue.

After his first effort to douse water over Ad and awaken him fails, Bugs decides that he needs to steer Nick away before Ad regains consciousness. Near the end of the story, Hemingway presents Bugs as offering a dramatic monologue—speaking at length to Nick but suavely registering and reacting to Nick's responses.[4] He politely dismisses Nick with a command ("No, don't thank me") and then presents a prop, the sandwich Nick later finds in his hand and moves to his pocket. In this dramatic monologue, Hemingway shows Bugs as adapting to Nick's implied responses. To Bugs's offer, "take some of that ham and bread with you?" Nick has apparently shaken his head. In response, Bugs registers Nick's refusal, but insists, "No? You better take a sandwich." Hemingway depicts Bugs with deft, calculated force, directing Nick to leave the camp—as firmly as when he knocked out Ad Francis—to avoid an escalation of a hostile conflict. Beginning tentatively with an "I wish you'd sort of pull out," Bugs quickly steers Nick to the next town, Mancelona, and explains that his staying the night is "just out of the question." Between two lines of the rough draft, Hemingway added by hand the sentences where Bugs directs Nick to resume walking: "You'll hit a town about two miles up the track. Mancelona they call it" (*CSS* 103). His pointing Nick to Mancelona suggests a precise knowledge of their geographical location—and even an understanding of the direction of Nick's journey. Hemingway's portrait of Bugs inverts Black and white roles, as Bugs controls the action, delivers a dramatic monologue smoothly but firmly, and dismisses Nick with the parting gift of a ham sandwich.[5] With Bugs's dramatic monologue, Hemingway depicts him as Nick's guide, steering him toward Mancelona and beyond. His offer of a sandwich is a sign of his giving Nick advice about steering clear of conflicts when he can.

"The Battler" turns when Bugs steps out of his stereotypical role as servant and issues clear commands to both Ad and Nick. In a story whose earlier drafts were initially laced with a racial slur when Nick refers to Bugs, Hemingway revised the story to replace most of the racist language with "negro." What may be easily missed is that Nick perceives Bugs's voice as insistent in speaking to the white boxer, Ad: "I spoke to you, Mister Francis" (*CSS* 101). Even though Nick hears Bugs's voice as spoken "softly," Bugs also persists in expecting an answer to his question of whether "Mister Adolph Francis" would have some bread dipped in ham fat. Bugs is in control of the conversation. Nick's mentor in "The Battler" is not his father, who is not present; nor Ad, whose counsel is to "Get him" (the brakeman who sucker-punched Nick) "with a rock sometime." His mentor is Bugs, who counsels Nick to move on—to continue his journey from home in Chicago to Mancelona in northern Michigan probably heading toward Petoskey (Svoboda 19).[6] Indeed, Ad's blunt counsel for Nick to avenge himself is in stark contrast with Bugs's steering Nick on his way. And his way—as we learn in chapter 6 of *In Our Time*—is far from the "summer people" of Hortons Bay.

Hemingway's powerful placement of "The Battler" between the Michigan stories and chapter 6 ("Nick sat against the wall of a church") portrays Nick as on the move from his home to his next field of battle. Bugs's counsel of strategic disengagement continues the mentoring that Dr. Adams provided in "The Doctor and the Doctor's Wife" and leads to Nick's disengagement from the battle in chapter 6 with the "separate peace" he offers to the silent Rinaldi.[7] The final sounds of Bugs's comforting Ad and the final vision of firelight suggest that Nick has learned from Bugs how to fight in close quarters and how to move on. Responding to Toni Morrison's indictment of Bugs as a "Tonto," Gary Edward Holcomb instead sees Bugs as "a kin of Invisible Man's grandfather . . . the disobedient New Negro" (311–12).[8] Bugs is less "Tonto" than handler. Bugs is also Nick's first mentor after he leaves his home, his first guide in how to navigate threats of violence.

On 31 March 1925, Hemingway mailed the Boni and Liveright contract and substituted "The Battler" as a replacement for "Up in Michigan." Rather stiffly, Hemingway wrote: "Enclosed is the signed contract and a new story to replace the one you are eliminating as censorable" (*Letters* vol. 2, 294). In the year between sending that letter with its enclosed contract and copy of "The Battler" and his probably completing "The Killers," Hemingway's writing life had been teeming. In April 1925 he met F. Scott Fitzgerald; in July he attended the *feria* in Pamplona that would become a central setting of *The Sun Also Rises* (which he began to write); by the end of September he finished the first handwritten draft of *Sun;* and on 14 October Sylvia Beach sold the first copy of *In Our Time* at her Shakespeare and Company bookstore. In November he finished the boxing story "Fifty Grand"; in late November and early December in a whirl he wrote (and mailed to Boni and Liveright) *The Torrents of Spring;* on December 30 in a cable telegram Boni and Liveright rejected *Torrents;* on 11 February 1926 in New York City he met Maxwell Perkins for the first time; and on February 17 he signed a contract with Scribner's and Sons for *The Torrents of Spring* and *The Sun Also Rises*. In April he wrote "An Alpine Idyll"; and on April 24 he sent the manuscript of *Sun* to Maxwell Perkins (Chamberlin 58–75; Smith, *Guide* 125–26, 132–33). On 21 May 1926, he wrote to his father from Madrid: "I've been writing some stories here" (*Letters* vol. 3, 85). One of those stories was probably "The Killers," a story he may have begun the previous fall.

In his second collection of short stories, *Men Without Women,* Hemingway included two stories involving boxers. In "Fifty Grand," the only reference to a Black character is to Bruce, the assistant who gives Jack, the boxer protagonist, a rubdown (*CSS* 242). As does the story's narrator, Jack uses a racial slur in taunting his opponent with having the name "Walcott," the name of the welterweight boxing champion from 1901 to 1904 (*CSS* 245; Flora, *Reading* 100). In "Fifty Grand," the presence of an African American is subservient, peripheral, stereotypical, and demeaned. In contrast, Sam in "The Killers" seems both peripheral as a character and central as the closest figure Nick has to a guide in the story. Furthermore, "The Killers" is a masterful example of what Paul Smith praises as "that remarkable revision so characteristic of [Hemingway's] craft" (*Guide* 139).

In his first draft for "The Killers," Hemingway presented George as the proprietor of "Harbor House" in Petoskey serving whiskey to Nick—no cook at all—before Al and Max appear (*SS-HLE* 215–17). As he revised his story,

Hemingway changed the title, striking out "Matadors" and writing by hand "Killers" after the word "The" (*SS-HLE* 219). On the top right of the type-script, by hand he wrote "Madrid—May 1926 Ernest Hemingway." Vertically along the right margin he wrote, "For uncle Gus! written between 2:15 and 8:00 p.m."—thus, dedicating the story to Pauline Pfeiffer's uncle and indicating that he worked on his revision that day (*SS-HLE* 218–19). Crossing out "Petoskey" by hand (the setting of the earlier draft of the story), he replaced it with "Summit," a suburb of Chicago (*SS-HLE* 220). In this revision Hemingway also added a cook, Sam (named six times in the story), and developed the story as, in part, a portrait of racial tension. One effect of shifting the location of the story was to move it much closer to the boxing and mob scene of Chicago, but another effect was to enable Hemingway to portray Sam as an African American in Summit, a more racially mixed city than Petoskey.[9]

Even though Sam is a less central character than Bugs in "The Battler," racial slurs are far more pervasive in "The Killers." The presence of the slurs is emphatic as Hemingway revised the story, more fully than he revised "The Battler," according to the manuscript evidence. In the first draft of the story, the racial slur does not appear once, as the characters are all white. In the second draft, signed "Madrid–May 1926," the racial slur appears eleven times, as it does in the final version. Moreover, in "The Killers," Hemingway depicts the characters who use the word as unsympathetic. The first to use the N-word is George, the counterman, who refers to Sam by repeating the word. Al, the more hostile of the two hit men, refers to Sam by the slur eight times—by far its most frequent use in the story. The narrator (perhaps reflecting what Nick observes) uses the word once to indicate that "the kitchen door opened," and the cook came into the counter area (*CSS* 217). Otherwise, Hemingway does not portray Nick as using the N-word, either in thought or in speech. In "The Killers," Hemingway deliberately uses the insult as a means of distinguishing the more sadistic of the two hit men, Al, from the passively observant Nick—and as a sign that there is a more overtly racist side to the killers and to George, the counterman, than there is to Nick. Unlike in "The Battler," where Hemingway deleted most of the uses of the racial slurs, he retained them in "The Killers," from the Madrid draft to the published version. By keeping the slur, he evoked the casual racism of both the killers and the counterman.[10]

At the beginning of "The Killers," Hemingway portrayed Nick, at first a relatively passive observer, as a means of focusing the third-person narration.[11] Although he does not reveal what Nick is thinking, he does make clear via the third-person narrator what Nick is doing: "From the other end of the counter Nick watched them." Hemingway kept this sentence virtually intact from the manuscript to the print version (*SS-HLE* 219; *CSS* 215). One of Hemingway's revisions relatively early in the story keeps the narration initially inside Nick's point of view. After hearing Max direct him with a homophobic slur to "go around to the other side of the counter with your boyfriend," Nick hears George refer to Sam with a racial slur, twice (*CSS* 217). Later, when George brings the two platters and side dishes to the two killers, Nick hears the counterman ask Al which order is his. During the following exchange between George and the two killers, Nick is watching George watch them eat. Initially, in the Madrid draft Hemingway had Max turn to Nick and ask him, "What are *you* looking at?" He crossed out "turned to Nick" and replaced it with "looked up at George." Initially, Nick responded to Max's question, "Nothing." By hand Hemingway crossed out "Nick" and replaced it with "George" as the one responding to Max's question (*SS-HLE* 220–21). These revisions make it more likely that readers hear this exchange from Nick's point of view if Max is directing his hostile query to George.

The most dramatic turning point of "The Killers" comes when Max and Al decide to leave the diner without killing Sam, George, or Nick. After Al ties Nick and Sam up in the kitchen, the narrative viewpoint gradually shifts from Nick to George. Even though bound, Nick can probably hear Max instruct George on what to do if anybody comes in the diner. He can hear George ask, "What are you going to do with us afterward?" (*CSS* 218). Max's response is chilling: "That's one of those things you never know at the time" (*CSS* 218). To that point the narrative and dialogue are identical in the Madrid draft and the published version of the story. Also identical are references to George's looking repeatedly at the clock. Right after Max's "one of those things" comment, Hemingway wrote, "George looked up at the clock. It was a quarter past six" (*SS-HLE* 223; *CSS* 218). After George steers a motorman outside the diner, the narrative point of view seems to remain with the counterman: "George looked at the clock. It was twenty minutes past six" (*SS-HLE* 223; *CSS* 219). Then two other people enter the lunchroom, and the narrator indicates the actual time is 6:55 p.m. when George declares, "He isn't coming." Hemingway revised the Madrid draft, striking out "forty-five" and replacing it with "fifty-five" to extend the time of the wait to 6:55 p.m. (*SS-HLE* 224; *CSS* 219). These references to the clock, while Nick and

Sam are bound together in the kitchen, signal that the narrative has shifted from Nick, who cannot see the clock above the counter. Furthermore, the repeated references contribute to the rising tension, as George keeps looking at the clock as a way of checking on the likelihood of the Swede's being killed upon entering the diner.

Subtly moving back in time, the narrator indicates that "once" during the period between 6:15 and 6:55 George had gone to the kitchen to make a ham-and-egg sandwich for one of the customers to take away. In the Madrid draft, Hemingway indicates that "Inside the kitchen he saw Al sitting by the wicket with a sawed ["a sawed" crossed out] cut-off shotgun resting on the ledge. Nick and the cook sat ["sat" crossed out] were back-to-back in the corner a towel tied in each of their mouths" (*SS-HLE* 224). In revising this passage, Hemingway replaced "cut-off" and restored "sawed-off." He added a visual detail—George saw Al's derby hat "tipped back," as if a slick vaudeville performer sat beside a sawed-off shotgun instead of a cane. In the published version, then, that sequence is: "Inside the kitchen he saw Al, his derby hat tipped back, sitting on a stool beside the wicket with the muzzle of a sawed-off shotgun resting on the ledge" (*CSS* 219). Hemingway added the reference to Al's derby hat and restored "sawed-off" instead of "cut-off" in an uncorrected typescript he sent Archibald MacLeish in the late summer of 1926 (KL/EH folder 536a; see Smith, *Guide* 140–41). This sentence, revised after the Madrid manuscript, is likely from George's point of view. He would be viewing Sam and Nick bound together on the floor of the kitchen, watched by Al with his sawed-off shotgun.

As Max and Al leave the diner, Nick and Sam are still bound inside the kitchen. The killers leave with parting shots directed at George, "You got a lot of luck" and "You ought to play the races, bright boy" (*SS-HLE* 224; *CSS* 219). Aside from an added comma, these lines are identical in the Madrid draft and the final version. So too are narrative markers that register the killers' departure from the counterman's point of view: "George watched them, through the window, pass under the arc light and cross the street" (*CSS* 219). The only change Hemingway made in this sentence is to cut "street" from before "arc light" (*SS-HLE* 225). Having already seen Al leave the kitchen with "a slight bulge" made by the shotgun under his overcoat, George watches the two literally turn their backs on the diner: "In their tight overcoats and derby hats they looked like a vaudeville team" (*CSS* 219). George's view of Al, his hat, and his gun likely contributes to the counterman's nervousness—and then to his relief at their comical appearance when they leave. Only as the killers disappear from view does George return to the kitchen to untie Nick and Sam. In short, while the story began as narrated from Nick's viewpoint, Hemingway shifts the middle of the story to George the counterman's point of view.

The narrative viewpoint clearly shifts back to Nick after George unbinds them, and Nick follows George's suggestion that he go to the boardinghouse to warn Ole Andreson. Before that sequence, Hemingway emphasizes Nick's listening to, and implicitly comparing, George's and Sam's responses to the killers and their advice to Nick. Sam is commonly discussed as a foil to highlight the manhood and courage of the white immigrant, the Swede, or that of the white "native," Nick Adams.[12] However, by the end of the story Nick follows Sam's sense of disengagement more than he follows the Swede's sense of defeat or George's sense of control. In both the Madrid draft and the published version, Sam speaks his words of disengagement firmly as the counsel of a mentor: "You better not have anything to do with it at all" (*SS-HLE* 226; *CSS* 220). Thus, once Hemingway gave Sam a strongly admonitory voice in the Madrid draft, he retained those words in the story published in *Men Without Women*. Hemingway portrays Sam as speaking with terse insistence.

In contrast, at the end of the story, George offers a pat explanation for why the hit men are pursuing the Swede: "Double-crossed somebody. That's what they kill them for" (*CSS* 222). George's tone of assurance, along with his vague references to "somebody" and "they," contrasts with Sam's physical reactions to being bound and gagged. Sam's shutting the door on George's and Nick's conversation seems a direct response to having a towel stuffed in his mouth. After being gagged (literally and figuratively) and unable to speak or be heard, Sam is determined to shut the door and block out the conversation between George and Nick. In response, initially Nick follows George's suggestion that he "better go see Ole Andreson" (*CSS* 220). By the end of the story, however, Nick follows Sam in his disengagement: "I'm going to get out of this town" (*CSS* 222). That decision to leave, or go into exile from Summit, seems to follow Sam's shutting the door after declaring, "I don't even listen to it" (*CSS* 222). Nick follows Sam's counsel of disengagement rather than either Ole's resignation ("There ain't anything to do") or George's simple advice with which the story ironically ends, "you better not think about it" (*CSS* 221–22). The Nick Adams stories that follow "The Killers" in *Men and Women*—"Ten Indians" and "Now I Lay Me"—show how unable or unwilling Nick is to follow that advice of not thinking.

As Mark Cirino points out, George's advice is akin to what Jake considers to be the advice of the Catholic Church concerning difficult questions in *The Sun Also Rises* (*SAR-HLE* 26; Cirino, *Thought* 95). In contrast to George and John's advice to Nick not to think, Sam warns Nick not to get involved: "You better stay way out of it" (*CSS* 220). His counsel seems to stem from his long-standing knowledge of practicing invisibility and silence whenever violence seems to erupt. "I don't want any more of that," he insists, after Nick and he have been tied up together by Al, in what must have seemed execution style to Sam, if not to Nick (*CSS* 220). Their being tied back-to-back is the first (and only?) time in any Nick Adams story that Nick is physically in touch with a Black man. Furthermore, Nick and Sam are equals at this point of the story—both are bound and gagged. The more practical advice in these two stories seems that offered by Bugs—"pull *out*"—and Sam—"You stay *out* of it" (*CSS* 103, 220, my emphases). In both cases, the Black mentors advise Nick to extricate himself from conflicts he cannot win. Their advice is close to what Dr. Adams asks Uncle George to do in "Indian Camp" after Nick sees the father's slashed neck: "Take Nick *out* of the shanty, George" (*CSS* 69, my emphasis). As mentors, Dr. Adams, Bugs, and Sam counsel Nick Adams in ways that resemble his broken monologue to Rinaldi about finding "a separate peace" from the war. Nick learns from his father, Bugs, and Sam that taking himself "out" of unwinnable battles is prudent and even wise, whereas seeking cures in armed conflict may lead nowhere.

At a pivotal part of the story, Hemingway suggests that Sam has overheard his white boss, George, refer to him with the racist slur. He has probably heard the yet unnamed Al repeat the slur as he orders Sam to come out of the kitchen and then leads Sam and Nick back into the kitchen with both a homophobic and a racist insult (*CSS* 217). Given Sam's immediate response to George's "Come in here a minute," Sam seems to have heard the entire conversation (*CSS* 217). It is understandable that, as he hears these comments, Sam would quietly size up his position and decide to stay quiet as long as the killers are present. However, as he rewrote the Madrid draft, Hemingway placed even more emphasis on Sam's standing up. In the Madrid draft, when told by Al to come out of the kitchen and stand by the door, Sam simply responds, "Yes sir," and looks at the two men. In revising the story, Hemingway added that Sam was "standing in his apron" while he "looked at the two men sitting" (*SS-HLE* 221–22; *CSS* 217). Conversely, Hemingway cut a reference from the Madrid draft to George's "standing behind the counter" as he "looked up at the clock" after Al's caustic remark about Sam and Nick's being "tied up like a couple of girl friends in the convent" (*SS-HLE* 223; *CSS* 218). From the Madrid draft to the published version, Hemingway revised the story so that Sam, not George, is standing. As he is standing, Sam is *not* looking at the two killers as if he were a passive or cowardly figure in the story but rather is studying them as a canny observer of a threat. "Standing" is almost always, in Hemingway, a positive assertion of self, as when Nick Adams "stood up" at the beginning of "The Battler," when he "stood up on the log" in the final paragraph of "Big Two-Hearted River," or when "Nick stood up" in this story after George untied Sam and him (*CSS* 97, 180, 220). In "The Killers," Sam's "standing in his apron" seems a reflection of his determination to navigate a dangerous intrusion into his ordinary life of work as a cook.[13]

In contrast to Nick, who "was trying to swagger it off" after the exit of the two white gangsters, Sam shows no bravado but rather maintains a resolute and understated firmness (*CSS* 220). At this point of the story, Nick's innocence is implicitly contrasted to Sam's experience. The narrator tells the reader that Nick "had never had a towel in his mouth before." The implication is that Sam *has* had a towel—or the equivalent—in his mouth.[14] Joseph Fruscione argues that Hemingway depicts Sam with "little, if any, interiority and autonomy" (104), but Hemingway's implication seems clear regarding what Sam is thinking. After George tells Nick that the two visitors were hit men, Sam "felt the corners of his mouth with his thumbs." That gesture does not exclude "interiority and autonomy." Sam's feeling the corners of his mouth seems a self-reassuring gesture that the gag is off and a reminder that silence is a weapon against oppression. In the earlier draft of the story, Hemingway does not have Sam feeling the corners of his mouth (*SS-HLE* 225). Instead, it is George who feels the perspiration under his shirt and then asks Sam to "Make us a couple of ham and egg sandwiches"—in effect, returning Sam to his domestic role as Black cook (*SS-HLE* 225). In revising the Madrid draft, Hemingway cut that line when George tells Sam to make Nick and him sandwiches; instead, George tells Nick, "You better go see Ole Andreson" (*CSS* 220). Hemingway's revision shifts the focus from Sam's role as George's short-order cook to Sam's role, along with George, as offering Nick advice.

Even though Nick, at this point, does not follow Sam's admonition and does go to warn Ole the Swede, Sam's counsel is clear and direct. In a late revision to "The Killers," not present in the Madrid draft, after Nick says that he will go see Ole Andreson, Hemingway added, as a one-sentence paragraph, "The cook turned away" (compare *SS-HLE* 226 with *CSS* 220). That narrative marker suggests Sam's disapproval of Nick's decision. In another late revision to the story, *also* not present in the earlier Madrid draft but present in the uncorrected typescript Hemingway sent to Archibald MacLeish, Hemingway has Sam mocking Nick: "Little boys always know what they want to do" (KL/EH folder 536A; *CSS* 220). Given the racial undertone in the word "boy," as applied by a white man to a Black man at the time, Sam's mocking Nick as a "little boy" seems a strong role reversal. (Is there another case in a work of American fiction of this period when a Black man calls a white man "boy"?)[15] Even more remarkable, Nick does not respond, either in speaking back to Sam or in his inner thoughts. Sam's line about "[l]ittle boys" seems ironically to seize the term "boy" from Max and Al, as repeatedly derisive of George and Nick as "bright boys" (thirty times in the story). Sam's appropriating "[l]ittle boys" from Max and Al's "bright boys" is a telltale sign of his outspoken and assertive self. As Hemingway revised the Madrid draft, Sam's response implies that Nick's willingness to follow George's suggestion and warn Ole Andreson shows his naiveté (Flora, *Reading* 65).

A valuable complement to reading "The Killers" is to compare Sam in Hemingway's story with Sam the cook in the *film noir* adaptation starring Burt Lancaster as Ole Andreson (Siodmark 1946). In Hemingway's story, Nick and Sam are "back to back in the corner, a towel tied in each of their mouths" (*CSS* 219). The narrator's emphasis is on how Sam and Nick are not just gagged but "tied" up together. In the film version, they are bound separately and never touch one another. As Ian Marshall argues, in the film version "Nick is tied up on a chair above Sam instead of tied to Sam seated on the floor" (184). Furthermore, in the film, with Nick seated above, Sam is looking up at Nick as if to a superior. After Al and Max have left the diner and George has untied him, in the film version Sam says only, "I don't like it. I don't like any part of it." In the story when George advises Nick to go see Ole Andreson, Sam responds more forcefully, "You better stay way out of it." He then repeats, even more strongly, "Mixing up in this ain't going to get you anywhere. . . . You stay out of it" (*CSS* 220). There is no such stern counsel from Sam to Nick in the film version. Sam's relative silence in the film underscores how outspoken and firm he is in the story Hemingway wrote. In the film, Sam is the Black cook whom most critics have regarded as Hemingway's portrait of a subservient coward, a foil to Nick's courage. But the movie's Sam is not Hemingway's Sam.[16]

Whereas Robert Siodmark, the director of the first Hollywood version of "The Killers," subordinates Sam as a character in the story, C. LeRoy Baldridge, who was commissioned by *Scribner's Magazine* to illustrate the story when it first appeared in the March 1927 issue, powerfully rendered Hemingway's complex portrait of the cook. Baldridge drew three illustrations for the story—one of George with Al and Max facing him over the counter, one of Sam's reacting to the killers' ordering him to "stand right there," and one of Nick in Ole Andreson's room. Of these three illustrations, Baldridge's portrait of Sam is the most arresting. From Sam's startled, angry face to his hands clenched together, Baldridge captured his importance to the story. Sam is the only character of the story Baldridge illustrated as an individual portrait—as opposed to the tableau of George and the killers, and the dual portrait of Nick and Ole Andreson. Although Hemingway apparently complained to Max Perkins about Baldridge's illustration of Nick Adams, there is no evidence of his being less than satisfied with the drawing of Sam. There *is* clear evidence that Hemingway knew about the illustrations.[17] The archives of *Scribner's Magazine* indicates that Scribner's paid Baldridge $125 for his illustrations, completed in pencil.[18] Baldridge's drawing is among the finest appreciations of Sam's importance to the story.

Sam in "The Killers" provides Nick with little protection, but with more lasting guidance than offered by the killers, by George the counterman, or by Ole the Swede.[19] In "The Killers," Sam the cook is as close as Nick has to a mentor in that story. Also striking is that, while Hemingway portrays Nick in "The Battler" as resorting to the N-word, particularly in moments of stress, he portrays Nick in "Killers" as not speaking the slur once. In contrast, George uses the word first, and Al, the more sadistic of the killers, uses the word eight times—the most of any character in the story. In "The Killers," Hemingway portrays Nick, in contrast with Max and Al, as sickened by the likely execution awaiting Ole, and the killers Max and Al bemused by their role as hit men and using racist language repeatedly in reference to Sam. In short, both "The Battler" and "The Killers" are important portraits of racial tensions and conflicts.

In "The Killers," Sam provides Nick with little protection (they are both bound together) but with an alternative to the guidance offered by the killers, by George, or by Ole the Swede. The killers' interactions with Sam as "other" seem akin to their interactions with "the Swede"—Al and Max are openly racist and homophobic, whereas Nick is respectful and responsive. Like Bugs, Sam guides Nick through a new, threatening experience. That said, neither the presence of a mentor nor a resolute sense of direction is clear at the end of "The Killers." Unlike at the end of "The Battler," Hemingway leaves Nick as neither looking forward at a bend in the tracks nor looking backward at a campfire. Sam's relative invisibility in "The Killers," in contrast to Bugs's voice in "The Battler," may be an indication that Nick is left without any discernible mentor as he leaves Summit. Nonetheless, in his essay on Hemingway, Fitzgerald, and Faulkner, James Baldwin singled out "The Killers" for praise as a story that expresses "almost impossible pain" (36). Hemingway's Bugs and Sam are important guides for Nick Adams in exposing him to that pain.

6

REVISING "NOW I LAY ME"

Hemingway and Maxwell Perkins had begun to discuss his second collection of stories almost as soon as he finished writing *The Sun Also Rises*. In a letter dated 26 August 1926, Hemingway wrote to Perkins that he would be sending the corrected proofs for *Sun* the next day (*Letters* vol. 3, 109, 110n1). Near the end of that letter, he wrote: "It is grand to have The Sun etc. off and to be able to start on something else without things to do on the book coming in and smashing up the production of anything else" (*Letters* vol. 3, 110). In a letter on 4 September 1926, Hemingway wrote Morley Callaghan that he "will have time between now and this time next year to write some stories for a book of Sht stories to come out a year from this fall" (*Letters* vol. 3, 112). In that letter Hemingway listed "The Undefeated," "Fifty Grand," and "three short ones" he had recently written—probably "An Alpine Idyll," "The Killers," and "A Canary for One" (*Letters* vol. 3, 112, 113n5). Four days later, Hemingway received a telegram and letter from Perkins accepting "The Killers" for *Scribner's Magazine* (*Letters* vol. 3, 119n3). On 23 November 1926, Hemingway wrote Perkins that he was working on "another Italian story"— probably "Now I Lay Me" (*Letters* vol. 3, 163, 163n3). On 4 December, Hemingway learned that "In Another Country" had been accepted for publication in *Scribner's Magazine,* where it would appear with "A Canary for One" in the April 1927 issue (*Letters* vol. 3, 162n1). Two days later, in a letter to Perkins, Hemingway focused on assembling "a book of stories" as the "next thing to figure on." Hemingway continued by emphasizing that he wanted the book to "be awfully good and not hurried" (*Letters* vol. 3, 176). In short, by the early fall of 1926 Hemingway was beginning to write about assembling his next collection of stories. By the end of the year, he had written eight or so of those stories and had probably begun composing "Now I Lay Me."

The collaboration of Hemingway and Perkins was crucial in their decision to place "Now I Lay Me" as the final story in *Men Without Women.* Hemingway first titled the story "Now I Lay Me" by hand above a typescript (KL/EH folder 620) dated by Paul Smith as late November 1926 "or shortly after" (*Guide* 172). Hemingway first cited the story within a list, "Stories for Next Book," dated mid-February 1927 (KL/EH folder 120B; *Letters* vol. 3, 205–8). This list, typed in red ink, along with numbers indicating possible placement in the collection, and pencil notes written in Hemingway's hand, represents his first substantial draft of a table of contents for *Men Without Women.* In this draft, Hemingway presented "The Undefeated" as the first story, labeled by hand to the right as a "Tour de Force." He listed "The Killers" as the fourth story and labeled it "all right." He placed "Up in Michigan" as the sixth or eighth story. And he included "Now I Lay Me," but the title of the story at this point was "In Another Country—Two," described along with "In Another Country" as "pretty good." Hemingway probably did *not* send this list to Perkins; in volume 3 of *The Letters of Ernest Hemingway,* the editors indicate in a note that this fragment was "apparently a draft of EH's following letter" (205). In the list of stories for his next book that Hemingway included in the letter he actually sent, there is mysteriously no reference to "Now I Lay Me" by either title. As Paul Smith explains, "between the end of November 1926 and nearly six months later, Hemingway did not mention the story to Perkins, at least in the published correspondence" (*Guide* 172). Instead, the story seemed to disappear from the drafts of tables of contents for *Men Without Women* that Hemingway shared with Perkins over several months.[1]

It is difficult to imagine two more different Nick Adams stories than "The Killers" and "Now I Lay Me": one set in a suburb of Chicago, the other on the Italian front during World War I; one with Nick encountering two killers armed with sawed-off shotguns in a diner, the other with Nick lying awake in the dark miles away from enemy guns; one with Nick bound and gagged with a Black cook, the other with Nick conversing in a room with his Italian adjutant; one with Nick without memories of fishing or war, the other with Nick remembering the streams where he fished and imagining the streams that he fished in his waking dreams. In May 1926 Hemingway finished "The Killers" in Madrid. About six months later he began "Now I

Lay Me" in Paris. Soon after finishing "The Killers," he submitted the story to *Scribner's Magazine,* where it was quickly accepted (Smith, *Guide* 141). For months after finishing "Now I Lay Me," Hemingway did not submit the story anywhere and did not mention it in letters he sent to Maxwell Perkins.

Hemingway composed one of his masterful war stories, "Now I Lay Me," while in Paris, living in a borrowed apartment on 69 rue Froidevaux and lying awake at nights while in turmoil over the dissolution of his marriage to his first wife, Hadley, and the uncertainty of his relationship with Pauline, later his second wife (Reynolds, *Homecoming* 55, 88–90, 230n7; Hemingway, *Letters* vol. 3, 137–41, 170–74; Justice 28–31; Vaill 184). Perhaps the most searing testaments to his insomnia are in letters to Pauline Pfeiffer in November and December 1926. In one letter, dated 12 November 1926, he confessed that "in the nights it is simply unbelievably terrible" (*Letters* vol. 3, 139). A month later he wrote Pauline about "the horrors at night and a black depression" (*Letters* vol. 3, 172). In the same letter he described the anguish of their separation as "almost as bad as an abortion" (172)—a stark comparison he might have remembered months later when he revised "Hills Like White Elephants" during their honeymoon (Justice 51–53). In language that seems closely related to his portrait of Nick Adams in "Now I Lay Me," he added in that letter: "You lie all night half funny in the head and pray and pray and pray you won't go crazy" (172). As he had written to F. Scott Fitzgerald earlier in that December 1926, the typewriter Hadley had given him six years before was "busted." In the same letter, he lamented to Fitzgerald that because of the broken typewriter he was typing a story on a "bloody borrowed typewriter" (*Letters* vol. 3, 164, 166nn2 and 3). That story probably was an early draft of "Now I Lay Me," a "better one" than the story he had already finished, "In Another Country."

Hemingway gradually shaped this story with the jagged edges of three stories stitched to one another: first, a soldier listening to silkworms feeding on mulberry leaves within earshot of "the noises of night seven kilometers behind the lines outside" (*CSS* 279); second, flashback memories of the soldier's mother burning snakes and arrowheads collected by his father; and third, a conversation between the American soldier and his Italian orderly about their trouble sleeping, about writing, and about marriage. Only after several drafts did Hemingway weave those parts together into a complex whole whose disparate combination itself contributes to the haunting power of the story. This chapter delves into what the manuscript history shows about Hemingway's transforming his original fragments concerning Nick's memories of listening to silkworms while he was at the Italian front and his memories of listening to his parents' confrontation over his father's burnt relics.

In the earliest fragments of "Now I Lay Me," Hemingway set the narrator lying on the floor of a room with two other men listening to the silkworms eating (KL/EH folder 618). Thus, Hemingway began "Now I Lay Me" as a story of three men, not only Nick and an Italian orderly, just as the earliest draft of "Big Two-Hearted River" initially presented Nick accompanied by two other fishermen. Rather, the initial fragment begins, "Three of us lay on the floor . . . and listened to the silk worms" (KL/EH folder 618; cited in Smith, *Guide* 172). There is no sign of a conversation between any of the men, who spend "all night" listening to the same "dropping sound in the leaves" that Nick hears in the first and final paragraphs of "Now I Lay Me" (*CSS* 276, 281). Furthermore, in this earliest manuscript fragment, Hemingway referred to a regiment that had been in a large battle, but by hand he crossed out those initial references to war. As Paul Smith observes, the second sentence of this manuscript fragment—with its references to a regiment of men marching in dust—looks ahead to the opening paragraph of *A Farewell to Arms* (*Guide* 172).

The longest of these early fragments includes two separate memories of deliberate fires in two separate childhood homes, both in Oak Park, a suburb of Chicago. The first home is based on Hemingway's birthplace in his grandfather's house on North Oak Park Avenue. In this first scene Nick remembers his mother's burning his father's collection of snakes soaked in alcohol in jars as a final house cleaning from this attic of those "things that were not to be moved" before the family's relocation to a "new home" (*CSS* 277–78). Ironically, the alcohol in which Nick's father had preserved the specimens served as fuel for his mother to burn them. The second home, in Nick's memory, is "a new house designed and built by my mother" (*CSS* 277), based on the Hemingway home on North Kenilworth where they moved after his grandfather's death. Hemingway set Nick's memory of the second fire at this second home: the scene of his mother's burning his father Clarence's collection of stone axes, arrowheads, and other Ojibway artifacts (Mellow, *Life Without Consequences* 19–20). In this draft, Hemingway initially had the mother identifying "Ernie" (crossed out, replaced by "Nicky") as having helped her with the burning (KL/EH folder 618; cited in Smith, *Guide* 173).

These earliest drafts of "Now I Lay Me" are dominated by Nick's memories of burnings in his childhood homes—the end points of his backward nocturnal mental exercises that he began just before the war and went as far in his past as "that attic in my grandfather's house" (*CSS* 277). In these early fragments, Nick remembers his mother and father in these burning scenes. In one fragment he is implicated by his mother as taking part in the burning. In neither fragment does he mention fishing actual or imagined streams, nor does he give even a hint of his work as a writer.[2]

The main conversation in the manuscript fragments is between Nick's parents, ending with his father telling Nick, as in the final draft of the story, "The best arrow-heads went all to pieces" (*CSS* 278). In the next draft of the story, Hemingway included neither the burning scenes nor the conversation in the second scene between Nick's mother and father (KL/EH folder 619). In the next draft (folder 620), Hemingway restored both the burning scenes and the parental conversations. As Hemingway revised his initial version of this scene, he added two telling details in the typescript version titled by hand "Now I Lay Me" that he preserved in the final draft. First, he added Nick's memory of "how they popped in the heat and the fire flamed up from the alcohol." Then he included Nick's thought: "But there were no people in that, only things" (*CSS* 278). In both cases, Hemingway added these sentences about the burning of the snakes and jars in the typescript draft. This second addition ("there were no people") implies that, had Nick's more recent memories not been blocked with the onset of his experiences in the war, he would have remembered when there *were* people in fire and when the sounds of loud popping were more menacing than the remembered popping of glass jars. As Hemingway revised the scenes of Nick's childhood memories, these references to the sound of popping jars and the sight of flames stoked by alcohol suggest that the Adams home was something of a war zone.[3]

In the manuscript fragment with the earliest version of the second burning scene, the only spoken words in that fragment are by Nick's father and mother (KL/EH folder 618). (Readers may wish to consult the appendix at the end of this chapter that summarizes each stage of Hemingway's revising "Now I Lay Me.") As he expanded that scene in the later typescript version (KL/EH folder 620), he included a comment by Nick's mother in which she tells his father that Nick helped her burn the things cleaned out of the basement—a statement Hemingway crossed out by hand in this draft and cut in the next version titled "In Another Country—Two" (KL/EH folder 622). Instead of the mother's statement implicating Nick in the burning, Hemingway added by hand a sentence he retained in the final draft: "She was standing there smiling, to meet him" (*CSS* 278). Her smile seems ambiguously defiant, and in Nick's memory he registers his father's initial reaction as physically aggressive: "My father looked at the fire and kicked at something" (*CSS* 278). Next, Nick observes his father quietly inspecting the remnants of the fire: "Then he leaned over and picked something out of the ashes," as if both the fire and its contents have been reduced to a mixed rubble (*CSS* 278). Then, Nick remembers his father's curt command: "Get a rake, Nick" (*CSS* 278). Without comment, Nick records these simple four words. Not until the next paragraph does he refer to his mother as having "gone inside the house" (*CSS* 278). Although Hemingway reworked the paragraph breaks, these sentences are almost identical with those in the earliest draft of the story (KL/EH folder 618).

Hemingway's striking revisions of this scene emphasize the efforts by Nick's father to gather himself into a measure of self-control. As in the original draft, Hemingway repeated the verb "rake" three times to describe the father's actions after Nick brought him a rake. In revising that draft he added in the print version a second "very carefully," repeating the phrase that emphasizes Nick's remembering how his father "raked them all out very carefully" from the fire (*CSS* 278). That is, Nick recollects not his father's losing his temper or his masculinity, but his gaining self-control after the initial kick in the fire. Another significant addition in Hemingway's revision of this scene indicates that Nick remembers his father's conduct as protecting him from trying to take on—or take in—too much during this scene. *Not* present in the original draft are his father's words when young Nick struggles to carry both the shotgun and the bags: "Don't try and carry too much at once" (*CSS* 278). This addition, also present in the typescript titled by hand "Now I Lay Me" (KL/EH folder 620), is striking: Nick remembers his father's counseling him to take the gun and the bags during separate trips. Moreover, his father's careful raking and his advice not to carry too much of a load at once surely resonate with Nick in the present, as he struggles at night to avoid carrying too much literally and emotionally, while hearing the "noises of night" seven kilometers away (*CSS* 279).

As Donald Daiker argues, this advice shows that Dr. Adams is in control of his anger and remains cognizant of his responsibilities "as Nick's father and teacher" ("Defending" 64n47). In "The Doctor and the Doctor's Wife," Nick probably does not witness directly the exchange between Dr. Adams and his wife inside the cabin (Daiker, "Defending" 58). In "Now I Lay Me," though Hemingway filters the narrative through an older Nick's memory of the scene, the young Nick is present and does witness the scene from "When my father came home" (*CSS* 278). Even *within* the narrative of the second burning (and not just retrospectively), Nick follows his father's advice. After returning with the newspaper, instead of making a second trip with the bags to reenter the house, he "stayed outside on the grass with the two game bags" (*CSS* 278). That is, Nick implicitly followed his father's advice by not reentering the cabin and witnessing a possible argument between his parents over the burned artifacts. To risk witnessing such a fight would be to carry too much weight emotionally. As he reworked this memory in his drafts, Hemingway preserved the scene of marital tension with laconic, terse conversation, leaving Nick outside the house that was, in effect, Nick's remembered domestic war zone. The most salient revision places Nick as remembering his father's advice, not to "carry too much at once," along with his final words registering a deep sense of loss: "The best arrow-heads went all to pieces" (*CSS* 278).[4]

Not until the typescript with the handwritten title "Now I Lay Me," dated by Paul Smith as late November 1926 or shortly thereafter, does Hemingway include the conversation on the Italian front between Nick as "Tenente" and John as orderly (KL/EH folder 620; Smith, *Guide* 172). Nick's conversation with his Italian orderly, John, dominates the last half of the finished story. John and Nick's exchanges about writing point to a distinct difference between their conversation and that of the major and Nick in "In Another Country," where Nick's role as a writer is not mentioned. Moreover, only with this typescript does Hemingway include the references to swamp grass, to grasshoppers, and to "made up" streams, all contributing to his metafictional self-reference to Nick as a writer and echoing the earlier Nick Adams story "Big Two-Hearted River" (KL/EH folder 620; discussed by Smith, *Guide* 172). In the early manuscript and typescript (folders 618 and 619), there is no reference to a "made up" stream, or any reference to a swamp. In the typescript contained in folder 620, Hemingway added the word "swamp" by hand in the phrase that eventually became "swamp meadows" (*CSS* 276). In the published version of "Now I Lay Me," Hemingway repeats the word "swamp," a word he used six times on the final page alone of "Big

Two-Hearted River" (*CSS* 180). These references to Nick's fishing and writing, hearkening back to "River," point to an essential element of his self-directed rehabilitation from the wounds of war.

The deepest wound is Nick's coping with the memory of feeling his soul leave him when an explosion struck him. Nick's memory left him afraid that, if he were to fall asleep at night, he "may lose his soul again, permanently" (Nickel 93). Hemingway worked to portray Nick's struggle to stay awake to keep his soul with his body. He drafted several versions of "Now I Lay Me" before he included, by hand, a powerful passage of Nick's remembering his soul's leaving his body. The language for Nick's out-of-body experience would not be present until a handwritten addition to a relatively late version of the story (KL/EH folder 622). Only then does Hemingway arrive at the language for Nick's out-of-body experience in which he shares his memory of losing his soul when he "had been blown up at night" (*CSS* 276). The initial pencil fragments of the story contain no reference to the narrator's being blown up; rather, as discussed above, the longest section of this draft presents the memory of his mother's burning of his father's collections (folder 618). The next draft, an untitled typescript, omits the memories of the burning but includes the first general reference to the narrator's feeling that, if he fell asleep in the dark, his soul would "sail" out of his body (KL/EH folder 619; cited by Reynolds, *The Homecoming* 89). In the next draft, the typescript titled in pencil "Now I Lay Me," the narrator retains the verb "sail" and refers for the first time to the "very great effort" it took to keep his soul with his body (KL/EH folder 620; *CSS* 276). As Paul Smith discusses, in this draft Hemingway included a curiously decorative simile, likening his soul to "a red silk handkerchief being pulled out of your pocket if your pocket was your body" (folder 620; quoted in Smith, *Guide* 173). Hemingway cut the simile in the next and final drafts of the story. Hemingway's effort to revise this account of Nick's out-of-body experience suggests its importance to the story, just as he would when he shifted to a "blast-furnace" in his narrative of Frederic Henry's out-of-body experience in *A Farewell to Arms* (47).

Initially, in the later typescript version titled "In Another Country—Two," Hemingway retained much of the language in his previous draft, except for cutting the "handkerchief" simile. Then he crossed out two sentences by hand and wrote a note to insert a page of pencil writing that was on the tenth and final page of the typescript (KL/EH folder 622). This handwritten passage contains perhaps the most powerful language of the story's first paragraph: "I had been that way for a long time, ever since I had been blown up at night and felt it go out of me and go off and then come back. I tried never to think about it, but it had started to go since, in the nights, just at the moment of going off to sleep, and I could only stop it by a very great effort" (*CSS* 276). This passage in the published version of the story replicates verbatim the handwritten addition at the end of the ten-page typescript. Only the phrase "a very great effort" appears in earlier drafts than this typescript. Nick's narrative is set in two different levels of the past tense—first, the "had been that way" past perfect of his fears that began as soon as he had been blown up at night. Hemingway presents these fears, albeit distanced in the past, as an enduring trauma: lasting "for a long time" and persisting "since, in the nights" after the initial explosion (*CSS* 276). Even in the more immediate past, when Nick "tried never to think about it," he did not seem able to let go of the fear of losing his soul if his body lost consciousness.[5] Thus, with this revision, Hemingway framed the entire sequence of memories—of catching grasshoppers and other insects for bait, of fishing the rivers, and of watching his father's collections burning in the backyard of one house and later in the road next to the new house—with a powerful passage of a soldier's out-of-body experience. His pauses with commas around the phrase "in the nights" (commas placed *after* the handwritten addition preserved in folder 622) emphasize these out-of-body experiences as Nick's dark night of his soul. He retained this language in the last draft, a carbon copy of a typescript, titled in ink "Now I Lay Me" (KL/EH folder 621). As Matt Nickel argues, Nick's "wounding experience" leads to his "composition of place" in his recollection of fishing trout streams as reflective of his strenuous effort to stay awake in the dark night of both his body and his spirit (Nickel 93, 96–97).

Central to Nick's "composition of place" is his remembering actual streams to recollect himself fishing in the past. Present for the first time in the initial typescript (KL/EH folder 619) is Nick's thinking "of a trout stream I had fished along when I was a boy and fish its whole length very carefully in my mind" (*CSS* 276). That sentence is virtually identical in the untitled first transcript (folder 619) and the published story. Hemingway simply cut "small" before "boy." Hemingway emphasizes Nick's present concentration on his memories of past fishing trips. In this first typescript, Nick's exercise in meditation focuses on *actual* streams in which he had fished. Hemingway's repetition of the phrase "very carefully" suggests the strenuous effort with which Nick concentrated on his "composition" of the places where he remembered fishing. That is, as first-person narrator, Nick remembers that he would fish the entire length of the trout stream "very carefully in my mind; fishing very carefully" (KL/EH folder 619; *CSS* 276). The second "carefully" was added by hand to the typescript in folder 619. Only later in the second typescript did Hemingway add "very" before the second "carefully" to emphasize Nick's mental concentration in meditating on the streams (KL/EH folder 620). This repetition points ahead to the later repetition of "very carefully" to describe his father raking the charred remains of his collection of arrowheads and pieces of pottery from the embers of the fire that consumed them (*CSS* 278). Although that repetition comes later in the narrative, in Nick's fictional life his father's *earlier* carefulness taught Nick by example how to concentrate on self-control. The model for Nick's meditation on fishing was his father's focus on "very carefully" raking the ruins in the fire.

Only with his second typescript (folder 620) does Hemingway include Nick's explicitly *inventing* streams as fictions: "Some nights too I made up streams, and some of them were very exciting, and it was like being awake and dreaming" (*CSS* 277). With each revision of this passage, Hemingway accentuates the metafictional nature of Nick's imagined dreams. For instance, in that typescript he added by hand the simile comparing the excitement of imagining the streams to that experienced in waking dreams. This simile suggests that for Nick the imaginary streams helped him to remain conscious, a waking dream-vision. Such an addition emphasizes how Nick wills himself to stay awake by remembering both the actual streams he fished *and* the imaginary ones he made up. Hemingway read about the "composition of place" as one of St. Ignatius of Loyola's spiritual exercises in Joyce's *Portrait of an Artist as a Young Man* (137). Hemingway's late revisions to "Now I Lay Me" develop the story in the direction of a nocturnal dream-vision.[6] Given what we learn later in the story about Nick's plan to write after the war, his recounting how he made up streams as part of his "composition of place" at night brings to mind fishing stories like "Big Two-Hearted River." In "Now I Lay Me," written roughly two years after "River," Hemingway suggests that making up fictional rivers is a creative part of Nick's self-administered therapy to cope with his fear of losing his soul.

Likewise, Hemingway's handwritten additions to this typescript underscore the importance of his imagined fishing. After Nick's reference to the imagined fishing as akin to "being awake and dreaming" (*CSS* 277), Hemingway's next (the third) typescript, titled "In Another Country—Two," includes the following sentence not in the second typescript: "Some of those streams I still remember and think that I have fished in them" (KL/EH folder 622; *CSS* 277). Thus, in his later typescript Hemingway has Nick emphasize with his adverb "still" the permanence of his *imagined* memories as equally present in his thoughts as those rivers he actually fished. Furthermore, by hand in this third typescript, Hemingway added an additional comparison between fictive and actual streams, as he remembers the imagined streams so well that "they are confused with streams I really know" (*CSS* 277). With this additional note about the streams Nick invented as "confused" with the streams he "really" knows, Hemingway conveys the importance of Nick's fictional fishing.

Not in the latest typescripts, including the even later carbon typescript (KL/EH folder 621), is a sentence Hemingway eventually added, at some point, for the published version of the story: "I gave them all names and went to them on the train and sometimes walked for miles to get to them" (*CSS* 277). This last *addition* seems subtly, but unmistakably, to connect the imagined streams of "Now I Lay Me" with "Big Two-Hearted River," a story about a river whose name Hemingway adapted, a story that begins with Nick's embarking from a train and walking miles to reach the section of the river where he decides to fish, a story that Hemingway explained in a letter to Gertrude Stein and Alice B. Toklas where he "made it all up" (*Letters* vol. 2, 141). In "Now I Lay Me," Hemingway's reference to the streams that Nick "made up" echoes his letter to Stein and Toklas sent on 15 August 1924, while he was writing "River." In his third typescript of "Now I Lay Me," Hemingway *did* name one of these rivers as "Wolf River" and then crossed out the name by hand (KL/EH folder 622), leaving unnamed "all" the rivers to which Nick says he gave names. In leaving out the names of the rivers, Hemingway leaves the reader guessing at what those names might have been. With each of these revisions, Hemingway presents Nick's imaginary and remembered fishing as essential to his keeping at bay his fears of being blown up, and as foreshadowing his development into the writer he becomes.

The most substantial addition to the earliest drafts of the story is the conversation between Nick and John that dominates the last half of the story. This conversation did not exist either in the manuscript fragments (KL/EH folder 618) or in the untitled typescript (folder 619). Not until the typescript titled by hand "Now I Lay Me" did Hemingway include, for the first time, the extended conversation between Nick and John, his Italian orderly. The dialogue emerges almost fully formed in that typescript revision (KL/EH folder 620). The revisions Hemingway made as he shaped their conversation suggest the importance of what might appear to be an idle conversation about writing. Not often discussed in the commentary on "Now I Lay Me" have been the references to Arthur Brisbane's columns in this exchange, from the first version of the dialogue to the print edition.[7] The references to writing in the conversation bring "Now I Lay Me" back to the importance of the bullfight critic's column for *El Heraldo* in "The Undefeated," the "very beautiful" writing with words like *fratellanza* and *abnegazione* on Nick's medals in "In Another Country," and the columns in *The Forum* that Hemingway mocks in "Banal Story." An important thread tying together many stories in *Men Without Women* is the implied distinction between the commercial, patriotic writing in popular culture and the writing Hemingway offers in his stories. In the final story of *Men Without Women,* the exchange between John and Nick about Arthur Brisbane's writings ties that thread with trenchant irony.

At first glance, Nick and John's conversation about writing seems incidental to the story. However, the context is Nick's answering John's question as to what he will do when he returns to "the States." Nick's answer is the one definitive indication in this story of his planning on a career in writing: "I'll get a job on a paper."[8] John's response—"In Chicago?"—implies that he has reason to suspect Nick will return to his home city. When Nick answers with an equivocal "maybe," John responds with a reference to "this fellow Brisbane," whose "editorials" his wife sends him. He asks Nick if he's ever read Brisbane. Nick's answer, "Sure," is rather noncommittal (*CSS* 280). This volleying back and forth is among the clearest of Hemingway's references to Nick as a writer in the Nick Adams stories. In one of the few revisions to this conversation, Hemingway included in the print version John's question, "Did you ever meet him?" and Nick's response, "No, but I've seen him." To that response, Hemingway also added John's statement, "I'd like to meet that fellow" (*CSS* 280). In revising his earlier version of the conversation, this brief exchange that Hemingway added to the typescript draft elongates the conversation and implies that, though Nick has not met Arthur Brisbane, he has seen him in person, presumably during one of his speaking engagements. Nick's lack of response to John's hope of meeting "that fellow" suggests his tacit skepticism about John's enthusiasm for Brisbane's writing—indeed, implies Nick's own lack of admiration for Brisbane.

With language present in the typescript titled by hand "Now I Lay Me," John resumes his praise: "He's a fine writer. My wife doesn't read English but she takes the paper just like when I was home and she cuts out the editorials and sports page and sends them to me" (KL/EH folder 620; *CSS* 280). John's praise of Brisbane's writing and his wife's thoughtfulness in serving his needs as a reader indicate quite clearly that, since his wife doesn't read English, she sends him Brisbane's columns because John must have enjoyed reading them before becoming a conscript in the war. Ironically, in John's set of values as a reader, Brisbane's columns have the same weight as the sports pages, as suggested by the paratactic syntax of his brief monologue. In this exchange, Hemingway seems to set John's appreciation for Brisbane as "a fine writer" against Nick's plans to become a writer. Nick is more definite about his future plan than in the explanation he had just offered as to why he became involved in the war: "I wanted to, then." When John responds, "That's a hell of a reason," Nick asks John to speak lower—perhaps not simply to avoid waking the soldiers up but rather to suggest that Nick does not need John to lecture him about what he has already thought for himself. It does not seem accidental that, after John tells Nick that his wife sends him Brisbane's editorials, Nick changes the subject by asking John about his children (*CSS* 280). Nick's lack of enthusiasm for Brisbane's writing suggests his lack of interest in writing in such a commercial vein.

What Hemingway knew of Brisbane's columns is a matter of conjecture, but his prewar columns were collected and published by the Hearst organization in 1906. Brisbane's column titled "The Vast Importance of Sleep" appears strikingly germane to Nick's struggle *not* to fall asleep in "Now I Lay Me." First Brisbane compares insomnia to suicide: "He might better open a vein and lose a pint of blood than lose the sleep, which is life itself" (Brisbane 339). Then Brisbane compares the insomniac to a "young spendthrift" who "squander[s] capital" and "throws away money." In this column, Brisbane's focus is squarely on conserving the body as akin to a financial savings account: "just so surely you bring irreparable loss upon yourself when you go without sleep" (Brisbane 340). Brisbane concludes his column with a comfortless prediction of doom to the soul who cannot sleep: "The man who loses sleep will make a failure of his life" (341). Even more apropos of John's advice to Nick at the end of "Now I Lay Me" is Brisbane's column,

"How Marriage Began." In that column, Brisbane wrote, "Marriage was brought about on this earth by the will and wisdom of God Almighty working through primitive babyhood" (Brisbane 99). Brisbane's glowing optimism about the biblical sanction of marriage would seem an ironic context for John's assurance to Nick that marriage "would fix up everything"—and for Nick's implied skepticism about such bromides (*CSS* 282). Given John's trying to persuade Nick to marry an Italian girl despite his limited knowledge of Italian, the fact that John's wife sends him editorial columns and sports news from the *Chicago Examiner* when she cannot read English seems doubly ironic. Nick appears to share neither John's confidence in marriage nor his enthusiasm for Brisbane's writing, as suggested by Hemingway's adding the understated line about Nick's having seen, but not met, the columnist—as if seeing him is enough.

The exchange between Nick and John—in particular, their exchange about Arthur Brisbane's writing—concludes the sequence in *Men Without Women* of repeated references to writers, beginning with the bullfighting critic of "The Undefeated," whose slick journalism and jingoism seem antithetical to the kind of writing to which Nick, or Hemingway, would aspire. Together with his advice about marriage, John's role as counselor seems limited, as suggested by Nick's skeptical invocation in the story's final sentence of what John "knew" about how marriage "would fix up everything" (*CSS* 282). In short, John's role as mentor in "Now I Lay Me" seems ironically to point readers back to the Major of "In Another Country," to whom Nick shows considerably more "profound empathy" and respect than he does to John (Flora, *Hemingway's Nick Adams* 143). Thus, "Now I Lay Me" completes a pattern of writing references such as the bullfight critic's review in "Undefeated" through the columnists' clichés in *The Forum* that Hemingway mocked in "Banal Story." In contrast, Nick's fictional imagination of rivers he had *not* fished evokes the redemptive power of writing and connects "Now I Lay Me" with "Big Two-Hearted River."

Hemingway's final revisions to "Now I Lay Me" signal the importance of prayer, from the child's prayer evoked by the title of the story to Nick's prayers for John in the final paragraph. In both the early fragment and the final version of the story, Nick's response to his memory of his mother's burning his father's collection "all to pieces" is to pray for both his parents. Hemingway ended the second manuscript fragment with two short sentences: "In that remembrance there were only two people. So I would pray for both of them and then go on" (KL/EH folder 618). These sentences are not in the first typescript (folder 619). In the second typescript, Hemingway combined the two short sentences into one, after the anecdote about his mother's burning his father's arrowheads and other artifacts (folder 620). He retained that sentence verbatim in the version of the story published in *Men Without Women:* "In remembering that, there were only two people, so I would pray for them both" (*CSS* 278). Hemingway's verb phrase "would pray" implies that Nick prayed recurrently whenever he recollected the burning scenes. In his second draft, an untitled typescript, Hemingway included for the first time Nick's references to specifically Catholic prayers, as he highlighted in this draft when he capitalized, by hand, "Hail Mary" and "Our Father" (KL/EH folder 619; *CSS* 277; see also Flora, *Reading* 166). Nick refers to these prayers as efficacious in helping him stay awake all night by tracing his memories back to the attic of his grandfather's house. That is, by praying for all of the "great many people" he remembered, "it took a long time and finally it would be light, and then you could go to sleep, if you were in a place where you could sleep in the daylight" (*CSS* 277). First appearing in the second typescript, this sentence was retained by Hemingway in the published story. This winding, forty-eight-word sentence suggests that Nick's prayers act as therapeutic ways to focus on his past memories. To the second transcript, Hemingway revised by hand a starting point for his backward movement through the past. After crossing out "now," he added by hand, "just before I went to the war" (KL/EH folder 620; *CSS* 277). That is, as he revised this passage, Hemingway specified that Nick started his efforts to "remember everything that had ever happened to me" just *before* he joined the war. Thus, he blotted out the time between his enlistment and "now," when Nick can hear the sounds of the war in the distance (*CSS* 277; see Flora, "Nick Adams in Italy" 188). Following after the references to Nick's fishing real and imagined streams, and to his praying for "a great many people," Nick's confession to blotting out memories of the war seems another strategy to cope with its traumas.

The untitled typescript in folder 619 includes the first reference not only to the Hail Mary and Our Father prayers, but also to the Lord's Prayer that he often could not remember beyond "On earth as it is in heaven" (*CSS* 278). Nick's memory of his parents' truncated conversation about the burning of artifacts seems connected to his being "absolutely unable" to complete the Lord's Prayer (*CSS* 278). That is, when Nick cannot complete the Lord's

Prayer, he does not reach the part of the prayer ("Forgive us our debts, as we forgive our debtors") that seems consistent with the spirit of forgiveness with which he prays for his parents ("them both") after the burning memories. Whether Hemingway includes the references to prayer as indicating Nick's "wavering religious faith" (Flora, *Reading* 169), as intimating his inability to "reconcile the living hell of combat with the promise of a peaceful afterlife" (Florczyk 123), or as reflecting his "contemplation of the soul" (Nickel 101), the inward recitation of his prayers becomes an increasingly central part of the story with each revision. And, although he only quotes from the Lord's Prayer he cannot complete, his final references to prayer in the story are to those for his Italian orderly, John.

Hemingway's further revisions in the typescript titled by hand "Now I Lay Me" accompany and complete his extended conversation with that Italian orderly. After John has fallen asleep, Nick, responding to John's advice about marriage, tried thinking of all the girls he had known. In language present in this second typescript, after trying to concentrate on retracing the girls in his past, Nick "gave up thinking about them almost altogether" when they became mixed up in his mind (*CSS* 282). Then he returned to praying, specifically for John: "But I kept on with my prayers and I prayed very often for John in the nights and his class was removed from active service before the October offensive" (*CSS* 282). Two changes that Hemingway made in the typescript to this sentence bear noting. First, by hand he added the words "kept on with my prayers," stressing his continuing to pray, in contrast to his giving up on the memories of girls. Second, in the typescript Hemingway has Nick date John's release from the service "in June before the Piave offensive," to which he refers by name (KL/EH folder 620). In revising the typescript, Hemingway removed Nick's reference to the Piave offensive and simply referred more generally to John's class as removed "before the October offensive," which could refer to a range of attacks in October 1918, the Battle of Vittorio Veneto, including attacks centered on the upper and middle Piave River (Thompson 364; see also Gilbert 482–83; and Banks 203). Nick was apparently wounded again during one of these attacks, and John came to visit him in the hospital in Milan "several months after" (*CSS* 282)—presumably, well after the Armistice of 11 November 1918. Hemingway's revisions during his composition of "Now I Lay Me" increasingly emphasize Nick's persistence in praying as part of a sequence of meditation including imagined rivers, memories of his childhood, and consciousness of the sounds of silkworms eating, with which the story begins.

Nick's final reference to prayer in "Now I Lay Me"—a story that is, in effect, an extended set of prayers—implies their efficacy. With his paratactic syntax, he seems to connect his prayers with John's being spared the risks of being wounded or killed in the Battle of Vittorio Veneto: after referring to his praying "very often for John in the nights," Nick follows with "and his class was removed from active service" (*CSS* 282). Although not necessarily implying a causal relationship between Nick's prayers and John's demobilization, Hemingway suggests that Nick's final thoughts about prayer in the story are positive. The syntax of the sentence does seem to suggest a connection between prayer and endurance. Likewise, in the present tense ("now") of the story, Nick seems to have healed sufficiently to be "fairly sure" that his soul would not leave his body if he fell asleep (*CSS* 276). In the final paragraph of the story, Nick's repeated references to prayers imply that they played a role in his healing. Although Nick as narrator reflects ironically on how John was "sure" marriage would "fix up" his life, his relief that John was spared the dangers of the October offensive seems a genuinely hopeful comment on the possible efficacy of his prayers. Nick's prayers are effective in keeping him awake until daylight; they may also have helped, he implies, in keeping John safe.

As is set forth in the appendix below, Hemingway went through a complex set of drafts and revisions in composing "Now I Lay Me." From the initial stages of the story's focusing on his childhood memories, Hemingway wove together threads of Nick's out-of-body experience while being wounded on the Italian front; his nocturnal meditations on streams (both actual and imaginary) where he fished; Nick's conversation with his orderly, John, about writing; and Nick's prayers throughout the story. Hemingway's complex process of revising "Now I Lay Me" makes clear how important those threads are. In "Now I Lay Me" his deft, brief allusions to Nick Adams's memories of past rivers evoke the redemptive power of imaginative writing.

In Hemingway's late, unfinished story "The Last Good Country," Nick and his sister Littless speak of the woods behind their house as like "cathedrals." When Littless challenges whether Nick has actually "seen a cathedral," Nick replies, "No. But I've read about them and I can imagine them. This is the best one we have around here" (*CSS* 517). In "Now I Lay Me,"

Hemingway portrays Nick's composing in his night thoughts the rituals of fishing and praying that help him construct an imagined sanctuary, "the best" he can fashion during the war near the front. In her essay about "A Pursuit Race," Ann Putnam connects "Now I Lay Me" with "Big Two-Hearted River" as showing that Nick Adams creates "certain rituals" that help him remain steady against the "fast currents" of the river ("Waiting for the End" 188; see also Flora, "Nick Adams in Italy" 189). Part of the beauty of "Now I Lay Me" is its juxtaposing the crackling family drama of Nick's childhood, the cannonades of war that he can hear behind the gnawing of silkworms on mulberry leaves, the fishing streams of his memory and imagination, and his prayers.

APPENDIX

Drafts of Hemingway's "Now I Lay Me"

KL/EH 618 (Kennedy Library, Ernest Hemingway Collection, folder 618)

- Not dated by Paul Smith in his *Reader's Guide.*
- Two false starts: in the first, "Three of us lay on the floor . . . and listened to the silk worms" (cited by Smith, *Guide* 172).
- In the second start: the two burning scenes, but with "Ernie" crossed out, instead of "Nicky" (only case of the Ernie/Nick substitution, cited by Smith, *Guide* 173). In this draft Ernie/Nicky helps his mother with the burning of the artifacts.

KL/EH 619

- The first typescript, an untitled typescript with many corrections in pencil by hand.
- Deletes the two burning scenes—retains the silkworms but with "we" (not "Three of us")
- Dated by Smith as late November 1926 (*Guide* 172).

KL/EH 620

- The second typescript, titled in pencil "Now I Lay Me." Dated by Smith as shortly after KL/EH 619 (*Guide* 172).
- Included the first instance of an out-of-body experience as "a red silk

handkerchief being pulled out of your pocket if the pocket was your body" (cited by Smith, *Guide* 173). Later cut.
- Restored the two burning scenes.
- First draft to include conversation between Nick and John, his orderly.

KL/EH 622

- The third typescript, titled "In Another Country—Two." Hemingway used this title in a tentative list he drew up in February 1927 for a table of contents for his collection *Men Without Women*. In a fragment of a letter, probably unsent, he listed the story as "In Another Country— Two" (*Letters* vol. 3, 205). In the letter he actually did send, dated 14 February 1927, Hemingway did not include "Now I Lay Me" by either title in his list of stories he wanted to call *Men Without Women* (*Letters,* vol. 3, 206–7) (see Smith, *Guide* 172).
- In this typescript, Hemingway adds by hand the description of Nick's being blown up that is present in the final draft: "I had been that way for a long time ever since I had been blown up at night and felt it go out of me and go off and then come back" (*CSS* 276).

KL/EH 621

- Carbon copy of a professional typescript, titled in ink "Now I Lay Me," probably a copy of the original sent to Scribner's for *Men Without Women* in late spring of 1927 (Smith, *Guide* 172).
- Retains the passage of Nick's being blown up but does not include the following about the streams Nick *imagined* fishing: "I gave them all names and went to them on the train and sometimes walked for miles to get to them" (*CSS* 277).

Men Without Women

- "Now I Lay Me" disappears from Hemingway's drafts of a table of contents from January to May 1927. In her biography, Mary Dearborn errs in claiming that the story was among those stories that "had been published before" *Men Without Women* and in asserting that the story first appeared in *Scribner's Magazine* (244) (see Smith, Guide 172– 73; see also my essay, "Hemingway's and Perkins's Formation of *Men Without Women*" 90–93).

- With Perkins's encouragement, after suppressing "Now I Lay Me" from his collection, Hemingway places it as the final story of *Men Without Women,* just as he had placed "Big Two-Hearted River" at the end of *In Our Time.*
- "Now I Lay Me" concludes *Men Without Women* with its pointed references to Arthur Brisbane's Chicago columns as another form of commercial writing. Thus, "Now I Lay Me" completes a pattern of such references to writing, beginning with the bullfight critic of "The Undefeated."

7

REVISING "HILLS LIKE WHITE ELEPHANTS"

As was the case when Hemingway assembled *In Our Time,* the last story Hemingway composed for *Men Without Women,* "Hills Like White Elephants," was not placed as the final story of the collection. Rather, like "The Battler," the last story he composed for *In Our Time,* Hemingway placed "Hills" earlier—in this case, as the third story after "The Undefeated" and "In Another Country" and before "The Killers." Hemingway regarded the story highly, pairing it with "In Another Country" as two stories he "did like" when he wrote F. Scott Fitzgerald in early November 1927 (*Letters* vol. 3, 323). Hemingway's process of revising the story resembled his process of composing "Cat in the Rain." In both stories an earlier draft presents a happily married couple exchanging pleasant thoughts about the landscape as they travel by train. In an earlier draft of both stories, Hemingway names Hadley, rendering the stories as initially autobiographical. In both stories an earlier draft names the exact place. A train from Genoa passes Portofino en route to Rapallo in the case of a "false start" for "Cat" (*SS-HLE* 74). In the case of an untitled early manuscript for "Hills Like White Elephants," after "a long hot trip from Pamplona" a train arrives at the station: "'That's Caseta,' the man at the next window said, 'Where you get off'" (*SS-HLE* 258–59). In both cases, Hemingway turns a sentimental travel vignette into a story of frosty marital tension.

Paul Smith conjectures that Hemingway wrote this draft in "the early summer of 1925," based on details that Hemingway included in a letter to Gertrude Stein of 15 July 1925 (*Guide* 204). Hemingway apparently based the untitled ink manuscript on his train trip with Hadley after the Festival of San Fermin in Pamplona (Pottle 44). Both the early draft contained in

KL/EH folder 472 (and now published in the Hemingway Library Edition) and the letter to Stein include references to traveling third-class by train from Pamplona, and to a standing-room-only crowd on the train from Caseta[s] to Madrid, where they shared a compartment with two priests and soldiers from the Guardia Civil. In both the early draft and the letter, the Guardia Civil helped Hadley (named in both the letter and the early draft) along the way (*Letters* vol. 2, 361; *SS-HLE* 258–59). It is not self-evident why Smith concludes that the early draft preceded the letter, rather than the other way around, but the similarity of details suggests that Hemingway composed both in the summer of 1925. If so, then "Hills Like White Elephants" was one of the first stories Hemingway began composing that would appear in *Men Without Women* and probably the last story he completed for the collection. Like "Cat in the Rain," it appears that Hemingway returned to his draft of the story a couple of years after he first sketched it.

That early draft reflects the aftermath of a trip the Hemingways took to Pamplona for the *feria*. The San Fermin fiesta began on 6 July 1925, and within a week or two Hemingway began *The Sun Also Rises* (Chamberlin 68). Thus, it seems safe to conclude that his beginning to write *The Sun Also Rises* contributed to Hemingway's setting aside the draft that begins: "The trains moved through the hot valley" (*SS-HLE* 258). The sounds of any marital discord are faint, at most. The first-person narrator says, "Look at those goddam White Mountains." Hadley replies, gushingly, "They are the most mysterious things I have ever seen" (*SS-HLE* 258). The narrator reflects quietly on the view of the two mountain ranges on either side of the Ebro River: "On a cloudy dark day they might have been gray as a white elephant is gray in a circus tent, but in the heat they shown white as white elephants in the sun" (*SS-HLE* 258). As Paul Smith points out, in this draft Hemingway attributes to himself, not to Hadley, the simile that eventually becomes the story's title (*Guide* 204). He suggests that the exchange between Hadley and the narrator represents the invention of the "white elephants" simile as "almost a connubial venture" (205).

Even in a line Hemingway crossed out and then restored, this early draft bears the marks of a travelogue, if not as gushing as an early draft of "Cat."[1] Passengers may seem like tourists standing or seated, looking at the countryside in the sentence Hemingway at first deleted: "Heads were out the open window" (*SS-HLE* 258). He then rewrote the sentence to stress that all of the windows were filled with the heads of passengers looking outside.

He placed the revised sentence below the paragraphs about the "mysterious White Mountains," as if to suggest that the source of interest was not the town of Caseta[s] itself: "Heads stuck out of all the car windows. Up ahead I saw a mud built town" (*SS-HLE* 258). At that point in the draft a man at the next window names the town. In this early draft most of the action takes place on the train. The couple's first view of what Hadley calls "the most mysterious things I have ever seen" is from the train (*SS-HLE* 258). Only a couple of paragraphs of the sketch take place "in the shade of the squat adobe railway restaurant" at the train station (*SS-HLE* 258). The couple orders and drinks two beers during the half-hour wait for the Barcelona express to Madrid.

The most dramatic event during their stay at the restaurant is that the "great swinging rattan curtain" between the bar and their table is caught in a gust of wind and "swept the beers off their pedestals onto the ground" (*SS-HLE* 258–59). There is very little dialogue, no discussion of a pregnancy or an operation; nor is there any strong indication of friction between the couple. Indeed, the rest of the draft takes place on the train the couple catches to Madrid. This third-class train carriage is crowded with their fellow passengers, including a boy of about fifteen wearing a straw hat and "reading a dime novel entitled 'More Man Than Curate,'" whose cover he shields to keep the priest next to him from seeing the title (*SS-HLE* 259). To say the least, this draft does not even rustle lightly with any sounds of tension or conflict. There is none of the dialogue that marks "Hills" as a vital part of Hemingway's contribution to a "new genre" of short fiction with a "heavy reliance on direct speech" (Lamb, "Hemingway and Dialogue" 474). In the case of "Hills Like White Elephants," that dialogue came about almost completely in the course of Hemingway's revisions.

Almost two years passed before any sign suggesting that Hemingway had returned to the story. On the back of the third page of a letter to F. Scott Fitzgerald dated 31 March 1927, there are apparently "typewritten first notes for the story 'Hills Like White Elephants'" (*Letters* vol. 3, 223, editors' note). His single sentence suggests that Hemingway intended to resume writing the story in the first person, as he had in the 1925 draft: "(We sat at a table in the shade of the station) this is the start of something or other" (*Letters* vol. 3, 223). Although still narrated in the first person, that sentence resembles a part of the opening paragraph in the final version of the story: "The American and the girl with him sat at a table in the shade, outside the building" (*CSS* 211). Thus, the line that Hemingway wrote could be "the start of something" was, instead, a return to the story he had begun to write in the summer of 1925. Preserved in folder 473 in the Hemingway Collection, the pencil manuscript titled "Hills Like White Elephants," published as part of the Hemingway Library Edition of the stories, is a radical departure from his earlier untitled ink manuscript.

This manuscript of the story likely was completed after the 31 March letter to Fitzgerald and before 10 June, the date Hemingway sent the typescript of the story with a letter to Max Perkins. That letter begins: "I am enclosing another story for the book—HILLS LIKE WHITE ELEPHANTS." He also enclosed a tentative list placing "Hills" immediately after "Now I Lay Me" as the eleventh story, whereas "Hills" ends up as the third story with "Now I Lay Me" as the last (*Letters* vol. 3, 246).[2] Between the 31 March letter to Fitzgerald and the 10 June letter to Perkins, Hemingway saw "A Canary for One" and "In Another Country" appear in the April issue of *Scribner's Magazine,* learned that the divorce decree from Hadley became final on 16 April, married Pauline Pfeiffer on 10 May, then honeymooned with her in Grau-du-Roi in Provence, and returned to Paris on 7 June (Chamberlin 80–81). Michael Reynolds concludes that Hemingway took the two-year-old sketch with him on the honeymoon (*Homecoming* 126). Reynolds also suggests the importance of the gypsy festival and religious pilgrimage located in Saintes-Maries-de-la-Mer, just forty kilometers from Grau-du-Roi, both of which Hemingway might have witnessed with Pauline (*Homecoming* 125–26). Matt Nickel also discusses the importance of the religious setting for Hemingway's revising "Hill" in the Camargue region of Southern France, with its "elephantine hills of salt white in the sun" (82–83). Hilary Justice speculates that "Hills" might have served as a wedding present for Pauline (40). Hemingway published the story first in the August 1927 issue of a magazine named *transition* (Smith, *Guide* 206). The editors placed "Hills" at the beginning, just before Joyce's "Continuation of a Work in Progress," an early draft of what became a section of *Finnegan's Wake.* Thus, just as "Indian Camp" first appeared in an issue of *Transatlantic* right before an early draft of Joyce's *Wake,* so "Hills" first appeared in an issue of *transition* next to an early draft of a different section of Joyce's novel-in-progress. During that time Hemingway wrote a new draft of the story much closer to the printed version than to the earlier draft. In this case his process of revision entailed completely redirecting the story from a travelogue portrait of Hadley's and his observing the Spanish landscape and fellow travelers. Instead, Hemingway rewrote the story as a taut portrait of an acid conversation about a medical procedure that neither the man nor the woman explicitly identifies.

Thus, as Hemingway revised the story, he shifted from a variation on a travel letter to Gertrude Stein about Hadley's and his train trip from Pamplona. Instead of beginning with the couple on the train from Pamplona to Caseta[s], Hemingway set the location as a café at an unidentified train station. The one-sentence note on the back of a letter to Fitzgerald had retained the first-person "we" of the 1925 draft. In the 1927 manuscript Hemingway changed that sentence to the third-person: "The American and the girl with him sat at a table in the shade outside the building" (KL/EH folder 473; *SS-HLE* 260). In the manuscript that sentence is placed at the end of the paragraph. In the print version, that sentence includes a comma after "in the shade," for a pause that serves to emphasize that the table outside the station is shaded from the hot sun (*CSS* 211). In the published story, that sentence is followed by two more sentences, to be discussed below.

The history of Hemingway's composing "Hills Like White Elephants" is less complicated than that of stories like "Now I Lay Me" and "Fathers and Sons." Once he completed the massive revisions to the 1925 manuscript reflected in the 1927 manuscript, he made relatively few changes, compared to those other stories. For example, at the end of the first paragraph in that manuscript draft, he concluded with the phrase "shade outside the building." In that manuscript the next two sentences form the second paragraph: "It was very hot and the express from Barcelona would come in forty minutes. It stopped at this junction for two minutes and went on to Madrid" (*SS-HLE* 260). Those two sentences set the stage for the increasingly heated conversation to follow, and they make clear that there is only a brief time for the couple to embark on the express to Madrid, explaining why the man would need to move their suitcases to the side of the track where they would board. As he revised the 1927 manuscript for the published story, Hemingway combined those sentences with the first paragraph and cut language identifying that the express from Barcelona would not come "from Zaragossa for an hour forty minutes" (*SS-HLE* 260). Thus, he combined the first two narrative paragraphs into one, and shortened the time of the couple's waiting for the express train by an hour: "It was very hot and the express from Barcelona would come in forty minutes" (*CSS* 211). Those decisions consolidated the prefatory stage-setting to one paragraph and compressed the time of the conversation to come.

The 1927 manuscript, titled "Hills Like White Elephants," contains virtually all of the elements of the story published in *Men Without Women,* including its taut dialogue. Instead of beginning with Hadley and the narrator on the train looking at the landscape with "[f]ields of ripe grain," Hemingway revised the story to begin *in medias res* at the train station with the American and the girl sitting at a table and looking at the "long and white" hills across the valley of the Ebro (*SS-HLE* 258, 260). Rather than include a crowd of "witnesses volunteer interpreters and innocent bystanders" surrounding the couple at the adobe railway restaurant in the earlier draft (*SS-HLE* 259), in the 1927 manuscript Hemingway set the entire action at the train station with the American and the girl sitting alone "at a table in the shade" (*SS-HLE* 260). No railway restaurant is mentioned. By taking away the crowd of "witnesses" from the 1925 draft, Hemingway rendered the scene as a more private conversation between the American man and the girl at the table outside a bar.

Moreover, Hemingway modified his description of the curtain separating the inside bar from the table outside. In the 1925 draft, the curtain was a "great swinging rattan curtain" (*SS-HLE* 258). In revising that description, Hemingway first wrote that "a door opened into the bar" (*SS-HLE* 260). He struck out "door opened into the bar" and instead referred to "a curtain made of ~~heavy~~ strings of bamboo beads" (*SS-HLE* 260). Especially once he struck out "heavy" and replaced "door" with "a curtain," Hemingway made the curtain between the table and the bar seem lighter, more permeable, easier to hear and see through. Thus, with the lighter curtain, the man can simply place the order for two *cervezas* "into the curtain" (*SS-HLE* 260; *CSS* 211). In both the 1927 manuscript and the published story, the repetition of "bead" and "curtain" reinforces the sense of permeable space between the bar inside and the table outside, with the waitress moving back and forth to bring the couple first two *cervesas* and then two Anis de Toro. As Joseph Flora observes, "That the woman speaks from the doorway keeps the image of thresholds before us" (*Reading* 44). Hemingway's revision also takes away the accident of the earlier draft, when a blustery breeze blows the heavier rattan curtain against their glasses and knocks them over, attracting the attention of a crowd of customers. In the revision there is a "warm wind" that "blew the bead curtain against the table," but no glasses are overturned or broken (*SS-HLE* 262; *CSS* 212). There are no sounds of broken glass to divert the reader's attention from the conversation between the man and woman sitting at the table. Thus, in this revised manuscript, Hemingway began the story in the middle of the couple's journey, left out any account of either train ride, and kept the focus on the dialogue between the couple.

Furthermore, as he revised the story, Hemingway developed the portrait of the waitress by reducing the narrative commentary and rendering more of her interactions by spoken words. In the 1925 draft, Hemingway merely describes the actions of the waitress, who does not speak a word. When the wind blows the curtain that then knocks over the beers, the waitress merely "came out in her own good time ... listened impassively ... and brought more beer" (*SS-HLE* 259). In the 1927 manuscript, Hemingway renders the waitress as an important third speaker in the story. Three times by hand on this manuscript, Hemingway struck references to this waitress as "girl" and replaced them with "woman," probably to distinguish her from the "girl" sitting with the American at the table, and perhaps to establish the waitress as an older observer of the interactions between the couple (*SS-HLE* 260–61). In the 1927 draft, she moves nimbly and speaks economically. When the man orders "*Dos cervezas*" into the curtain, the waitress responds "from the doorway," as if poised to take the order. Her response—"Big ones?"—is a question suggesting that the man order two large beers and implying that the couple has plenty of time to drink them (*SS-HLE* 261; *CSS* 211). To that point the American's conversation with both the girl and the waitress is rather relaxed and ordinary.

Hemingway also carefully rephrased the sentence describing how the waitress set the beer glasses on the table. His revision slowed down her delivery and placement of the glasses on the table. At first, she "put the beer glasses on the felt pads" (crossed out), as if the pads were already on the table before she brought the beer. Hemingway rewrote the sentence so that she brings both the felt pads and the two glasses of beer, puts the felt pads on the table, and then places the beers on the felt pads (*SS-HLE* 261; *CSS* 211). However, he did not end the sentence narrating her actions with the pads and glasses. Rather, Hemingway made the subtle point that she "looked at the man and the girl. The girl was looking off at the line of hills" (*SS-HLE* 261; *CSS* 211). Implicit in the sequence is that, aside from completing her business tasks as a waitress, the woman is also observing her customers. To that extent, when she emerges from behind the bead curtain, the waitress is reading the couple's actions and spoken words. By repeating the forms of "looking" (the waitress "looked" at the couple, while the girl "was looking off"), Hemingway introduces the importance to the story of the girl's "looking off" as part of her means of keeping her distance. Thus, instead of crowds of bystanders, Hemingway focuses on just one—the waitress who takes their orders, brings them their drinks, and quietly observes them.

In the 1925 draft, the verb "Look" is first a rather brusque directive from the narrator to Hadley: "Look at those goddam White Mountains" (*SS-HLE* 258). Then the verb is the narrator's observation of how crowded the Barcelona Express is that Hadley and he boarded at Caseta[s]: "There looked to be no places" (*SS-HLE* 259). The only two instances of the verb are dominated by the male narrator, either truculently telling the woman to look at "those goddam" mountains, or pessimistically noting that the train is standing room only. In no sense is this draft focused on dramas of looking and observing. In the 1927 manuscript, Hemingway repeatedly focuses on what the American girl looks at during their conversation. Thus, references to her looking provide important signs as to how she reacts to what she hears. In revising the 1925 draft, Hemingway refers several times to the girl's looking at or away from her surroundings. As just mentioned, while the waitress is setting the beers on the table, she sees the girl "looking off at the line of hills" (*SS-HLE* 261). That she is "looking off" implies that she is looking at the hills not simply to admire their beauty but to avoid eye contact with the man sitting with her at the table. Instead, while looking at the line of hills, she almost whimsically utters the simile, "They look like white elephants" (*SS-HLE* 261; *CSS* 211). Instead of responding to her impressionistic simile, the man reacts both literally and self-importantly with a line that suggests his lack of imaginative vision: "I've never seen one" (*SS-HLE* 261; *CSS* 211). That quick exchange—the beginning of the extended dialogue that dominates the story—intimates the contrast between the girl's imaginative vision and the man's self-absorption.[3]

The couple continues their conversation with a series of terse, thinly disguised barbs. To his literal response that he has never seen "one" (a white elephant), she retorts: "No you wouldn't have." In defense, he offers a tentative "I might have." He then adds, more aggressively, a mocking repetition of her comment: "Just because you say I wouldn't have doesn't prove anything" (*SS-HLE* 261; *CSS* 211). As Joseph Flora argues, the man's "response is like an adolescent taunt" (*Reading* 44). Aside from a comma that Hemingway added to the 1927 manuscript, he retained this exchange in the published version of the story. In the middle of their conversation about the mountains, the narrator indicates that "The girl looked at the bead curtain" (*SS-HLE* 261; *CSS* 211). For the second time in the story, she seems to avert making eye contact with the man. Instead, she notices that the curtain serves as a strange canvas for painted words. Perhaps only noticing the painted letters after she draws his attention toward the curtain, the man identifies the words as "Anis de Toro." He then explains: "It's a drink" (*SS-HLE* 261). What she regards as a curious piece of artwork, he quickly turns into an opportunity both to display his knowledge of Spanish drinks and to place himself in the position of guide to the girl, offering her an experience with a drink she has apparently never tasted.

After a series of tart exchanges about the licorice taste of the Anis and the girl's repeating her simile about the white elephants, she acerbically sums up the state of their frayed relationship: "That's all we do isn't it? Look at things and try new drinks" (*SS-HLE* 262). In revising the story as it appeared in *transition* for publication in *Men Without Women,* Hemingway made few changes, aside from adding commas for pauses, and apostrophes to indicate possession. One of the most striking changes, however, came with Jig's reference to "That's all we do." In both the manuscript published in the Hemingway Library Edition and in the version published in *transition,* Hemingway divides Jig's derisive statements into two sentences: "That's all we do isn't it? Look at things and try new drinks" (*SS-HLE* 262). The version published in *transition* is the same as in the Hemingway Library Edition, except that before "isn't it?" a comma is added ("Hills" in *transition* 10). When the story appeared in *Men Without Women,* Hemingway combined the sentences into one: "That's all we do, isn't it—look at things and try new drinks?" (*CSS* 212). In the final version, with a dash replacing the question mark, Hemingway presents the entire sentence as Jig's sharp-edged, rhetorical question mocking the man's assuming the role as her guide. Thus, after the first two instances of "look" as narrative comments on what the girl is doing (looking at the distant hills, then at the bead curtain), the girl uses "look" as a verb summing up pejoratively what the couple has been doing. She sums up their relationship as that of tourists who "[l]ook at things" like paintings in museums and who "try new drinks" as part of the traveling experience. Implied in her "all we do" is what they do *not* do—make affectionate physical contact, speak tenderly to one another, or share each other's point of view with any empathy.

Then, departing from her life as a tourist looking at famous sights and tasting novel drinks, the girl "looked across at the hills" for the second time (*SS-HLE* 262; *CSS* 212). Apparently, she chooses to look back at the landscape along the river rather than to look at the man sitting across the table from her. She then recants her simile—the most imaginative comment either the man or she has made: "The [*sic*] don't really look like white elephants. I just meant the coloring of their skin through the trees" (*SS-HLE* 262). Even in recanting, she offers an explanation for her original impression that suggests her artistic intuition. In painterly terms she explains her impression that led to her simile: "the coloring of their skin" (the white slope of the distant hills in the background) as seen "though the trees" (presumably trees on the other side of the Ebro River, in the nearer foreground). The phrase "through the trees" sharpens the portrait of the girl's sense of depth and perspective. Even as she concedes that the hills do not look like white elephants, she offers an explanation about how the green foliage of the trees affects the "coloring" of the "skin" of the hills. Furthermore, this phrase referring to the trees in the foreground prepares for an echoing of the same phrase in a sentence that Hemingway added while revising the manuscript: "The shadow of a cloud moved across the field of grain and she saw the river through the trees" (cited by Justice 48; *SS-HLE* 263; *CSS* 213). That sentence with the repetition of the phrase "through the trees" is not shown as an added revision to the manuscript in the Hemingway Library Edition. Taken together, Hemingway's repeating "through the trees" in this revision places even more emphasis on the depth of the girl's vision. Apparently unresponsive to her reason for seeing the hills as like white elephants, the man asks, "Should we have another beer?" (*SS-HLE* 262; *CSS* 212). He seems no more interested in her painterly explanation—with its reference to how trees in the foreground affect the appearance of hills in the background—than in her original simile.[4]

At that point, seemingly out of nowhere, but likely a return to previous conversations, the man introduces the topic that becomes central to the rest of their dialogue. Aside from the striking difference between the relative lack of spoken words in the 1925 draft and the dominance of dialogue in the 1927 manuscript, perhaps the most striking revision is the next topic of conversation. After the relatively small talk about the landscape, the hot weather, and the drinks, the man introduces the topic of "an awfully simple operation . . . not really an operation at all" (*SS-HLE* 262). In the published story, the man addresses the girl by name or nickname: "It's really an awfully simple operation, Jig" (*CSS* 212). Neither in the revised manuscript nor in the version of the story published in *transition* does the American man address the girl as "Jig" in this reference to a "simple operation" (*SS-HLE* 262; "Hills" in *transition* 11). By adding her name, Hemingway portrays the man as attempting to be personal, and even appear affectionate, at the very moment he turns the conversation in a direction that escalates rather quickly. Addressing her by name when continuing the topic of an operation also makes the second time he does so an echo, or repetition, of the first time: "I know you wouldn't mind it, Jig" (*SS-HLE* 262; *CSS* 212). By that point the gulf between the man's addressing her by name, and his assuming he knows she wouldn't "mind" the operation, is deep.

In response to this line suggesting the man's complete lack of understanding of, or empathy for, her feelings about the "operation," the girl "looked ~~away~~ at the ground the table legs rested on" (*SS-HLE* 262). Deleting "away" to leave the point implied, Hemingway indicates that the girl "looked at the ground" to turn away from eye contact with the man who has just proposed that she undergo an operation. Her silence speaks volumes. After a series of exchanges about whether the "operation" would restore the couple "[j]ust like we were before" by taking away "the only thing that makes us unhappy," the girl again looks away, as if resisting the man's assumptions about her feelings, as implied by his pronouns "we" and "us." In the manuscript draft, Hemingway struck "away" a second time to imply more subtly that, in looking at her surroundings, she is looking away from the man. This time she "looked at the bead curtains, put her hand out and took hold of two of the strings of beads" (*SS-HLE* 262). Not shown in the Hemingway Library Edition of "Hills" is that Hemingway added this sentence by hand above the following line of dialogue: "And you think we'll be all right and be happy?" (KL/EH folder 473, 6; *SS-HLE* 262). Thus, by adding this sentence about the girl's looking at the bead curtain, Hemingway suggests her resistance to the man's assumptions, as she turns to look at the curtain before asking, "And you think . . . ?" Hemingway also echoes the earlier point in the story when the girl looks at the bead curtain after the man responds to her comment that he "wouldn't have" seen a white elephant (*SS-HLE* 261; *CSS* 211). This time, instead of asking the man a question about the letters painted on the curtain, the girl engages in the first act of touching in the story. Her taking hold of "two of the strings of beads" seems an alternative to taking hold of the man who promises a return to whatever their relationship has been if she will agree to the operation. The girl's looking away seems a counterpoint to her engaging in even a terse conversation. Rather, as she touches the strings of beads, "the man can see Jig considering her options and deciding" what to do next (Justice 48).[5]

The girl's next act toward looking rather than talking comes after one of the longest sequences of pure dialogue without intervening narrative bridges. The section of the story from her asking him, "And you really want to?" to her saying, "Then I'll do it and everything will be fine" is virtually identical in the 1927 manuscript draft and the printed version of "Hills" (*SS-HLE* 262–63; *CSS* 213). During that sequence, Hemingway leaves the stichomythic dialogue without narrative commentary or even an indication of who is speaking. At the end of that sequence, she voices agreement with the man's assurance that if she goes through with the operation, "then everything will be fine." Apparently catching the touch of irony or sarcasm in her voice, he responds, perhaps with feigned empathy: "I don't want you to do it if you feel that way" (*SS-HLE* 263; *CSS* 213). His nonconcession concession suggests that her feeling "that way" is wrong and selfish—ironic, given his part in the conversation. As Robert Paul Lamb argues, "what he wants is not just for her to have the abortion but to acknowledge that she *wants* to have it, that is, to feign volition, thus absolving him from responsibility for the actions he demands" (*Art Matters* 200). Again, she responds not by talking but by standing up and walking "to the end of the station"—an act that seems both to put distance between the man and herself and to keep from screaming at him.

At this point the narrative suggests that she is studying the landscape, seeing fertile "fields of grain" that seem to reflect her sense of beauty and birth in the distance that is unlike her experience of what is nearby: "Across, on the other side, were fields of grain and trees along the banks of the Ebro. Far away, beyond the river, were mountains. The shadow of a cloud moved across the field of grain and she saw the river through the trees" (*CSS* 213). That moment of penetrating vision—perhaps the high point for the girl of the time waiting at the train station—leads her to resume the conversation with a comment summing up her view of their deteriorating relationship. Presumably, she has walked back toward the table, close enough for the man to hear her, but not close enough for him to understand the words she spoke: "We could have all this.... And we could have everything and every day we make it more impossible" (*SS-HLE* 263; *CSS* 213). The Hemingway Library Edition shows these two sentences as part of the paragraph that starts with "The girl stood up." A close reexamination of the manuscript shows that Hemingway indented "We could have all this" to start a new paragraph, as is the case in the story as printed in *transition* and later in *Men Without Women* (KL/EH folder 473, 8). By setting off the girl's "could have all this" statement as a new paragraph, Hemingway emphasizes how her repetition of absolutes ratchets up her part of the conversation into a dramatic state of conclusions about their relationship. Although they "could have all this ... everything and every day," they have lost everything they could have had. The man's response is literally tone-deaf, indicative of his steady lack of understanding her: "What did you say?" (*SS-HLE* 263; *CSS* 213). Perhaps, as Hilary Justice suggests, he genuinely did not hear what the girl said (43–44). Ironically, that question is more responsive to what the girl has said than earlier, when he changed the subject and asked her if she'd like another beer after she explained why the hills looked to her like white elephants.[6]

In the manuscript, the girl's reference to "all this" begins with her stating "We could have all this." In revising the manuscript for publication in the August 1927 issue of *transition* and in the version published in *Men Without Women,* Hemingway added a single word: "And we could have all this" ("Hills" in *transition* 12; *CSS* 213). By adding "And" at the beginning of her statement, Hemingway suggests that her spoken words may be a continuation of her unspoken thoughts, as "all this" likely includes the view of the fields of grain in the foreground and the mountains in the background. The additional "And" also provides an ironic sequence of three: "And we could have all this.... And we could have everything and every day we make it impossible" (*CSS* 213). One might expect the third "and" logically to be "but": "And we could have everything, but every day we make it impossible." Instead, with an accumulating force of three identical conjunctions, the girl gives voice to her emotional sense of cumulative losses in the couple's life together.

Another slight change Hemingway made in this conversation contributes to the girl's emphatic insistence on her feelings of loss. In the manuscript, she responds in one sentence to the man's claim that "It is ours"—"it" seeming to refer to "the whole world" that lies before them if they continue their travels. (Ironically, the American man's "it" does not seem to refer to the child they have conceived. In his mind, at least at this point of the story, only if the child is aborted will the "it" of the world ahead of them, and of their happiness with each other, be "ours.") Her response in the 1927 manuscript is a brief compound sentence: "No it isn't and once they take it away you never get it back" (*SS-HLE* 263). At some point before the story appeared in *transition,* Hemingway split Jig's response into two sentences, a simple and a complex. For the version published in *Men Without Women* he added a comma: "No it isn't. And once they take it away, you never get it back" ("Hills" in *transition* 12; *CSS* 213). Checking his absolute claim of "We can have the whole world," she replies firmly. By separating "No it isn't," Hemingway gave her response a stronger tone of terse finality. He then started a new sentence with the dependent clause, "And once they take it away," giving the American girl's statement a tone of fatalistic resolution. Although she leaves unclear who "they" are taking "it" away (the couple themselves?), she leaves no doubt that "you" (meaning "we") "never get it back" ("it" possibly referring not just to their relationship but to their unborn child). When the man responds, as if taking her words literally, "But they haven't taken it away," she answers him with words that may seem concessional but that sound grimly prophetic: "We'll wait and see" (*CSS* 213). Her "wait and see" seems foreboding but may allow for the possibility that the man could change and let her "see" a different side of him than the insensitive cad he has shown himself to be so far in the story (Justice 49–50).

In revising the 1927 manuscript, Hemingway changed very little of the dialogue from the point where the girl repeats herself after the man asks what she just said ("I said we could have everything") until the conversation after "[t]hey sat down at the table" (*SS-HLE* 263–64; *CSS* 213). Hemingway implied that she remains at the end of the station's platform, where she walked after the man's half-hearted concession: "I don't want you to do it if . . ." During the next series of terse exchanges, the girl repeats "No, we can't" or "No, it isn't" four times. Each time the man tries to counter with an affirmative "We can" or "It's ours." After his claim that "they haven't taken it away," the girl's response changes slightly, suggesting that this stage of the conversation has reached an impasse: "We'll wait and see" (*SS-HLE* 263; *CSS* 313). Seemingly checked by her open-ended, slightly defiant response, the man asks her to "Come on back in the shade." The "come back" implies either that he has walked out of the shade over to her at the end of the platform or that he is asking her to return to the shade, where he has remained. Either way, his next comment offers little comfort: "You mustn't feel that way." To which she responds, "I don't feel any way," refusing point-blank to allow the man to dictate her feelings. She adds, "I just know things," implying that she knows more than he does, without specifying what "things" she knows (*SS-HLE* 263–64; *CSS* 214). Without revising any part of this sequence of dialogue, Hemingway retained this section intact from the manuscript to the publication of "Hills Like White Elephants" in *Men Without Women*.

As discussed above, a salient revision from the 1925 to the 1927 man-uscript drafts is the man's bringing up the topic of an operation he would like the girl to have. His references to the operation are vague and suggest his lack of medical knowledge or sensitivity: "It's not really an operation at all" (*SS-HLE* 262; *CSS* 212). In working on the 1927 manuscript, Hemingway carefully excised references, explicit or implicit, to the girl's state of being pregnant. When the man agrees "to go through with it if it means anything to you," he leaves unspoken what "it" is that he is willing to "go through," but "it" here implies his willingness to "go through" with her giving birth to their child (*SS-HLE* 264; *CSS* 214). After the man says that he is "per-fectly willing to go through with it," the girl asks, "Doesn't it mean anything to you?" She then begins her next sentence: "Three of us" (*SS-HLE* 264). At that point Hemingway crossed out "Three of us," taking out her explicit reference to their unborn child. The phrase Hemingway cut "is too direct, too obvious" for this conversation (Justice 47). Robert Paul Lamb concludes about the ten times the pronoun "it" is used: "These uses of *it* not only mir-ror the shorthand manner by which people refer to matters they both under-stand (or think that they understand), 'it' also creates the ironic ambiguity that makes for relevance. By subsuming such radically incompatible an-tecedents within one pronoun, Hemingway demonstrates how, in dialogue, all hope of communication may become impossible" (*Art Matters* 202). In this part of the dialogue, the American man apparently uses "it" at first to refer to the unspoken word "abortion": "It's not really an operation." Then he uses "it" to refer to her going through with the pregnancy, suggesting a hesitation, an uncertainty, on his part. As Lamb argues, "it" refers to mul-tiple possible referents: having the abortion, having the baby, the baby it-self, the girl's sense of the entire conversation, an implied explicative, and the man's "knowledge" that an abortion is "perfectly simple," accentuated by the man's emphatic "but I do know it" (*CSS* 214; *Art Matters* 202). In the case of the girl's question, "Doesn't it mean anything to you?" she seems to include in "it" a conflation of the baby, the abortion, the girl's feelings, and the relationship itself.

According to Hilary Justice, at this point of the manuscript, "Two lines from this section of dialogue proved the most elusive to Hemingway as he reworked them through no fewer than four complete versions" (46). In each version that Hilary Justice discusses, after the girl asks, "Doesn't it mean anything to you?" the man responds, "Of course it does" (*SS-HLE* 264; *CSS* 214). As discussed above, Hemingway leaves open whether "it" refers to the unborn child, the abortion, the girl's feelings, or the couple's relationship. In one version that Hemingway struck from the manuscript draft, the man follows "Of course it does" with "But it's just a matter of expediency. And I know it's perfectly simple" (*SS-HLE* 264). In this draft Hemingway suggests that the second "it" is the abortion, euphemistically referred to as "an expediency," with the man's repeating his earlier assurance that he knows the operation is "awfully simple" and "perfectly simple" (*SS-HLE* 262–63). In what Justice discusses as a different version of this dialogue, the man's response is, "Of course it does. But I don't want anybody but you. I don't want anyone else. I know how the other thing is. And I know it's perfectly simple" (cited by Justice 46; *SS-HLE* 264). This version of the man's reply is clearly detectable in the Hemingway Library Edition, although that edition shows that Hemingway crossed out "I know how the other thing is" after crossing out the sentence "But it's just a question of expediency" (*SS-HLE* 264). In the version of this exchange published in both *transition* and *Men Without Women,* Hemingway has cut the man's reference to the operation as an "expediency" and "the other thing," as perhaps too obviously callous and utilitarian. He retains the man's repeated emphasis on not wanting "anybody but you" or "anyone else." And he retains the man's repeated assurance, "And I know it's perfectly simple" ("Hills" in *transition* 13; *CSS* 214). At that point the girl repeats "it" to mock his simplistic view of the operation: "Yes, you know it's perfectly simple" (*SS-HLE* 264; *CSS* 214).

Moreover, at just this point of their intensifying conversation, Hemingway's deleting "expediency" and "the other thing" leaves unspoken these euphemistic references to the girl's pregnancy. After the man repeats that he does not want "anybody" or "anyone else" (such as a child), he adds: "I know how the other thing is" (*SS-HLE* 264). Hemingway struck through this sentence in the manuscript and deleted it from the published story.

The "other thing" the man apparently "knows" is having an abortion. Hemingway cut both references to the operation as "a question of expediency" and as a "thing," as perhaps too clearly giving away the nature of the operation. Then, the girl pleads with seven "Please" intensifiers for silence, one of which, as Hilary Justice points out, Hemingway added during his process of revision (48). After the girl's crescendo of "Please" admonitions that he "stop talking," the man is left speechless, briefly. Instead of responding immediately to her plea, he "looked at ~~her~~ the bags against the wall of the station" (*SS-HLE* 264). By crossing out "her," Hemingway again leaves implied what he doesn't need to spell out: the man looks at the suitcases as a way to avoid eye contact with the girl who has told him to "please" shut up. As Joseph Flora points out, "In contrast to Jig's looking from the platform across the fertile plain, the man looks at their bags against the wall, an impasse" (*Reading* 51). In revising the 1927 manuscript, Hemingway made two more changes at this point that might seem incidental but are fine touches. As he described the man looking at the suitcase in response to the girl's "please" admonitions, Hemingway struck "stickers" and replaced the word with "labels" (*SS-HLE* 264; *CSS* 214). Referring to the labels on suitcases that presumably identify the places the couple has traveled, he revised the reference to seem a bit more formal—"stickers" seeming more childlike. Likewise, in the same sentence, he replaced "spent nights" with "stayed" in referring to the hotels identified by the labels on the suitcases (*SS-HLE* 264). In the version of the story published in *transition,* Hemingway changed "stayed" to "had stopped." In the final version of the story, he reverted back to "spent nights," a phrase that implies a more transitory passing through tourist stops than the verbs "stayed" or "had stopped" ("Hills" in *transition* 13; *CSS* 214). The verb "spent" also suggests a more commercial, impersonal aspect of their travels. As Russ Pottle argues, "In its final form the phrase ['spent nights'] strikes the ear with the empty rings of coins falling, an echo of the tourist's commercial passage" (53). Finally, "spent nights" may suggest lovemaking, but perhaps with the added sense that by the time of the story the couple has expended what love they once had. Joseph Flora reads "spent" as suggesting both sexual and emotional waste in the couple's present and future: "The sexual energy will be spent, with nothing other than the spending as the reward" (*Reading* 52). Hemingway's restoration of "spent nights" preserves a possible financial pun akin to Shakespeare's sonnet 129, "Th'expense of spirit in a waste of shame."

After turning away to look at the suitcase, the man speaks again: "But I don't want you to . . . I don't care anything about it—" (*SS-HLE* 264). Presumably, he is suggesting to the girl that he doesn't want her to go through with the operation if she doesn't want to. Perhaps more tellingly, in trying to back away from insisting that she have the operation, he states that he doesn't "care anything about it"—where "it" seems most clearly to be the operation, but could be the unborn child, or (as the girl might understand it) their entire relationship. In the manuscript Hemingway stresses her interrupting the man by placing a dash after "I don't care anything about it—" (*SS-HLE* 264). In the published version he replaces the dash with a simple period (*CSS* 214). Furthermore, at that point in the manuscript, Hemingway crossed out "Three of us could get," with what the three could "get" left incomplete (*SS-HLE* 264). However, this time it is the man who starts a sentence with "Three of us." Hemingway seemed about to have the man say, "The three of us could get along." By cutting the reference to "three of us," Hemingway again deleted an explicit allusion to an unborn child. By keeping the man from completing his statement, Hemingway also stopped short of having the man concede to the girl's apparent reluctance to have the operation. Instead, the girl escalates her vehement repetition of "please" into a threat: "I'll scream" (*SS-HLE* 264; *CSS* 214). By deleting both references to "Three of us," Hemingway removed the only clear references to the girl's pregnancy—and, thereby, took out strong indications of what operation the man wants the girl to undertake. Those excisions contribute to the fruitful ambiguity of the story, leaving the reader to guess or infer what topic the couple is discussing—or talking around—and leaving open whether they decide to raise a child or not, to stay together or not.[7]

Then, once the girl threatens to scream in order to stop the man from renewing his protestations, the waitress reappears carrying the two more beers that the girl requested. In contrast to her first spoken words of the story, when she asked if the couple wanted "Big ones," here she alerts them that the train is due in ("ten" crossed out) five minutes (*SS-HLE* 264). By revising the waitress's reference to the time left for the couple to drink their second beers, Hemingway adds to the sense of urgency about what they will do next.[8] For the first time in the story, the girl smiles—first, "smiling brightly at the woman, to thank her." To that sentence in the manuscript, Hemingway added a comma after "woman," with a pause for emphasis on the girl's gratitude for being given the warning—and her gratitude for a time to change locations, topics of conversation, and perhaps more. Once the American man declares that he had "better take the bags over to the other side of the station," she "smiled at him" (*SS-HLE* 264; *CSS* 214)—with the second smile added as Hemingway revised the story (Justice 48). In both cases, her smiles come without speech, silently. Particularly in the case of her smile at the man, Hemingway leaves ambiguous why she is smiling or what she is thinking. Whereas he emphasizes that the girl smiles at the waitress "to thank her," Hemingway leaves to the reader's conjectures whether she is smiling at the man in gratitude for his initiative in moving the suitcases, relief at his leaving her for a time, or simply to present a smile that Joseph Flora sees "as enigmatic as that of the *Mona Lisa*" (*Reading* 52).[9]

Hemingway's last revisions to the manuscript of 1927 are a pair of deletions in the final narrative paragraph of the story, concentrating in a single sentence a brief glimpse into the thoughts of the American man. Carrying the bags "to the other tracks," the man "looked up the tracks but could not see the train" (*SS-HLE* 265; *CSS* 214). Hemingway leaves unspecified whether the "other" tracks lead to Madrid or to Barcelona, to an operation or to an eventual delivery. After the man leaves the suitcases next to "the other tracks," he stops on the way back to have an Anis at the bar before rejoining the girl. He enters the bar and "drank an Anis and looked at the people" (*SS-HLE* 265; *CSS* 214). Right after he refers to the man's looking at the people in the bar, Hemingway cut two sentences: "There must be some actual world. There must be some place you could touch where people were calm and reasonable" (*SS-HLE* 265). As these sentences brought readers inside the man's thoughts, these cuts suggest Hemingway's desire to strip the story of "access to any character's consciousness," as Robert Paul Lamb argues ("Hemingway and Dialogue" 469). However, between those deleted sentences, Hemingway added by hand one brief sentence where he brings us inside the viewpoint of the man, who observes the customers at the bar: "They were all waiting reasonably for the train" (*SS-HLE* 265). Hemingway retained this simple sentence in the final version of the story (*CSS* 214). The man's observation implies that, while these customers inside the bar are "waiting reasonably," the girl at the table outside has not been doing so. After so many references to the girl's looking at or away, in the second half of the story Hemingway refers four times to the man's looking—first, at the girl and the table; second, at their suitcases; then, at the empty tracks; and, finally, at the people drinking at the bar. That final look leads the American man to contrast, in his brief thought, the customers "waiting reasonably" with the girl at the table who, presumably, is not. Then after the sentence about the customers "waiting reasonably for the train," Hemingway deleted another sentence presenting the man's interior reflection: "Once it had all been as simple as this bar" (*SS-HLE* 265). Presumably, "it all" included especially his relationship with the girl. Hemingway's cuts remove what seem excessive insistence, even by this man, on his rectitude and the girl's irrationality. The cuts also let the one sentence do the work. "They were all waiting reasonably for the train" is all the reader needs to know is running through the man's mind as he drinks his Anis fast enough to finish it in time to return to the girl before catching the express train.[10]

As inveterate a reviser as he often was, with the 1927 manuscript for "Hills" he recognized that the spoken words, including the final words of the story, needed to remain as they were. In one last solicitous gesture, the American man, having just drunk another Anis del Toro in the bar, asks the girl, "Do you feel better?" His question might imply the hope that her discontentment would be like a brief fever, passing into a reasonable acquiescence to his advocacy for a "perfectly simple" operation (*CSS* 213). Or his question might be conciliatory: do you feel better now that you see where I placed the suitcases to catch the train? After smiling at him enigmatically, she says simply, "I feel fine." Then she speaks the final words of the story: "There's nothing wrong with me. I feel fine" (*SS-HLE* 265; *CSS* 214). With words identical to those in the manuscript draft, Hemingway closed the story with an ambiguous ending that leaves questions unanswered: Has she decided to agree to the operation, or not? Has she decided whether to leave the American man? What is she thinking inside? When the express train for Madrid (or Barcelona) arrives, do both the man and the girl board it together? Does the couple reconcile, or do they split up? As Verna Kale concludes, Hemingway "built ambivalence and ambiguity into the story so that, whichever ending the reader chooses, the story holds tightly together" (*Ernest Hemingway* 74).[11]

8

REVISING "A WAY YOU'LL NEVER BE"

Five years passed between Hemingway's composing "Hills Like White Elephants" in May 1927 and his later story "A Way You'll Never Be," begun around May 1932 (Smith, *Guide* 268). In between the two stories came *A Farewell to Arms,* appearing in installments beginning with the May 1929 issue of *Scribner's Magazine,* and published as a novel by Scribner's on 27 September 1929 (Chamberlin 86, 94, 97). After such compact, tightly interwoven stories as "Now I Lay Me" and "Hills Like White Elephants," and after such a monumental and successful novel as *A Farewell to Arms,* one might wonder why, roughly three years after publication of his novel, Hemingway would begin around May 1932 another Nick Adams story set on the Italian front during World War I.

During the previous and subsequent months of 1932, he had been hard at work on a number of stories that would join "A Way" in forming his next collection, *Winner Take Nothing.* For example, "God Rest You Merry, Gentlemen" is a strangely compelling story of self-mutilation during Christmas. The three-part "Homage to Switzerland" is a story with the same beginning and three different endings, one of which likely alludes to Hemingway's father's suicide (Smith, *Guide* 246–47, 252–53). If not as experimental or modernist in formation as was *In Our Time,* the subject matter and treatment of these stories show Hemingway's testing the limits of new ground for short fiction. This chapter explores how his massive revisions to his story "A Way You'll Never Be" illustrate his experimenting with complex interior monologues and a comical, extended spoken monologue, both developing Hemingway's portrait of Nick Adams's struggle to cope with the traumas of war.

Almost a year after he began writing "A Way," in a letter to Maxwell Perkins on 8 April 1933, Hemingway proposed "After the storm and other stories" as a possible title for his next collection (*Letters* vol. 5, 369). In a letter dated 13 July 1933, Hemingway shared with Perkins his proposed order of the stories, with "A Way You'll Never Be" placed between "The Sea Change" and "The Mother of a Queen," stories exploring anxieties about sexuality (*Letters* vol. 5, 436). Hemingway was charting relatively new waters navigated by misfits, loners, castoffs, and divergent rebels.[1] Like the narrator in "After the Storm," he seemed to be diving for treasure in a sunken ship whose glass portholes he could not break open with a wrench, only to learn that Greek divers later "got the safe out with dynamite" and "got it all"—all the gold the ship was carrying (*CSS* 286). In an unpublished letter to Hemingway dated 7 August 1933, Ezra Pound insinuated that Hemingway had sold out as an artist to commercial interests and popular appeal.[2] However, stories like "A Way You'll Never Be" and others in *Winner Take Nothing* would seem anything but wrapped in a commercial package designed for sale to mainstream readers.

One answer to the question of why Hemingway would return to the Italian front after "Now I Lay Me," "Hills Like White Elephants," and *A Farewell to Arms* is that "A Way You'll Never Be" presents a stream-of-consciousness interior monologue and a darkly manic spoken monologue that explore new terrain in Hemingway's short fiction. In a long paragraph that Hemingway added to an earlier draft of "A Way," Nick veers wildly from memories of battlefields in Italy to Paris and back to Italy. "A Way" offers a zany, dark comedy in Hemingway's final Nick Adams war story set on the Italian front in World War I—and one of his last Nick Adams stories. Hemingway's story begins as a collage of pornographic postcards, scattered papers, military paraphernalia, and corpses on a battlefield. Later in the story, Hemingway shifts from an interior monologue to a manic, spoken monologue when Nick addresses Italian combatants, who are signaling for runners to find their commander to take control of the American. At the climax of the story, Hemingway composes Nick's mock lecture about grasshoppers and locusts in a key of stand-up, absurdist comedy. Nick's references to grasshoppers and locusts are mocking, as he pokes fun at American enlistment posters, messianic assumptions about Americans as deliverers, schemes involving grasshoppers in insect warfare, and his own, earlier story, "Big Two-Hearted River." In "A Way You'll Never Be," Hemingway portrays Nick Adams as using humor to gain a measure of control over his stream-of-consciousness memories and hallucinations.

Such unusual elements of fractured narrative have led some scholars to be less than enamored with the story. In his *Reader's Guide,* Paul Smith laments that the challenge posed by "A Way You'll Never Be" had not yet been met in the discussions of the story, despite its being one of Hemingway's "most original, even daring fictions" (275). Joseph Flora's discussion in *Hemingway's Nick Adams* remains the most comprehensive reading of the story, along with Ellen Andrews Knodt's more recent essays, "Towards a Better Understanding" and "Getting Closer to 'It.'" Mark Cirino argues that this story "is surely the most harrowing depiction of shellshock Hemingway ever wrote" ("A Way You'll Never Be" 99).[3] Few, if any, have focused on the role of comedy in the story. Although he does not refer specifically to "A Way," Scott Donaldson describes the "increasingly dark" and "macabre" humor of Hemingway's later stories (*Fitzgerald and Hemingway* 325). Donaldson aptly cites Sheldon Grebstein's comment about Hemingway's being a "magnificent craftsman" with "the ability to laugh" (*Hemingway's Craft* 201). However, Grebstein does not discuss the role of comedy in "A Way," instead commenting on Nick's "garbled fragments" and "incoherence" in the story (18–19, 119). Robert Paul Lamb follows Grebstein in characterizing Nick's monologues as rambling "incoherently" (*Art Matters* 67). Especially by focusing on Hemingway's extensive revisions to "A Way You'll Never Be," this chapter will make a case for reading the story as a powerful portrait of Nick Adams's wacky humor as a means of coping with the trauma of war.

Recently published correspondence from Hemingway to Maxwell Perkins shows that, after beginning the story around May 1932, he continued to revise "A Way" into April 1933. In March 1933, he wrote Perkins that he "[f]inished long one about the war but it needs going over" (*Letters* vol. 5, 360). On 8 April, he wrote Perkins referring to a story "I just finished about the war" (*Letters* vol. 5, 369). Even in that letter he informed Perkins: "Wrote that Piave story, no time to re-write it yet" (*Letters* vol. 5, 370). These letters indicate that Hemingway continued revising the story months later than indicated by Paul Smith. He conjecturally dated the penultimate draft—a typescript with pencil corrections (KL/EH folder 815)—as composed during late October or November 1932, some years after the previous manuscript of "A Way" (KL/EH folder 746a) he dated as "late 1920s" (*Guide* 269–70). Hemingway's letters to Maxwell Perkins indicate that he continued to re-write the story for several more months later than November 1932—at least until mid-April 1933 after his letter of April 8 in which he wrote that he had not had time to "re-write it yet." In a letter to Perkins on 13 July 1933, Hemingway listed all of the stories that would appear in *Winner Take Nothing*, except "Fathers and Sons." In the same letter he indicated that he was revising a story called "Tomb of His Grandfather," later retitled "Fathers and Sons" as the final story in that collection. Hemingway added that he could have sold "A Way You'll Never Be," but he wanted to have "plenty of good unpublished stories to sell the book" (*Letters* vol. 5, 437). This correspondence with Max Perkins strongly suggests that Hemingway extended his period of revising "A Way" and decided to reserve it for *Winner Take Nothing* as one of the new, unpublished stories.

In Hemingway's first draft, an untitled manuscript draft, he narrates the story in the first person, whose "I" walked his bicycle along a street to avoid the shell holes (KL/EH folder 813; Smith, *Guide* 271; Cirino, "A Way You'll Never Be" 101). Hemingway crossed out this beginning and replaced it with a paragraph where the first-person narrator is pushing his bicycle into a town with houses demolished by shells and three bodies in the streets. This fragmentary sketch includes several elements of the opening paragraphs of the published story—an approach from Fornaci by bicycle, three corpses in the street, houses in the town shattered by shelling, and guns hidden behind mulberry leaves that can be detected by the heat waves of the sun reflecting off the metal (*CSS* 306–7). It is as if Hemingway, with the sketching pencil in hand, drew a few strokes on the page that he saved for future shadings and details.

Then comes a four-page typescript draft, titled "War in Italy," that begins again in the first person (KL/EH folder 814; Smith, *Guide* 271). The narrator sets the scene by repeating in two of the fragmented paragraphs a sentence that is virtually identical with the first sentence of the published story: "The attack had gone across the field, been held up by machine-gun fire from the sunken road and from the group of farm houses, encountered no resistance in the town, and reached the bank of the river" (*CSS* 306). For the first time, this typescript draft includes an early version of the paraphernalia Nick finds scattered on the battlefield. In the published version of the story, this detritus includes "mass prayer books . . . propaganda postcards" (*CSS* 306). In this draft, Hemingway refers to a smell that would have overwhelmed even Clausewitz, an expert on war. The final two fragments appear to shift to the third person, referring to a character for whom July was a bad month. Present in this draft—but not in later drafts—is the date of this character's being wounded, 8 July, the same date Hemingway himself was wounded at Fossalta, Italy. In this draft, Hemingway first included, but then crossed out, the location as the Piave River. Also present for the first time is a reference to the letters Nick finds, along with the photographs and postcards, as litter on the battlefield. However, in this draft Nick refers only once to the letters, whereas in the published version of the story he repeats the reference three times to "the letters, letters, letters" (*CSS* 307). Such repetition suggests, early in the story, the compulsive quality of Nick's narration that will culminate in his monologue to the Italian adjutant about locusts (*CSS* 312–13). Without yet naming the main character, this typescript introduces an observer filling out a mental report about signs of battle and drawing inferences about the nature of the attack from the positions of the dead bodies and the papers scattered around them.

Hemingway's next draft of "A Way You'll Never Be," an untitled handwritten pencil manuscript, is now reprinted in the Hemingway Library Edition of *The Short Stories* (KL/EH folder 746a; *SS-HLE* 327–41). In this revised version of the story's beginning, the first-person narrator, not yet identified as Nick Adams, is pushing a bicycle, later identified in this handwritten draft as "the machine" (*SS-HLE* 327; *CSS* 306). The double participial phrase about the bicycle remains the same from the manuscript version to the published edition: "Coming along the road on a bicycle, getting off to push the machine" (*SS-HLE* 327; *CSS* 306). Retaining the basic elements of his earlier drafts, Hemingway adds details about the equipment and weapons the narrator observes, now including "calfskin covered haversacks," "stick bombs," and "star shelled pistols" (*SS-HLE* 327). His earlier references to postcards become much more vivid and are largely retained in the opening paragraphs of the published story: "group postcards showing the machine gun unit . . . as in a football picture for the college annual" and "propaganda postcards showing a soldier in Austrian uniform" in the process of raping a woman bent backwards over a bed (*SS-HLE* 327).

Furthermore, the narrator observes the corpses in details added to the earlier drafts and retained in the published version: "The hot weather had swollen them all regardless of nationality" (*SS-HLE* 327). To this sentence, Hemingway simply added "alike" after "them all," thus emphasizing the similar bloating of both the Austrian and the Italian corpses (*CSS* 307). In this handwritten draft, Hemingway included a reference to "many holes" left by the shelling, "some of them yellow-edged from the mustard gas" (*CSS* 307). Perhaps most significantly, Hemingway added to earlier drafts the emphasis on the narrator's *returning* to a battlefield alongside a riverbank whose foliage had grown back "very lush and over-grown since I had seen it last" (*SS-HLE* 328). By changing "over-grown" to "over-green" in the final draft, Hemingway added to Nick's ironic observation that the landscape is now dominated by greenery (*CSS* 307). Thus, the first elements of this draft shade in the essential features of the narrator's observations of the battle scene—the weapons, paraphernalia, corpses, and signs of bombardment and gas warfare amid a verdant riverbed. In this draft, Hemingway intimates for the first time that a story will unfold about a soldier's returning to a battlefield where, at least this time, the Italian troops have been the victors. Although it is unclear how much time passed between Hemingway's writing this draft by hand and the next draft of the story, a typescript with pencil corrections (folder 815), he clearly retained his essential additions that set the stage for "A Way You'll Never Be."

The fifteen-page typescript draft in folder 815 bridges between the handwritten manuscript in folder 746a and the final draft. The story's title was added later by hand to this typescript (Smith, *Guide* 269). One notable change comes in Hemingway's initial reference to Nick's riding a bicycle. In the typescript he crossed out "you could see" and replaced it with "Nicholas Adams saw." Not until this later typescript, conjecturally dated by Smith as November 1932, did Hemingway identity "Nicholas Adams" as the character on whom the story is centered. That is how the first paragraph of the story ends in the collection *Winner Take Nothing:* "Nicholas Adams saw what had happened by the position of the dead" (*CSS* 306). In that simple sentence Hemingway establishes Nick as a clinical analyst of a battlefield. In this typescript draft Hemingway added the long paragraph of Nick's interior monologue that began, "Nick lay on the bunk" (*CSS* 310). He replaced Paravicini's lecture scolding his lieutenant for raising a storm about catching two soldiers in a sexual coupling—"doing this in one of the old dugouts" (folder 746a; *SS-HLE* 332). Instead, Hemingway centered the story around Nick's spoken monologue that follows his interior monologue. In short, the pencil manuscript records substantial revisions and expansions of earlier drafts, and the fifteen-page typescript contains the essential diptych of Nick's unspoken and spoken monologues, instead of Paravicini's scolding lecture to his lieutenant.

This naming of Nicholas Adams is one of only four times in Hemingway's stories that he gave his protagonist's full name—twice in "Fathers and Sons" and once in "Summer People" (*CSS* 369 and 497). In naming Nick Adams more formally as "Nicholas," Hemingway places him in a role as a forensic archaeologist of battle—reconstructing the battle movements from the positions in which he found the corpses and debris. Such a role is distinctive, especially when one compares the observations of the dead and debris at the beginning of "A Way" with those in Henri Barbusse's *Under Fire,* a novel published in 1916 (English translation, 1917) that Hemingway praised in a letter to Evan Shipman dated 24 August 1929. In that letter Hemingway stated that *All Quiet on the Western Front* was "no improvement" over "Le Feu" (*Letters* vol. 4, 73, 74n13). In his introduction to *Men at War,* he further declared that *Under Fire* was "[t]he only good war book to come out during the last war." He praised its "protest" of "the gigantic useless slaughter" in that war (xv). Nick's survey of prayer books, postcards, pamphlets, and letters strewn among corpses on the battlefield bears a striking resemblance to a passage in Barbusse's novel.[4] In each substantial draft of this story, Hemingway begins with the narrator's reconstructing the movements of the battle: the first sentence of the story is virtually identical in the manuscripts, typescript, and published versions.

As Hemingway revised his drafts of these first paragraphs, he added the ironic presence of a "field kitchen" (*CSS* 306), and the debris, including gas mask cans, that remained strewn on the battleground. None of these features of the battlefield that Nick observes are present in the opening chapters of *A Farewell to Arms,* the major work Hemingway completed before he wrote "A Way You'll Never Be." In his opening description of Nick's observations, the battleground itself includes gas warfare in the final draft, as among the equipment scattered on the field are "gas masks, empty gas-mask cans" (*CSS* 306), suggesting that the masks and cans survive as debris, not as life preservers. There is no reference to gas masks in the manuscript version, though that narrator observes the vestiges of mustard gas in the "yellow-edged" bomb craters (*SS-HLE* 328). Hemingway refers to gas masks in the later typescript (KL/EH folder 815). To that typescript, Hemingway added by hand the phrase "empty gas mask cans" included in the printed version of the story—revising the description to imply that the cans were depleted during a gas attack (compare *CSS-HLE* 328 with *CSS* 306). His reference in the final version to the empty cans leaves ambiguous whether or not the masks were effective in repelling the gas attack—and, indeed, leaves unspecified which side used the mustard gas. The added reference to gas masks adds a note of irony, as neither masks nor helmets protect soldiers like Nick from the traumatic aftershocks of battle. As I will discuss below, the presence of mustard gas as an element of the battle whose debris Nick is observing bears a connection to his being haunted by a memory of a yellow house along the river.[5]

Furthermore, Hemingway added the ironic reference to a kitchen, per-haps echoing the raucous comedy of the kitchen-chef narrator in chapter 1 of *In Our Time* as a prelude to "Indian Camp"—perhaps more tragically an oblique reference to the kitchen chef who was the first American killed on the Italian front. In the manuscript draft, there is no reference to the "field kitchen" whose presence evokes that period "when things were going well" (compare *SS-HLE* 327 with *CSS* 306). Hemingway added that reference to a kitchen in the fifteen-page typescript with a handwritten addition, sug-gesting its relatively late presence in the story (KL/EH folder 815). By add-ing the reference to a roving kitchen, Hemingway implies that, at the time of the story, "things" are not going as well for the troops fed by the portable kitchen—implying, but not explicitly stating, that the battle was "going well" at one point for the Austrians. The added reference to the "field kitchen," the first in Hemingway's list of battle debris that Nick sees, suggests the irony that what once fed the troops now lies as a relic, along with the "stick bombs" and the "full belts" of ammunition among the detritus of battle (*SS-HLE* 327; *CSS* 306). In short, as Hemingway revised his final Nick Adams story set on the Italian front of World War I, he enhanced both the horror and the comedy of the battle scene that Nick sizes up as a rather detached military analyst.[6] This exposition establishes a baseline of Nick's circum-spect self-control that underscores the desultory course of his interior monologue about Paris and Fossalta, as well as the manic quality of his lec-ture about locusts to troops in Paravicini's regiment.

The early manuscripts end after the opening paragraphs where Hem-ingway depicts Nick alone, silently studying the battleground (KL/EH fold-ers 813–14). Only with the handwritten manuscript does Nick encounter a "young second lieutenant with a stubble of beard" and bloodshot eyes (*SS-HLE* 328). The tense exchange between the lieutenant and Nick is virtually the same in the manuscript, typescript, and published version of the story. In the transcript, Hemingway did add the passage where Nick observes that the lieutenant is dangerously tense. He retained this language in the final version: "the face of a man during a bombardment," a tight voice that "did not sound natural," and a pistol that understandably "made Nick nervous" (KL/EH folder 815; *CSS* 308). Likewise, in the typescript and then in the final draft, Nick's observations lead him to tell the lieutenant to put the gun away, explaining that "There's the whole river between them and you"—another reference to the river that Nick remembers from previous combat (*CSS* 308). Once Nick sees Captain Paravicini in the dugout serving as his headquarters, their conversation begins virtually the same in the manuscript and later versions. As shown in the transcript of the manuscript with Hemingway's revisions, he crossed out Nick's comment about his role circulating as a goodwill ambassador in an American uniform: "It's fairly disgusting, isn't it" (*SS-HLE* 330). In the typescript and the published story, he replaced that strong language with Nick's wittier remark, "Like a bloody politician" (compare *SS-HLE* 330 with *CSS* 309). His revisions to the story's exposition build more gradually and subtly toward the conflict between the Italian soldiers under Paravicini and Nick.

By far the major revision in this section of the story comes when Paravicini asks how Nick is doing. In the manuscript draft, he asks, "How are you yourself, really? Not joking" (*SS-HLE* 331). Although the language of his question is slightly modified in the print version, Hemingway's more striking revision comes with Nick's reply: "I'm all right. I can't sleep without a light of some sort. That's all I have now" (*CSS* 309). Nick's reference to insomnia, hearkening back to "Now I Lay Me," is not in the manuscript draft of this conversation. Implied in Nick's response is his intimation that, while "now" he suffers only from insomnia, previously his maladies have been more severe. In the manuscript, at this point of the narrative, the second lieutenant, pistol in his hand, appears with the two soldiers, "young, shamefaced looking" that he caught in some type of sexual activity (*SS-HLE* 331–32). The focus at this point is on Paravicini's conversation with the lieutenant who caught the two soldiers "doing this in one of the old dugouts," with a "gesture" to show what they had been doing (*SS-HLE* 332). In the manuscript, the lieutenant's report leads to Paravicini's lecturing him about his intolerance. Instead of Captain Paravicini's stern lecture to the lieutenant about overreacting to "a childish nastiness" (*SS-HLE* 333), Hemingway focuses on the captain's opinion that Nick's wound "should have been trepanned," on his reassuring comment that Nick now seems to be "in top-hole shape," and on his encouraging him amiably to "take a nap, Nicolo" (*CSS* 310). The revision places Paravicini's focus directly on Nick's state of mind.

At this point, in both the typescript and the published story, Hemingway includes Nick's manic, disjointed, difficult interior monologue. Nick's wayward, often abrupt shifts evoke his confusing struggle to cope with his traumatic memories of battles, including the one where he is shot. These interior monologues also frame Nick's spoken performance of an extended, sardonic lecture about "untold millions" of American soldiers "swarming like locusts" (*CSS* 312). The difficulties in sorting out Nick's stream-of-consciousness monologues, with their abrupt dislocations in time and place, reflect Hemingway's craft of revision. Through his late addition of a long interior monologue, followed by shorter monologues and his inclusion of Nick's lecture about American locusts, Hemingway completed a story whose difficulties are central to its powerful portrait of Nick's struggle for self-command.

A long, circular paragraph at the center of the story begins with a simple narrative marker: "Nick lay on the bunk" (*CSS* 310). It ends with another simple statement as the narrator remarks: "He [Nick] lay down again" (*CSS* 311). This circular narration signals that the paragraph's motion is interior, that it all takes place inside Nick's troubled consciousness. In between those plain, physical references to Nick's lying on the bunk, the narrator briefly indicates one action: "He sat up and looked around" (*CSS* 311). That brief statement is the only physical movement in the paragraph. Notably, this paragraph was not present in the earlier drafts of the story, including the manuscript reprinted from folder 746a (*SS-HLE* 327–41). Not until the later draft contained in folder 815, conjecturally dated November 1932 by Smith (269), but possibly as late as April 1933, does this long, circular paragraph dominated by Nick's interior monologue appear. This added paragraph is among the weirdest—and most agitated—Hemingway ever wrote in a Nick Adams story. In "A Way You'll Never Be," this interior monologue is quickly followed by a second, shorter monologue after Nick "lay down again." Together with two shorter interior monologues later in the story, these reflect Nick's attempts to gain control over his memories and nightmares associated with his trauma of being wounded.[7]

While lying awake on the bunk in Paravicini's battalion headquarters, Nick's first stream-of-consciousness interior monologue begins with his memory of the only attack he had *not* made "stinking" drunk (*CSS* 310).

From the beginning of his monologue, Nick vacillates, like Hamlet, between scoffing at authority and mulling over his own fragility. He refers to himself as part of a "platoon of the class of 1899" (the year of Hemingway's birth), "just out at the front"—that is, in its first line of fire. This memory sequence commences when Nick remembers the time that some Italian soldiers "got hysterics during the bombardment before the attack" (*CSS* 310)—the only time in Hemingway's fiction a word related to "hysteria" applies to soldiers in action.[8] Nick remembers wearing his chin strap so tightly "to keep his lips quiet"—presumably, to keep his teeth from chattering (*CSS* 310). That detail about his helmet evokes Nick's past fears before the charge. Hemingway presents Nick's prebattle fears next to his understanding of the futility of the battle charge: "Knowing they could not hold it when they took it." That is, an Austrian counterattack would force the Italians to retreat from the position they had taken. By hand, Hemingway added to this typescript an even more derisive and vulgar fragment in Nick's interior monologue: "Knowing it was all a bloody balls" (KL/EH folder 815; *CSS* 310). This latter sentence fragment is one of the rare times that Nick Adams swears obscenely—a sign of his distress on the eve of an attack. At this point, Nick's interior monologue presents him not only as fearful and resentful, but also as relatively stable.

"Savoia" is the only word in the paragraph that Hemingway placed in quotation marks, as if Nick hears the word spoken and/or speaks the word himself. Robert W. Lewis and Michael Kim Roos explain that "'Savoia' is an Italian war cry that dates at least to the 19th century, abbreviated from '*Avanti* Savoia!' meaning 'Go Savoia!' It was used to exhort soldiers in the Italian army into battle in support of the King and the Royal Family, which was known as the House of Savoy" (94–95). In his interior monologue, Nick comments that he looks at his watch as if checking for the time of attack, after having already observed that it has been postponed. Then he hears or gives the command for a charge, "in that quiet tone, that valuable quiet tone, 'Savoia'" (*CSS* 310). Framed by pauses, Nick's repetition of "that valuable quiet tone" (a phrase Hemingway added by hand to the typescript in folder 815) seems a muted command to charge, with "valuable" as inwardly sarcastic. As Nick reflects back on the "Savoia" call to arms, his repetition sounds caustic, implying that the cry was valueless to the soldiers on either side who died during the battle. Thus, this first reference to "Savoia" is self-mocking, as Nick remembers his inglorious venture in trying to make this charge "cold" (stone cold sober) and lacking time to "get it" (perhaps a bottle of grappa, his shot of courage). This charge is the "only time he hadn't done it stinking"—that is, the only time he had not made a charge stinking drunk, as he confessed to Paravicini out loud before this interior monologue.[9]

As Nick mentally replays his commanding officer's orders, ending in "Savoia," he becomes agitated. One can discern the actual sequence of events that are scrambled in Nick's recollection. At an undetermined time, Nick observes the Italian troops, "just out at the front" (in their first battle), becoming hysterical during a bombardment before the attack (310). He recalls that the attack was "put back" (delayed) "to five-twenty" (310). He recalls "Para" instructing him to "walk them two at a time outside to show them nothing would happen"—that is, show the soldiers that the bombardment was benign (310). Presumably, the other instructions ("Break his nose" and so on) also came from Paravicini. He then waits for a command, hears "Savoia" spoken, and then quietly repeats (perhaps both internally to himself and aloud to his men) the order to charge. Aside from the command "Savoia," Nick recalls that the cave-in "started them"—that is, forced the soldiers out of their dugouts and into an attack "up that slope" (310). Such an unscrambled chronology loses the force of Nick's disoriented recollection that leaves less clear, for example, when the trench cave-in occurred in relationship to the "Savoia" cry and the charge up the hill. The actual paragraph conveys more powerfully Nick's memory of tensely waiting for the futile charge.

In this interior monologue, a relatively late addition in Hemingway's process of revising the story, Nick sounds increasingly unstable, veering toward delirium. Nick mentally replays an officer's commands, along with his observation that the battle charge has been delayed: "Break his nose. They've put it back to five-twenty. Break that other silly bugger's nose and kick his silly ass out of here" (*CSS* 310). The image of Nick's marshalling a line of soldiers by breaking noses (while keeping his chin strap tightly over his mouth) is a mock-heroic sequence. Then Nick asks himself: "Do you think they'll go over?" He answers himself with what sounds like an even more extreme form of leading a charge—shooting malingerers in the back: "If they don't, shoot two and try to scoop the others out some way" (*CSS* 310). The first part of this internalized directive sounds as if Nick remembers that an officer (probably Captain Paravicini) commanded him to "shoot two" soldiers as an example to the other troops. The second part, "try to scoop the others out," sounds like Nick ridiculing the absurdity of the orders. "To scoop" soldiers out of trenches would be done most often with shovels scooping out corpses—not part of an orderly charge following a battle cry like "Savoia." Then Nick remembers a command that is the one sign of his rank at this point: "Keep behind them, sergeant" (a lesser rank than Nick held as "tenente" in "Now I Lay Me"). Sergeant Adams is to stay behind the men under his command, apparently because no one would follow if he led an attack. Nick remembers his officer's admonition: "It's no use to walk ahead and find there's nothing coming behind you" (*CSS* 310). The admonition builds tension, as "behind" Nick presumably is a higher officer who might shoot him if he does not lead his troops forward. He is more commanded than in command.

At that point Nick's sense of humor turns grimly ironic as he puns on the word "bail." "Bail them out as you go" implies to force the soldiers out of the trenches, ironically the opposite of "bail them out" by rescuing them (*CSS* 310). According to *The Oxford English Dictionary*, the verb "bail" originated from the Old French and entered Middle English in the judicial sense of money paid to liberate a prisoner from jail before trial. Since the 1500s the word "bail" has come more broadly and figuratively to mean "to liberate from imprisonment."[10] In that sense, the command for Nick to "bail them out as you go" means to "liberate" the soldiers from their trenches. Nick's memory of the command is sarcastic: he is ordered to "free" his soldiers from their protective trenches and expose them to the fusillade of enemy fire. Then, in his unspoken interior monologue, Nick repeats, tersely, the "bloody balls" curse, followed by his apparent effort to regain his equilibrium just before the moment of a charge: "All right. That's right" (*CSS* 310). Nick repeats these words in an effort to calm and comfort himself. Ironically, his simple words imply, following his cursing, that neither the battle nor he is "All right." The entire sequence builds tension as Nick anticipates hearing the Italian word for "charge."

Nick's memory of the battle cry "Savoia" is ironically at odds with the chin strap he had wrapped tightly to keep his teeth from chattering. Rather than evoking a call to glory, "Savoia" is heard shortly before Nick's loss of orientation: "he couldn't find his own after the cave-in" (*CSS* 310). In Nick's jumbled memories the sequence including the cry "Savoia" and the "cave-in" of part of the trench is disjointed. In a slapstick sequence, tinged with horror, Nick hears the battle call but reacts by fumbling for, and not finding, something he had lost in the cave-in. Nick repeats the phrase "Making it cold"—first before "no time to get it," without making clear exactly what "it"

is. Then he repeats the phrase in a way that suggests "it" was a bottle of liquor: "making it cold up that slope the only time he hadn't done it stinking"
(310). Thus, Nick remembers the chaos of this charge as keeping him from
drinking before battle. Earlier he told Paravicini: "I was stinking in every
attack" (309). His recollection of being unable to find his bottle during the
attack with the cave-in implies that he was *not* "stinking" in that attack.[11]
His hectic struggle to retrieve his bottle ("find his own") after "one whole
end" of the trench caved in is mirrored in his present straining to restore
his composure while remembering his dual roles as a receiver and giver of
commands during an infantry charge. The phrase "it was that started them"
refers to the cave-in as what "started" the charge, even more than the cry of
"Savoia"—at least in Nick's recollection. Worth noting is that, in the setting
copy Hemingway used in compiling *Winner Take Nothing,* he added by hand
the clauses "one whole end had caved in; it was that started them" (KL/EH
folder 222; *CSS* 310). This late addition suggests that the cave-in forced the
soldiers out of the trench. The interior monologue registers the beginning
of an infantry charge as a series of disconnected memories, as Nick struggles to hold his mind together. Yet the multiple antecedents of the pronoun
"it" (referring both to the infantry charge and also apparently to a bottle of
liquor) convey Nick's mind as absorbed in his memories. Nick's first reference to "Savoia" is part of a hallucinatory sequence, where it is hard to make
out whether Nick is speaking to himself, or remembering an officer's orders
to shoot malingerers, or both. His interior monologue contributes to a sense
of confused tension about the sequence of events in the battle charge and
dramatizes Nick's persistent disorientation and trauma.[12]

"Savoia" is the word Nick remembers as the signal for leading a charge;
"teleferica" is the word that he uses in reference to a rescue mission in
which he apparently participated. In Nick's scrambled flashback while lying on a cot in an Italian bunker, his memory has none of the glory of an Alpine charge implied in the cover illustration for the 20 July 1918 issue of
Scientific American—published within two weeks of Hemingway's being
wounded at Fossalta on 8 July. The "teleferica," similar to a ski lift but used
to transport soldiers and equipment up and down a mountain, reminds Nick
of the chaos of the retreat and the losses sustained by the attack. The word
comes to stand for the failure of an aerial transportation either to defeat the
Austrian enemy or to rescue the Italian wounded. As such, the "teleferica"
is akin to the ambulances that Frederic Henry and others drive during the

disastrous retreat of Caporetto portrayed in *A Farewell to Arms*—a part of the chaos of battle rather than a means of orderly rescue.[13]

In contrast to the *Scientific American* cover image of a ski lift's wires buoyantly holding two machine-gunners aloft in their ascent, Nick's memory involves no heroic picture of a warrior with a mountainous backdrop. Nick's means of ascent up the mountainside is not clear—certainly, he makes no reference to a teleferica. Instead, Hemingway focuses on Nick's journeys *down* the mountain. Hemingway's presentation of Nick's memory of descent is more in keeping with an image later in the same *Scientific American* issue of a teleferica carrying wounded soldiers down the mountain. In this second image, a wounded soldier with a head bandage is lifted onto a makeshift stretcher. At least one of the figures lifting the soldier onto a stretcher is wearing a Red Cross armband.

Much of this memory sequence involving a teleferica is present in the typescript before Hemingway's handwritten corrections and revisions (KL/EH folder 815). However, one key phrase he added by hand, so that in the printed version the sentence begins: "And after they came back the *teleferica* house burned, it seemed" (*CSS* 310). By hand, Hemingway added the words "after they came back" to make clear that the teleferica was intact and working when Nick participated in a charge from the trenches—and presumably ascended up the mountain. Only "after they came back" did the teleferica house burn. Hemingway's handwritten addition to the typescript places the burning down of the teleferica as clearly following the initial charge and preceding Nick's subsequent return "four days later" (*CSS* 310). It bears noting that Hemingway also added by hand to the typescript, "and we came down, we always came down" (KL/EH folder 815; *CSS* 310). His repeated addition of "we came down" contributes to Nick's memory of survival, apparently climbing and descending the mountain a second time by foot. In other words, especially as Hemingway revised the typescript by hand, Nick's interior monologue includes a memory of descent as a scrambled rescue operation, without the benefit of the teleferica, because its house had burned. This memory of ascending and descending a mountain is separate from Nick's memory of being wounded, presumably at some point after this mountain assault, at a river "outside of Fossalta" near a "low house painted yellow" (*CSS* 310). Adding further to the irony of Nick's repeating "we came down" is his reflection that "some did not get down"—that is, some did not survive the attack and, perhaps, some of the corpses were left in the mountain snow. In short, Nick's turning into a transporter of the wounded or dead is ironically Sisyphean—recurrently futile. Nick went up, he came down; he went back up, he came back down. Nick's thoughts about the teleferica suggest that he is shadowed by survivor's guilt. As he wrestles with this guilt, his interior monologue becomes increasingly jarring.

The most difficult element of this paragraph, however, comes not so much from Nick's memory of battle scenes as from his jumbling those recollections with fantasies about himself as a performer opposite a dance-hall Madonna of the early twentieth century, Gaby Deslys. Nick's allusion to Gaby Deslys follows immediately after his repeating that "we always came down"—as if performing with the star actress was what he came down to: "And there was Gaby Delys [sic], oddly enough, with feathers on" (CSS 310). That shift from Fornaci to Paris comes with the pauses around "oddly enough," a phrase that Hemingway added by hand to the typescript. The revised sentence suggests that what is odd is the performer's having her feathers on—not Nick's shifting abruptly in his interior monologue from the Italian front to a Parisian show hall. "A Way You'll Never Be" is the only Nick Adams story with explicit references to Paris—to "the great Gaby," a Parisian star entertainer; to the cathedral of Sacré Coeur; and to a girl who was sometimes with Nick and sometimes with "some one else" (CSS 310). Nick's free-associating from surrealistic memories of the battlefield to recollections of Paris is not just a spatial but also a temporal movement, a movement further back in time: "The Paris part came earlier" (CSS 311). As he lies on the cot, Nick's reverie takes him from the more recent past of the battlefields to the more distant past of scenes in Paris. Such rapid shifts reflect the fluidity of Nick's memories and his disconnection from the present battalion of soldiers under Paravicini's command. In his fantasy of a performance with "the great Gaby" in a Parisian dance hall, Nick may be compensating for his lack of command in the past and present.

In this odd memory, Nick imagines himself as Gaby's dance partner, Harry Pilcer: "and my name's Harry Pilcer too" (CSS 310). He remembers stepping out of a taxi during a steep climb up Sacré Coeur, presumably with Gaby Deslys: "we used to step out of the far side of the taxis" (CSS 310). In this hallucinatory sequence, Nick associates himself with these two dance-hall entertainers and film stars, on a taxi ride up to Montmartre, where Sacré Coeur seems "blown white, like a soap bubble" (CSS 310). The simile is strange, as if the monumental church on top of the hill becomes in Nick's imagination a soap bubble ready to burst. This sequence of hallucinatory memories is a mixture of the erotic and the sacred: a show-dancer remembered "with feathers on, with feathers off," and connected in Nick's fantasy with a ride up to Montmartre and Sacré Coeur.[14]

Contributing to this strange sequence is Nick Adams's fancying himself as singing "you called me baby doll a year ago tadada" (*CSS* 310). The lyrics are from Al Jolson's 1916 song "A Broken Doll" (Lloyd-Kimbrel).[15] That Nick imagines himself as Harry Pilcer seems an uncanny doubling of stage stars in Nick's erotic fantasy. Nick freely shifts from identifying with Harry Pilcer, Gaby's dance partner, to identifying with Al Jolson (who also performed with her) in singing the line "you called me baby doll a year ago" (*CSS* 310). This puzzling interlude of entertainment in Paris lies between Nick's memory of helping to rescue wounded soldiers and his haunting vision of a yellow house by a river. This interlude also associates Al Jolson's lilting song of "A Broken Doll" with Nick Adams's broken head. Nick's punning on "A Broken Doll" adds a musical dimension to this unnerving sequence of non sequiturs. This sequence with Nick's recollections of Paris seems, as Steve Florczyk puts it, "a jumble of memories recalled ... while in the battle zone" (103). Nick's "tadada" refrain strikes a strangely comical note in this dreamlike song-and-dance routine. With his "tadada," Nick presents himself lightly as a performer whose "girl," however, is often not with him but with someone else. By comparing himself to Harry Pilcer, Nick seems to wish for more control of his performance than he had as a sergeant under Captain Paravicini or has now on show "demonstrating the American uniform" (*CSS* 312). It bears reemphasizing that Hemingway added this entire sequence of memories and fantasies of the Italian front and Paris when he revised the manuscript published in the Hemingway Library Edition of *The Stories of Ernest Hemingway*.

From his memories and fantasies of Paris, Nick's interior monologue shifts abruptly back to the Italian front. The transition takes place within the same sentence that begins romantically in Paris ("Sometimes his girl was there") and ends nightmarishly on the Italian front ("only it frightened him"). The nightmare image involves a yellow house that seems to stand for Nick's memory of being shot during a battle. Hemingway's first reference to the color yellow in the story is related to the color of mustard gas: holes tinted "yellow-edged from the mustard gas" that Nick is studying at the beginning of the story as an archaeologist of a battlefield (*CSS* 307). That reference to "yellow-edged" holes is not present in either of the first drafts of the story (folders 813 and 814), but it is consistent from the manuscript draft (folder 646a in *SS-HLE* 328) to the final print text (*CSS* 307). Thus, in revising "A Way," Hemingway includes the color yellow as associated with mustard gas early in the story. The only other references to mustard gas in any of Hemingway's stories is in a comparable battlefield scene in "A Natural History of the Dead" (*CSS* 338). None of Hemingway's previous Nick Adams stories set on the Italian front in World War I—chapter 6 of *In Our Time,* "In Another Country," or "Now I Lay Me"—includes mustard gas as part of the military menace that Nick has faced. The tone of Nick's narrative when observing the "yellow-edged" holes is calm and objective—no sign of fear in the repeated intransitive clauses "These were" and "there were" (*CSS* 307). Even when Nick notes that Paravicini's smile shows "yellowed teeth," there is no emotion (*CSS* 309; Knodt, "Towards a Better Understanding" 80). In other words, the story's first references to the color yellow present Nick as a rather detached, studious observer of his environment. However, the mention of gas masks, gas canisters, and "yellow-edged" holes adds a note of menace to the landscape.

During Nick's interior monologue while he lies on the bunk, Hemingway presents a sudden transition from the Paris of Sacré Coeur to the battle site near the Piave River. Such a syntactic disjuncture suggests Nick's fractured psyche. Right after his allusion to "the great Gaby" and Harry Pilcer, Nick's interior monologue shifts in midsentence from Paris to that combat zone in Italy: "Sometimes his girl was there . . ., but those were the nights" (*CSS* 310). Here the conjunction "but" lurches midsentence from Sacré Coeur in Paris to a haunting yellow house on a river near Fossalta. Nick's reverie turns to the mystery of why "those were the nights the river ran so much wider and stiller than it should" (*CSS* 310). The clause "those were the nights" links Nick's nocturnal dreams of Paris and his nocturnal memories of the river where he witnessed battles—and, presumably, where he was wounded. But why is Nick disturbed by the river's seeming fuller and "stiller than it should"—as if the natural state of the river were a turbulent current? These memories of Paris also serve Nick as distractions from the war, though the currents of memory keep returning him to the traumas of battle. As in his nocturnal meditations in "Now I Lay Me," rivers serve as a deep part of his memories and efforts to cope with the pressures of combat.

This winding sentence, present for the first time in the typescript revision of the story, begins "Sometimes his girl was there," where "there" is the hill in Paris with Sacré Coeur, of which Nick dreamed "every night." Thus, the sentence *begins* with Nick's remembering the presence of "his girl" with him in a romantic or spiritual dream of Sacré Coeur. The sentence turns at "but," shifting location from his dreams of Sacré Coeur to his memory of the river "outside of Fossalta" with the yellow house (*CSS* 310). The shift of location is clear—Paris to Fossalta. Less clear is that Nick is free-associating from one dream to another—from a dream of Sacré Coeur at the top of the hill of Montmartre with "his girl" present, to a nightmare of the river and the yellow house. Nick stresses that he sees both dream-visions every night: "he could see that hill every night when he dreamed with Sacré Coeur" (*CSS* 310). Likewise, "every night" Nick has been "there a thousand times and never seen it," where "there" is the river scene with the yellow house (*CSS* 310). As Hemingway revised the story, he placed more emphasis on the presence of Nick's nocturnal dream-visions in his daytime reveries lying on a bunk in Paravicini's dugout.

The middle of this long sentence evokes Nick's sense of confusion, mystery, and terror. The sentence shifts from the puzzling calmness of the river to include his haunted memory of a yellow house: "and outside of Fossalta there was a low house painted yellow with willows all around it and a low stable" (*CSS* 310). To this point, the tableau is of a yellow house surrounded by what seem like peaceful willows and a stable for farm horses. However, the sentence continues with another conjunction (no pause) introducing another independent clause with a final detail about that photographic composition: "and there was a canal." For whatever reason, a canal that at first appears to be a benign presence in Nick's memory introduces its psychological impact as a haunting recurrence in his dream-vision of the yellow house.[16]

Following the reference to a canal, this long, paratactic sentence leads to a final note of Nick's traumatic memory: "and he had been there a thousand times and never seen it, but there it was every night as plain as the hill, only it frightened him" (*CSS* 310). The first turn comes with the repeated conjunction "and" joining what seem to be opposites. That is, Hemingway presents Nick as certain *both* of his having been "there a thousand times"—the river, the yellow house, and the canal—*and* of his never having "seen it." Hemingway implies that Nick has never seen that exact tableau with a waking vision, but that he has seen it "every night" in his nightmares. Connecting this vision with that "plain" memory of "the hill" suggests Nick's psychological association of the Parisian visions when he "dreamed with Sacré Coeur" with the visions of a yellow house where he has been "a thousand times." The sentence *ends* with Nick's remembering that the river and yellow house leave him in a state of fear: "only it frightened him (*CSS* 310). Thus, Nick's memories are in stark contrast: a dream of innocence with a Paris church on a hill and a nightmare of a yellow house by a river. Nick's recollecting both dreams in the same sentence may be logically confusing, but the sentence evokes the fluidity of his memories, as he gropes for a cohesive sense of identity from fragments of memory. Or, as Stephen Dedalus puts it in one of his interior monologues in James Joyce's *Ulysses,* he constructs his identity "by memory . . . under everchanging forms" (156).

After completing this winding sentence, Nick reflects upon the effect of the yellow house on him: "That house meant more than anything and every night he had it" (*CSS* 310). Again, one has to guess what "it" is that Nick had: presumably, the terrifying vision of the yellow house. Nick's confiding to himself—and earlier to Paravicini—that he was terrified during the attacks is presented not as an indication of cowardly shirking of battle but as the haunting effect of this memory.[17] In repeating this admission that the memory "frightened him," Nick adds another enigma—that the terror was intense "especially when the boat lay there quietly in the willows on the canal, but the banks weren't like this river" (*CSS* 310-11). Why does the presence of a boat lying quietly on a canal in what would seem protective camouflage of the willows arouse fear? Why were the banks unlike "this river"? Does Nick refer to one river, or two? Has Nick repressed whatever part of this scene would explain its effect on him? Such questions suggest how disorienting Nick's interior monologue becomes.

An answer to these questions may come, in part, in the final sentences of this paragraph. In these sentences Hemingway adds a third location to Nick's inner meditation on memories. Just as Paris shifted without transition to the battle places at Fossalta, so the paragraph ends by shifting, with barely a transition, from a river and canal at Fossalta to a different river at Portogrande. Connecting the two rivers, Nick remembers the banks of the river in his dream of the yellow house as "all lower, as it was in Portogrande" (311). In this third location, Hemingway returns to the inclusion of human actors in the scene. Whereas in the memories of the river and yellow house, Nick's memories are without any reference to human presence, at Portogrande "they had seen them wallowing across the flooded ground holding the rifles high until they fell with them in the water" (*CSS* 311). In this case, Nick's memory includes a distinct battle scene where "they" (probably the Italians with whom Nick was serving) had watched "them" (the Austrians attacking across a river) fall with their rifles in the water. In remembering that scene of Austrians shot as they were trying to cross a flooded river while holding their rifles in the air, Nick finally meditates on what *might* answer questions about why he seems traumatized by a vision of a yellow house. He follows this memory of Portogrande with a rhetorical question that echoes his earlier sarcasm about the "bloody balls" exclamation during the Italian attack. Now Nick seems to empathize with the Austrian soldiers whose deaths he apparently witnessed: "Who ordered that one?" (*CSS* 311). Nick's question would seem rational, were it not near the end of such a centrifugal meditation. This interior monologue of memories nears its end with Nick having imaginatively switched sides from the Italians to the Austrians to ask another of his sardonic questions challenging military commands. Like the yellow house near Fossalta, the river at Portogrande serves in Nick's interior monologues as a fictional locus of Nick's wartime trauma, whereas Paris is the locus of his peacetime fantasies of romantic song and dance.[18]

This paragraph concludes with five sentences that bring Nick, lying on a bunk in an Italian dugout, back to the fictional present in which he is in an American uniform returning to a scene of battle—and to the Italian commander under whom he served. Hemingway begins this transition by having Nick reflect on how jumbled his own memory is: "If it didn't get so damned mixed up he could follow it all right" (*CSS* 311). As Mark Cirino concludes in his engaging analysis of this sentence, "No writer used the word 'it' as evocatively and carefully as Hemingway" ("A Way You'll Never Be" 115). In contrast to the beginning of the story, when Nick was studying the scene of battle with such a clinical precision and archaeological reconstruction of the attack, he now struggles to "keep it all straight" and reorient himself to know "just where he was" (*CSS* 311). However, Nick's ability to collect himself in this interior monologue is momentary—"but suddenly it confused without reason as now"—leaving unclear what "it" is that still discombobulates him. Hemingway then uses two participial phrases to highlight Nick's loss of a role of command: "he lying in a bunk at battalion headquarters, with Para commanding a battalion" (*CSS* 311). Though parallel in structure, the two participial phrases imply that, just as Paravicini is *not* lying down racked by memories, Nick is *not* in command either of a group of soldiers, or even of himself. Accenting that irony, Nick repeats the vulgar "bloody," suggesting that his American uniform is an obscene costume that alienates him from the Italian troops to whom he has been sent as a kind of walking wartime poster. With this third "bloody" oath in the paragraph, Nick sarcastically laughs at military command, at his acting role, and at himself, diagnosed and "certified as nutty" (*CSS* 310). Near the end of the paragraph comes the one action Nick takes: "He sat up and looked around" (*CSS* 311). When he sits up, Nick sees that "they [are] all watching him" (*CSS* 311). By hand, Hemingway added to the typescript these words about Nick's seeing that the Italians are "all watching him" (KL/EH folder 815; *CSS* 311). It is as if, instead of being the observer that he was at the start of the story, in command of piecing together what happened in the battle, Nick feels that he has exposed himself to the soldiers around him. Nick sees the Italians watching him, as if he has *spoken* aloud as an unintended performance what Hemingway presented as his interior, stream-of-consciousness monologue.

The fused memories of Paris and the yellow house could have ended with Nick's sense that all eyes are on him when he sits up on the bunk. Hemingway could have moved directly to the sequence when Nick *does* actually speak to the Italians present. He also added that spoken monologue in the typescript when he revised his earlier manuscript of the story. Instead of moving directly to his spoken monologue about "demonstrating" the American uniform and heralding the onset of "the American locust" (*CSS* 311–12), Hemingway included a paragraph with another interior monologue in which Nick revisits his association of Paris and Fossalta. In this paragraph, Hemingway changed very little in the typescript preserved in folder 815 at the Kennedy Library. First, Hemingway began by reiterating that "the Paris part came earlier" than the memories of the yellow house (*CSS* 311). That is, Nick reminds himself that there is a chronological order to his recollections: Paris before the Italian front. Then comes a strange association of his fears that connect the taxi scene in Paris with the scenes along the river during the war: "he was not frightened of it except when she had gone off with some one else" (*CSS* 311). Nick's pronoun "it" refers generally to "The Paris part," and he focuses first on his fears aroused when his girl "had gone off with some one else." As was the case with Jake Barnes in *A Sun Also Rises,* the knowledge that "she" had gone off with someone else might trigger Nick's ruminations of being wounded.[19] However, that is not clearly the case here.

Rather, Nick focuses second on his inscrutable anxiety that "they might have taken the same driver twice" (*CSS* 311). Why would it matter to Nick, in a city with many taxi drivers, whether he and his girl happened to be driven by the same driver on two separate occasions? And yet, Hemingway portrays Nick as so definite that he becomes tautological in his thoughts: "That was what frightened about that" (*CSS* 311). The circularity of the vague pronoun "that" leaves one unsure what, exactly, "that" is, but Nick is sure that it frightened him. The vague pronouns, weird syntax, and non sequiturs present Nick's mind as suppressing, evading, or distancing himself from the source of his traumatic fears aroused by the war.

Nick's claim that his fears have nothing to do with the war seems dubious. Yet, with laconic certitude, Nick insists to himself that his fears were "Never about the front" (*CSS* 311). Nick's extending his claim to his dream life ("he never dreamed about the front") only reinforces one's sense that the dreams of the yellow house are somehow associated with the front, in ways that, at this stage of interior monologues, Nick denies. By hand, Hemingway added "now" after "front," accentuating Nick's insistence to himself that "He never dreamed about the front now any more" (KL/EH folder 815; *CSS* 311). Even as he tells himself that he no longer dreams about the front, his denial comes alongside his being haunted "now" in his waking visions. The transitions in Nick's thoughts turn on conjunctions without a pause: "but what frightened him so that he could not get rid of it was that long yellow house and the different width of the river" (*CSS* 311). The paratactic syntax is unsettling—why is Nick disturbed by a yellow house? And why does the "different width of the river" matter, unless part of his memory is that the river was wider and more turbulent when he was wounded?

Nick seems to calm himself by noting that what he remembered in his haunted memories is not what he witnessed on his recent return to the same battle ground. He assures himself with a series of past-tense clauses: "Now he was back here at the river, he had gone through that same town, and there was no house. Nor was the river that way" (*CSS* 311). Hemingway portrays Nick as focusing on his certitude upon revisiting the battle scene: "he *was* back here" and "he *had* gone through," "there *was*," and "Nor *was*" (emphasis added). Likewise, Nick is certain that, now, the house and the river of his dream-vision are no longer the same features of the landscape. Because he has revisited the battle scene, Nick *knows* that the yellow house and river of his nightmares are either not there or have changed.[20] And yet, he also knows that the river and the house still haunt his dreams. The paragraph concludes with Nick's asking himself: "Then where did he go each night and what was the peril and why would he wake, soaking wet, more frightened than he had ever been in a bombardment, because of a house and a long stable and a canal?" (*CSS* 311). These seem genuinely haunting questions: what is so important about a house, a stable, and a canal that leaves Nick more traumatized than he ever remembers being when the bombs were falling? Even in "Now I Lay Me," Nick is not "soaking wet" during his nocturnal meditations. At this point of the story, such "why" questions are unresolved, except by Nick's next action: "He sat up" (*CSS* 311). Nick's sitting up is not the affirmative standing up that occurs at the end of "Big Two-Hearted River." As if waking from a traumatic nightmare, he stirs, soon to launch into a manic, spoken lecture about grasshoppers and locusts.[21]

To reiterate, the pairing of Nick's unspoken, interior monologue and his lecture, spoken to the Italians who remain in the dugout, reflects Hemingway's massive revision of "A Way You'll Never Be." In his thirty-five-page manuscript reprinted in the Hemingway Library Edition of the short stories, Hemingway included neither Nick's interior monologues during his daydream nightmares nor his extended lecture to the adjutant (*SS-HLE* 327–41). The lecture in the manuscript version is from Paravicini concerning the practice of homosexuality in the Italian army. Speaking to a second lieutenant who has brought him two soldiers engaged in a sexual act, Paravicini addresses him "in the tone of a lecturer in a popular course at a university" (*SS-HLE* 332). Nick hears Paravicini lecture the lieutenant and then scold the two soldiers for their "nasty tricks" (*SS-HLE* 333). Not until the subsequent typescript does Hemingway compose the absurdly comical monologue in which Nick lectures about "medium-brown" grasshoppers (the color of the American uniforms), American troops as locusts (perhaps a biblical plague of locusts), and two officers who could hold a net as a "seine" (a word repeated in Nick's lecture, perhaps as a pun on the Seine River) to capture the grasshoppers (*CSS* 312–13). This scene of two officers holding a net to catch locusts seems to be Hemingway's parody of officers' mismanagement of war to which he alludes acerbically in his remarks about World War I as a "gigantic useless slaughter" led by incompetent officers in his introduction to *Men at War* (xv). As Joseph Flora points out, Nick's lecture is "the longest uninterrupted speech in any Hemingway short story" ("Nick

Adams in Italy" 195). Nick's lecture is also perhaps the funniest monologue Hemingway ever wrote.

The transition from the long interior monologue while Nick lies on a bunk comes with the second time "Nick sat up"—this time after he asks himself the question about why his memory of a yellow house, stable, and canal leads him to wake up "soaking wet" with sweat night after night. When Nick sits up, he again becomes aware of his being watched by the adjutant, signalers, and two runners. Rather than interacting with the Italians as allies, Nick seems immediately tense: he "returned the stares" of the Italian soldiers (CSS 311). His next act seems hostile: he puts on his trench helmet, as if readying himself for a charge. In a tone that sounds defensive, Nick seems to apologize for his lack of supplies like chocolate and cigarettes but insists that he is "wearing the uniform." His tone apparently aroused concerns among the Italians, as the adjutant responds: "The Major is coming back at once" (CSS 311). Nick's silent retort is to remind himself that in the Italian army an adjutant is not commissioned—as if to dismiss his stature or credibility. In the manuscript version of the story, there is little or no conversation between any of the Italian soldiers (besides Paravicini) and Nick. As Hemingway revised the story, he presented an increasingly hostile conversation between Nick and an Italian adjutant as a prelude to his manic lecture about American locusts.

After Nick's edgy apology for not bringing chocolate, postcards, and cigarettes, he gives a messianic proclamation that seems hyperbolic about his role as representative of masses of soldiers to come: "There will be several millions of Americans here shortly." He adds sardonically that these Americans will be "twice as large as myself, healthy, with clean hearts . . . wonderful chaps" (CSS 311). Nick seems to mock the image of purity in American soldiers projected by Norman Rockwell's cover illustration for the 31 January 1918 issue of *Life Magazine*—and later used as the sheet music cover for George Cohen's "Over There."[22] David Lubin describes the image as a chorus of "four fresh-faced, practically juvenile doughboys singing, strumming a banjo, and merrily snapping their fingers. They gather around a campfire like scouts on a weekend retreat" (85). Nick's parody of the idealized image of American soldiers gains its edginess from self-ironic references to his own military career—"never been wounded, never been blown up, never had their heads caved in" (CSS 311)—a rising tricolon that echoes

Paravicini's earlier opinion that Nick's head should have been trepanned. Rockwell depicted the soldiers in their freshly minted, brown American uniforms and with spirited looks of camaraderie on their faces. Rockwell's soldiers have no marks of either physical wounds or psychological trauma.

The adjutant's questions about Nick's nationality serve to intensify his defensiveness. When asked if he is Italian (perhaps a compliment to Nick's fluency with the language), he responds: "No, American. Look at the uniform." About his "uniform," Nick jokes about its being made by Spagnolini, a premier Milanese designer, but then adds that "it's not quite correct" (*CSS* 311). As this exchange continues, Nick becomes increasingly irritated. The adjutant asks a question that seems innocently inane ("A North or South American?") but for whatever reason initiates Nick's sense that he is veering out of control: "He felt it coming on now" (*CSS* 311). The Italian adjutant's next comment ("But you speak Italian") sets Nick further on edge. His response is a triplet of increasingly hostile questions: "Why not? Do you mind if I speak Italian? Haven't I a right to speak Italian?"[23] To the adjutant's concession implying that Nick's Italian medals give him the right to speak his language, Nick responds tartly: "Just the ribbons and the papers. The medals come later. Or you give them to people to keep and the people go away; or they are lost with your baggage. You can purchase others in Milan. It is the papers that are of importance" (*CSS* 311–12). Nick's repeating "papers" ironically echoes the beginning of the story when he observes with apparent detachment the various types of papers strewn with the dead. This terse dialogue—one of the edgiest conversations in any Hemingway short story—leads to Nick's strange admission that he has been "reformed out of the war" (*CSS* 312). At some point *after* his handwritten revisions to the typescript, Hemingway added this sentence where Nick refers to having been "reformed out of the war." As if he has been sent to a reform school, Nick alludes with veiled sarcasm to his apparent role as a showman of American military might. His reference to being "reformed" then leads to Nick's re-forming himself as a grasshopper/locust that, instead of serving as bait for trout, seems a metaphor for a biblical plague of locusts to come.

One common denominator between Nick and the locusts is the brown color of his uniform. Whereas the grasshopper in America is "small and green," the locusts Nick invokes are "medium-brown," like his uniform (*CSS* 312). Nick's reference to the "medium-brown" color of the grasshopper/locust hearkens explicitly back to the role grasshoppers play in the trout fishing of "Big Two-Hearted River" and "Now I Lay Me." Immediately after connecting the color of his uniform with the color of the grasshoppers, Nick explains why they are ideal trout bait: "They last the best in the water and fish prefer them" (*CSS* 312). In this simple compound sentence, Hemingway suggests that Nick, knowingly or not, contrasts the grasshoppers that "last best" with his own role as bait to attract soldiers to the front. In his manic lecture Nick suggests that he is lousy fish bait without so much as a chocolate bar to hook Italian troops. Rather, in his monologue about the types of grasshoppers, Nick seems to identify himself with the bright-red or blackened grasshoppers whose wings "go to pieces in the water"—an apt metaphor for his mental state in this monologue (*CSS* 312). That is, while his uniform might signify Nick's belonging to the "millions" who "swarm like locusts," Nick's monologue suggests that he has gone to pieces before the swarm has arrived.

Nick's spoken "locust" lecture in "A Way" is self-mocking but with an edgy sense of humor. Instead of speaking to himself, Nick addresses a resistant, if not openly hostile, audience: "I must insist" (*CSS* 312). Nick's monologue begins immediately after the adjutant motions with his hand for a "second runner" to summon Paravicini. That signal follows Nick's reference to the importance of grasshoppers in his past—perhaps a metafictional reference to Hemingway's past Nick Adams trout fishing/grasshopper stories. "These insects at one time played a very important part in my life," Nick confides to the adjutant (*CSS* 312). Then he begins his lecture with comments on the "medium-brown" locusts preferable as bait "for a day's fishing" (*CSS* 312). Nick responds to his Italian audience mockingly, as if the Italians are staring at him on exhibition. Although Hemingway revised very little of Nick's grasshopper lecture, here he inserted two sentences into the typescript: "It's perfectly all right for you to look. You can stare if you like" (KL/EH folder 815; *CSS* 312). The added sentences accentuate Nick's hostility and self-consciousness as he begins his lecture. In what seems another self-reference to his earlier Nick Adams story, Hemingway has Nick mock the practice of harvesting grasshoppers by hand, even though he did so himself in "Big Two-Hearted River" when he picked up "only the medium-sized brown ones" as fishing bait (*CSS* 173). In "A Way," Nick insists that his listeners will "never gather a sufficient supply of these insects for a day's fishing by pursuing them with your hands or trying to hit them with a bat" (*CSS* 312). Nick's sarcasm here is darker than his bemused comment in "Big Two-

Hearted River" about picking up fifty "hoppers" by hand when harvesting them in "a grasshopper lodging house" (*CSS* 173). As if addressing children, idiots, or madmen, Nick dismisses with deadpan humor using hands or bats to catch grasshoppers—a far cry from his carefully harvesting grasshoppers in "Big Two-Hearted River" early in the morning before the dew had dried.[24]

Another level of comedy in Nick's locust lecture is in its taking "medium-brown locusts" as a metaphor for infantry troops and weapons of war. Part of the sharpness of Hemingway's humor here may be that grasshoppers were actually envisioned as potential weapons in warfare. In the same 20 July 1918 issue of *Scientific American* with a cover story about the teleferica as a means of transporting Italian soldiers and weapons into the mountains, Hemingway could have read, in the very next article, a piece about insect warfare. Titled "Fifty Billion German Allies Already in the American Field," the article is a quite serious discussion of the possibility that Germans were using insects like aphids, Hessian flies, army worms, and grasshoppers to conduct unconventional attacks on America's farm industry. With martial language, the article refers to the insects as "hostile," connects the naming of the "Hessian flies" to "Hessian soldiers," and refers to defensive tactics to trap and crush "marching army worms" ("Fifty Billion" 47). At the end of the article, the descriptive tone turns editorial: a call is issued to defend prize crops "worth fighting for," as the "guerrilla fighting to which this interest has been left in the past will no longer suffice—has never sufficed, in fact" (59). Rather, the *Scientific American* summons Americans to engage in "[c]arefully planned campaigns" (59).[25] Not only could Hemingway have read such an article about efforts to defend against insect warfare, in Italy he also could have read or heard about a patent applied for to develop a "grasshopper bomb" to "destroy the wheat crops of Germany and Austria" (cited in Florczyk 115). As far-fetched as these schemes of insect warfare might seem, they add comic bite to Hemingway's portrait of Nick's lecture about swarms of American troops.

Following his dismissal of trying to catch grasshoppers by hand or with a bat, Nick evokes an even more absurd scenario of two officers holding a skein of netting to catch grasshoppers blowing in the wind—a scene that seems to foreshadow the dark humor of Joseph Heller, J. D. Salinger, or Tim O'Brien.[26] Nick refers informally to "the hoppers" (as he did in "River") as if they were bit actors—like Nick himself—in a scene of capture: "flying with the wind," the grasshoppers would "fly against the length of netting and are imprisoned in its folds" (*CSS* 313). Breezing on, Nick continues by insisting that any officer training program should include training with mosquito netting to capture grasshoppers—a proposition that sounds like a *Monty Python* skit. Concluding his lecture, Nick mockingly asks his audience if there are "any questions" (*CSS* 313). In the setting copy that he used for assembling the stories in *Winnter Take Nothing*, Hemingway added a sentence that contributes to Nick's self-mockery of his role as lecturer: "If there is anything else in the course you do not understand please ask questions" (KL/EH folder 222; *CSS* 313). Apparently, there are no questions, as the adjutant has been too busy sending word to Paravicini to follow Nick's lecture-soliloquy. Nick ends his lecture to an audience of one, the adjutant (if he is listening), with a repeated mock address by citing the words of Sir Henry Wilson: "Gentlemen, either you must govern or be governed" (*CSS* 313). He repeats himself with a valediction to the "gentlemen" to whom he bids "Good-day." His words sound as if the story has come to its end. And yet it hasn't.

In the manuscript version, the story approaches its close with a rather confusing set of interactions between Paravicini and Nick over his possibly walking to the river to survey the troops on the other side. On the one hand, Paravicini encourages Nick to "go up and look across the river and see them," if he wants to see the troops there (*SS-HLE* 334). On the other hand, when Nick insists on "making a little tour," Paravicini tells him to wait until dark, and Nick responds by mocking him as "Grandma Paravicini" (*SS-HLE* 336). As he revised this manuscript draft, Hemingway sharpened the conflict between Paravicini and Nick and focused more clearly on Nick's fear of having another manic fit.

When Paravicini returns at the end of his lecture about locusts, Nick and he have their most overt conflict of the story. As Nick is preparing to walk to the river to wet his helmet, Paravicini leads Nick back inside the dugout and tells him to sit down. In response, Nick concedes that he does not have to go to the river and that helmets are a "damned nuisance" anyway. Nick then adds, "I've seen them full of brains too many times" (*CSS* 313). After Paravicini objects to Nick's presence as likely to cause his soldiers to bunch together and "invite shelling," he responds that he came because he was sent and because he thought he might see Paravicini. Nick then mentions to Paravicini that, instead of coming to visit this brigade, he "could have gone to Zenzon or San Dona" (*CSS* 313). Both Zenzon and San Dona are in the region of the Piave River where the Austrians and Italians fought. Striking is that Nick adds, "I'd like to go to San Dona to see the bridge again" (*CSS* 313). Implicit in Nick's wish is that he took part in a battle at that bridge. Paravicini seems unmoved by Nick's comment that he could have visited San Dona instead. He tells Nick at first gently and then firmly that he "won't have you circulating around to no purpose" (*CSS* 313). At that point Nick agrees and then "felt it coming on again" (*CSS* 313). The "it" to which Nick refers is another fit—as when he felt "it" coming on shortly before his manic lecture about locusts. After Paravicini insists that any "circulating" should be done at night, Nick thought to himself, "He knew he could not stop it now" (*CSS* 314). Nick then rants about how Paravicini should see to the burial of the dead. In response, Paravicini patiently encourages him to "Lie down a little while, Nicolo" (*CSS* 314). This exchange, with Nick's going back to the bunk on which he had his first two interior monologues, leads to a third, short, revelatory memory about a yellow house by a river.

There are three references in Nick's interior monologues to a yellow house as part of his dream-visions. First is his vision of a "house painted yellow" outside of Fossalta, associated in his mind with his dreams of Sacré Coeur. In that section of his interior monologue, Nick is certain that "every night he had it"—the night vision of the yellow house next to willows, a stable, and a canal (*CSS* 310). The next stage of Nick's dwelling on the yellow house comes in its recurrence as part of his second interior monologue after Nick "lay down again" on the cot once he sees the Italians in the room staring at him after Paravicini had left. In this second stage, Nick continues questioning himself, *after* insisting that "he never dreamed any more about the front" (*CSS* 311). Having asserted unequivocally his disassociation of the yellow house from his experiences on the Italian front, Nick nonetheless asks himself a direct question about his dreams of a yellow house, stable, and canal: "why would he wake, soaking wet, more frightened than he had ever been in a bombardment" (*CSS* 311). By asking himself this question, Nick seems to move closer to recognizing that his recurrent nightmares *might* be anchored to the war, after all.

The third stage of Nick's mental journey to understand the significance of the yellow house comes *after* his comic monologue about American locusts. In his third interior monologue, once he follows Paravicini's suggestion that he lie back on the bunk, and after he shuts his eyes, Nick has a vision, for the first time in the story, of "the man with the beard who looked at him over the sights of the rifle, quite calmly before squeezing off" (*CSS* 314). That is, Nick reenvisions the moment before he felt the bullet's "club-like impact" and fell to his knees, coughing "it" (blood) "onto the rock" (*CSS* 314). In remembering this moment, Nick now sees clearly that his vision of "a long, yellow house" was a displacement of the traumatic memory of being wounded badly enough for Paravicini to insist that he should have been trepanned (*CSS* 310). Whatever the precise physical nature of where Nick was wounded, he seems to face his traumatic memory in this vision of a bearded man who shot him.[27] He seems now to recognize that his nightmarish dreams *have* been about the war. In remembering this moment, Nick now sees that his vision of "a long, yellow house" was a displacement of the traumatic memory of being wounded. Nick explicitly understands that the vision is "in the place of the man" who shot him (*CSS* 314). That is a far more traumatic memory of losing control than that of a man (or men) with whom his girl went in Paris when she was not with him. Near the end of the story, this short paragraph—the briefest of the three about the yellow house—leads Nick to complete his interior monologue by speaking to himself: "Christ ... I might as well go" (*CSS* 314).

Nick's "Christ" near the end of "A Way" seems a note of accommodation to Paravicini's guidance away from the battleground. He realizes that he has no place metaphorically showing the American flag to the Italians on the front, or lecturing soldiers about harvesting locusts for grasshopper bombs or the like. Underscoring this affirming resolution to leave the battlefield, Hemingway follows with a one-sentence narrative marker: "Nick stood up" (*CSS* 314). After twice noting Nick's tentative actions of lying down, then sitting up, then lying down again, and then sitting up again, Hemingway here emphasizes that Nick stood up. Nick's standing up is a positive motion of determination and resilience, as was the case at the beginning of "The Battler" and at the ending of "Big Two-Hearted River" (*CSS* 97, 180). Informally addressing Paravicini with affection as "Para," Nick declares simply that "I'll ride back now in the afternoon" and that he will return only "when I have something to bring" (*CSS* 314). Nick's simple statements are pragmatic, accommodating, and simple—far from the circuitous, rambling interior monologue and spoken lecture that are so central to "A Way You'll Never Be." Nick seems, implicitly, to have renewed his ability to laugh at himself and move on.

Ironically, after Paravicini's admonishing Nick not to mingle with his troops "to no purpose," Nick's underlying purpose in returning to the Italian battlefield—and probably to the river scene of his being wounded—is fulfilled, at least in part. Ostensibly, Nick came bearing gifts foreshadowing the arrival of American troops. However, Nick admits to Paravicini that he has no chocolates, postcards, or cigarettes to offer (*CSS* 309). Nick remembers watching from a relatively protected position as Italian soldiers shot Austrians who were crossing a river at Portogrande. He both revisits and remembers a more traumatic location with a river, where he was shot by an Austrian soldier. By revisiting the river scene where he was shot, Nick confronts the source of his nightmares involving a yellow house and gains more understanding and self-command. His underlying purpose in returning, Hemingway implies, is his coming to terms with his trauma of being wounded. He "may as well go" away from the battle camp because he has fulfilled his deeper purpose of his journey back—confronting the fears haunting him after he was wounded.

Hemingway ends the story with a final interior monologue—Nick's humorously confused meditation about where he saw a "Terza Savoia cavalry regiment riding in the snow"—apparently a reference to an elite cavalry unit. This final monologue was not present in the manuscript (*SS-HLE* 340–41). Hemingway added this monologue as part of his revision preserved in the typescript. To that typescript, Hemingway made further alterations, evident in the published version of the story. For example, by hand he added the sentence: "The horses' breath made plumes in the cold air" (KL/EH folder 815; *CSS* 315). This addition contributes a note of comedy, as the "plumes" seem decorative, like plumes of feathers worn by horses marching on parade. This second reference to "Savoia" initially seems to be a sign of Nick's trying to reorient himself, as he remembers a time when, earlier in the war, he had passed the "cavalry regiment riding in the snow" (*CSS* 314). At first, Nick remembers that the horses' breath "made plumes"; then he corrects himself ("No, that was somewhere else"). His self-correction of his own misdirection ironically echoes his initial reference to the battle charge, "Savoia." Nick associates the initial battle cry with his subsequent sighting of cavalry horses whose breath in the freezing cold air made decorative "plumes." Revising his own memory of where he saw the Terza Savoia cavalry, Nick now asks in his final, silent, interior monologue, "Where was that?" (*CSS* 315).[28] That question leads Nick to set aside his uncertainty of where he saw the Terza Savoia cavalry and to focus instead on where he left his bicycle. Nick's simple questions suggest his disorientation even after he emerges from his disjointed interior monologues to accept Paravicini's suggestion that he return to his bicycle.

Earlier in the story Nick reminded Paravicini of the night when they rode from Mestre to Portogrande. He was drunk and "used the bicycle for a blanket" (*CSS* 309). Here is another case where Nick's bicycle serves him as an improvised shelter, but there is an important difference. Here Nick is not drunk, and he is not contemplating the bicycle as a blanket for sleeping but, rather, as a practical means of returning back to Fornaci. Whereas "A Way" begins with Nick's meticulously reconstructing the way a battle was fought, it ends with his speaking aloud to himself: first, "I'd better get to that damned bicycle"; then, "I don't want to lose the way to Fornaci" (*CSS* 315). His silent interior monologues have now become a spoken interior monologue, as Nick's bicycle becomes a "damned" way from self-damnation. This mild curse points to his quest for balance.

The end of the story in its earlier version is simply an exchange of "Ciaou" [*sic*] after Nick and Paravicini trade apologies for talking too much (*SS-HLE* 341). This revised ending takes readers from a rather perfunctory dialogue in the earlier draft between Nick and the Italian Captain Paravicini to an interior monologue presented as if spoken. Nick's speaking to himself straddles the border between his manic, shell-shocked voice and his rational, poised voice. He is still speaking to himself, if not to the Italians; he is speaking about his bicycle, if not about locusts. Furthermore, Nick is speaking to himself in his rational, poised voice: he curses lightly to himself, and he resolves not to "lose the way" to his destination.

In a letter to Maxwell Perkins on 8 April 1933, Hemingway wrote that he once thought that "A Way You'll Never Be," the story he had "just finished about the war," could be "one more simple story of action" that his collection of stories needed. Instead, as he confided to his editor, that story "turned out to be a hell of a difficult one" (*Letters* vol. 5, 369). During an astounding period of revision, Hemingway's incorporation of Nick's interior monologues and his spoken lectures about American locusts contribute to the story's power. In this balance between mania and sanity, Nick in "A Way" is as close as Hemingway's Nick Adams ever came to Shakespeare's Hamlet—the mad prince and the logician, the monomaniacal Nick lecturing about how to catch grasshoppers and the witty mocker of military authority as two sides of the same mind. The final word Nick speaks to himself in the story, "Fornaci," is equivalent to "sanity," and balancing while riding his bicycle is equivalent to balancing his mind. Nick's resolving not to lose his way to For-naci is, I think, an indication of his awareness of a destination, a path, and a means to follow that path—that is, Nick's resolve not to "lose the way." His resolution does not remove the elements of hysteria, trauma, and alienation from the story: with the humor remain traces of horror. As George Meredith wrote in his "Essay on Comedy" about Cervantes's *Don Quixote,* the "gro-tesque" can coexist with "the burlesque." In the "great humorist" there can be "lights of tragedy with his laughter." Or, as Meredith described the "test of true comedy" later in his essay, "it shall awaken thoughtful laughter" (45, 47). That "thoughtful laughter" is what Hemingway gives us in "A Way You'll Never Be."

9

REVISING "THE GAMBLER, THE NUN, AND THE RADIO"

"A Way You'll Never Be" represents a return to a setting and conflict Hemingway had depicted before—from the "Nick sat against the wall" chapter in *in our time* through "Now I Lay Me" and *A Farewell to Arms*. In contrast, "The Gambler, the Nun, and the Radio" reflects relatively new terrain—revisiting the American West of "Wine of Wyoming"—but with a more traditional narrative structure than "A Way." Set in a hospital in a fictional Hailey, Montana, the story has a central narrative focus—a writer—and two other major characters, the Mexican gambler Cayetano Ruiz and the nun Sister Cecilia. The story offers clear transitions—unlike parts of "A Way"—and a relatively simple three-part structure. Hemingway developed the story, however, as a striking departure from traditional elements of the Western novel that was familiar to him. There is no heroic gunslinger or archvillain—no shootout between the Virginian and Trampas, as there is in Owen Wister's *The Virginian*. In "Gambler," instead of filling the role of a stereotypical villain, the Mexican, Cayetano Ruiz, embodies cool under pressure. And the anodyne for pain is neither a landscape of "virgin wilderness" as an idyllic refuge (*The Virginian* 270), nor an idealized marriage of eastern sophistication and western Wild West, but a radio that plays tunes like "Little Lies" all night. This chapter will explore the significance of four major elements in Hemingway's revisions to the original drafts of "The Gambler, the Nun, and the Radio": the shift in narrative viewpoint from first person to third person; the portrait of Cayetano as a witty, self-ironic, and empathetic character; the revisions to the ending that swerve from the stereotypical climax and denouement of the Western; and the changes in the story's title. Hemingway's "Gambler, Nun, and Radio" revises the traditional Western, as embodied by

Owen Wister's *Virginian,* and in the course of Hemingway's revisions becomes a complex, comical portrait of human frailty and humor.[1]

In his *Hemingway: The 1930s,* Michael Reynolds recounts the events of the summer of 1930 leading up to an automobile accident in Wyoming that left Hemingway immobilized and unable to write for months. In late June (or, according to Brewster Chamberlin, 2 July), Hemingway, Pauline, and Jack drove from Piggot, Arkansas, to Kansas City and then made the long drive to Clarks Fork, Wyoming (Chamberlin 103). On 13 July they settled into the L-Bar T Ranch located at 6,800 feet altitude on the floodplain of the Clarks Fork of the Yellowstone River (Reynolds, *Hemingway: The 1930s* 45). On 1 November, riding in a car with John Dos Passos, Hemingway swerved off the road to avoid an oncoming car. The accident landed him in the emergency room at St. Vincent Hospital in Billings with a severely broken arm (Reynolds, *Hemingway: The 1930s* 52–53; Chamberlin 104).

Taken off morphine after five days, Hemingway was immobilized in his hospital bed. As Michael Reynolds puts it, "For three weeks unable to move for fear of ruining his writing arm, he has plenty of time to think, too much time" (*Hemingway: The 1930s* 54). During this convalescence, he learned about two new patients, a Russian beet worker who groaned loud and often from the pain of his thigh wound, and a Mexican, despite a more severe stomach wound, who remained stoically quiet. Cared for by a Catholic nun, Sister Florence Cloonan, whose secular passions were the Philadelphia Athletics and the Notre Dame football team under Knute Rockne, Hemingway at some point thought of a new story based on his observations in the hospital (Reynolds, *Hemingway: The 1930s* 54–56). This story is far different from those based on his recuperation in Milan from the wounds caused by mortar shrapnel: far different, that is, from "A Very Short Story" and the hospital scenes of *A Farewell to Arms.* In "The Gambler, the Nun, and the Radio," there is no romance, no sex, and no doctor or nurse's administration of anesthesia. Rather, there is a tight-lipped, witty Mexican gambler, a nun whose passion for her favorite teams rivals her ambition of becoming a saint, and a radio that serves the writer Mr. Frazer as an all-night distraction, just as remembering and imagining the rivers he had fished served Nick in "Now I Lay Me."

Whether or not he had begun to write the story in his head, in a letter he dictated via Pauline to Archibald MacLeish, probably on 22 November 1930, he sketched the essential elements of the story. Referring to his writing arm whose broken bones the doctor had tied together with kangaroo tendons, Hemingway confided that he was not sure about his writing arm's prognosis: "There is some kind of numbness that will either clear up or can be relieved by another operation" (*Letters* vol. 4, 403). After dictating a section of the letter about the plans for an African safari and information about guns, Hemingway turned to the subject of the radio in his room: "any time day or night I can get Rudy Vallee, the somethingless crooner—remember I'm dictating—singing in a thin voice about that Big Blue TEAM" (*Letters* vol. 4, 404). He was referring to Vallee's recording of the Yale fight song, "Goodbye Harvard," recorded the previous month (*Letters* vol. 4, 406n3). Next, he referred to the Russian and Mexican across the hall, and then to two Mexicans with whom he shared drinks of Scotch. He then remarked that "This is Will James country here," referring to the author and illustrator of *Smoky the Cowhorse,* awarded the 1927 Newbery Medal for children's literature (*Letters* vol. 4, 406n7). Calling James a "dog-eared moth-eaten, shifty-eyed, fake imitation of old C. W. Rossell [sic], who was a real cowboy artist" (*Letters* vol. 4, 405), Hemingway began to associate two of the major characters of his story—the gambler and the radio—with the genre of Western fiction and art. Comparable to the earliest sketches for a work of short fiction, this letter was the foundation for the initial draft of the story.

On 17 November 1933, Hemingway wrote Maxwell Perkins that "Gambler" is an example of a story that is "word for word as it happened" (*Letters* vol. 5, 542). However much his earlier letter to MacLeish, dictated to Pauline while he was in his hospital bed, might confirm that claim, the numerous revisions Hemingway made in the course of composing the story—and even changing its title—suggest that the "Gambler" includes its fictional elements and narrative decisions. As autobiographical as the story may be, "Gambler" still bears the clear signs of Hemingway as artist. His process of revising "The Gambler, the Nun, and the Radio" illustrates his artistic craft, even in a story whose roots come from his personal experiences. As Ann L. Putnam put it, "the facts are wonderfully transformed into a rich tapestry" ("Opiates, Laughter" 159).

According to Paul Smith, in its first version, Hemingway titled the story "Three Ambitions"—and crossed out that title. This early draft, contained in folder 417 at the Kennedy Library, is printed in the Hemingway Library Edition of the short stories (*SS-HLE* 371–86). While this draft includes the major elements of the story, Hemingway wrote it in the first person, after a few fragments in the third person, two of which are contradictory: "He heard them brought" and "He did not hear them brought in" (*SS-HLE* 371). Then, before shifting to the first-person viewpoint, the story begins with virtually the same sentence as the final version: "They brought them in around midnight and then, all night long everyone along the corridor heard the Russian" (*SS-HLE* 371). In beginning the story largely in a first-person point of view, Hemingway followed Owen Wister, whose *Virginian* is narrated by a visitor from the East who recounts the main storyline of the Virginian and a schoolteacher from Vermont—that is, settlers in the West who grew up in southern and northern states in the East.

In Hemingway's initial drafts for the story, he composed "Gambler" in the first person. For example, in a typescript fragment, the opening paragraphs and dialogue are identical with the version published in *Winer Take Nothing,* with one exception. This earlier version has "I asked the night nurse" instead of the later "Mr. Frazer asked the night nurse" (KL/EH folder 420a; *CSS* 355). Likewise, in a typescript of the story, reproduced in full in the Hemingway Library Edition, the story is completely narrated in the first person (KL/EH folder 417; *SS-HLE* 371–86). Later, in a manuscript fragment on the back of Hotel Brevoort, New York, stationery, Hemingway crossed out the first-person "I" and replaced it with the third-person "he." For example, in a paragraph that began "Mr. Frazer lay there and listened to the radio," Hemingway crossed out "I" twice and replaced it with "he." At the same time, near the ending of the story, Hemingway left the viewpoint in the first person, twice writing, "'Listen,' I said" (KL/EH folder 421; *SS-HLE* 388). Eventually, Hemingway was more consistent in replacing the narrative "I" with "Mr. Frazer" and "he." Clearly later than that manuscript fragment is a typescript version of the story that was published in *Scribner's Magazine,* "titled, signed, noted for serial rights, and addressed at Key West" (Smith, *Guide* 290). On the first page of this typescript, Hemingway crossed out "I" by hand and replaced it with "Mr. Frazer" (KL/EH folder 420, 1). He did so as well on subsequent pages of the typescript. For example, on page two he crossed out "me" and wrote "Mr. Frazer" by hand (KL/EH folder 420, 2). In short, by the time Hemingway revised his early typescript of "Gambler" for the version published in *Scribner's* as "Give Us a Prescription, Doctor," he had firmly settled on shifting to a third-person narration.

The first significant revision in the early draft of the story illustrates the benefits of Hemingway's shifting to third-person narration. This revision comes in a sequence describing the view from the window of the hospital, including the account of an accident that leaves a scar on Mr. Frazer. The shift from first person to third person strengthens the slapstick comedy of the reading light's falling on Mr. Frazer's head. In the draft, the first-person narrator keeps insisting that the event was funny at the time, but his account of the incident does not seem that humorous. Once the narrative shifts to third person, there is a comical alternation between the repetition of the formal "Mr. Frazer" and the "leaded base of the lamp" that, "hitting the top of his head," knocked him out (*CSS* 358). To the earlier draft, Hemingway added the clause, "who was a most excellent doctor," underscoring the irony that a doctor whose job was to heal Mr. Frazer knocked out his patient while trying to move furniture so he could see two pheasants outside the window (compare *SS-HLE* 375 with *CSS* 358). Enhancing the humor in his revision, Hemingway likened the accident to a comic strip, "just as in a comic section" (*CSS* 358), reinforcing the slapstick sequence of spotting pheasants, moving the patient's bed toward the window, and then accidentally knocking him out before he could actually see the pheasants.

The most striking revision in this section of the story involves the list of contemporary songs that the narrator/Mr. Frazer listens to on the radio. In both versions, the list includes "Sing Something Simple," "Singsong Girl," and "Little White Lies."[2] However, in revising the story, Hemingway added "Betty Co-ed," a popular Rudy Vallée song (compare *SS-HLE* 376 with *CSS* 359). Not only did Hemingway add the song to the list of tunes Mr. Frazer hears on the radio, but he also referred to Frazer's parodying the song with lewdly improvised lyrics: "the parody of the words which came unavoidably into Mr. Frazer's mind, grew so steadily and increasingly obscene that there being no one to appreciate it, he finally abandoned it and let the song go back to football" (*CSS* 359). In the revision, it is as if Mr. Frazer tries to spice up the song's lyrics with obscene transformations, just as he might wish to embellish the view out the window where he sees "a field with tumbleweed coming out of the snow, and a bare clay butte" (*CSS* 358). Even before introducing Mr. Frazer in the next section of the story as a writer, Hemingway suggests the limits and constraints on his imagination, while virtually immobile in his hospital bed.

The next major revision comes deep into the story, after the narrator has listened to the Notre Dame game on the radio, after he was visited for the first time by three Mexicans, and after a night of listening to radio stations from Denver to Minneapolis. In the early typescript draft, the first-person narrator indicated that every time the nun saw him crying, she would ask, "What's the matter?" He continued by sharing his response: "I would explain that it was my nerves which were all shot. They really were" (*SS-HLE* 381–82). As Hemingway reworked that draft, he crossed out both the nun's question and the first-person narrator's response. Instead of a brief conversation with the nun's asking the narrator why he has been crying, Hemingway shifted to Frazer's interior monologue presented via third-person narration: "His nerves went bad at the end of five weeks, and while he was pleased they lasted that long yet he resented being forced to make the same experiment when he already knew the answer. Mr. Frazer had been through all this before. The only thing which was new to him was the radio. He played it all night long" (*CSS* 363). Noteworthy is that in the earlier version, the first-person narrator makes no reference to an "experiment." Instead, he records the gist of his conversation with the nurse (*SS-HLE* 381–82). By hand, Hemingway added the sentence about Mr. Frazer's resentment at having to go through "the same experiment" to the typescript on which he based "Prescription" for *Scribner's* (KL/EH folder 420, 11). Hemingway's shift to a third-person narrative is much more enigmatic and effective in raising questions. What experiment? What was "all this" he had been through before? The "experiment" sounds like Nick's in "Now I Lay Me" when he forced himself to stay awake all night so his soul would not fly out of his body: "that summer, I was unwilling to make the experiment" (*CSS* 376). Whatever "through this" and "all this" refer to, the new aspect of Mr. Frazer's coping strategy has been to use the radio as a distraction, as Nick had meditated on real and imagined fishing streams—in Frazer's case, a way of keeping his anxieties at bay, his nerves from cracking up.

Hemingway's portrait of Cayetano subverts common stereotypes of Mexicans prevalent in popular Western fiction and films. Such a derogatory portrait is present in an early story by Owen Wister, "A Pilgrim on the Gila," first published in November 1895 (*The West of Owen Wister* xvi). In that story, Wister refers to Mexicans as "old shriveled cigarette smoking apes" (*The West of Owen Wister* 157). A decade later, the stereotypes were present in Everett McNeil's 1908 book *In Texas with Davy Crockett*. Repeatedly referring to Mexicans as "greasers," Davy Crockett and his friend Sam McNally laugh together at the notion that "the good lord . . . made Mexicans so they can't shoot straight" (McNeil n.p.). In 1925, Will James's *Smoky the*

Cowhorse was published, and won the Newbery Medal in 1927. In his November 1930 letter to Archibald MacLeish, in which he sketched the characters for "Gambler," Hemingway derided James as a writer about the West—a "false imitation" of Charles Russell as a "cowboy artist." Until about midway through *Smoky the Cowhorse*, Will James portrays a charming, if sentimental, comradeship between Smoky and his rider Clint, "the bronc twister of the Rocking R outfit"—that is, a cowboy who broke and tamed wild horses (87). That sentimental portrait of a bronco buster taming a wild mustang itself might have raised Hemingway's acerbic ire. However, the sentimental tale turns bleak when Smoky is stolen by a half-Mexican referred to as "a half-breed of Mexican and other blood that's darker" (220), "the breed" (222), and "the half breed" (236). Striking about the racist slurs and stereotypes is not just their sudden appearance, but their appearance as if natural and normative accounts of Mexican characters as rustlers who cruelly manhandle animals. Although Hemingway's scoffing at Will James as a writer of a Western may or may not be centered on his racist stereotyping of the rustler, his portrait of Cayetano in "Gambler" runs counter to James's novel.

Likewise, in the films of the early twentieth century, Hemingway could have seen such stereotypes as pervasive in the Western genre. Hemingway showed his familiarity with the genre when he wrote a disclaimer for Maxwell Perkins to circulate in order to correct some of the sensational tales included in newspaper stories about him. Taking particular aim at the film industry, he wrote Perkins on 7 December 1932 that corrective statement. Part of his disclaimer refers specifically to the cowboy film star Tom Mix: "While Mr. H appreciates the publicity attempt to build him into a glamorous personality like Floyd Gibbons or Tom Mix's horse Tony he deprecates it and asks the motion picture people to leave his private life alone—" (*Letters* vol. 5, 293). In the 1915 film *The Man from Texas,* Tom Mix starred as a heroic cowboy who rescues the leading lady from the clutches of a Mexican character who enters roughly twenty-four minutes into the film, leads a stagecoach robbery, ties up the heroine, and gloats. Tom Mix, the "Man from Texas," enters the cabin, rescues the girl, and ties up the Mexican.[3] That part of the film seems a thinly disguised allegory of the triumph of Texas over Mexico.

In *Martyrs of the Alamo,* directed in 1915 by Christy Cabanne and produced by D. W. Griffith, the stereotypes of Mexicans are outright racist. Seven minutes into the movie, a Mexican officer, dressed in uniform, is depicted as a drunken assaulter of women. At about fifty minutes, the Mexicans attacking the Alamo are shown to savagely shoot women, their babies, and young boys. At fifty-five minutes, a Mexican soldier grabs a small, blond boy around the neck, apparently stabs him, and throws him aside. At fifty-nine minutes and forty-three seconds, the text on the screen offers this description of the Mexican commander Santa Ana: "An inveterate drug fiend, the Dictator of Mexico also famous for his shameful orgies" (Cabanne). The film depicts Sam Houston's victory at the Battle of San Jacinto as a result, in no small part, of Santa Ana's preoccupation with a virtual harem of Mexican dancing girls.

Even the 1929 film version of Owen Wister's *The Virginian* includes stereotypes of Mexicans, for which the novel itself offers little basis (V. Fleming). Virtually the only reference to a Mexican in the novel is in a list of absurd rumors that Molly, the eventual wife of the Virginian, has been "engaged to a gambler, a gold miner, an escaped stage robber, and a Mexican bandit" (*The Virginian* 151). The list of her alleged suitors is a virtual catalogue of stereotypical figures of the Wild West. On no more basis than that rumor in the novel, the film version (a movie Hemingway might have seen while working on "Gambler") portrays some of the villain Trampas's gang as poker-playing, sombrero-wearing *bandidos*. Trampas, who leads a gang of cattle rustlers, at times in the film commands the attention of a Mexican prostitute. At one point shortly before the Virginian leads a posse to capture three members of the gang, one stereotypical *bandido* serenades his fellow thieves with song.

In contrast to these frequently racist stereotypes of Mexicans, Hemingway portrays Cayetano as a sympathetic, witty, and empathetic character. His revisions enrich his portrait of the Mexican gambler Cayetano's relationship with Mr. Frazer, who serves as the focal viewpoint once the narration shifts to the third person. Mr. Frazer and Cayetano share a wry sense of humor that, implicitly, provides Mr. Frazer another means of controlling his nerves. Most of the funniest moments in the middle of the story are present in the early typescript reprinted in the Hemingway Library Edition of the stories. For instance, during the conversation with the three Mexicans about Cayetano, the first-person narrator in the earlier draft (and Mr. Frazer in the published version) learns that Cayetano has won hundreds of dollars playing cards with "the smallest one" and "the thin one." Correcting Mr. Frazer's assumption that Cayetano must be "very rich," the small Mexican replies, "He is poorer than we.... He has no more than the shirt on his back."

Mr. Frazer replies with a witty play on words: "And that shirt is of little value now . . . Perforated as it is" (*SS-HLE* 379; *CSS* 361–62). Whatever the Spanish word Mr. Frazer presumably used that is rendered as "perforated," the euphemistic reference to the shirt's holes suggests bullet holes. The only revision Hemingway made in this exchange was the shift from first-person narration to third-person with the conversation presented through Mr. Frazer's point of view.

In the early draft, the first-person narrator shared with Sister Cecilia that he was suffering from "shot" nerves. By cutting this section, Hemingway shifted the discussion about Frazer's nerves to his later conversation with Cayetano. In that conversation, Frazer and Cayetano show concern for each other. With Sister Cecilia looking on, "observing them happily," Mr. Frazer and Cayetano hold an extended conversation in which they share empathy, honesty, and witty humor in discussing their psychological and physical conditions. Since the conversation includes a discussion about the radio Mr. Frazer listens to, this penultimate section brings together the three title characters of the story—the gambler, the nun, and the radio. Cayetano enters the scene in a wheelchair, but with "his eyes very laughing," he addresses Mr. Frazer in Spanish, *"Hola amigo! Que tal?"* To Mr. Frazer's question about his condition, he responds, "Alive and with the leg paralyzed." Frazer offers in return words of commiseration and encouragement, "Bad. . . . But the nerve can regenerate and be as good as new" (*CSS* 364). Cayetano then asks Mr. Frazer, "What class of pain do you have?" In response, Frazer is open about his emotional pain and fragility: "When the nurse goes out I cry an hour, two hours. It rests me. My nerves are bad now" (*CSS* 365). Cayetano responds with his own words of encouragement, "You have the radio," as if the radio is for Mr. Frazer the equivalent for Cayetano of the hope that the nerve in his leg will regenerate. Although this part of the conversation is identical in the typescript draft and the version published in *Winner Take Nothing*, Hemingway's cutting the narrator's references to his nerves in the earlier scene with Sister Cecilia places more emphasis on the empathy shared between Cayetano and Frazer.

After Cayetano and Frazer discuss each other's nerves—Cayetano's in his leg, Frazer's in his head—they switch to the topic of the *cabrón* who shot Cayetano. Whereas he was evasive in answering the detective's questions about the incident, Cayetano tells Frazer the probable motive for the shooting: "I won thirty-eight dollars from him at cards" (*CSS* 365). He corrects the newspaper account that he was shot before the Russian. Hemingway revised Cayetano's narrative about the shooting to set up his joke about the man who shot him. In the typescript draft Cayetano tells Frazer that "The first shot he fires is intercepted by a poor Russian" (*SS-HLE* 384). That is, in this earlier draft, the *cabrón* doesn't miss. Hemingway revised this account so that the first shot hits no one, building up to Cayetano's wry humor about the shooting. After the shooter fired a first shot "into nothing," his second shot was "intercepted by a poor Russian. That would seem to be luck. What happens? He shoots me twice in the belly. He is a lucky man. I have no luck. He could not hit the side of a horse if he were holding the stirrup. All luck" (*CSS* 365). In a witty joke leveled at the stereotype of Mexicans who can't shoot straight, he scoffs at the man who shot him as a lucky bumbler whose bullets somehow found his gut. With equal good humor, he scoffs at Mr. Frazer's complimenting him as "a philosopher." In language identical in the typescript and published versions, Cayetano offers a self-mocking summary of his career history: "No, hombre. A gambler of the small towns. One small town, then another, another, then a big town, then start over again" (*CSS* 367). Cayetano's ability to laugh at stereotypes about Mexicans—and, indeed, to laugh at himself—establishes a bond of bemused irony between Frazer and him.

Cayetano's ability to laugh at his assailant leads to the end of their final conversation when Frazer and he exchange wishes that the pain "passes quickly." Their echoing each other's "[e]qually" conveys a comradeship superior to that of the three Mexicans (*CSS* 366). As Scott Donaldson observes, Hemingway portrays Cayetano not as a stereotypical gambler or bad-luck, down-and-out loser but as belonging to the group of "admirable men, all of Spanish heritage," ranging from Romero of *The Sun Also Rises* to Santiago of *The Old Man and the Sea* (*By Force of Will* 189). As Donaldson's connecting Cayetano to Romero and Santiago suggests, Hemingway's sympathetic portrait of Cayetano reflects his love for Spanish-speaking cultures. Hemingway portrays Cayetano as the most balanced, witty, and empathetic character in "Gambler." Discussing the context of the story in the tradition of the Western, Seth Bovey argues that Cayetano's sense of humor marks him as an "ideal cowboy." Although he does not compare Cayetano with Wister's wry Virginian, his point is well-taken: "Cayetano's 'laughing' eyes also tell us that he is very much an ideal cowboy in the sense that he can face adversity without having his spirit broken. . . . Cayetano's spirit is further revealed by his ability to laugh at himself as he is feeling great pain" (89). Whether or not one sees Cayetano as a cowboy, his ability to laugh at himself marks him as a guide for the writer, Frazer.[4]

As was the case with Hemingway's portrait of the hit men in "The Killers," the least sympathetic character in "The Gambler, the Nun, and the Radio" repeatedly uses a racist slur when the detective sergeant says in frustration over Cayetano's speaking in Spanish that he wishes he could "talk spick" (*CSS* 357). After Frazer tartly asks him, "Why don't you learn?" the detective repeats the epithet twice: "I don't get any fun out of asking that spick questions. If I could talk spick it would be different" (*CSS* 357). Frazer's response to his racist slurs is a joke, the irony of which the detective does not comprehend. Mocking the detective's earlier scoffing at Cayetano's claim that he was shot in the back, Frazer's parting shot is, "Don't let anybody shoot you in the back" (*CSS* 357). As the story evolved from his initial sketch of the characters in his letter of 22 November 1930 to Archibald MacLeish, Hemingway humanized and enriched his portrait to present Cayetano Ruiz, the gambler, as a source of sophisticated wit, stoic self-control, and empathy. In so doing, Hemingway subverts the stereotypes of Mexicans as inept fumblers, criminal *bandidos,* corrupt *federales,* or political revolutionaries armed with bandeliers like Pancho Villa. In short, Hemingway's sympathetic portrait of Cayetano is a striking re-vision of common stereotypes of Mexicans, as portrayed in texts and films of the early 1900s.

Aside from departing from the stereotypical portrait of Mexicans in Western fiction and film, Hemingway also turned from the typical climax of a shootout between the hero and the villain. About one hour and eighteen minutes into the 1929 film version of *The Virginian,* there is a clear example of such a conventional climax. Trampas throws down his shot of liquor, confronts the Virginian with "Hey you," and issues his challenge: "I'm having a showdown with you here and now." That challenge leads to Trampas's threat to kill the Virginian if he is still in town after sunset. In the film version, the Virginian (played by Gary Cooper) wheels, fires twice, and kills Trampas, who was stealthily approaching from behind. The novel itself sets that showdown offstage, as the two shots are heard by Molly while she is waiting in the hotel to learn whether her fiancé will survive the gunfight. Unlike Wister's steady development toward a climactic showdown between the Virginian and Trampas, Hemingway's story never identifies the Mexican who shot Cayetano and the Russian, presents the shooting as part of the backstory that occurs "offstage," offers as a motive "nothing to kill about" (265), and does not build toward a showdown between a hero and a villain. All we know is that the shooter left town and left a legacy of consummate guitar playing that the remaining Mexican musicians do not match.

In what might have been a fitting ending to the story, the gambler and the writer exchange their kind wishes that each will have luck and each will have the pain pass quickly. Hemingway might have concluded the story with a mutual blessing ("equally") in their valedictions. Indeed, his first draft of the ending comes just a paragraph after Cayetano and the first-person narrator both wish each other that "the pain passes quickly" (*SS-HLE* 385). The early typescript draft of "Gambler" drew to a conclusion not with a showdown of either gunfire or a spoken dispute but with mutually benevolent wishes of good luck and an end to pain. As Hemingway revised that conversation, he made the exchange even more emotionally generous. In the typescript draft, Cayetano tells Frazer that he hopes "the pain passes quickly" (*SS-HLE* 385). In the published version, his farewell wish is even stronger: "And that the pain stops" (*CSS* 366). In the typescript, the first-person narrator responds laconically, "It is passing. It is nothing" (*SS-HLE* 385). In the story published in *Winner Take Nothing,* Mr. Frazer's response is: "It will not last, certainly. It is passing. It is of no importance" (*CSS* 366). Instead of a climactic standoff or shootout here, there is a mutual concord captured in the word "[e]qually" that Cayetano and Frazer speak in wishing each other well.

Hemingway's first version of the story's ending was a paragraph he included after that last conversation with Cayetano: "Those are the last two conversations that I remember with Sister Cecilia and with Cayetano Ruiz" (*SS-HLE* 385). He then added a list of places that he had visited via the radio—and has not revisited since (*SS-HLE* 385). That is, in his first ending, Hemingway concluded with mutually empathetic farewell wishes between Cayetano and the narrator, along with the narrator's references to his recovery and release from the hospital. Following his reference to having left the hospital, the narrator then lists the cities he visited vicariously through the radio, as if the radio contributed to his recuperation. However, the narrator emphasized: "I have not been back to Billings nor have I visited Denver, Salt Lake City, Los Angeles or Minneapolis" (*SS-HLE* 385). In listing these as places he has never visited, the narrator almost sounds as if he is willfully placing as much distance between himself and the radio stations with which he distracted himself during his hospital stay in Billings. Combined with the first-person narration, the reference to Billings makes the narrator seem close to Hemingway himself, who spent weeks in a Billings hospital recuperating from the auto accident that badly damaged his writing arm. This first ending of the story makes it difficult to distinguish memoir from fiction.

Instead, in a process set forth clearly by Paul Smith, Hemingway repeatedly revised the ending of the story (*Guide* 290–91). For the second version of the conclusion, Hemingway added two pages of text by hand in pencil. In this case, after Cayetano and the first-person narrator exchange their wishes that the pain would "pass quickly," he designated a break with three asterisks, followed by three paragraphs, the last of which he crossed out (*SS-HLE* 385–86). In the first and longest of these additional paragraphs, the narrator recounts how the Mexican musicians "played the accordion and other instruments in the ward . . . the bells, the traps and the drum" (*SS-HLE* 386).[5] He then lists the other patients on the ward—a rodeo rider with a broken back, a carpenter who broke both ankles and wrists from a fall off of a ladder, a boy with a broken leg, and Cayetano Ruiz, "a small-town gambler, with a paralyzed leg" (*SS-HLE* 386). Hemingway preserved this list of patients in his final drafts, both the version published in the May 1933 issue of *Scribner's Magazine* and the version that appeared as the penultimate story in *Winner Takes Nothing*. The second paragraph of these three added paragraphs is a one-sentence summary: "It was not logical nor was anything that happened in that hospital logical nor was the time I spent there wasted" (*SS-HLE* 386). Presumably, the motley crew of bad-luck patients suffered from accidents that escape rational logic, but the time was not "wasted" for the patient narrating the story. As he revised the story, Hemingway did not retain this second paragraph added to the initial draft of the ending. Cutting that one-sentence paragraph made sense: in this second version the narrator leaves the reader with the paradox that there was no logic behind the patients' landing in the hospital and yet that he profited from the time spent there—perhaps by assembling materials for telling a story. Such a conclusion suggests that the narrator-writer has no compunctions about profiting from the patients' pain by composing stories about them.

In both the early typescript draft and a later manuscript fragment, Hemingway concluded this version of the ending with the sweeping statement that "assuredly it is not entirely to be solved by economics"—crossed out in the typescript, retained in a manuscript fragment (KL/EH folders 417 and

421; printed in *SS-HLE* 386–87). Such a general observation—perhaps a verbal swipe at Marxist writers, perhaps a side comment leveled at the economic writings of Ezra Pound—seems a polemic departure from the endings of Western novels or films.[6] In a sign of his uncertainty about the ending, he retained and then struck the sentence, "Assuredly it is not entirely to be explained by economics" (KL/EH folder 420; *SS-HLE* 389). In this version, Hemingway has softened the statement, first by replacing "solved" with "explained," then by striking that paragraph and continuing the story so that "economics" is not the last word.

Then, in what Paul Smith describes as "the third tentative ending" (*Guide* 290), for the first time Hemingway provided a weird twist on the Western shootout. This version is preserved in a handwritten pencil manuscript "on the back of Hotel Brevoort, New York, stationery" (KL/EH folder 421, cited in *SS-HLE* 387). In this draft, he departed from two elements of the Western, as illustrated by Owen Wister's *The Virginian:* a climactic shootout and a fadeaway shot of the hero riding off into the sunset. Even in the initial drafts, Hemingway ended "Gambler" without a shootout between the hero and the villain, such as occurs between the Virginian and Trampas near the end of Wister's novel. In this third tentative ending, Hemingway concludes with a discussion between the thin Mexican and the narrator (eventually, Mr. Frazer) about political revolutions. After listing in an interior monologue various opiums of the people, the first-person narrator asks the nurse, "Get me that little thin Mexican will you please?" (*SS-HLE* 388). What follows is a "shootout" of wits between the "thin Mexican" and the narrator on the subject of "La Cucaracha" as an "historic tune . . . the tune of the real revolution," according to the Mexican (*SS-HLE* 388). To this pronouncement of the song's anthemic power, the narrator responds skeptically, "Why should the people be operated on without an anaesthetic?" (*SS-HLE* 388). After the Mexican replies, "I do not understand," the narrator resumes the verbal sparring.

The showdown is anticlimactic, as neither Frazer nor the Mexican fires a fatal argument. Rather, the Mexican maintains his belief that the people "should be rescued from ignorance"—presumably, by the educational value of "La Cucaracha." Frazer maintains with equal conviction that "Education is an opium of the people" (*SS-HLE* 388). Not understanding Frazer's distinction between education and knowledge, the Mexican expresses his confusion for the second time: "I do not follow you." The narrator responds with an edgy, elusive, self-deprecatory comment: "Many times I do not follow myself with pleasure" (*SS-HLE* 388). The Mexican then asks, "You want to hear the Cucaracha another time?" Accepting the peace offering, Frazer replies, probably with a disingenuous compliment, "Play the Cucaracha another time. It's better than the radio" (*SS-HLE* 388). The Mexican clearly does not understand that, given the quality of lyrics Mr. Frazer has been listening to, his compliment is, at best, faint praise. So ends the typescript of the story—with "La Cucaracha" as the equivalent of the combatants throwing down their guns. This reconciliation in the third version of the story's ending is a far cry from the showdowns in the films *The Man from Texas, Martyrs of the Alamo,* and *The Virginian.* Neither the Mexican nor the first-person narrator is vanquished; neither walks away with a clear victory. The thin Mexican, verbally agile, is hardly a stereotypical *bandido* with bandoliers of bullets wrapped around his shoulders. Nor is the thin Mexican anywhere near the racist stereotype of D. W. Griffith's version of General Santa Ana. Rather, Hemingway's portrait of the thin Mexican in this version of the ending contributes to what Ann L. Putnam described as "vaudevillian comic dialogue" ("Opiates, Laughter" 161).

Hemingway revised the ending again in a fourth version that preserved much of this exchange between Frazer and the thin Mexican in a typescript for the story titled "Give Us a Prescription, Doctor" that appeared in the May 1933 issue of *Scribner's Magazine* (KL/EH folder 420, reprinted in *SS-HLE* 388–91). In this fourth draft, now a third-person narration with Mr. Frazer as the observer-writer, Hemingway incorporated much of the third ending. However, in this version, Hemingway established a clearer distance between the third-person narrator and Mr. Frazer. In the previous draft, there was a confusing shift in point of view after the Mexicans' musical performance: "In spite of this introduction of emotion Mr. Frazer went on thinking. I was thinking about the opium of the people" (KL/EH folder 421; *SS-HLE* 387). In the fourth draft of the ending, Hemingway stabilized the narrative point of view: "In spite of this introduction of emotion Mr. Frazer went on thinking. He avoided thinking all he could except when he was writing but now he was thinking about the opium of the people" (KL/EH folder 420; *SS-HLE* 389). Thus, even though Hemingway in this draft establishes Frazer as a thinking writer, he also maintains a sharper distinction between narrator and character. When the thin Mexican asks Frazer if he would like to hear "La Cucaracha" again, he responds with the same comment ("better than the radio") that ended the third version ("Give Us a Prescription" 278; discussed by Smith, *Guide* 290). The typescript to which Hemingway added pages handwritten in ink contains much of this newly revised version of the ending. However, even in this late version, Hemingway made at least four notable changes that appear in the story published in *Scribner's Magazine.*

First, Hemingway deleted what had been the narrator's reflection that nothing in the hospital was logical, "nor was the time I spent there wasted" (KL/EH folder 420; *SS-HLE* 389). Aside from deleting the first-person aspect of this passage, Hemingway also took out language suggesting that Frazer had gleaned profitable material for writing from his observations of his fellow patients. Furthermore, he cut the superfluous side remark about economics. Second, less noticeable is Hemingway's cutting from the typescript two sentences from the paragraph listing various opiums of the people. After including sexual intercourse as an opium for "some of the people," he deleted: "But not with a broken leg. No not with a broken leg" (*SS-HLE* 390). That seems a clear reference to Frazer's broken leg. Thus, in Frazer's interior monologue about these opiums, he excluded himself from those for whom sex could serve as an opiate. Perhaps Hemingway cut those sentences as seeming too obviously self-pitying.

Aside from these two deletions from the late typescript of the story, the version published as "Give Us a Prescription, Doctor" illustrates Hemingway's craft of revision by addition. The list of opiates in the Key West typescript included "Ambition . . . along with a belief in any form of government" (*SS-HLE* 390). In "Prescription," Hemingway added "new" before "form of government," so that Frazer's broadside focused on popular enthusiasm for "new" political movements. Then he added three sentences to the text of the typescript: "What you wanted was the minimum of government; always less government. Liberty, what we believed in, now the name of a MacFadden publication. We believed in that although they had not found a new name for it yet" ("Give Us a Prescription" 278). Hemingway retained these sentences in "Gambler," as published in *Winner Take Nothing* (*CSS* 367). These added sentences portray Frazer as supporting minimal government, such as Hemingway advocated in a letter to Ezra Pound dated 22 July 1933, just a few months before the publication of "Gambler" in *Winner Take Nothing* in October 1933: "I hate the whole conception of the state with a small or a big s. . . . Wish to be let alone. The more you organize it the more officials the more beaurocrats [sic] the more lousy injustice and everybody working for someone else instead of themselves. Or for the machine" (*Letters* vol. 5, 443–44). Frazer's inward reflection about "less government" and "liberty" seems sincere. However, in his interior monologue, Frazer ironically connects the ideal of "liberty" to a "Macfadden publication" bearing that name, as if the ideal of liberty has become just another marketing device to sell magazines. As Nicole J. Camastra points out, in the magazine *Liberty* that he purchased in 1931, Bernarr Macfadden "suggested martial law and dictatorship as solutions to the nation's economic depression" (264). Hemingway's references to liberty and a "Macfadden publication" by that name are bitingly ironic additions to Frazer's meditation on opiates of the people.

Fourth, after conceding to the thin Mexican that "La Cucaracha" was "better than the radio," Hemingway added a paragraph in "Prescription" with three sentences of Frazer's interior monologue. These sentences did not appear in the ending of the typescript draft labeled with Hemingway's Key West post office box (folder 420; *SS-HLE* 388–89). Rather, Hemingway must have added this three-sentence paragraph after the typescript but before publication of the story "Give Us a Prescription, Doctor. The added paragraph ends "Prescription" on a dark note about political "opiates" as needed to soothe a populace bludgeoned and bloodied during the tyrannies that accompany revolutions: "Revolution, Mr. Frazer thought, is no opium. Revolution is a catharsis; an ecstasy which can only be prolonged by tyranny. The opiums are for before and after" ("Give Us a Prescription" 278). These three sentences reflect Mr. Frazer's cynicism about political revolutions as "prolonged by tyranny"—perhaps bearing in mind the Reign of Terror after the French Revolution, or the bloodshed during and after the Bolshevik Revolution. In the final version of "Gambler" published in *Winner Take Nothing,* Hemingway retained these sentences, while adding a fourth sentence that ends Frazer's interior monologue on an ironic note, as discussed below.

As Hemingway rewrote the ending of "Gambler" again and again, his revisions are generally accretional. That is, although in some revisions he cut material, the revisions tend to keep adding on to the story. Hemingway kept the story going with one afterthought following another: the "sinister lightness" of "La Cucaracha" leading to an edgy catalogue of the opiums of the people, leading to a conversation with the thin Mexican, leading to a reflection about revolution as a catharsis "prolonged by tyranny." As Mr. Frazer reflected in a paragraph after he listened to the Mexicans playing "La Cucaracha," "Usually he avoided thinking all he could, except when he was writing, but now he was thinking about those who were playing and what the little one had said" ("Give Us a Prescription" 278; *CSS* 367). Even that sentence is an expansion of a comparable sentence in the Key West typescript, where there was no reference to Frazer's thinking "about those who were playing"—that is, the musicians who had come to perform "La Cucaracha" for him (compare *SS-HLE* 389 with "Give Us a Prescription" 278 and *CSS* 367). As he revised the first, second, and third drafts of the ending, Hemingway increasingly centered the conclusion on Mr. Frazer's barbed reflections about political revolutions, various types of anesthetics, and the prophetic sense that the "ecstasy" of revolutions leads to the sharp pains of tyranny. Unlike Nick Adams in "Big Two-Hearted River," who can choke off his train of thinking, Mr. Frazer, without the distraction of the radio's tunes, cannot. Increasingly in each revision, Hemingway focused on Frazer's nocturnal thinking about revolutions and opiates for the masses, a far cry from the topics occupying the Virginian and his wife at the end of Wister's novel— "Western questions: irrigation, the Indians, the forests" (*The Virginian* 280).

Some readers might wish that he had ended the story at Cayetano and Mr. Frazer's farewell exchange—a rather sentimental and feel-good ending. Instead, with his final revisions to the ending, Hemingway added the list of badly injured patients on the same floor as Mr. Frazer. Then he incorporated references to the Mexican revolutionary song "La Cucaracha." He then added Frazer's extended interior monologue about Karl Marx's phrase "opium of the people," a phrase parroted earlier in the story by the thin Mexican: "It is alcohol that mounts to my head. Religion is the opium of the poor" (*CSS* 362). Hemingway then added Frazer's conversation with that Mexican. Instead of ending on a conciliatory note with the sympathetic, noble Cayetano, Mr. Frazer's final conversation is a combative exchange with the thin Mexican about revolution.

Hemingway wrote the final draft of the ending by adding it to the tear sheets from the story as it appeared in *Scribner's Magazine* that he used as the setting copy for *Winner Take Nothing* (Smith, *Guide* 290). On that tear sheet, he wrote another sentence and a final paragraph. The sentence is Frazer's commenting to himself about his thought that opiums serve as anesthesia before and after, but not during, a revolution: "He was thinking well, a little too well" (*CSS* 368). That critical self-reflection echoes his earlier remark that he usually "avoided thinking all he could, except when he was writing" (*CSS* 367). Here, without connecting his thinking and his writing, Frazer again implies that he is overthinking the significance of the thin Mexican's comments about "La Cucaracha." Thus, immediately following Frazer's sardonic comment about revolutions and tyranny, he includes a self-ironic note suggesting that he takes no refuge even in his clever cynicism. Although Cayetano is not physically present in this version of the ending, his spirit of self-mockery seems to be.

Then Hemingway added a final paragraph to this fifth revision of the ending—a continuation of Frazer's interior monologue that begins, "Revolution, Mr. Frazer thought, is no opium" (*CSS* 368). As he anticipates the departure of the Mexican musicians, he reverses his earlier comment that "La Cucaracha" is better than the radio: "They would go now in a little while, he thought, and they would take the Cucaracha with them. Then he would have a little spot of the giant killer and play the radio, you could play the radio so that you could hardly hear it" (*CSS* 368). As is the case with the endings of some of Hemingway's finest stories, this final draft leaves questions open and unanswered: What is the significance of the return of the radio as the ultimate anesthetic or self-medication? Will Rudy Vallée's singing "Betty Co-ed" soothe his thoughts and comfort Frazer's nerves? Is Frazer's turning to the radio, with a taste of "the giant killer" to spike the sounds, a surrender or a temporary relief?[7] Hemingway's revision by addition leaves readers with an ending where the gambler and the nun have both disappeared, and are silent, leaving the radio, accompanied by liquor, as the last refuge in Frazer's interior monologue about painkillers. Cayetano's ability to laugh at himself does not seem to be as strong a presence in the final version of the story's ending.

In both "Give Us a Prescription, Doctor" and the final version of "Gambler," Hemingway revised the ending by adding two paragraphs of interior monologue as Frazer continues thinking. Both paragraphs complicate the stereotypical ending of a Western with the extended "ride into the sunset" conclusion of Owen Wister's *The Virginian*. After he kills Trampas in the shootout and Molly relinquishes her threat to call off their wedding if he engages in the gunfight, the couple rides their horses to the location of a pine-sheltered island that the Virginian has selected for their wedding night. For pages in the novel's final chapter, they ride out of town, past "the last sign of wagon wheels," into "deep canyons" and toward the piney island. As Molly views the island for the first time, she focuses on the beauty of the landscape at sunset: "The sun was throwing upon the pine boughs a light of deepening red gold. . . . In this forerunning glow of the sunset, the pasture spread like an emerald" (*The Virginian* 271–72). Even once they are no longer riding far out of town, and have set up their camp, the couple "sat together, watching the last of the twilight and the gentle oncoming of the dusk" (*The Virginian* 273). Wister's novel imbues a highly charged romantic glow onto the sunset. The ending Hemingway wrote for "Gambler" could not be more different. In all of these endings—from the early typescript, through "Prescription," to "Gambler"—Mr. Frazer is riding nowhere. He is, presumably, lying in his hospital bed, thinking.

Hemingway's change in titles is a final element in his revising the story. In the first version of the story, the working title was "Three Ambitions," a title he cut from the story's early typescript (KL/EH folder 417; *SS-HLE* 371). Ironically, the most clearly ambitious character in the story is Sister Cecilia, whose ambition is to be canonized as a saint. Cayetano Ruiz, the gambler, is notably without lofty ambitions. The narrator's ambition is perhaps to write the story itself, but that is not clear. In a letter to Maxwell Perkins dated 4 January 1933, Hemingway referred to the story as one of the three he sent as submissions to *Scribner's Magazine* (*Letters* vol. 5, 310, 310n1). He referred to the story by its present title ("The Gambler, The Nun, and the Radio") in a letter to Perkins dated 6 February 1933, where he indicated that Pauline was typing the story. He gave its length as "about 19 pages of this foolscap double-spaced" (*Letters* vol. 5, 323). He referred to the story again in a cable to Perkins on 9 February 1933, in which he indicated that he "would like to let it lie for a week then cut to between five and six thousand [words]. Also working on title" (*Letters* vol. 5, 327–28). These letters strongly suggest, as was the case with "A Way You'll Never Be," that Hemingway was revising the story for months later than conjectured by Paul Smith (*Guide* 289–90). He enclosed the story in his letter to Perkins of 23 February 1933, in which he explained, "I had to wait on this to get the title right" (*Letters* vol. 5, 334). The title, as the story appeared in the May 1933 issue of *Scribner's Magazine,* was "Give Us a Prescription, Doctor." It did not take Hemingway long to decide that he had not gotten the title "right," as he claimed in his February 1933 letter to Perkins. In a letter to Arnold Gingrich dated 24 May 1933, Hemingway wrote: "You didn't have to tell me that title turned out lousily." He pledged that "it wont be called that in the book" (*Letters* vol. 5, 389). Likewise, in a provisional list of the stories for his next collection, Hemingway wrote Gingrich again on 7 June 1933 that he had restored the original title of "The Gambler, The Nun, and the Radio" (*Letters* vol. 5, 402). On the setting copy taken from the story as published in *Scribner's*, the title "Give Us a Prescription, Doctor" is crossed out by hand and replaced by "The Gambler, the Nun, and the Radio" (KL/EH folder 222). In a letter to Maxwell Perkins with a revised list of the stories, he again gave "The Gambler The Nun and The Radio" as the title of the final story in the collection, though he added that a story he was revising called "The Tomb of His Grandfather" might become "last in the book" (*Letters* vol. 5, 436–37).

Hemingway's revision of the title complemented his shift from first- to third-person narration. Instead of a self-pitying narrator asking a doctor for a stronger pain medication, Hemingway shifted the title to a more ambiguous, less personal title focused on the strange triad of the story—the gambler Cayetano Ruiz, the nun Sister Cecilia, and the radio that is the only voice that Frazer contemplates at the end of the story. By shifting titles, Hemingway also focused readers on the three-part structure of the story—with sections alternating between the gambler, the nun, and the radio. Not only did he change the title of the story for publication in *Winner Take Nothing*, but he added sentences that conclude the story with the final focus on the radio: "you could play the radio so you could hardly hear it" (*CSS* 368). That ending fits Hemingway's revised title. As Edward Stone notes, that new title gave the radio a prominent place—a place fitting an era when the radio became more and more prevalent as a medium for music, theater, presidential addresses, and commercial advertisements ("Hemingway's Mr. Frazer" 387).

In conclusion, Hemingway's affirming portrait of the Mexican gambler Cayetano works against the grain of negative portraits of Mexicans in many Westerns. In contrast to his critical portrait of the staid, shallow detective in "Gambler," Hemingway's Cayetano is a gambler who mirrors the writer Frazer's irreverence and sharp-edged humor. When praised by the writer Mr. Frazer as a philosopher, Cayetano responds: "No, hombre. A gambler of the small towns. One small town, then another, another, then a big town, then start over again" (366). Hemingway's gambler offers his life's story in fragments and repetitions and a chiasmus: "then another, another, then..." One "small town" led to another and then to a big town and then to another start: a new round of pushing a rock up a hill before it fell down again. The voice

of the gambler—a rolling stone—seems to echo Frazer's own life's story—
a writer in a hospital bed with a broken leg from falling off a horse listening
all night to tunes like "Betty Co-Ed" on the radio. Cayetano's and Frazer's
midlife, tumbleweed stories, whatever quest they were on in this strange
Western, seem to mirror one another.[8]

10

FROM "TOMB OF MY GRANDFATHER" TO "FATHERS AND SONS"

Hemingway ended each collection of his stories with a Nick Adams story: "Big Two-Hearted River" to conclude *In Our Time,* "Now I Lay Me" as the final story of *Men Without Women,* and "Fathers and Sons" to end *Winner Take Nothing* as its "anchor story" (Reynolds, *Hemingway: The 1930s* 138). His extensive revisions for each of these culminating stories provide a window into how carefully he crafted them. In revising "Big Two-Hearted River," Hemingway worked to capture Nick's American idiom, his watchful eye, and his keen sense of touch. In revising "Fathers and Sons," Hemingway enriched the portrait of Nick Adams as son and father with a lyrical elegy of the midwestern landscapes where his father and the Ojibway taught him. As Paul Smith observes, "No other manuscripts show more extensive and detailed revisions" (*Guide* 310). If Hemingway's fishing story "Big Two-Hearted River" portrays Nick Adams in solitude, "Fathers and Sons" is a story crowded with a father's evening memories of *his* father, memories of his sexual initiation, and memories of his son's innocent questions. In a letter to Hemingway dated 22 September 1933, Maxwell Perkins wrote: "I do not think you ever wrote a better story than 'Fathers and Sons'" (Bruccoli, *Only Thing* 200). Until recently, however, "Fathers and Sons" has received relatively little attention from scholars writing about Hemingway.[1] His revisions of "Fathers and Sons" show that Hemingway, again at the height of his art, transformed what began as a tale about a sexual initiation into a comical and elegiac story about Nick Adams's recognition of his responsibilities as a son remembering his father, as a man remembering the Ojibway people, as a father responding to his son, and as an artist crafting his work of art.

This chapter will focus on Hemingway's careful and complex process of drafting and revising his story, examining closely six different stages in his composition: (1) the earliest draft, a pencil manuscript fragment (KL/EH folder 382, printed in *SS-HLE* 404–5); (2) two different fragments in pencil on two different numbered pages (KL/EH folder 384, printed in *SS-HLE* 413–14); (3) an extensive pencil manuscript titled "The Tomb of My Grandfather," twenty-five pages (KL/EH folder 383, printed in *SS-HLE* 405–13); (4) a typescript, fourteen pages, with three inserted, handwritten pages (folder 385a, printed in *SS-HLE* 415–24); (5) the "setting" copy for "Fathers and Sons" as located with the "setting" copies for the stories collected in *Winner Take Nothing* (folder 222); and (6) the print edition, including material not present even in the handwritten revisions to the setting copy. This section of the Hemingway Library Edition of *The Short Stories* is one of the most complete publications of handwritten pencil manuscripts and typescripts with pencil corrections. Thus, one can examine closely the multiple stages of Hemingway's composition of this complex, powerful story. The narrative structure of "Fathers and Sons" is as intricate and nuanced as any in Hemingway's collection of stories—with at least nine different flashbacks in Nick's memories, several different interior monologues during which Nick reflects upon his responsibilities as a father and as a son and as a writer, and a two-part conversation with his son presented mostly as dialogue. Thus, the extent of Hemingway's careful revisions and additions over several different stages of composition reflects the richness evoked by the plural nouns in its title. Hemingway's revisions to "Fathers and Sons," like his extensive work in composing "Big Two-Hearted River," are consummate examples of artistic craftsmanship.

FOLDER 382: THE EARLIEST FRAGMENT

In the draft that Paul Smith determined was "clearly the earliest fragment" (*Guide* 307), Hemingway begins with the first-person, unnamed narrator remembering his father's keen eyesight and his teaching about sexual life. With three "et ceteras" in the sketchy fragment, Hemingway seems to be jotting down quickly two traits of his father that the story eventually develops: "My father was etc eyes built like etc but all he ever told me about sexual life was that etc" (*SS-HLE* 404). This early draft presents several aspects of the narrator's father that Hemingway picks up in the story. For instance, the narrator mentions part of his father's practice in teaching him to hunt was to limit him to three gun shells a day: "My father used to give me three shells because he said it was all right for a boy to hunt all day but ~~not to~~ that you'd never learn to hunt if you had lots of shells" (*SS-HLE* 404). With that sentence the narrator adds a trait about his father that becomes crucial to the story—the father's legacy of teaching his son to hunt.

In the final paragraph of this early draft, Hemingway circles back to consider what he learned from his father. He ends by presenting the gist of a conversation with his father as free indirect discourse: "when I asked him what the Indians were like when he was a boy he said that ~~they~~ he had very good friends among them, that he was very fond of them and that they called him We-Tek-Ta-La which means Eagle Eye" (*SS-HLE* 405). Having returned to his memory of his father's keen vision, the narrator now includes his father's memory of mutual affection and respect for the Ojibway. He ends this early sketch by including their Ojibway nickname for his father. After introducing his memories of his father in the first fragment, the narrator then brings the narrative into the present, as answering his son's spoken question about what it was like growing up with the Ojibway people when he was a boy. He quotes his son's question directly in language very close to the version of the story published in *Winner Take Nothing:* "what was it like Papa when you lived with the Indians when you were a boy?" Only missing from this early draft is the son's placing his father's childhood as the time when he "used to hunt with the Indians" (*SS-HLE* 404; *CSS* 375). By adding the son's comment about the time Nick used to hunt with the Ojibway, Hemingway suggests that Nick actively shared hunting experiences and was not just "living aside" (or nearby) them. The addition also sets up the irony that, for teenage Nick, hunting squirrels became a pretext for his sexual initiation.

The center of this early draft focuses on the narrator's spoken conversation with his son and on his silent memories about the role of "an Indian girl named Prudy Gilby" in his sexual education. In a conversation that Hemingway did not retain in subsequent drafts, the narrator's son asks him, "What happened to her?" In the story's final version, Hemingway includes neither that question nor the narrator's crude answer, "She went away to be a hooker." From this early draft he strikes even the narrator's silent reflections about what happened to Prudy: "nor how it was when I came back and found she was a whore, a hooker we said then" (*SS-HLE* 404). This draft *does* include an early version of what becomes the inward memories of Prudy's sexual power. With her "quick searching tongue," recounted in language that Hemingway retains in the final draft, "she did first what no one has done better" (*SS-HLE* 404; *CSS* 375). Even as early as this initial sketch for the story, the narrator contrasts what he learned about sex from his father's lessons and what he learned from direct experience with Prudy Gilby.

Thus, in the middle of this draft is the evocative and explicit interior monologue in which the narrator remembers what he cannot tell his son—his sexual initiation with a girl whose "thin brown legs, flat belly, hard little breasts" are physical memories in the published story that are present in this very first draft (*SS-HLE* 404; *CSS* 375). From its beginning, this untitled draft is focused on sexual activity as a revelation, an awakening to flight in a story that, unlike "Summer People," Hemingway decided to publish. Perhaps most striking of all the elements in this original version of "Fathers and Sons" are the references to the smell of Prudy/Trudy.[2] If one bears in mind the offensive references that the Garners make comparing the odor of Native Americans to that of skunks in "Ten Indians," then the narrator's lyrical evocation of Trudy's smell could not be more distant from the Garners' racist derision (see *CSS* 253–57). In "Ten Indians," Nick Adams's friend Carl Garner taunts him about his knowledge of skunks: "You ought to. You got an Indian girl" (*CSS* 254).[3] Neither the first-person narrator of this first draft, nor the younger Nick, nor his father in the published version, speaks or thinks with similar derision about Trudy. Likewise, in "Fathers and Sons" an older Nick explicitly rejects "any jokes about them nor old squaws" (*CSS* 376). In "Fathers and Sons," a mature and adult Nick Adams strongly rejects either racist jibes at, or stereotypes of, Ojibway women.

Furthermore, even in this earliest draft, Hemingway portrays Nick as remembering the "smell" of the Ojibway people, not just Trudy, as powerfully redolent. Hemingway's language in the print version of the story is close to the language in this earliest draft referring to the narrator's memory of the Ojibway: "all the empty pain killer bottles and the flies that buzz do not turn against the sweetgrass smell, the smoke smell" (*SS-HLE* 404; *CSS* 376). Their smell is what the narrator knows from direct experience and remembers fondly. Thus, this original draft contains at least five kernels of "Fathers and Sons"—the narrator's memory of his eagle-eyed father, his memories of his father's "nonsense" about sexual life, the narrator's son asking him about his youthful experiences with the Ojibway, the narrator's interior monologue about his sexual initiation, and his memory of the fragrant aroma of the Ojibway.

In the final version of the story, Nick Adams's son does not speak until the concluding section of the story, breaking what until that point are mostly flashbacks cast as interior monologues. In contrast, this earliest fragment ends with the narrator's asking himself his own version of his son's question; that is, the narrator wonders what *his own* father knew "besides the nonsense he fed me" (*SS-HLE* 405). In the beginning of this fragment Hemingway makes clear that the "nonsense" from his father was "about sexual life." The narrator answers his own question about what his father knew by attributing his father's useful knowledge to his keen, inborn eyesight and to his connection with the Ojibway people. This fragment presents the narrator's conversation with his son first, then his inward meditation; in the version of the story published in *Winner Take Nothing*, these elements are reversed.

NEXT FRAGMENTS: FOLDER 384

In what Paul Smith identifies as the "second fragment" of the story, Hemingway actually has *two* separate fragments, one numbered page 5 and one on page 6 of a manuscript (KL/EH folder 384; *SS-HLE* 413–14). Although Smith quotes at length from the first fragment and almost all of the second fragment (*Guide* 308–9), he does not point out that Hemingway crossed out *all* of the first fragment on page 5 but did not cross out the second fragment on page 6. Smith characterizes the first fragment as approaching "uncontrollable rage" (*Guide* 308). One can see why, even at this early stage, Hemingway canceled entirely a passage in which the narrator advises his father to "get rid of" his wife "with whom he has nothing in common" (*SS-HLE* 414). The narrator is downright brutal in his portrait of a marriage dominated by a woman who is full of "utter selfishness and hysterical emotionalism." He is equally brutal in advising the husband to try physical beating before a complete break: "He might try to whip her first but it would probably be no good" (*SS-HLE* 414). The narrator's anger at the mother is searing as he hears her remind him how "mother carried you, darling, over her heart all those months and her heart beat in your heart" (*SS-HLE* 414). The narrator virtually snarls back at her sentimental memory of their mutual heartbeats.

The frostiness in the Adamses' marriage, a chill that Hemingway keeps relatively under the surface in "The Doctor and the Doctor's Wife" and in "Now I Lay Me," is in this manuscript fragment an iceberg jutting clear out of the frigid waters. This fragment illustrates how much Hemingway left out of the published version of "Fathers and Sons" about the marriage of Nick's parents.

This second fragment begins after the narrator's reference to his mother's "heartbeat" speech, the last sentence in the first fragment that Hemingway crossed out with a big X. The narrator then shifts to the memory of his father: "I've seen him when we used to row in the boat in the evening, trolling, the lake quiet, the sun behind the hills" (*SS-HLE* 414). The second fragment in folder 384, not crossed out, continues from there. In the second fragment, the first-person narrator is baffled by his father's surprising weakness. Tired from rowing a boat in the evening, the father asks the narrator to take over the rowing "because it was uncomfortable." The father in this fragment seems to feel "uncomfortable" out of heat exhaustion and fatigue. The narrator cites his father's explanations for his discomfort: "It's the hot weather," he said. "And the exercise" (*SS-HLE* 414). The unnamed first-person narrator then describes himself in a boat looking at his father sitting in the stern, a reversal of the position of Nick and his father in a boat at the end of "Indian Camp." The narrator describes his father as black: "sitting in the stern the big bulk of him, the blackness of him, he was very big and his hair and beard were black, his skin was dark and he had an indian nose and those wonderful eyes" (*SS-HLE* 414). Although the narrator wonders why his father turned over the oars to him, he seems more focused on his father's bulk, black skin color, and Ojibway features than on his physical weakness.

The narrator's vision of his father as other than a white, middle-class professional stands in tension with his comical summary of his father's sexual education as tantamount to claiming that "masturbation produced blindness, insanity and death" (*SS-HLE* 414; *CSS* 371). The fragment ends as the narrator indicates that his father's warning about prostitutes and venereal disease came when they were squirrel hunting. The passage in folder 384 ends in midsentence: "and once when we were squirrel" (*SS-HLE* 414). In this early fragment, as is the case in the published story, squirrel hunting provides the context for his father's lectures about the maladies to follow sexual misconduct. These lectures are what seemed to make the narrator begin "to feel uncomfortable" in his father's presence—a word repeated to describe first the father's physical discomfort rowing in the heat, then the narrator's feeling "uncomfortable" when his father began to lecture him about how "prostitutes gave you gonorrhea and syphilis" (*SS-HLE* 414). In this second fragment, Hemingway suggests the fragility and weakness of the narrator's father—first physically, as he seems too tired or weak to row, and then emotionally, as his efforts to educate his son about sex seem feeble and lead the narrator to awkward discomfort. As he revised his story, Hemingway completely removed the first fragment about the narrator's parents' marriage. He preserved part of the second fragment now in folder 384, both fragments printed in the Hemingway Library Edition. Although he did not retain the vivid portrait of his father's black beard and black skin color in describing Dr. Adams's "big frame" (*CSS* 370), he did include, almost verbatim, the father's lessons about the dire consequences of masturbation and sex with prostitutes (*CSS* 371). This second fragment in folder 384 deepens the contrast presented in the earliest draft between the narrator's admiration for his father's keen sight and his bemusement at his sexual teachings. Taken together, these two fragments show Hemingway's early ventures in this story toward a stark narrative of his parents' marriage.

"THE TOMB OF MY GRANDFATHER": FOLDER 383

The first full-length pencil manuscript of the story, still in the first person but for the first time identifying the narrator as Nicholas and Nickie, is titled "The Tomb of My Grandfather" (KL/EH folder 383, printed in *SS-HLE* 405–13). Hemingway's correspondence suggests how carefully he was revising the story. Hemingway probably referred to "Tomb of My Grandfather" as the "24 page story" that he mentioned in his letter to Maxwell Perkins on 13 June 1933 as having finished the previous day (*Letters* vol. 5, 410). In a later letter to Perkins, dated 13 July 1933, Hemingway referred to "The Tomb of His Grandfather" as "one more story I am re-writing," the same story he described as "[f]inished" in his letter of 13 June. That is, a full month after he had written Perkins that he had completed "Tomb," he told his editor that he was still revising the story.

This twenty-five-page manuscript incorporates key elements of the earlier fragments: the contrast between the father's eagle eyes and advice about masturbation and prostitutes, Trudy's sexual initiation of the narrator, and the memory of the fragrant "sweet Indian smell of sweetgrass"—

evocative language in the earliest manuscript largely retained in "Tomb of My Grandfather" (*SS-HLE* 404, 412). Hemingway continues to tell the story of "Tomb" in the first person and refers to his father as "my father." However, for the first time, "The Tomb of My Grandfather" begins with the narrator's driving in a car. For the first time, this draft presents the initial setting as the "main street of this town" surrounded by fields of cotton, corn, red sorghum, soybeans, and peas, locating the start of the story in the South (*SS-HLE* 405–6). In the opening paragraph of "Tomb," Hemingway suggests a contrast between this landscape—"It was not my country" (*SS-HLE* 405)—and the midwestern landscapes of the narrator's past, both those landscapes in which his father and he hunted, and the forest where he spent time with the Ojibway. In this draft, Hemingway crossed out by hand "The boy was asleep," the only reference in the first paragraph to his son (*SS-HLE* 405). In this opening paragraph he also did not refer to his son's presence (here named "Schatz," as in the story "A Day's Wait") until the end of the story (*SS-HLE* 412; *CSS* 332). The conversation between Nick Adams and his son at the end of the story in this draft is almost identical with the ending in the print story, except that in "Tomb" the narrator's son doesn't mention his grandfather's gift of an air rifle (compare *SS-HLE* 412 and *CSS* 376). In short, although he has not yet made "Tomb" a Nick Adams story narrated in the third person, Hemingway has much of the frame of the story in place.

Noteworthy is that, once he introduces the narrator's son as a speaker near the end of "Tomb," Hemingway renders the conversation almost exactly as it remains in the print version, from "You might not like them but I think you would" (*SS-HLE* 412). And the ending of "Tomb" is identical (punctuation aside) to the print version—from the son's question, "Why do we never go to pray at the tomb of my grandfather?" to the father's answer at the end: "I can see we'll have to go" (compare *SS-HLE* 413 with *CSS* 376–77). Unlike his process of revising "Big Two-Hearted River," when Hemingway made major deletions and revisions to his initial ending of the story, with "Fathers and Sons" he settled firmly on the ending of the manuscript draft titled "Tomb of My Grandfather." The final revisions of "Fathers and Sons" leave intact most of the conversation when Nick Adams, instead of being guided by his father, becomes the struggling mentor for his son.

In comparison to the earlier drafts and fragments, Hemingway fleshed out his portrait of the narrator's father substantially in "Grandfather's Tomb." For instance, to the initial references to his father's eagle eye, he added the flashback of a vignette about Dr. Adams asking Nick if he can see that his sister has run the flag up the flagpole and about his father's counting sheep that, to the narrator, appear dimly as "grey on the grey green of the hill" (*SS-HLE* 406). In the final draft Hemingway revised this phrase to sharpen the picture of what Nick barely sees: "They were a whitish patch on the grey-green of the hill" (*CSS* 370). This vignette sharpens the portrait of the father's keen vision, in contrast to his son's cloudy sight. However, Hemingway included in "Tomb" three different images of the narrator's father's physique that he deleted when revising the story. First, the narrator compared his father's build to pictures of James J. Jeffries, a heavyweight boxing champion who was coaxed out of retirement as the "great white hope" to face Jack Johnson, the African American heavyweight who defeated him (Rozen n.p.). In the "Tomb" draft, Hemingway deleted and then restored that comparison: "and he was built, then, like pictures of James J. Jeffries in the Police Gazette" (*SS-HLE* 407). The second image was of his father's fatigue when rowing a boat on a lake in the hot weather—the anecdote from the second fragment in folder 384, discussed above. In the third reference, Hemingway's narrator remembers his father, "undressed to go swimming," as "built like the pictures of James J. Jeffries (*SS-HLE* 408). He crossed out that sentence in the "Tomb" manuscript. By deleting such comparisons from his final version of the story, Hemingway keeps the focus on Nick's father's temperament and vision more than on his physique or weakness. Rather, as in the final draft of the story, the narrator emphasizes most of all his father's eyes: "They saw much farther and much quicker than the human eye sees" (*SS-HLE* 406). In the published version, Hemingway retained that language and added two comparisons: "They saw much farther and much quicker than the human eye sees. . . . His father saw as a bighorn ram or as an eagle sees, literally" (*CSS* 370). Rather than compare his father's physique to a heavyweight boxer's, Hemingway chose to emphasize his father's extraordinary vision as his most memorable physical trait. In adding the comparisons, he also connected his father's eyesight to the natural world of rams and eagles.

Likewise, in addition to the father's attempts at sexual education in the earliest fragment of the story, Hemingway included two comical anecdotes as narrative flashbacks in "Tomb." First, the father's definition of "bugger" as "a man who has intercourse with animals" leads the narrator to think "of various animals but none seemed attractive or practical"—language in the anecdote added in "Tomb" that Hemingway retained (*SS-HLE* 408; *CSS* 371). The father's reference to bestiality ironically incites, rather than curbs, his son's sexual imagination. That the father seems unaware that "bugger" is also British slang for sodomite is surely part of the humor added to the story in this manuscript version. Ironically, the young Nick's swearing at the squirrel that bit him as a "bugger" also fits the sense of "bugger" as a crude, homophobic insult.[4] The references to the flagpole scene and to the father's definition of "bugger" intensify the contrast between the father as keen hunter and as fumbling sex educator.

Even funnier is the anecdote associating Enrico Caruso with "mashing" —a vignette present for the first time in "Tomb." Hemingway's comical reference is to the arrest of Caruso for allegedly groping women in the Monkey House of the Central Park Zoo in 1906, a front-page story in the *New York Times* when Hemingway was a young boy ("Signor Caruso"; see also Bauerle 140n2). In portraying the father's account of "mashing" as "the most heinous of crimes," Hemingway presents the mature narrator as mocking his father's hyperbole. His portrait of the narrator's reaction is laughable: as a boy, Nick assumed that Caruso did something "strange, bizarre and heinous to a beautiful lady with a potato masher" (*SS-HLE* 408). Thus, in language present for the first time in "Tomb," the first-person narrator "resolved, with considerable horror, that when I was old enough I would try mashing ~~perhaps~~ once at least" (*SS-HLE* 408). Again, his father's effort to curb his son's imagination only spurs his wayward thoughts. By striking "perhaps," Hemingway made the narrator's resolve even stronger and more comical. Thus, the two anecdotes about his father's sexual education contribute a level of humor present for the first time in "Tomb of My Grandfather."

Hemingway's original source for the anecdote may well be his father, the model for Dr. Adams, but another source for this story in his comical portrait of Nick's sexual education is probably James Joyce. In the "Sirens" chapter of *Ulysses,* Joyce puns on both meanings of "mash": as turning ripe potatoes into a liquid form of "mashed potatoes," and as sexually accosting another person.[5] At the same time as Leopold Bloom hears Blazes Boylan's "flick of whip" on his "mare's glossy rump" as he rides toward his assignation with Bloom's wife, Molly, Bloom "mashed mashed potatoes" as he dines in the bar of the Ormond Hotel (*Ulysses* 222). Bloom is mashing potatoes while Boylan rides a carriage toward Bloom's wife, whom he will "mash." Hemingway's recounting of the "mashing" incident with Caruso seems to follow Joyce in his sexual puns, albeit from the older narrator's viewpoint in bemusedly reflecting on the story about Caruso.⁶ Hemingway's jocular allusion to the Caruso "mashing" would seem to place Joyce over his father as his mentor in such matters of sexuality. Hemingway presents the narrator's remembering himself as an innocent American boy, caught in an intrigue that excites his imagination but eludes his understanding. In the manuscript of "Tomb," with the anecdotes of "bugger" and "mashing," Hemingway builds a comical portrait of a father's flawed teachings about sexual malpractice.

Conversely to ways that "Tomb" expands the portrait of the narrator's father, Hemingway kept out of the story a searing, graphic indictment of the father's marriage to his wife. In "Tomb" Hemingway again considered including—and then cut—references to the narrator's mother. On the bottom of page 4 of this manuscript, Hemingway crossed out with a large *X* a passage referring to the narrator's father as a "coyote" married to a "white French poodle"—another return to the topic of his parents' marriage that he struck out in the first of two earlier fragments preserved in folder 384 and that he deleted from the draft of "Tomb" now in folder 383 (*SS-HLE* 413–14, 407). In the earlier draft, the narrator's venom seems more directed at the mother's "utter selfishness and hysterical emotionalism" (*SS-HLE* 414). Initially in "Tomb," when Hemingway revisited his portrait of a dismal marriage, he adopted harsher, more searing language, particularly toward the father. Before striking out the passage, Hemingway has the narrator using language like "very nervous," "sentimental," and "cruel." In what would seem a caustic reference to the father's self-pitying, suicidal weakness, the narrator concludes: "he had too many emotions and when everything was gone to pieces he went in for martyrdom" (*SS-HLE* 407). The very next line after the entire passage that Hemingway deleted explains the cut. The first-person narrator, a writer, declares: "There are too many people alive for me to write about my father yet" (*SS-HLE* 407). Hemingway did not strike that sentence from "Tomb." As he revised the story, shifting to the third-person narration focused on Nick Adams, Hemingway incorporated a variation of that line (*CSS* 371).

In "Tomb of My Grandfather," Hemingway significantly expanded the conversations between Trudy and the narrator. The earliest draft of the story presented their speaking with minimalist dialogue, with her asking, "You want?" The narrator responds gutturally, "Uh huh" (*SS-HLE* 405). Before he used exactly the same words to present the beginning of their conversation, in "Tomb" Hemingway richly evoked the landscape, "virgin forest where the trees grew very high before there were any branches" (*SS-HLE* 409; *CSS* 372). With language he preserved verbatim in "Fathers and Sons," Hemingway set the narrator's sexual initiation in a paradise lost where he hunts squirrels with Trudy and her brother Billy and has sex with her. This powerful evocation of the lost landscape of the Ojibway serves in "Tomb," as in "Fathers and Sons," as a poignant transition between the comedy of his father's miseducation and the narrator's sexual initiation with an Ojibway girl. Among the many vivid aspects of this passage is the narrator's reference to the hemlock bark "piled in long rows of stacks roofed over with more bark like houses and the peeled logs lay huge and yellow where the trees had been felled" (*SS-HLE* 409; *CSS* 372). This sentence, with a few commas added later by Hemingway, is present at this point in "Tomb" as the Edenic setting in a forest of sexual freedom. Hemingway's comparison of the high stacks of bark to the roofs of houses seems ironic, connecting the narrator's sexual dalliances with the Ojibways' loss of their home. Furthermore, although the peeling of tree bark in "Indian Camp" may have as much to do with Native medicine as with industrial production (*CSS* 67), here the narrator explicitly indicates that the Ojibway people are stripping and selling their native forests to a "tannery at Boyne City" and leaving those forests "open, hot, shadeless, weed-grown slashing"—language in the print version that is identical to that in the "Tomb" manuscript (*SS-HLE* 409; *CSS* 372).[7] The setting suggests a contrast between Dr. Adams's pedantic, prudish sense of "heinous" sex crimes discussed with Nick during their squirrel hunting and the narrator's sexual initiation, in which hunting for squirrels seems a pretext for sex in the forest that is becoming a lost homeland for the Ojibway people.

A central section of "Tomb" returns to a focus of the earliest draft: the narrator's flashback to Trudy's encouraging him to have sex. Although this draft retains what Marc Kevin Dudley terms "broken descriptors" (60), Hemingway revised and deepened his portrait of Trudy in a scene of mounting intensity and climactic power. In "Tomb," she addresses the narrator as "Nickie," first by encouraging him to shoot a squirrel, later in insisting that the narrator leave her half brother alone (*SS-HLE* 409–10). (She is, incidentally, the first character in "Tomb" to address the narrator as "Nickie.") Her language when she first speaks is, admittedly, broken and crude: "You shoot Nickie. Scare him. We see him jump" (*SS-HLE* 409). Then, confirming her brother's reporting that Eddie, their older half brother, wants to sleep with Nick's sister, she says, simply, "That's all he want to do" (*SS-HLE* 410). Then, while placing her hand inside the narrator's pocket, Trudy insists that her half brother is not serious: "He's big bluff" (*SS-HLE* 410). To that point, she seems rather like a caricature of a young, barely articulate, sexually assertive girl.

Once the narrator enacts a scene where he shoots and then scalps Eddie Gilby, Trudy reacts strongly at this threat to inflict a stereotypically Indian execution. In "Tomb," the narrator repeats: "'I'd scalp him,' I said happily" and then "I'd scalp him and send it to his mother" (*SS-HLE* 410). In "Fathers and Sons," Nick's threat is even more forceful: "I'd" becomes "I'll scalp him" (*CSS* 373). Trudy's responses are as strong and insistent as Nick's are brutally demeaning. After Nick's threat to scalp Eddie, Trudy responds by fondling Nick as a means of persuasion: "She put her hand in my pocket" (*SS-HLE* 410). Hemingway is even more explicit in his print version that she "was exploring with her hand in Nick's pocket" (*CSS* 373). At the same time, she responds with a direct judgment about scalping that ironically subverts the stereotype of Native Americans: "'No,' said Trudy, 'That's dirty.'" And when Nick responds with even more savagery, "'I'd scalp him and send it to his mother,'" Trudy's reply is insistent, pragmatic, and personal: "His mother dead. . . . Don't you kill him Nickie. Don't you kill him for me." The language in this exchange is identical in "Tomb" and "Fathers" (*SS-HLE* 410; *CSS* 373). Despite her plea, Nick's threats become more brutal and dehumanizing: "After I scalped him I'd throw him to the dogs" (*SS-HLE* 410; *CSS* 373). Nick then acts out in pantomime how he would scalp "that half-breed renegade," perhaps the ugliest slur Hemingway ascribes to Nick in any of the Nick Adams stories, present verbatim in "Tomb" and "Fathers and Sons" (*SS-HLE* 410; *CSS* 373). Hemingway portrays the young Nick here as a racist brute. Billy's response to Nick's threats is morose. Based on his facial expression, Nick observes that he "was very depressed." After Nick's threats, Billy speaks ominously about Eddie in language present in both "Tomb" and "Fathers": "He better watch out" (*SS-HLE* 410; *CSS* 373). Although Billy does give voice to a possible warning he may carry to Eddie, his rather weak response underscores how forcefully Trudy checks and diverts Nick from his savage threats.[8]

As was the case with his manuscript of "Tomb," Hemingway's language in this scene of "Fathers and Sons" clearly shows Trudy's physically opposing Nick's blustering threats. As soon as the narrator imagines scalping Eddie Gilby, he brutally envisions "standing watching the dogs tear him" (*SS-HLE* 410; *CSS* 373). In all his stories about Nick Adams, this moment portrays Nick at his most savage. From watching the dogs tear Eddie's corpse to pieces in his murderous fantasy, the narrator suddenly senses himself falling: "I fell backwards against the tree, held tight around the neck Prudy holding, tight squeezing, and crying, 'No kill him. No kill him. No kill him. No. No. No. Nickie, Nickie, Nickie'" (*SS-HLE* 410). In the climax of this scene—arguably the climax of the entire story—Trudy has thrown herself upon Nick, pushed him back onto the tree, and begun strangling him to literally beat sense into him.

The major difference in this scene between "Tomb" and "Fathers and Sons" is the shift from first-person to third-person narration—from "I fell back" to "he fell backward" when Trudy reacts powerfully to Nick's threat. Indeed, in the print version Hemingway restored language that he struck from the manuscript of "Tomb." Whereas he crossed out "holding, tight" in the draft, he makes clear in the final draft that she began to strangle Nick—"held tight around the neck, Trudy holding, choking him" (*SS-HLE* 410; *CSS* 373). Her own physical action shifts, that is, from gently erotic caresses to actions and words that are among the most forceful of any of Hemingway's female characters. Her repetition of "No" six times is reminiscent of Jig's repeating "Please" seven times when she tells the man to "please stop talking" near the end of "Hills Like White Elephants" (*CSS* 214). That Nick presents the scene as if he fell backward, for no apparent reason, indicates how shocked he was, as suggested by his feeble question, also present in the "Tomb" draft: "What's the matter with you?" Trudy's response to his question is to repeat her three-word command: "No kill him" (*SS-HLE* 410; *CSS* 373). Her words suggest that nothing is the matter with her; what is wrong is Nick's threatening to kill Eddie Gilby. Trudy's speech may be fractured and basic, but it is clear, moral, and effective. Trudy's English is as forceful as any words spoken in the story. My reading of this scene in "Fathers and Sons" is quite different from Joseph Flora's reference to it as "an amusing account" of Nick as a "sexual athlete" (*Hemingway's Nick Adams* 241). Trudy is neither a mute spectator nor a passive receptacle for Nick's sexual sport. Rather, Hemingway has constructed this scene, first present in "Tomb" and largely preserved in "Fathers and Sons," as a powerful and mounting portrait of interracial conflict where an Ojibway girl revolts against a white boy's threat to scalp her half brother.

Even the young Nick shows signs of having been deeply affected by Trudy's vehemently repeated command. One sign of Nick's disturbance is his insisting that her brother must leave before their next act of sex. When Hemingway first mentions her as a partner for Nick, both in "Tomb" and in "Fathers and Sons," her brother serves as a kind of panderer, asking, "You want Prudy again?" (*SS-HLE* 409). When she affirms that she wants to have sex, Nick bids her come away: "Come on." When he objects to having sex in front of Billy, she responds, "He my brother" (*SS-HLE* 409). Since that part of the scene ends there, Hemingway implies Nick's acquiescence in having sex in the presence of Trudy's brother. After the three-way conflict about Eddie Gilby's interest in Nick's sister, Billy is far less accommodating, and Nick is insistent that Trudy send her brother away. Clearly perturbed by Nick's vicious threats about Eddie, Billy responds with disgust that his sister is willing to having sex with the young man who just threatened to kill their half brother. After Nick concedes that he will not kill Eddie "unless he comes around the house," Trudy seems to offer herself as a reward for his change of mind: "'That's good,' Trudy said. 'You want to do anything now? I feel good now.'" Nick responds that he will "do anything" only "If Billy goes away." Billy's response is one of the most obscene oaths spoken in the story: "'Son a bitch,' Billy said. 'I get tired this. What we come? Hunt or what?'" Hemingway preserved this exchange from the "Tomb" manuscript to "Fathers and Sons" (*SS-HLE* 410–11; *CSS* 373–74). Although rendered in broken English, Billy's response in "Tomb" and in later drafts evokes his anger at Nick and his sister. He is not quite "all but mute," as Marc Kevin Dudley claimed (60). He acquiesces and takes Nick's offer of a gun, but he swears, utters his frustration clearly, and asks harsh questions. Nonetheless, his half-mute response highlights Trudy's strong insistence on Nick's backing down from his threats.

Moreover, a simple narrative comment about this exchange suggests the adult Nick's distance from his boyish self. After the younger Nick's condition for sex, "If Billy goes away," the narrator adds, "I had killed Eddie Gilbey, then pardoned his life, and I was a man now" (*SS-HLE* 411). In "Fathers and Sons," Hemingway includes this sentence but shifts to the third-person point of view. In shifting the narrative point of view from the first person of "Tomb" to the third-person limited narrator, Nicholas Adams, Hemingway enhances his story by implying a distance between the younger and older Nick. The older Nick Adams seems to be mocking the ease with which, as a boy, he convinced himself of his manhood by a sexual conquest after acceding to Trudy's pleas in defense of her half brother. Hemingway's shift from the past perfect ("Nick had killed Eddie Gilby") to the past tense ("then pardoned him") to the imperfect ("he was a man now") is more effective in the third-person perspective of "Fathers and Sons" (*SS-HLE* 411; *CSS* 373). Nick even offers to let Billy take his gun—an offer that seems part of the sexual comedy after a deeply serious interracial conflict.[9] While most of this exchange is contained in the earlier draft, "The Tomb of My Grandfather," Hemingway's crucial change from the first person of "Tomb" to the third person in "Fathers and Sons" distances Nick Adams as the ruminating father from Nickie as an irascible, sexually aroused, and hypocritically blustering brother.

The final reference to Trudy is in the older Nick Adams's nostalgic memory of their sexual activity that he does not share with his son. All he tells his son about his hunting with the Indians is that he went "nearly every day all one summer" with Eddie Gilby and his sister Trudy (*SS-HLE* 412). Nick's reference to his daily contact is clearly limited to their going "all day to hunt black squirrels" (*SS-HLE* 412). When his son asks, "what were they like to be with?" Nick responds simply, "It's hard to say" (*SS-HLE* 412). Then comes his memory of his sexual initiation that he does not share with his son. Some of the language in his reverie is in the early sketch, and some of the language is present in a brief fragment that Paul Smith neither identifies nor discusses but that is printed in the Hemingway Library Edition (KL/EH folder 385; *SS-HLE* 414). In this fragment the narrator emphasizes what he could not tell his son: "brown legs, smooth belly and hard little breasts" (*SS-HLE* 414). In "Tomb," Hemingway added even more erotic language that makes the girl seem like a fantasized object of the narrator's sexual nostalgia: "I could not tell him of the plump brown legs, the flat belly, the hard little breasts, nor the quick searching tongue nor the flat eyes, nor how she first did what no one ever has done better" (*SS-HLE* 412). With its pulsating repetitions and rhythms, this interior monologue suggests the sexual arousal of the first-person narrator, not only in the past, but in his present reminiscence.

UNTITLED TYPESCRIPT WITH PENCIL CORRECTIONS AND THREE-PAGE PENCIL INSERT: FOLDER 385A

The next significant stage in Hemingway's composition of "Fathers and Sons" is the untitled fourteen-page typescript "with pencil corrections and a three-page pencil insert" contained in folder 385a of the Hemingway Collection at the Kennedy Library (*SS-HLE* 415). This typescript shifts the narrative point of view from first to third person. As is the case in the print version, Nicholas Adams is named in the winding first sentence of the story. In this typescript Hemingway introduces the presence of Nick Adams's son in the opening paragraph. This typescript takes out all of the narrator's references in "Tomb" to his father as physically resembling the boxer James Jeffries; likewise, the rowing scene in which the father feels too "uncomfortable" to row the boat is completely cut except for the reference to his father's counsel about masturbation, prostitutes, and venereal disease. To the anecdote about "mashing," in this typescript Hemingway has the young Nick imagining the "beautiful lady" as resembling "the pictures of Anna Held on the inside of cigar boxes," a fine touch he added to "Tomb" that he kept in the print edition (*SS-HLE* 417; *CSS* 371).

In this untitled typescript, Hemingway added a series of adverbs to intensify Nick's erotic memory of his sexual arousal: "quick searching tongue, the flat eyes, good taste of mouth then uncomfortably, sweetly, moistly, lovely, tightly, achingly, fully, finally, unendingly, never-endingly, never-to-endingly, suddenly ended the great bird flown like an owl in the twilight only it XXXX daylight in the woods and hemlock needles stuck against your belly" (folder 385a; *SS-HLE* 422). In "Fathers and Sons," Hemingway retained that rhapsodically erotic language, almost word for word, with its simile of an owl's twilight flight evoking sexual climax (*CSS* 375–76). Although this passage has been praised by some readers, it seems another example of Hemingway's tendency to use overwrought language to evoke sexual arousal and climax—for example, in the scenes with Robert Jordan and Maria in *For Whom the Bell Tolls* and the gondola scene in *Across the River and into the Trees*.[10] In this case, by adding twelve adverbs in the untitled transcript that were not present in "Tomb," Hemingway's process of revision seems to render a male-centered fantasy of erotic pleasure. The male narrator imagines himself flying like an owl, while the girl's eyes remain "flat," virtually lifeless.

On the other hand, some of the revisions and additions to this typescript that Hemingway made are striking in their references to Nick Adams as a conscientious writer. In the paragraph that begins "Like all men" (in both the typescript and print version), Hemingway added a crucial phrase to a sentence when Nick refers to himself as a writer. In the typescript, Nick refers to the "trap" that led to his father's death. Hemingway also restored some of the harsh language about Nick's father that he had crossed out in "Tomb": "Then too he was sentimental and like most sentimental people he was both cruel and abused" (compare *SS-HLE* 407 with *SS-HLE* 416). With just a slight change, Hemingway then included Nick's brief reference to writing in this typescript: "Nick could not write about him yet although he would later truly and fully, but the quail country made him remember him as he was when Nick was a boy, and he was very grateful to him for two things: fishing and shooting" (*SS-HLE* 416). By hand, Hemingway added to Nick's interior monologue the words, "although he would, later truly and fully" (*SS-HLE* 416; *CSS* 370). This addition contributes a moment of metanarrative early in the story, as Nick reflects upon his knowledge that he *would,* in the future, write the story of his father's death, even if he is not yet ready to do so in the present.

Later in this typescript, Hemingway adds another reference in Nick's interior monologue to his writing. After the sentence when Nick muses over his father's advice that he should keep his "hands off of people," Hemingway added, by hand, the following sequence of Nick's interior monologue in which he contemplates writing about his father: "On the other hand his father had the finest pair of eyes he had ever seen and Nick had loved him very much and when he thought about him it always made him sad. If he wrote it he could get rid of it. But it was too early for that. He would tell it all or tell nothing. So he decided to think of something else" (KL/EH folder 385a; *SS-HLE* 417). In this monologue, Hemingway's revisions evoke Nick's inner conflict as a writer—between the catharsis that writing could bring to "get rid of" his emotional pain, and the pain that his writing might bring to others—hence, making it "too early" for Nick to write the story yet. Hemingway leaves ambiguous what "it all" is that Nick could tell about his father beyond what he has already told about his bumbling efforts at sexual education. By deepening the portrait of the older Nick Adams as a writer with a sense of responsibilities, Hemingway enriches and complicates the portrait of the younger Nick in the woods with Trudy and her brother—or with his father hunting squirrels and receiving warnings about promiscuity.

In by far the most substantial revision to this typescript, Hemingway wrote "insert" in reference to three handwritten pages that he placed between two pages of the typescript (*SS-HLE* 421–22). He inserted these pages after the scene with the three-way exchange between Billy, Trudy, and Nick Adams about Eddie Gilby that ends with Trudy asking Nick for a "kiss on the face" (*SS-HLE* 421; *CSS* 374). After portraying the young Nick Adams as a racist boor, Hemingway's addition of another flashback humanizes Nick as loving the father who taught him how to fish and hunt but also as hating the father whose body odor repulsed him. His addition evokes Nick's revulsion—with almost the fury of Swift's Gulliver at the end of his travels—at the smell of his father. This handwritten addition complicates the portrait of the young Nick. His murderous hatred of the father who beat him for hiding the underwear he forced his son to wear seems a world apart from the tenderness Nick shows toward his own son at the end of the story. The three pages Hemingway added at this stage of composition are comparable to the three pages Hemingway added about Nick's watching a kingfisher fly above the trout stream in "Big Two-Hearted River." Yet there is a world of difference between the three pages added to "River" of Nick's silently and carefully observing a kingfisher and trout in a Michigan stream and the three pages added here with Nick's thinking of blowing his father's brains out with the gun in his hands.

In the first section of his handwritten additions, Hemingway presents a poignant elegy to Nick's father. In a winding sentence that begins, "His father came back to him," Hemingway wrote by hand a gorgeous word painting of the midwestern landscapes where he remembered his father in various seasons and places: "His father came back to him in the fall of the year, or in the early spring when there had been jacksnipe on the prairie, or when he saw shocks of corn, or when he saw a lake, or if he ever saw a horse and buggy, or in a duck blind; remembering the time a golden eagle dropped through the whirling snow to strike a canvas covered decoy, rising, his wings beating, the talons caught on the canvas" (*SS-HLE* 421).[11] Here Hemingway's repetition of "or" underscores how Nick remembers his father's presence in different seasons and in a variety of hunters' landscapes. The repetitions in this winding crescendo affirm that Nick's father *did* return to him in spirit when Nick found himself in landscapes like those where he learned to hear, see, and hunt the wild geese and ducks.

In this handwritten insertion, the sentence continues as Nick encounters the memory of his father whenever he saw landscapes reminding him of their times outdoors together: "and in all deserted orchards and in all new plowed fields, in all thickets, in small hills or when going through dead grass, whenever splitting wood or hauling water by grist mills, cider mills and dams and always with open fires" (*SS-HLE* 421). This lyrical passage remains virtually intact in "Fathers and Sons" (*CSS* 375). Hemingway evokes the landscape here as a nurturing presence—working mills, warming fires—that sets a different scene from the denuded setting at the beginning of "The End of Something," the burnt-out terrain at the beginning of "Big Two-Hearted River," or the "weed-grown slashing" that replaced the "virgin forest" of the Ojibway people in the earlier section of this story (*SS-HLE* 409; *CSS* 372). Here, in Nick's interior monologue, the mills are working, literally and figuratively, as these mills are the places where Nick remembers sensing his father's spirit. Among the most important revisions after the manuscript of "Tomb," this handwritten addition to the typescript, preserved in "Fathers and Sons," records Nick's flashbacks of his father's visitations.

This elegy is rhythmically rhapsodic, poetically memorializing how a variety of seasonal scenes helps Nick in his interior monologue as a father see *his* father. In his later fine-tunings of this passage, Hemingway retained its elegiac power. Aside from cutting the repeated phrase "in all" to tighten the list, he added the clause, "or when he saw, or heard, wild geese" right after "or if he ever saw a horse and buggy" (*CSS* 374). With the pause accenting "or heard," Hemingway emphasized that merely the honking of far-off geese sufficed to trigger Nick's memories of his father. Hemingway decided to begin a new sentence after referring to the eagle's talons "caught in the canvas." Instead of continuing the sentence with its memories of "deserted orchards" and "new ploughed fields," he began the next sentence with "His father was with him, suddenly, in deserted orchards" (*CSS* 374–75). After a fall harvest and before a spring planting, Nick's father appears to him with arresting force, particularly with the pauses around "suddenly" in the sentence he added. Hemingway portrays Nick's memories as lyrically bringing his father to his consciousness.

Even in this lyrically gorgeous set of recollections, Hemingway interlaced hints of Nick's severely qualifying his fond memories of his father. Hemingway's later decision to end the sentence with "the talons caught on the canvas" underscores Nick's associating his father with an eagle before the transition to the vignette about his father's underwear. Here Hemingway remembers his father as an eagle—not only as powerfully sharp-sighted and swift but also as misguided, striking a "decoy" and catching its talons on the decoy's canvas. At times the eagle's eye that Nick compares to his father's vision seems myopic. Then, in the handwritten insert to the typescript, Hemingway resumes Nick's recollection of his father's spirit present "whenever splitting wood or hauling water, by grist mills, cider mills and dams and always with open fires" (*SS-HLE* 421; *CSS* 375). In "Fathers and Sons," Hemingway then added a pair of pivotal transitional sentences not present in the handwritten addition to the transcript: "The towns he lived in were not towns his father knew. After he was fifteen he had shared nothing with him" (compare *SS-HLE* 421 with *CSS* 375). Furthermore, in "Fathers and Sons" Hemingway began a new paragraph with the transitional reference to his father's frosted beard (*CSS* 375). That image leads to Nick's recollection that his father also liked "to work in the sun on the farm" despite the fact that "in hot weather he sweated very much" (*SS-HLE* 421; *CSS* 375). By starting a new paragraph with the reference to Nick's father's beard, Hemingway placed more emphasis on the transition from nostalgic memories to Nick's recollection of the time his father whipped him and he felt like shooting his father.

Thus, the powerful elegy is a prelude to Hemingway's evocation of Nick's deep hatred of his father's smell in contrast to the sweet smell he remembers of the Ojibway people with whom he grew up. In this three-page handwritten insertion, Hemingway adds layers of narrative complication. After the part of the addition that memorializes his father's spirit in the landscape, Hemingway follows his pastoral elegy with a simple statement of deep ambivalence: "Nick loved his father but hated the smell of him" (*SS-HLE* 421; *CSS* 375). He then recalls the time when he was forced to wear his father's underwear: "it made him feel sick all day and he took it off and put it under two stones in the creek and said he had lost it" (*SS-HLE* 421). Aside from cutting the words "all day," Hemingway preserved that language in "Fathers and Sons" (*CSS* 375). When Nick came home from fishing and was caught lying about having lost his father's underwear, "he was whipped for lying" (*SS-HLE* 422; *CSS* 375). To this point Hemingway presented the scene with virtually the same words in the handwritten insert and in "Fathers and Sons."

The most salient change evident at this point is that Hemingway started a new paragraph in the published story to mark the transition between Nick's being whipped and sitting in "the woodshed with the door open, his shotgun cocked" (*SS-HLE* 422). To this sentence, in the published version Hemingway added that Nick's shotgun was "loaded and cocked"—stressing the live ammunition in the shotgun. Nick then remembers holding a gun in his hand and thinking, "I can blow him to hell. I can kill him" (*SS-HLE* 422; *CSS* 375). These simple thoughts echo Nick's earlier thoughts about killing

Eddie Gilby. Nick's holding the gun as he thinks of shooting his father is far distant from the restraint Dr. Adams shows in placing his shotgun behind the dresser in "The Doctor and the Doctor's Wife" (*CSS* 75). In these three pages Hemingway completed after "Tomb" and added to the typescript preserved in folder 385a, he set in Nick's interior monologue both elegiac and vengeful memories as a powerful juxtaposition of extreme emotional conflict between love and hatred. As Richard McCann puts it, Nick is "torn between love and guilt" about his father (267–68). Moreover, his portrait of Nick reflecting upon his memory of hating his father develops the story from an interracial conflict with Eddie Gilby into a fierce family duel, with the unmentioned mother below the surface.

"FATHERS AND SONS" SETTING COPY WITH HANDWRITTEN TITLE: FOLDER 222

The next substantial stage in Hemingway's composition of "Fathers and Sons" is the setting copy on which the author worked while assembling separate stories into the collection *Winner Take Nothing*. This setting copy is preserved in folder 222 in the Hemingway Collection of the Kennedy Library. Some of these are tear sheets of previously published stories, and some are typescripts. Hemingway left a story like "A Clean, Well-Lighted Place" intact without a single change in the tear sheet. On the other hand, to a typescript of "The Light of the World," Hemingway made a total of almost thirty changes by hand—none of which seems to alter the story substantially. To the typescript of "A Way You'll Never Be," Hemingway made roughly forty changes. Of all the stories he was assembling in *Winner Take Nothing*, the most substantial revisions came in the typescript of "Fathers and Sons," also contained in folder 222. In a letter to Maxwell Perkins dated 2 September 1933, Hemingway apologized for the extent of his late revisions on the setting copy: "Sorry I had so much correcting on last story. Please go over that *very carefully* before sending final proof. It's a damned good story—It's a good book. Having just read it for 6th straight time feel pretty good about it" (*Letters* vol. 5, 481). Hemingway's letter attests to how long and how hard he worked on revising "Tomb of My Grandfather" until it became "Fathers and Sons."

There are three layers of revision between the untitled typescript contained in folder 385a and the final version of "Fathers and Sons" printed in

Winner Take Nothing. First, there are the changes Hemingway made between the typescript contained in folder 385a and the typescript in the setting copy of folder 222. Second, there are the changes he made by hand via insertions and cross-outs on the typescript in folder 222. Third, there are the changes in "Fathers and Sons" evident only in the first edition of *Winner Take Nothing*—changes that were not present even in the handwritten revisions in the folder 222 typescript. In these late revisions Hemingway fleshes out the intense ambivalence in Nick Adams toward his father—vacillating between deeply fond memories and increasingly horrific details about his death. Nick's aversion to his father's smell contrasts even more strongly with Nick's positive memories of the smells he associates with the Ojibway people with whom he grew up. As Hemingway continued to revise "Fathers and Sons," he associated Nick Adams more with the Ojibway and the father of his childhood, and less with the father whose death he suggests was an act of violence plastered over by a mortician's cosmetic art.

A vital layer of revisions came in framing the scene with Nick, Trudy, and Billy with a reminiscence of his father *after* that scene in the forest. As discussed above, Hemingway first added the flashback in the three-page, handwritten insert to the transcript preserved in folder 385a, the next version after the manuscript "Tomb of My Grandfather." While a substantial part of that addition appears in the typescript of folder 385a, the later typescript in folder 222 includes several important revisions. For instance, Hemingway provided a smoother bridge from the fierce argument between Nick and Trudy to his tender memories of his father. After Nick and Trudy resolve their conflict, the transcript in folder 385a simply has a one-sentence transition: "Now as he rode along the highway in the car and it was getting dark Nick was all through thinking about his father" (*SS-HLE* 421). Then comes the three-page pencil insert that suggests, to the contrary, Hemingway was not ready to portray the adult Nick as "all through thinking about his father." To the setting copy in folder 222, Hemingway added, by hand, a sentence that remains in the print version: "The end of the day never made him think of him" (*CSS* 374). After editing this typescript used as the setting copy, Hemingway added another sentence to the final print version: "The end of the day had always belonged to Nick and he never felt right unless he was alone with it" (*CSS* 374). These two sentences—one added by hand to the typescript in folder 222, one added later—are richly ironic. Even as Nick banishes his father from his evening reveries, the paragraphs that follow show Nick's being haunted by the presence of his father in various scenes of hunting, wild life, and "cider mills and dams" (*CSS* 375), as if the father's spirit brings Nick back to pastoral landscapes. Hemingway bracketed the nostalgic lure of these memories with another pair of sentences that did not appear in any manuscript or typescript until the first edition of *Winner Take Nothing:* "The towns he lived in were not towns his father knew. After he was fifteen he had shared nothing with him" (*CSS* 375). Thus, Hemingway's last revisions of "Fathers and Sons" qualify Nick's romantic memory of his father as an eagle-eyed hunter visiting him in spirit. Instead, the revisions emphasize his firm recognition of the distance he had drifted from his father after his childhood, culminating in his break with his father when he was fifteen and ultimately ending with his father's funeral.

Hemingway makes that distance most palpable in the scene when Nick's father forces him to wear his underwear and Nick recoils at the smell. However, Hemingway's revisions to this scene also intensify the guilt Nick feels in remembering his thought of shooting his father, after his father had whipped him. In the transcript that he used as a setting copy for "Fathers and Sons," Hemingway inserted a paragraph symbol to set apart the paragraph beginning "Afterwards, he had sat inside the woodshed" (*CSS* 375). Setting that paragraph apart places an emphasis on its contents: Nick's murderous thought that "I can blow him to hell. I can kill him" (*CSS* 375). Furthermore, Hemingway's revisions make Nick's guilt at remembering these patricidal thoughts more graphic. He wrote by hand in the typescript contained in folder 222 the words "that his father had given him," preserved with another slight addition in the print version as "he felt a little sick about it being the gun his father had given him" (*CSS* 375). Again, Hemingway sharpens the contrast between young Nick, full of murderous fury, and the older Nick, wincing at having pointed at his father the very gun his father had given him for hunting. Such a contrast enriches the later conversation when Nick's own son asks him when he can have a gun, as the layers of fathers, guns, and sons deepen.

Moreover, Hemingway's late revisions paint an even starker picture of the death of Nick's father and of Nick's self-restraint as an adult writer. In one of the most important revisions that Hemingway included, for the first time, in the setting copy in folder 222, Nick refers to the indelible image of his father's dead face in his coffin: "The handsome job the undertaker had done on his father's face had not blurred in his mind" (*CSS* 371). In the typescript that served as the setting copy, the sentence ends there. At some later point, Hemingway continued the sentence with another layer of Nick's reaction to his father's death—his responsibility to others still living. In "Fathers and Sons," the entire sentence refers both to the undertaker's "handsome job" and to Nick's sense of duty: "The handsome job the undertaker had done on his father's face had not blurred in his mind and all the rest of it was quite clear, including the responsibilities" (*CSS* 371). That language, partly contained in the typescript of folder 222 of the Hemingway Collection, was not present in earlier drafts. At some point, while working with this setting copy, Hemingway added by hand the sentence "There were still too many people" (*CSS* 371). That is, there were still survivors alive who would be affected if Nick were to write the complete story of his father's death. Hemingway's revisions make clearer Nick's sense of responsibilities as a writer.

Finally, in three phrases included in his handwritten revisions to the transcript that served as the setting copy for "Fathers and Sons" in *Winner Take Nothing,* Hemingway conveys the retrospective affection the older Nick Adams feels in remembering Trudy, the girl who "did first what no one has ever done better" (*CSS* 375). First, after "hard little breasts" in the typescript in folder 222, Hemingway added by hand, "well holding arms" to make the blazon of Trudy's body include the very arms with which she had wrung his neck for threatening to scalp Eddie Gilby (*CSS* 375). That the thirty-eight-year-old Nick Adams remembers her arms as "well holding" suggests his fondness for her physical intimacy. Second, again by hand, Hemingway added to the typescript the word "smell" twice, leaving the sentence in the print version as: "all the pain killer bottles and the flies that buzz do not kill the sweetgrass smell and the smoke smell" (*CSS* 376). Nick's repeating "smell" amounts to a recollection of the Ojibways' fragrance as an antidote to his father's rancid odor. Whatever pain led to the prescription for painkillers, and whatever odors attracted the flies, the adult Nick seems soothed by the memories of the Ojibway companions of his childhood. In context, the reference to "smell" is not just to Trudy but to all of the Ojibway who have vanished: "So that when you go in a place where Indians have lived you smell them gone" (*CSS* 376). Nick's thought here mourns the passing of the aromas of the Ojibway in his childhood and regrets their replacement by the smells of his father's underwear.

Third, to the transcript in folder 222, Hemingway added by hand the following sentences in Nick's meditation on the loss of the Ojibway from his childhood home: "They all ended the same. Long ago good. Now no good" (*CSS* 376). These curt sentences are virtually the final thoughts the elder Nick Adams has in reflecting upon his childhood. Ironically, these late additions give the mature Nick Adams the fractured English that Trudy and Billy spoke earlier in the story.[12] "Long ago good. Now no good," sounds like a father's private meditation about a lost paradise of childhood before turning to his son with fatherly, simple, deferential comments. In a delayed response to his son's question about whether he would like the Ojibway people, Nick says, "You might not like them. . . . But I think you would" (*CSS* 376). When his son asks when he will be old enough to handle a shotgun and hunt by himself, Nick answers: "Twelve years old if I see you are careful" (*CSS* 376). After his son confides that he doesn't "feel good never to have even visited the tomb of my grandfather," Nick says, "I can see we'll have to go" (*CSS* 377). In each case, Hemingway presents a two-way conversation, not a father-to-son lecture. He portrays Nick as acceding to his son's wishes, but tentatively, until the boy's open desire to see his grandfather's tomb elicits an absolute concession. Nick Adams's final words in the story, presented as directly spoken, are caring words from a father in response to his son's queries and lament. Hemingway's handwritten additions to the typescript he used as the setting copy soften the portrait of the younger, angrier, more violent Nick to an older, tender, nostalgic father who tries to convey his affection for the Ojibway people to his son—and his poignant sense of their loss.

"FATHERS AND SONS": THE FINAL DRAFT

Hemingway's handwritten additions to the typescript that served as the setting copy for *Winner Take Nothing* were not his final revisions. In the setting copy, as noted above, Hemingway added by hand the sentence, "There were still too many people." However, in the setting copy the explanation "too many people for him to write it" is not present. Not until later did Hemingway add Nick's repeated explanation of why he could not yet write the story: "It was a good story but there were still too many people alive for him to write it" (*CSS* 371). This sentence is not completely present in *any* draft before it appeared in the first edition of *Winner Take Nothing*. Thus, only in his final version of the story does Hemingway make clear what kept Nick from feeling free "to write it" (the story of Dr. Adams's death)—his concern for the living members of his family. Moreover, earlier in that paragraph,

Hemingway added a sentence, not present before the print version, explaining why he would like to write about the death, at some point: "He had gotten rid of many things by writing them" (*CSS* 371). That sentence in "Fathers and Sons" follows a sentence that *was* in the setting copy: "If he wrote it he could get rid of it" (*CSS* 321). By adding the sentence referring to the "many things" that Nick had previously "gotten rid of," Hemingway suggests that writing had *already* served Nick as cathartic—perhaps alluding to stories like "Big Two-Hearted River," "Now I Lay Me," and "A Way You'll Never Be."

Now, with "Fathers and Sons," his father's death tempts Nick into writing about it to cleanse himself of his pain and anger. Thus, these two additions *after* the handwritten revisions made in the typescript used as the setting copy convey the conflict in Nick Adams as a son for whom the memory of his father carries responsibilities to his family *not* to record his father's cause of death. On the other hand, writing about his father's death would be cathartic, a way of setting troubling memories to rest (Meyers 249; Young 61). However, he had to consider the feelings of other "people alive," his family members. Only in the version published in the first edition of *Winner Take Nothing* does the sentence that begins "The handsome job the undertaker had done" end with the words "and all the rest of it was quite clear, including the responsibilities" (*CSS* 371). This carefully crafted paragraph portrays the older Nick—even more clearly than in the earlier typescripts—as a mature writer aware of his responsibilities about what to tell and what not to tell now. That portrait of Nick as an adult writer is a vital prelude to the depiction later in the story of the much less responsible younger Nick who blusters about scalping Trudy's half brother to protect his sister and his sense of racial purity. Hemingway's final revisions to "Fathers and Sons" balance such bravado in the younger Nick with the older, more considerate writer Nicholas Adams.

At this point it can be helpful to slow down and compare the context and content of Hemingway's references to Nick's ambivalence as a writer between the typescript present in folder 385a and the published version of "Fathers and Sons." In both the typescript and the published version, the passage is in the same paragraph as the one where Nick contemplates his father's warnings against masturbation and sex with prostitutes. Despite Nick's clear reaction against his father as sexual educator, Hemingway wrote: "On the other hand his father had the finest pair of eyes he had ever seen and Nick had loved him very much and when he thought about him it always made him sad. If he wrote it he could get rid of it. But it was still too early for that. He would tell it all or nothing" (KL/EH folder 385a; *SS-HLE* 417). In this earlier draft, Nick is much clearer in his interior monologue about what he admires—his father's eyes—than about what "it" is that he would like to "get rid of" through the cathartic process of writing. In the published version of the story, Hemingway intimates more clearly that "it" involves his father's death: "If he wrote it he could get rid of it. He had gotten rid of many things by writing them. But it was still too early for that. There were still too many people. So he decided to think of something else. There was nothing to do about his father and he had thought it all through many times. The handsome job the undertaker had done on his father's face had not blurred in his mind and all the rest of it was quite clear, including the responsibilities" (*CSS* 371). The most striking difference between the passage in the typescript in folder 385a and the final version is Nick's reference to the undertaker's "handsome job" cosmetically preparing "his father's face" for a casket viewing. Without specifying exactly what had happened to Nick's father, and by including other references in the story to his father's having "died in a trap," Hemingway implies that Nick's father's death was not natural or accidental. As he revised the typescript draft, Hemingway portrays Nick's discretion in writing only so much about his father's death as even more clearly discrete and poignant.

At the same time as Hemingway's final layers of revision portray Nick Adams as a self-conscious son and writer, they also offer more grotesque details about Dr. Adams's appearance at his funeral. Even as he depicts Nicholas Adams as a writer restrained about what to include about his father's death, Hemingway added, after editing the transcript in folder 222, details that strongly suggest a gunshot wound to Dr. Adams's head: "He had complimented the undertaker. The undertaker had been proud and smugly pleased. But it was not the undertaker who had given him that face. The undertaker had only made certain dashingly executed repairs of doubtful artistic merit" (*CSS* 371). This entire excerpt does not appear until the publication of "Fathers and Sons" in the first edition of *Winner Take Nothing.* Hemingway's repetition of "the undertaker," with particular emphasis on his smug pride in his cosmetic art, suggests that his art is a sham—one can see its marks and one can see the signs of the wound it does not completely efface. Even though Hemingway restrains from identifying how Nick's father died, he implies that a gunshot wound led to "dashingly executed repairs," an art that Nick ponders mockingly.[13] Nick admires his father's face as having fashioned itself, more than the false face doctored up by an undertaker's cosmetics: "The face had been making itself and being made for a long time. It had modeled fast in the last three years" (*CSS* 371). Again, this language is not in the text of the setting copy. Hemingway must have added this passage even after marking that copy by hand. The phrase "modeled fast" ironically implies a swift decline in the face of Nick's aging father, as opposed to the mortician's cosmetic illusion. Given the number of references Nick makes to his own writing, implicit in his rather sarcastic reflections is that he has a scant regard for the mortician's cosmetic art.[14]

CODA

In Nick's conversation with his son at the end of the story, the shift in verb tenses marks how central the memory of past time and anticipation of future time is to the story. The very first fragment of the story is dominated by the past tense, as in the question the narrator's son asks him, "What was it like, Papa" (*SS-HLE* 404). However, even in this first draft, the first-person narrator reflects on his awareness in the present of what has been lost from the past: "So now if I go in a place where Indians have lived I smell them gone" (*SS-HLE* 404). With the narrator's conversation with his son at the end of "Tomb of My Grandfather," Hemingway adds the future conditional that becomes so central to the end of the story. Without so much as a transition from his memory of sex with Trudy, the first-person narrator says to his son about the Ojibway, "You might not like them but I think you would" (*SS-HLE* 412). With considerably more transition to prepare for that line, Hemingway keeps the same "might . . . would" sentence in the typescript in folder 385a (*SS-HLE* 423) and in the published version of "Fathers and Sons" (*CSS* 376). Likewise, consistent from "Tomb" through "Fathers and Sons" is the son's "could" verb in his asking: "Couldn't we all be buried out at the ranch?" (*SS-HLE* 413, 424; *CSS* 377). Also unchanged from "Tomb" through "Fathers and Sons" is the rationale for a family burial site at the ranch: "Then I could stop and pray at the tomb of my grandfather on the way to the ranch" (*SS-HLE* 413, 424; *CSS* 377). Whereas the earliest draft of "Fathers and Sons" is dominated by the past tense, from "Tomb of My Grandfather" to "Fathers and Sons" the future conditional ("could") becomes important to Nick's conversation with his son about a family burial plot.

At the same time, the story, so dominated by layers of memories, ends in the present and future—the present of Nick's son's feelings about his grandfather, the conditional future of his son's contemplated prayers "at the tomb of my grandfather on the way to the ranch," and the imperative future of Nick's promise: "I can see we'll have to go" (377). From the manuscript of "Tomb" to the printed version of the story, Hemingway deftly interweaves verbs in the present, future conditional, and future tenses, as the father and son look ahead to visiting the tomb together. Unlike the composition of a story like "Now I Lay Me," when the final conversation between Nick and John is a late addition, Hemingway left the conversation between Nick and his son virtually unchanged from "Tomb" on.

In that conversation he portrays two sides of Nick as a father. On the one hand, for most of the story, Nick is so absorbed in his own reminiscences that he "had not even noticed the boy was awake," language not present in "Tomb of My Grandfather" that Hemingway included in the late draft preserved in folder 385a and in the published story (compare *SS-HLE* 412 and 422 with *CSS* 375). His son's question snaps Nick out of his reveries about the past, oblivious to his son's being awake, and brings him into the present as they are driving on a highway in the South. On the other hand, Hemingway portrays Nick, in the conversation itself, as a patient and caring listener to his son. While unwilling to agree to be buried in France, he accepts the emotional plea from his son: "I think I ought to go pray at the tomb of my grandfather" (*SS-HLE* 413, 423; *CSS* 376). Nick's first response offers a conditional promise in the future tense: "Sometime we'll go" (*SS-HLE* 413, 423; *CSS* 376). Pressed when his son shares his strong feelings ("Well, I don't feel good"), Nick shifts to mix the present with an imperative future tense: "I can see we'll have to go" (*SS-HLE* 413, 424; *CSS* 376). Nick's last word ends the story on a positive note of his promise to his son to visit the tomb of his own father, whatever memories of disappointment and anger he might have. For all the substantial revisions he made in his lengthy process of composing the story, Hemingway let that final conversation end the story on a note of reconciliation, conciliation, and caring.[15]

The final revisions of "Fathers and Sons" leave intact most of the conversation when Nick, instead of being mentored by his father, becomes a mentor for his son. Particularly as he revised the story, Hemingway presents Nick in "Fathers and Sons" as a rounded, humane, and complex character. As such, the Nicholas Adams of this story brings *Winner Take Noth-*

ing to a close with a far less cynical figure than the loners and misfits who generally populate the collection—doctors who cannot heal a self-mutilated boy ("God Rest You"), Nick at the front as an hysterical advance man showing the American flag ("A Way"), a son whose father shot himself (part 3 of "Homage to Switzerland"), and a writer whose "nerves are bad now" ("The Gambler, the Nun, and the Radio" [*CSS* 365]). The Nicholas Adams of "Fathers and Sons" is closer, I think, to the Nick of "Indian Camp," "Cross-Country Snow" and "Big Two-Hearted River"—independent, complex, and caring for his father (and, in this case, his son). The brilliance of this story is Hemingway's placing Nicholas Adams as a father meditating about two stories he cannot tell his son—the erotic story of his own sexual initiation and the grim story of his father's death. The story blends elegy with comedy, as Nick remembers his father and, with a quiet smile, accommodates his son's wish to pray at his father's tomb. Hemingway's revisions to "Fathers and Sons," like his extensive work in composing "Big Two-Hearted River," are consummate examples of artistic craftsmanship.

CONCLUSION

I can work slow and I can see the words when I say them.
If they're wrong I hear them wrong and I can do them over
and work on them until I get them right.

—ERNEST HEMINGWAY, "Get a Seeing-Eyed Dog"

In "Get a Seeing-Eyed Dog," one of the last stories Hemingway ever published, Hemingway imagines himself as a writer, blind, who depends upon a tape recorder and his wife to help him draft his stories, listen to the words in the drafts, and continue working on the words until they sound right to his ear. Inside a hotel in Venice, with the rain pouring steadily outside, the writer contemplates his writing in the dark, in the limited time he has left, with his mind focused on releasing his wife from the burdens of taking care of a blind, dying man. "Seeing-Eyed Dog" bears some resemblance to "The Snows of Kilimanjaro," except that the narrator, Philip, is focused less on the stories he will not be able to write and more on the words he can see and hear in his mind and do over.

From almost the beginning of his career as one of the greatest short story writers, Hemingway learned the importance of revision in the craft of fiction. The future study of Hemingway's art of revision has been enhanced by the publication of the Hemingway Library Edition of some of his stories, along with the publication of some of the manuscript and typescript drafts. For example, as discussed above, an understanding of "A Way You'll Never Be," "The Gambler, the Nun, and the Radio," and "Fathers and Sons" is substantially aided by the extensive publication of manuscripts and typescripts of those three stories. Indeed, the chapter devoted to "A Way" relies heavily on the publication of an early untitled pencil manuscript of the story (KL/

EH folder 746a; *SS-HLE* 327–41). Similarly, the chapter on "The Gambler, the Nun, and the Radio" relies heavily upon an early typescript of the story, then titled "Three Ambitions" (KL/EH folder 417; *SS-HLE* 371–86). The discussion of Hemingway's various drafts for the story's ending depends upon the inclusion of manuscripts in the Library Edition (KL/EH folders 421, 420; *SS-HLE* 386–91). Finally, the chapter about the composition of "Fathers and Sons" focuses on an early untitled pencil manuscript, an early handwritten draft titled "Tomb of My Grandfather," a discarded pencil manuscript, a sentence fragment written by hand on the back side of Hotel Ambos Mundos stationery, and an untitled typescript with pencil corrections and a three-page pencil insert (KL/EH folders 382, 383, 384, 385, 385a; *SS-HLE* 404–24). This wealth of resources to explore Hemingway's composition and revision of "Fathers and Sons" represents close to an ideal publication of Hemingway's short fiction, along with a nearly complete set of drafts. Even so, the opportunities and challenges for future manuscript studies of Hemingway's short stories are significant. Ongoing study of Hemingway's manuscripts can, as Seán Hemingway put it in his introduction to the Library Edition, "tell us a great deal about his writing technique, especially how he worked to perfect the beginnings and endings of his stories and how he continued to refine them through multiple drafts" (*SS-HLE* xxvii).

Just to illustrate the opportunities and constraints facing teachers and scholars wishing to study Hemingway's process of composition, I would like to discuss the example of "The Snows of Kilimanjaro," a story that is widely regarded as one of the finest of his stories published after *Winner Take Nothing*. Teachers and scholars have more access to some of Hemingway's drafts of "Snows" than was the case a few years ago. Three of the drafts to "Snows" are printed in the Hemingway Library Edition of *The Short Stories*. One is the earliest typescript of the story, then titled by hand "The Happy Ending" (KL/EH folder 702; *SS-HLE* 487–508; discussed by Smith in *Guide* 349). A second draft records a flashback to a scene in Shruns, Austria—a flashback that Hemingway decided not to include as part of the story (*SS-HLE* 508–9). The third is a penciled draft for the epigraph for "Snows" (*SS-HLE* 509–10). All three reproductions of drafts for "Snows" are important resources for readers, teachers, and scholars. One would be hard-pressed to challenge the decision to include those drafts. And the single-volume edition of some of the drafts of some of Hemingway's stories must, perforce, leave out much of value.

However, two of the most important drafts are not included in the Hemingway Library Edition. One is a later typescript than that titled "The Happy Ending." That transcript is now preserved in the archives of the University of Delaware's library (discussed by Smith, *Guide* 349–51). Thanks to a research archivist of the Special Collections Library at the University of Delaware, I was able to obtain a scanned copy of that typescript. Another is a later typescript, with Hemingway's revisions by hand, of "The Snows of Kilimanjaro," now preserved in the Ransom Center of the University of Texas. Thanks to the staff in Reference and Research Services at the Ransom Center, I was able to obtain a scanned copy of that transcript. Furthermore, thanks to research archivists at the Hemingway Collection of the Kennedy Library, I received a copy of essays signed by Robert W. Lewis Jr. and Max Westbrook (Lewis; Lewis and Westbrook, "Texas Manuscript"; Lewis and Westbrook, "Snows"). These two scholars discussed the genesis and evolution of "Snows" in essays Paul Smith described as "the first endeavor to introduce manuscript evidence into Hemingway scholarship" (*Guide* 350). Lewis and Westbrook reprinted images of pages of Hemingway's transcript, with his handwritten revisions. They even published the entire typescript as part of the essay that appeared in the summer 1970 issue of the *Texas Quarterly*. This late typescript of "The Snows of Kilimanjaro" was, essentially, Hemingway's final draft before the version published in *Esquire* in August 1936 (Lewis and Westbrook, "Texas Manuscript"; Lewis and Westbrook, "Snows"). Today teachers and scholars are allowed to quote extensively from that typescript only because Lewis and Westbrook published it before the copyright restrictions became more stringent.

Thus, one can study the evolution of "Snows" in three stages. The first is the "earliest typescript" (Smith, *Guide* 349), preserved at the Kennedy Library (KL/EH folder 702) and now published in the Hemingway Library Edition (*SS-HLE* 487–508). The second is the typescript now at the University of Delaware, a typescript that incorporates the "many revisions" made in the earlier draft at the Kennedy Library (Smith, *Guide* 349). The "third and final typescript" is that located at the Harry Ransom Center of the University of Texas—the transcripts collated and annotated by Lewis and Westbrook that were published in the summer 1970 issue of the *Texas Quarterly* (Smith, *Guide* 350–51). To illustrate the potential benefits of future manuscript study, I will focus on three revisions to "Snows"—Hemingway's adding historical details to his paragraph about the execution of the Paris Communards, his adding and then deleting a reference to the countries about which Harry had written well, and his adding a passage in the Texas typescript following Harry's addressing death as "You stinking bastard" (*SS-HLE* 506; *CSS* 54). A discussion of such opportunities for future study of these revisions is offered in the spirit of Paul Smith's observation made decades ago: "Now with the manuscripts in the Kennedy Library, there is more than enough material to warrant a revised version of their [Lewis and Westbrook's] original work including the story's three typescripts" (*Guide* 351).

In the Texas typescript of "The Snows of Kilimanjaro," the most dramatic and visible revision comes with Hemingway's underlining each line of the sections he wanted the printer to italicize. As is the case in the published story, these italics mark each of Harry's interior monologues, dominated by flashbacks. The third such section combines his memories of a log house that was burned down, along with the rifles owned by Harry's grandfather. That flashback then shifts quickly to the Black Forest and Harry's memory of the two ways to walk to a trout stream where he fished. Ending with a reference to the hotel proprietor's suicide, that memory then shifts to Paris. In both the first transcript and the published story, that section begins with Harry's ambivalent statement: "You could dictate that, but you could not dictate the Place Contrescarpe where the flower sellers dyed their flowers in the street" (*SS-HLE* 501; *CSS* 51). After asking Helen whether she could take dictation (surely knowing she could not), Harry then reflects upon his inability to write (or dictate) stories about the Place Contrescarpe near the rue Cardinal LeMoine and the rue Mouffetard, streets to which he refers in this flashback. In this typescript, Harry's reference to the local drunkards is relatively brief: "They were the descendants of the Communards and it was no struggle for them to know their politics. They knew who had shot their fathers, their relatives, their brothers, and their friends." Following that reference is Harry's recollection of his early days as a writer. In that neighborhood, "he had written the start of all he was to do" (*SS-HLE* 502). That passage in the second (Delaware) typescript is precisely the same, word for word, as in the earlier (Kennedy) typescript.

Then, in the third (Texas) typescript, Hemingway recorded by hand a striking addition to this passage. In the earlier version, the sentence referring to the Communards ended with "their brothers, and their friends." Hemingway deleted the period that marked the sentence as ending there. He replaced the period with a comma and added the words "when the Versailles troops came in and took the town after the Commune and executed any one they could catch with calloused hands, or who wore a cap, or who carried any other sign he was a working man" (Lewis and Westbrook, "Snows," 124n167.32–35; see also *CSS* 51). As Lewis and Westbrook note about this revised part of the typescript, "the pencilled addition from 'carried' on was added, canceled, then restored" (124n167.32–35). Thus, both stages of Hemingway's additions to this passage intensify Harry's connecting the drunkards hanging around the Place Contrescarpe with the Communards hunted and shot down by the "Versailles troops." Hemingway's penciled additions render as more forceful Harry's words sympathizing with the working-class rebels of the Commune and excoriating the brutal repression of the French government. He retained them in the published version of "Snows" (*CSS* 51). Among the questions one might ask about these additions: what is the significance of Hemingway's decision to include—among Harry's memories of a log house consumed by fire, a trout stream in the Black Forest, and the area near the Place Contrescarpe from which he traced his beginnings as a writer—this biting reflection about the persecution and execution of the Communards?

In the earliest typescript preserved at the Kennedy Library, Harry's penultimate flashback focuses on a story he had not told about a "half wit chore boy" who worked on a ranch in the West (*SS-HLE* 503). In that typescript, and in the published story, the flashback begins with Harry's insistence that "he had never written about Paris. Not the Paris that he cared about" (*SS-HLE* 503; *CSS* 52). As recorded in the Hemingway Library Edition publication of that draft, Hemingway then deleted a sentence, a fragment, and a question that Harry asks to himself: "Of two other countries he had written well and of the place where he had been a boy he had written well enough. As well as he could then. But what about the rest?" (*SS-HLE* 503). Perhaps to keep some distance between Harry and himself, Hemingway does not identify the "two other countries" about which he had written well. That passage about the stories Harry had written is clearly marked for deletion in the Kennedy typescript, as printed in the Library Edition. Just as clearly, the passage is restored, word for word, in the later typescript preserved at the University of Delaware. Then, in the latest typescript at the Ransom Center, most of the passage is crossed out, again, with a few new words added. Hemingway crossed out, as recorded in the Texas transcript, "Of two other countries he had written well and of the place where he had been a boy he had written well enough. As well as he could then." In this third transcript, he retained the question, "But what about the rest?" To that question, Hemingway then added, by hand, the words, "that he had never written" (Lewis and Westbrook, "Snows," 129n169.18). Thus, with his deletions and additions, the Texas typescript reads exactly as does this passage in the published story: "No, he had never written about Paris. Not the Paris that he cared about. But what about the rest that he had never written?" (Lewis and Westbrook, "Snows," 129n169.18; see also *CSS* 52).

This sequence of revisions gives rise to a number of questions. After his claim that he had never written about the Paris "he cared about," why did Hemingway add and then strike in the early typescript his reference to two other countries that he *had* written about "well"? Why, in the second (Delaware) typescript, did he restore that sentence about the two countries of which he had written well? Why, in the third (Texas) typescript, did he again strike the sentence about the two other countries? Why, in the end, did he add the words "that he had never written"? Aside from suggesting Hemingway's uncertainty about what to include in Harry's references to his past writing, the final draft of the sentences in "Snows" serves to emphasize his bleak pessimism while reflecting upon his writing career. Instead of referring to two countries about which he had written well, and to the place where he grew up about which he had written "well enough," Hemingway left only negative statements and a negative rhetorical question: he had *never* written about Paris—at least not the Paris he cared about. Harry then asks himself more emphatically about "the rest that he had never written." A study of the evolution of this passage in the three transcripts suggests how, after wavering, Hemingway settled on leaving Harry's meditation completely self-critical as a preface to the story about "that old bastard from the Forks" and the boy who shot him—one of "at least twenty good stories from out there and he had never written one" (*CSS* 52–53). Thus, Henry's berating himself about the Paris stories that he had never written is the stripped-down preface to the stories of the ranch and the Wild West "out there" that he had also never written. As Hemingway revised this passage, Harry's meditation becomes darker and darker.

Another instance of Hemingway's revision by addition comes immediately after Harry addresses death, moving like a hyena, as "You stinking bastard" (*SS-HLE* 506; *CSS* 54). In the earliest typescript, after a line break, Hemingway shifts to the final section of the story, beginning "Just then it was morning" (*SS-HLE* 506). In the Delaware typescript that line break is shown by two solid horizontal lines drawn by hand. Then, the story continues, just as it did in the earliest typescript, "Just then." At this point of the story, in the latest transcript at the Harry Ransom Center, almost identical with the manuscript fragment at the Kennedy Library labeled "(26) Insert," Hemingway added by hand the following passage:

> It moved up closer to him still and now he could not speak to it, and when it saw he could not speak it came a little closer, and now he tried to send it away without speaking, but now it moved in on him so its weight was all upon his chest, and while it crouched there and he could not move, or speak, he heard the woman say, "Bwana is asleep now. Take up the cot very gently and carry it into the tent." He could not speak to tell her to make it go away and it crouched now, heavier, so he could not breathe. And then, while they lifted the cot, suddenly it was all right and the weight went from his chest (KL/EH folder 705; Lewis and Westbrook, "Snows" 137n172.29–36, 137n173.1–6).

This addition is one of the most powerful interior monologues in one of his stories. In this passage, Hemingway evokes Harry's sense of helpless paralysis, as he senses that death, like a hyena who seems attracted to the smell of death, is moving closer and closer. Paralyzed and muted, Harry cannot speak, but he hears the woman speak and tell the African servants to move his cot indoors.

Here, in the manuscript fragment at the Kennedy Library and in the published version of the story, Hemingway began a new paragraph after Harry hears Helen say, "Take up the cot gently and carry it into the tent" (KL/EH folder 705; *CSS* 54). Thus, separated into its own paragraph is the account of Harry's last sensations before he seems to lose consciousness. Still unable to speak, Harry feels "it" crouching, "heavier" on his chest, "so he could not breathe." Seemingly awake but appearing asleep to Helen, Harry loses all power of motion, sight, speech, and even breathing. Near suffocation, he can only feel "it" weighing upon him. The passage that Hemingway added by hand ends with Harry's feeling the weight lifted as the servants lift his cot. He appears to pass out or fall asleep, as the next sensation is his hearing a plane, whether he is awakened or in a dream.

With this added passage, Hemingway enhances the drama within Harry's consciousness before the final section of the story. The first and second typescripts, those housed at the Kennedy Library and the University of Delaware, move directly from Harry's swearing at the "stinking bastard" to his hearing the sounds of an airplane. By adding this inserted passage, Hemingway takes the reader inside Harry's last waking thoughts about the stalking approach and weight of death. However much his misogynistic attacks on Helen render Harry one of Hemingway's least sympathetic male characters, his final sensations and thoughts evoke one's empathy for his feeling numbed and paralyzed. As Paul Smith noted, the contents of folder 705 at the Kennedy Library describe "the last approach of the hyena before Harry's dream-flight" (*Guide* 349). The paragraph break after Helen's "take up the cot" is the one aspect of the manuscript fragment in the Kennedy Library that reflects a late change Hemingway preserved in the published form of the story.

By a combination of factors, the study of Hemingway's process of composing and revising "Snows" is much less fraught with challenges than are other stories. Thanks to the recent publication of the Hemingway Library Edition, the earliest typescript (KL/EH folder 702) is now available for study and for quotation in scholarly publications. The second typescript, preserved at the University of Delaware, is available for study but is protected by copyright from extensive quotation. The third typescript, and perhaps the most important, has already been transcribed and published (with all its handwritten revisions). The transcript, commentary, and essays by Lewis and Westbrook were completed before the copyright owners of Hemingway's drafts tightened control over what scholars could do with the manuscripts.

My hope is that, at some point in the not-too-distant future, the copyright holders will become more generous about granting access to, and wider quotation of, the manuscripts and typescripts in the collection. That said, I am grateful to Seán Hemingway, the editor of the Hemingway Library Edition, for publishing some of the drafts of some of Hemingway's short stories. Particularly given the COVID-19 years, when I could not return to the Hemingway Collection at the Kennedy Library, I was able to complete this book thanks to his work on the Library Edition.

This book ends with a chapter devoted to the final story, "Fathers and Sons," that Hemingway placed at the end of the last collection of new stories he would compile in his lifetime, *Winner Take Nothing*. As I hope that chapter shows, his manuscripts and drafts of "Fathers and Sons" demonstrate how powerfully he learned the importance of sketching, composing, and revising works of art. He learned those lessons principally from his most important mentors during his education and development as a young artist: Pound, Joyce, and Stein. Looking back a decade after his work with Pound on *in our time,* Hemingway wrote to him on 22 July 1933: "I learned more about how to write and how not to write from you than from any son of a bitch alive and have always said so" (*Letters* vol. 5, 445). Like Pound, James Joyce and Gertrude Stein taught him how to jar, jostle, and provoke readers with ironic juxtapositions in their narratives. Joyce became for Hemingway a model of exhaustive revision. In a letter to Ernest Walsh and Ethel Moorhead dated 30 November 1925, Hemingway enclosed the proof of his story "The Undefeated" with "4 changes in words and have corrected 61 typographical errors." He then added a comment about his restraint in not making as many changes as he "wanted badly" to make. "So don't think I'm being like Joyce about the proof and wanting to re-write the story every time a proof is sent" (*Letters,* vol. 2, 420).

At the other extreme in the art of revision was Gertrude Stein, whose *Geography and Plays* he praised lavishly in his review, and part of whose mammoth novel *The Making of Americans* he edited in serial form for the *Transatlantic.* In contrast to Joyce's massive revisions, Stein came to represent for Hemingway (rightly or wrongly) an example of a writer who generally declined to revise her work. In a letter to Ezra Pound of 28 February 1930, Hemingway wrote about Stein: "I think at the start she had something and was writing good stuff. . . . Then because she did not have to make it give a kick to the one who reads as well as the one who writes she could do it right off like automatic writing—However some of the short pieces in Geography and plays and some others are damn good legitimate stuff—(To me)" (*Letters* vol. 4, 246). Noteworthy about this assessment, aside from its balance of praise and criticism, is Hemingway's reference to "automatic writing"—a process that for him meant no revision of a writer's original sketching, jotting, and brainstorming. The pervasive nature of early drafts, false starts, and multiple sketches in the Hemingway Collection at the Kennedy Library illustrate how much distance he placed between automatic writing and his own art. The early masterpieces like "Indian Camp" and

"Big Two-Hearted River" reflect Hemingway's transformational revisions by cutting, modifying, and adding to his earliest drafts. Even after Hemingway became a best-selling writer, he composed stories like "Now I Lay Me," "Hills Like White Elephants," "A Way You'll Never Be," and "Fathers and Sons" that became more daring and difficult and powerful as he extensively revised them. My deepest hope is that readers of Hemingway's powerful short stories will come away with an appreciation for how much he practiced the craft of revision in composing his short fiction.

NOTES

1. POUND'S INFLUENCE ON HEMINGWAY'S REVISION OF *IN OUR TIME*

1. Bill Bird to Ernest Hemingway, The Hemingway Collection at the John F. Kennedy Presidential Library and Museum, Series Three: Incoming Correspondence, Box IC02, folder marked "Bill Bird."

2. I will cite subsequent quotations from this essay as "Essay on Inquest." About the probable dates for Pound's unpublished "Inquest Sketch" and "Essay on Inquest," see Brita Lindberg-Seyested's note 40 in *Letters to Ford Maddox Ford* 190–91. Pound's account of the inception of the "Inquest" series in this "Essay" is consistent with his account in a letter to John Quinn of 21 September 1922 (unpublished, in the John Quinn Memorial Collection at the New York Public Library).

3. This fictional story is reflected in Pound's reference in Canto XVI to Hemingway's being "buried for four days" (*Cantos* 71). In the Three Mountains Press edition of *A Draft of XVI Cantos*, Pound had Cyril Hammerton—not the "Ernie Hemingway" of the current New Directions edition—as buried alive. On the subject of Cyril Hammerton as a pseudonym for Hemingway in Pound's original *Draft of XVI Cantos*, see my essay "Pound's Composition of Canto 16."

4. The drafts for chapter 7 of *in our time* are preserved in Box 18, folder 94a, Hemingway Collection, Kennedy Library. For reasons of copyright, I will quote only from drafts as reprinted by Derounian.

5. This note to "Dearest Old Izz" can be found at Ernest Hemingway Personal Papers, Series 1.1 Manuscripts: Books, Box MS18, folder 94a, at the John F. Kennedy Presidential Library and Museum. See Cohen 245n62. John Peale Bishop reported in his 1936 essay "Homage to Hemingway" that "In Paris Hemingway submitted much of his work in fiction to Pound. It came back to him blue-penciled, most of the adjectives gone. The comments were unsparing" (40–41). Malcolm Cowley later claimed that Hemingway learned from Pound "to bluepencil most of his adjectives and adverbs" (50). It is not clear on what basis Bishop and Cowley make their claims about Pound's marking Hemingway's drafts (see Hurwitz 476, 482). However, there can be little doubt that Pound's editing of Hemingway's chapters for *in our time* was influential in his development as a writer whose "respect for craftsmanship became manifest during the Paris years because of Ezra's prodding" (Hurwitz 480).

6. These drafts of the fictional chapter of Maera's supposed death can be found at KL/EH Box 54, folders 564 and 564a.

7. While Pound does not explicitly identify which works he regarded as of less value, he likely had in mind Hemingway's commercially successfully works like *The Sun Also Rises*. For evidence supporting that conjecture in an unpublished letter Pound wrote Hemingway on 7 August 1933, see my essay "Hemingway's Marlin and Pound's Canto 40" 124–25.

8. Michael Reynolds records that "the Pounds and Hemingways went on a walking tour" during the month they spent in Rapallo (*Paris Years* 112–13). Pound's biographer David Moody goes into more detail about their walking tour of February 1923: "the four of them toured Sigismondo's old battlefields in Tuscany" during the period when Pound was researching archives and libraries for historical documents pertinent to the Malatesta cantos (46–47). For a discussion of Pound's extensive process of revision while composing *A Draft of XVI Cantos,* see my essay "Pound's Composition of Canto 16."

2. JOYCE'S "THE SISTERS" AND HEMINGWAY'S REVISION OF "INDIAN CAMP"

1. Hemingway's earliest manuscript of "Indian Camp" is preserved in KL/EH folder 493, reprinted in *SS-HLE* 60–67. As Paul Smith and the editors of volume 2 of Hemingway's *Letters* note, on the verso of page 9 of this manuscript Hemingway started typing a letter to Lawrence Gains. Since this unfinished letter, dated 4 November 1923, is on the letterhead of the *Toronto Star,* it seems likely that Hemingway began writing "Indian Camp" in the autumn of 1923 and resumed work on the story when he returned to Paris that winter (Smith, *Guide* 34). Stacey Chandler, archivist at the Kennedy Library, noted that the first eight pages "are on white unlined paper, about 7.5 × 9.5 inches," whereas page 9 is on *Toronto Star* letterhead, "a slightly smaller page . . . with a brownish tone" (e-mail to the author, 1 August 2022). For two succinct accounts of the impact of Hemingway's return to a role as journalist in Toronto, see Lamb, *Short Story* 5–6; and Kennedy, Introduction, *In Our Time: A Norton Critical Edition* xiii.

2. At the end of an unpublished letter dated 3 December 1923, Pound wrote Hemingway: "Wot's the use your pore ole grandpa Ford sitting in a damp cottage sweatin 'is nek off to perduce a revoo where the Young can express 'emselves IF you aren't going ter com across wif de PUNCH. I think, myself, you'd better come bak here and direk the policy of the damn thing. I want a little leisure for composition." This summons suggests Pound's rather remarkable confidence in the young Hemingway's ability to provide the "PUNCH" for the *Transatlantic Review* that "old grandpa Ford" could not give and to relieve Pound of some editorial responsibilities so that he would have more time to write. Indeed, Pound's encouraging Hemingway to return to Paris, in part so that he could "direk the policy of the damn thing," seems to have worked. That is, by mid-December, almost immediately after receiving Pound's letter of 3 December, he wrote Gertrude Stein and Alice B. Toklas that he was going to "chuck journalism." I am grateful to Abigail Malangone of the Kennedy Library for scanning and sending me a copy of Pound's letter.

3. For a blistering critique of this flashback-within-a-flashback explaining how the church hymn triggered Nick's fear of death, see Lamb, *Short Story* 20–21.

4. Lamb's comments about Nick's being literally and figuratively in the dark, as he crosses the lake and approaches the Indian camp, bear particular emphasis: "Because he does not know where he is going and why, Nick has nothing around which to structure these impressions.

They are unprocessed because his journey is unfocused. Therefore they are reported as he consciously experiences them, randomly" (*Short Story* 30–31).

5. In their edition of *Dubliners,* Robert Scholes and A. Walton Litz include an earlier draft of "The Sisters" as part of their supplementary section titled "The Composition and Revision of the Stories." I am not suggesting that Hemingway was aware of, or was influenced by, the specific revisions Joyce made in the story. Rather, as an editor of the *Transatlantic Review* that published some of Joyce's "Works in Progress" that became *Finnegans Wake,* Hemingway was quite aware of the extent to which Joyce exhaustively revised his work.

6. For a carefully argued defense of Dr. Adams's actions and comments during the Caesarean section he performs, see Daiker, "In Defense." For a more critical assessment of Dr. Adams's comments to Nick, see Lamb, *Short Story* 51–60.

7. Robert Paul Lamb's reading of this passage (and of the entire story) is quite complex and astute, but I differ from his analysis in one respect. Lamb argues that "Nick begins to fade from the narrative" (*Art Matters* 91); that Hemingway presents the discovery of the Indian's suicide as it "would have felt to the doctor at the precise moment he made it" (92); that the discovery has the "most revealing effect" on the doctor (92); and that the "camera eye" for that scene is Nick's father's (94). He resumes that line of argument in *The Hemingway Short Story.* On the one hand, Lamb notes that "In rendering this scene, Hemingway was determined not to let anything undermine the focalization" through Nick's point of view (*Short Story* 63). On the other hand, he argues that "the discovery paragraph . . . seems perilously close to being focalized through the doctor" (*Short Story* 66). Lamb then suggests a reconciliation of these two lines of reading: "Hemingway manages to focalize through the doctor—reaping the dramatic benefits enumerated above—while still making it seem as though he is focalizing through Nick" (*Short Story* 66). That is, Lamb suggests that Hemingway broke the thread of the focalization through Nick's point of view. At the same time, Lamb seems to suggest that Hemingway deftly finessed that break so that it is hardly noticeable. Lamb does not discuss Hemingway's revisions from the manuscript to the printed text. My reading is that Hemingway revised the passage to keep the "camera eye" as Nick's. I believe that Hemingway maintains a strict internal third-person focalization through Nick in "Indian Camp." I agree that Nick's father is deeply affected by his discovery not only of the Indian's suicide but also of his son's witnessing the bloody scene. However, I do not see the "revealing effect" as more focused on Dr. Adams than on Nick, as the conversation that ends the story suggests the questions triggered by Nick's shock. I agree with Lamb's comment that the simile comparing Dr. Adams, "exalted" after the surgery, to a football player after a game is "the only real mistake in the story" (*Short Story* 59).

8. For a persuasive argument that "we do not know why the Indian husband took his life," see Lamb, *Short Story* 78–79. For a superb discussion of the dialogue at the end of "Indian Camp," see Lamb, "Hemingway and the Creation of Twentieth-Century Dialogue" 457–61.

3. STEIN, JOYCE, AND HEMINGWAY'S REWRITING "CAT IN THE RAIN"

1. Michael S. Reynolds reprinted and discussed Hemingway's review of Stein's *Geography and Plays* in Reynolds, "Hemingway's Stein."

2. Joyce sent his instructions for sending Hemingway a press copy to Harriett Weaver in a letter dated 25 November 1922, who must have relayed word to Sylvia Beach (Smith, *Guide* 45; Joyce, *Letters* vol. 3, 69). Beach's record of sending a copy of *Ulysses* to Hemingway is in a

notebook titled "lettres et paquets recommendées pour la France 1922" (Sylvia Beach Archives, The Firestone Library of Princeton University, Series 2: Shakespeare and Company, Box 63, folder 1). In her note, she wrote the Hemingways' address as Chamby Sur Montreaux; the same address is recorded in Hemingway, *Letters* vol. 2, 3–8. This unbound press copy now resides in the Hemingway Collection at the John F. Kennedy Memorial Library, where an archivist, Stacey Chandler, showed it to me. See my essay "Hemingway's Reading of Joyce's *Ulysses*." I am grateful to Gabriel Swift (Special Collections reference librarian), Sandra Calabrese (Special Collections assistant), and their colleagues at the Rare Books and Special Collections division of the Firestone Library at Princeton University for their support during my research.

3. Picasso's *Architect's Table* is now at the Museum of Modern Art in New York. For the influence of cubist art on Hemingway's design for *In Our Time*, see Brogan; Kennedy, Introduction, *In Our Time: A Norton Critical Edition;* Reynolds, "Hemingway's *In Our Time*"; Strychacz, "In Our Time, Out of Season"; and my essay "Hemingway's Formation of *In Our Time.*"

4. George Plimpton's interview of Hemingway originally appeared as "The Art of Fiction No. 21," in the spring 1958 issue of the *Paris Review;* it was later reprinted in *Writers at Work: The Paris Review Interviews, Second Series* (Hemingway, Interview by Plimpton).

5. Joyce composed his stories in *Dubliners* during 1904–7 (Ellmann 163, 207–11, 264). Stein wrote her stories in *Three Lives* during 1905–6 (Mellow, *Charmed Circle* 77; Stein, *Writings* 920). Their *Ulysses* and *Geography and Plays* were both published in 1922 (Pondrom viii).

6. Bacigalupo 119–25; Kennedy and Curnutt 5; Lamb, *Art Matters* 113–35; Perloff; Ryan.

7. Joyce probably learned the power of concatenated repetition from Dante Alighieri. Here is one example—Beatrice's words to the pilgrim Dante, as she leads him to the Empyrean:

> We have issued
> from the largest body to the Heaven of pure light,
> light intellectual, full of love,
> love of true good, full of joy,
> joy that surpasses every sweetness.
> (Alighieri, *Paradiso*, trans. Hollander and Hollander, 30:38–42)

For an account of Joyce's "reciting long passages of Dante in rolling sonorous Italian," see McAlmon and Boyle 28. For a general discussion of Joyce's identifying his *Ulysses* with Dante's *Commedia*, see Ellmann 4, 361, 393.

8. In his second attempt at this story in late February, Hemingway has the outline of this first paragraph but not its rhythmic repetitions. This second draft also traces the couple's train journey from Genoa past Portofino toward Rapallo. Only in the third draft, dated in Hemingway's hand "March 1924," do the basic elements of the first paragraph appear *in medias res,* and not after a narrative of a train ride from Genoa (KL/EH folder 319; *SS-HLE* 75).

9. My translation from Bacigalupo.

10. Also quoted in Smith, *Guide* 43; and in Eby, *Hemingway's Festishism* 135.

11. David Lodge analyzed this opening paragraph as an overture of the central oppositions in the story, but he did not discuss Hemingway's rhythmic repetitions (18).

12. See the exchange of extended monologues between Melanctha Herbert and Dr. Jeff Campbell about his disdain for "excitements" (Stein, *Writings* 148–54). In contrast, see Joyce's dialogue at the end of "Counterparts" (*Dubliners* 97–98); the conversation between Stephen

Dedalus and Cranly about his refusing his mother's request to make his Easter duty (*Portrait* 259–69); and Stephen's exchange in Italian with Artifoni (*Ulysses* 188).

13. Hemingway had already portrayed the miscommunications of an American husband trying to converse in Italian in "Out of Season," a story Hemingway completed in April 1923, shortly after the first start to "Cat in the Rain" in February 1923 (Smith, *Guide* 16).

14. The detachment of George from his wife as she brushes her hair is strikingly different from the intimacy at a similar moment in *A Farewell to Arms* (223–24). In a letter commenting on a typescript of *A Farewell to Arms*, Fitzgerald praised "Cat in the Rain" and "Hills Like White Elephants" as stories when Hemingway was "really listening to women" (Bruccoli, *Fitzgerald: A Life* 165).

15. The bullfighter Belmonte gave rise to three extremely different portraits: Stein's rather farcical portrait in "The History of Belmonte"; Hemingway's portrait of Belmonte as unwell, awkward, and wolf-faced in *The Sun Also Rises* (216–25), a stark foil to the graceful Pedro Romero (Stoneback 268–69); and Hemingway's tribute to Belmonte in *Death in the Afternoon*. In the latter work, Hemingway refers to Belmonte eighty-three times and praises him as "a genius and a great artist" (69).

16. Stein's nickname for Alice B. Toklas was apparently "pussy" (Reynolds, *Hemingway: The 1930s* 29), as would seem to be the case given the pun "push sea push sea" in "Sacred Emily" (Stein, *Geography and Plays* 178; see also Pondrom xlvii). "Feather Cat" was also one of Hemingway's nicknames for Hadley (*Letters* vol. 2, 30, and 31n8; McAlmon and Boyle 160; Eby, *Hemingway's Fetishism* 122). For evidence that Hemingway read Havelock Ellis's discussion of fetishism involving animals like cats, see *Letters* vol. 1, 271n4; and Reynolds, *Paris Years* 120–22.

17. See, for instance, David Lodge's consideration of whether the wife is pregnant (16), along with the discussions by Kennedy, "What Hemingway Omitted" 76; Comley and Scholes 13–14; Smith, "1924" 44; *Guide* 47; and Bennett 247. I question Griffin's argument that, since male tortoiseshell cats are generally sterile, George probably is as well (102). The American critics and the Italian translators of "Cat" consistently assume that the "tortoise-shell" is male (Bennett; Griffin; West). Bacigalupo cites the first Italian translation in 1953 as referring to the "big tortoise-shell cat" as male, "un grosso gatto di maiolica" (123). That translation is followed by Vincenzo Mantovani, who renders the "tortoise-shell" as male: "un gattone" and "questo" (Hemingway, *I quarantanove racconti*, trans. Mantovani 180). However, the authors of two books in Hemingway's library indicate that tortoiseshell cats are almost always female (Gay 45; Méry 148–49; see also Brasch and Sigman). In Joyce's *Ulysses*, Leopold Bloom remembers "That half tabbywhite tortoiseshell in the City Arms with the letter em on her forehead" (*Ulysses* 309). Whereas Joyce's cat is explicitly feminine ("em" as a reminder of Molly Bloom), Hemingway does not specify the gender of the "tortoise-shell" in "Cat." Whatever the gender, I follow Carl Eby in seeing the "tortoise-shell" in the story as a "replacement cat" for the pleasure the wife is missing in her marriage (*Hemingway's Fetishism* 137). See also Tetlow 80–81.

18. Here I disagree with Robert Gajdusek, who regarded the wife in "Cat," like Maria in Joyce's "Clay," as the "victim of masculine, sterilizing dichotomies" (*Hemingway in His Own Country* 213). Worth noting is that the monument in Rapallo, *Monumento ai caduto*, erected in 1922, later melted down in the late 1930s, showed a female winged victory over a male fallen soldier (Neel 104). After my presentation of an earlier form of this chapter at the 16th Biennial Hemingway Conference in Venice, an Italian couple was kind enough to point that fact out to

me. For a photograph of this monument, see Bacigalupo (194) or Neel (103). I am not suggesting that the American wife embodies a female winged victory; nor do I believe George represents a fallen, heroic soldier. Rather, Hemingway's reference to the statue three times in the opening paragraph seems a prelude to the story's mock-heroic comedy. The inscription at the base of the monument was: "Brotherly soldiers in the supreme sacrifice, gloriously joined, in the greatest Italian victory" (Neel 104).

19. The American wife's conversation with her husband about her desire to grow her short hair out seems distant from Catherine's in *The Garden of Eden*, as she decides to have her hair cut short and then persuades her husband to have his hair cut short to match hers. However, the wife in "Cat" is an early example of strong-willed women in Hemingway's fiction.

20. See, for example, Cohen 233n11; Gajdusek, *Hemingway in His Own Country* 208–9; Meyers 83, 144; and O'Connor 150–55.

21. These sheets of Câblogramme Western Union paper are preserved in KL/EH folder 97A. For a discussion of the importance of this folder in documenting Hemingway's process of arranging the stories and chapters, see my essay "Hemingway's Formation of *In Our Time*."

22. These observations derive from my examination of the Paris *in our time* at the Berg Collection of the New York Public Library. I am thankful to the curators of that collection, especially to Lyndsi Barnes, for their assistance.

23. Milton Cohen notes that the chapter ends without resolving whether or not the bull will charge (178). Benson makes this point in comparing the hesitant bull with "Elliott's sexual uncertainty" (Benson 116–17), but the uncertain bull also evokes the immobile George in "Cat in the Rain." As such, the chapter complements the ambiguous endings of the stories it both follows and precedes.

24. I read the story differently than Warren Bennett, who sees the wife as "[t]he tragic figure in 'Cat in the Rain'" (256). I am more drawn to the comical reading of Vila-Matas, who discusses the story in his novel *Never Any End to Paris*. See West's discussion of Vila-Matas's reading of "Cat."

4. REVISING "BIG TWO-HEARTED RIVER"

1. Several scholars have discussed Hemingway's extensive process of revising the story. Paul Smith notes the "false start" of the original beginning (*Guide* 85). Bernard Oldsey discusses the references to war in this early draft of "River" (219–20). Smith discusses Hemingway's addition of three manuscript pages to the early part of "River" ("Hemingway's Early Manuscripts" 280–81). Michael Reynolds quotes and discusses Hemingway's draft of the story's ending with a flooded fishing site (Reynolds, *Hemingway: The Homecoming*, 209; see also Cirino, *Thought* 22; and Wyatt 165).

2. As shown in this version printed in the Hemingway Library Edition, Hemingway not only started the story in the first person but began the story with Nick Adams joined by two fishing companions in what resembles a war zone (*SS-HLE* 126). For two discussions of the presence of war within the absence of explicit references to combat, see Cirino, *Thought* 20–36; and Vernon, "War, Gender."

3. Robert Paul Lamb observes: "The exhilaration that Nick feels in setting up camp is the joy a writer feels in sitting down to write" (*Short Story* 180). See also note 5 below regarding his discussion of the original ending to "Big Two-Hearted River."

4. In a lovely discussion of the original ending of "Big Two-Hearted River," Kennedy argues that the original ending "portrays Nick Adams in Michigan, thinking back to his life in Paris and—from that exilic perspective—remembering the Michigan that he has already lost" (*Imagining Paris* 95).

5. Without retracting his critique of the original ending, Lamb offers a fascinating discussion of that earlier draft as Hemingway's metafictional meditation on his ambitions and innermost feelings about his writing (*Short Story* 167–92, esp. 175–80). In his biography of Hemingway, James Mellow argues that, had Hemingway been able to bring together "the objective account of his experience of the river and Nick Adams's subjective ruminations on writing . . . he would have accomplished a tour de force in modern writing" (*A Life* 276). Debra A. Moddelmog, in "The Unifying Consciousness of a Divided Conscience," uses the original ending to argue that Nick Adams is the implied author of *In Our Time* (reprinted in part in the Norton Critical Edition of *In Our Time* edited by J. Gerald Kennedy, 209–25).

6. For a discussion of Stein's role in Hemingway's revising the original ending, see J. Gerald Kennedy, "An Introduction to the Volume," *Letters* vol. 2, liii. See also Hemingway's letter to Robert McAlmon referring to the "shit" of the "mental conversation" as "the stuff I've got to cut" and his letter to Donald Ogden Stewart about the "fecal matter" of the original ending (*Letters* vol. 2, 170–72).

7. For a discussion of those two scenes of Jake's fishing and bathing, see Ng 36–39, 41–43.

8. Responding to Hemingway's letter of 15 August 1924 (*Letters* vol. 2, 141), Stein wrote in a letter postmarked 17 August 1924, "I am glad you are doing a good fishing story and I want awfully to see it" (KL/EH, Box 77, Series 3: Incoming Correspondence). By acceding to Stein's suggestion about cutting the original ending, Hemingway preserved the "fishing story" as cleared of explicit references to Nick's writing, aside from the brief reference to his "need to write" (*CSS* 164). Paul Smith saw the influence of Joyce's "The Dead" on Hemingway's revised ending to "Big Two-Hearted River." Arguing that the revised ending pays "silent homage to Joyce," Smith compares "Gabriel's communion with the falling snow" at the end of "The Dead" to Nick's "contemplation of the cedared swamp" ("Hemingway's Senses of an Ending" 235).

9. KL/EH folder 281, as cited by Reynolds (*Paris Years* 209, 378n6); also quoted by Wyatt 165.

5. REVISING "THE BATTLER" AND "THE KILLERS"

1. This story is contained in KL/EH, Personal Papers, Box OM07, High School Literary Magazine. For a brief discussion of this story, see Fenton. Elizabeth Lloyd-Kimbrel read earlier versions of this chapter before and after I presented it at the Hemingway Society Conference in Oak Park on 21 July 2016. I am grateful to Elizabeth for her suggestions. I also thank Michael Kim Roos and Donald A. Daiker for their comments about later drafts of this chapter.

2. See Norman Marcus, "Joe Gans and Ernest Hemingway," at "pauldavisoncrime.com." The following year, Hemingway wrote a sketch of a boxer, "Kerensky, the Fighting Flea," for the *Kansas City Star*, 16 December 1917, published in Paul 187–89. Racial identity and conflict do not figure in that story.

3. Quoting Kenneth Lynn, Toni Morrison refers to Bugs's blackjack as the weapon of a sadist (83). Joseph Flora sees Bugs's use of the blackjack as skillful and careful (*Nick Adams* 90). Likewise, Flora fails to see any hint of a sexual relationship between Ad and Bugs (*Nick Adams in Italy* 92), as has been suggested by DeFalco (72, 77); Mellow, *Life Without Consequences*

(410); Strychacz, "Masculinity" (281); and Young (39–40). Hemingway himself apparently rejected this view of a homosexual relationship between Bugs and Ad (Baker 509).

4. On the relationship between the speaker and the implied listener in a dramatic monologue, see Mermin. In this dramatic monologue, Nick's silence is indicative of Bugs's dominating the conversation.

5. As Grebstein argues, Bugs's "gentle mode of address, which seems only to suggest and cajole . . . really communicates a series of commands that compel obedience" (106).

6. Michael S. Reynolds claims that when Hemingway sent the story to Boni and Liveright he removed "every use" of the racial slur (*Paris Years* 279). It is not clear on what evidence he bases that claim, since the published version includes the slur four times, if far less often than in an earlier draft. Discussions of Bugs's role in "The Battler" vary (Morrison 82; Monteiro 226–28, Marshall 203, Wright-Cleveland 161, Holcomb and Scruggs 60). My reading is closest to that of Sheldon Grebstein, who sees Bugs as "revealing an entire galaxy of experience Nick knows nothing about" (106). Likewise, Joseph Flora implies that Bugs was Nick's mentor, "helping to shape Nick's understanding of life" (*Reading* 59–60; see also Reynolds, *Paris Years* 280). Similarly, H. R. Stoneback writes that Bugs is "the clear exemplar of the tale, the tutor in values for Nick Adams" (107).

7. For persuasive discussions of Dr. Adams as a positive father for Nick, see Daiker, "In Defense of Hemingway's Dr. Adams" and "Defending Hemingway's Henry Adams."

8. See also Holcomb and Scruggs 17–18; and Dudley 70, 78, 79, 81. As Dudley argues, "Even as he dons the garb of servility, Bugs directs the exchange, propels the narrative, and becomes the oracle of personal history for the crew" (79). So far as I know, no one has commented on the importance of Bugs's dramatic monologue as the form of his directing Nick to move on.

9. Joseph Fruscione claims that Sam is referred to by name only twice by the narrator (103). The narrator refers to "Sam" by name four times, and he is named twice by George. For the demographics of Summit, Illinois, see the entry for Summit, Illinois, in the online *Encyclopedia of Chicago*. According to Andrew Chevron, a reference librarian at the Petoskey Public Library, in 1920 whites constituted 97.9 percent of the residents, and Blacks constituted 0.003 percent (e-mail to the author, 10 August 2018). Summit had a considerably higher population of Blacks than did Petoskey.

10. In revising the Madrid typescript, Hemingway also deleted the word "wop" three times, replacing it by hand with "Swede," and replacing Dominick Nerone with Ole Anderson (later spelled Andreson) as the name of the boxer who is marked for the hit (*SS-HLE* 222–23).

11. For a brief discussion of the "external focalization" of third-person narration in "The Killers," see Lamb, *Art Matters* 81.

12. Paul Smith and Gary Edward Holcomb are the only critics I have found who defend Sam's insistence on noninvolvement. Paraphrasing Sam's comments as "let those white folks kill each other," Smith suggests: "in a way his is the most intelligent response" (147). Likewise, as Holcomb argues, "Sam's is a rational response for a black man living in the first decade of the twentieth-century America, when the story is set" (312). The more common view is either to ignore Sam as a character (Dudley 28; Fleming, "Hemingway's 'The Killers'"; Lamb, *Art Matters* 190–93; Meyers 196; Williams 94–95) or to argue that Sam is a foil for Ole Andreson and Nick (Brooks and Warren 187–96; DeFalco 67–68; Flora, *Hemingway's Nick Adams;* Marshall 181, 183, 185; Young 49). Flora's appreciation of Sam's role in "The Killers" seems to have evolved, as his discussion of Sam in *Reading* suggests (see esp. *Reading* 60 and 65).

13. See Joseph Flora's persuasive argument: "When Sam is addressed with the epithet, he knows that there is an implicit threat, knows the behavior that is expected—submission" (*Reading* 60).

14. As Joseph Flora observes, Sam's reaction to being bound and gagged highlights Nick's youthful innocence: "There is nothing of the youthful in Sam's reaction to the towel in his mouth; he has probably endured humiliation often.... There is no swagger in him" (*Reading* 65).

15. The closest example to Sam's addressing Nick as "boy" may be Hemingway's in the unfinished, unpublished novel "The New Slain Knight," started in September 1929 (Dudley 93). Part of that novel was later published separately as "The Porter." In that story, the porter addresses Jimmy Breen as "boy" in a tone that seems ambiguously solicitous (*CSS* 573). In this case, Jimmy Breen *is* a young boy, whereas in "The Killers" Nick seems to be older. However, the porter may be wittily mocking whites' racist use of "boy" to denote a Black man. For a fine reading of "The Porter," see Dudley (91–110).

16. In contrast, the television film of "The Battler," with Paul Newman playing the role of Ad in the *Playwrights '56* adaptation of the story, features a stronger performance by Frederick O'Neal as Bugs than is given by Bill Walker as Sam in Richard Siodmark's film version of "The Killers."

17. In a letter to Hemingway dated 21 February 1927, Max Perkins wrote: "I am sending you an advance copy of the Scribner's which contains 'The Killers,' a story of which Mr. Scribner, Sr., who read it first in the form in which you now see it pronounced, 'not only a good story, but a great story.' I am sorry for the picture of Nick. Except for Nick, I think the characters are pretty well presented in drawing" (KL/EH Box IC29). Perkins's letter implies that Hemingway registered his objection to Baldridge's drawing of Nick with Ole Andreson, the third of his three illustrations for the story. Perkins's letter also suggests that Hemingway did *not* criticize Baldridge's portrait of Sam.

18. Scribner's Card File, card 41247, Collections of The Walter and Leonore Annenberg Research Center, Brandywine River Museum of Art, Pennsylvania. Baldridge's drawing of Sam is from the March 1927 issue of *Scribner's Magazine*. This drawing is reprinted on page 53 of my essay "Bugs and Sam," published in the *Hemingway Review*, spring 2019. The essay is accessible via MUSE.

19. Joseph Flora briefly refers to Sam as having "met the brutality of the world before" (Hemingway's *Nick Adams* 101). In his later commentary on "The Killers," he also refers to Sam's "admonition of avoidance" (*Reading* 65). He does not discuss Hemingway's process of revising the story.

6. REVISING "NOW I LAY ME"

1. Aside from its absence in the list that Hemingway attached to the letter dated 14 February that he sent Perkins, Hemingway did not include the story in the list he sent on 4 May 1927 (*Letters* vol. 3, 232). Paul Smith conjectures that Hemingway did not submit "Now I Lay Me" to a journal because he may have thought the story was "too revealing, too obviously autobiographical" (*Guide* 173). For a fuller discussion of Hemingway's revisions in the multiple drafts of plans for the sequence of stories in *Men Without Women,* see my essay "Hemingway's and Perkins's Formation."

2. James Mellow makes the connection between Hemingway's birthplace and Nick's mem-

ories of the attic of his birth home, an attic in "my grandfather's house" where his father's collection of "snakes and other specimens" lay alongside "my mother's and father's wedding-cake in a tin box hanging from one of the rafters" (*CSS* 277–78; Mellow, *Life Without Consequences* 10). Mellow raises the question as to whether these scenes of burning are purely fictional or are based on memories of actual events (19–20). Scott Donaldson assumes that Hemingway witnessed his mother's gathering up his father's collection of artifacts and tossing them "into a back-yard bonfire" (*Hemingway vs. Fitzgerald* 171). Both Hemingway homes still exist in Oak Park, Illinois. His birthplace is a museum operated by the Ernest Hemingway Foundation of Oak Park.

3. In his piece for the *Toronto Star*, "A Veteran Visits the Home Front," Hemingway wrote about revisiting Fossalta, the site of his wounding, where he remarked that the Austrians "were hunted down" in the same location and "had died in rubble- and debris-strewn streets and had been smoked out of its cellars with *flammenwerfers* during the house-to-house work" (*DLT* 179). In "Now I Lay Me," Hemingway suggests that Nick's childhood memories may overlay and cover over his traumatic sights of war on the front.

4. Unlike "The Doctor and the Doctor's Wife," set in the family's summer home on Walloon Lake (Daiker, "Defending" 45–47), Nick's memories of the burnings in "Now I Lay Me" place them outside the homes where he grew up. In her memoir, Hemingway's sister Marcelline recalled how her father assembled "a remarkable collection" of Indian artifacts he gathered along the Des Plaines River (Sanford 21, 28). The wisdom of Dr. Adams's advice to Nick suggests that he is neither a failed guide nor an "emasculated or ineffectual father" (DeFalco 107, 110), nor a father who raises "the child's feared wound of emasculation" (Hovey 186), nor a husband whose wife has "emasculated" him (Bell; Donaldson, "Hemingway vs. Fitzgerald" 306) and silenced him "without even a hint of protest" (Flora, "Nick Adams in Italy" 196). In short, especially as Hemingway revised the drafts, he portrayed Nick as remembering his father as self-controlled and protective. Nick remembers not a "symbolic castration" of his mother's destroying his father's artifacts (Sempreora 22–24) but rather his father's gathering himself in a temperate masculinity.

5. For a different interpretation of the verb tenses and repetitions in "Now I Lay Me," see Lamb, *Art Matters* 128–33.

6. In his chapter "The Dark Night," Matthew Nickel discusses the possible influence of Dante on Hemingway's *Farewell to Arms* (106–9). Hemingway's comparing Nick's meditation on imagined streams places "Now I Lay Me," even before *Farewell to Arms*, in the tradition of the medieval dream-vision, of which Dante's *Commedia* is the pinnacle in presenting dream-like fiction as visionary truth. In the edition of the *Commedia* that Hemingway owned, Henry Wadsworth Longfellow followed his translation of the *Inferno* with notes about, and excerpts from, the dream-vision genre (Alighieri, *Divine Comedy: Inferno* 181–82, 417–46; see also Reynolds, *Hemingway's Reading* 115). In his first-edition copy of Pound's *Draft of XVI Cantos* (now preserved in the Hemingway Collection at the Kennedy Library), Hemingway would have read Pound's invoking Dante in the opening stanzas of Canto 16, with its dream-visions to follow. Pound's extensive lecturing and writing about Dante, and his influence on the early Hemingway discussed in chapter 1, make it quite possible that he was aware of this dream-vision genre. Another influence leading Hemingway to Dante could also have been Joyce's *Portrait*. For a comparison of the original ending of "Big Two-Hearted River" with *Portrait*, see Michael Reynolds's "Hemingway's *In Our Time:* Biography of a Book," in the Norton Critical Edition edited

by J. Gerald Kennedy (202–3). Hemingway's allusions to Dante's *Inferno* are most repeatedly explicit in his later novel *Across the River and into the Trees*. See Mark Cirino's glossary and commentary on that novel.

7. Joseph Flora discusses the conversation between John and Nick about Brisbane as a writer (*Reading* 173–74). In her extensive discussion of "the metafictional nature of Nick the writer," Margot Sempreora does not mention John and Nick's exchange about Brisbane.

8. Nick's reference to newspaper writing here echoes Krebs in "Soldier's Home." When Krebs considers moving to Kansas City to get a job away from his hometown, he thinks of this plan for himself in a brief interior monologue at the end of the story. Krebs does not share the plan out loud with his mother, even though earlier in the story she handed him the *Kansas City Star* (*CSS* 114, 116). In his conversation with John, Nick speaks aloud and explicitly identifies writing as his likely occupation when he returns to America (*CSS* 280).

7. REVISING "HILLS LIKE WHITE ELEPHANTS"

1. For a discussion of "Hills Like White Elephants" as an allegory of the difference between travel and tourism, see Pottle. The early sketch portrays Hadley and the narrator as tourists. Hemingway revised the sketch so that, as Pottle puts it, "'Hills' is certainly not guide-book fiction" (56). For a photograph of the train station at Caseta[s], identified as a setting in this early draft of the story, see Joseph Flora's *Reading*, the fourth photograph after page 110.

2. Paul Smith was probably mistaken in dating the letter in which Hemingway enclosed "Hills Like White Elephants" as 27 May 1927 (*Guide* 205). Perhaps following Smith, Brewster Chamberlin made the same mistake (81). The editors of Hemingway's letters indicate that the stories he enclosed with that 27 May letter were probably "Ten Indians" and "Now I Lay Me," previously titled "In Another Country-Two" (*Letters* vol. 3, 241n1).

3. As Sheldon Grebstein notes, "The girl looks at the distant hills, the bead curtain, the ground, the curtain again, the river, and the hills once more. Each of these looks corresponds with a phase in the conversation" (113). See also Donaldson, *Fitzgerald and Hemingway: Works and Days* 278.

4. For a comparison of the description of this landscape with the landscape in Cézanne's paintings, see Grebstein 164; and Watts 151.

5. For a reading of the girl's taking hold of two of the strings of beads as carrying the religious significance of rosary beads and a "Hail Mary" prayer, see Nickel 82.

6. John Hollander interprets the phrase "all this" as including "the nearby growth of grain and tree, the promise of plenitude and the promise of continuity in the glimpse of the river—all of these lost before to the beyondness of the elephantine hills" (214–15). Pamela Smiley discusses the significance of this moment when Jig "turns her back on the sterile, burnt hills and the American and looks out onto the fertile fields" (296).

7. Hilary Justice discusses another variation on this exchange. In this version, the girl asks, "Doesn't it mean anything to you? Three of us could get along." The man answers, "Of course it does. And I know we could" (47). This version strongly suggests that the man agrees that "it" (the unborn child, her feelings, their relationship?) "does" mean something to him. His second sentence also suggests that, in agreeing that the three "could get along," the man agrees that the couple should stay together and that she could deliver the child. The version of this manuscript published in the Hemingway Library Edition, with Hemingway's revisions, provides a basis for

the girl's question and statement but does not include the man's replying, "I know we could" (crossed out just under the "t" in "anything). In an e-mail message on 24 February 2023, Stacey Chandler, an archivist at the Kennedy Library, confirms that the draft on page 10 in folder 273 includes the deleted words "I know we could." In my examination and reexamination of this manuscript, I confirmed that Hemingway added—and then crossed out—the sentence "I know we could" immediately above the words "Of course it does." In any event, this version, one that Hemingway did not keep, suggests that he revised this exchange to leave unresolved and open to question what the couple decides to do. Also worth noting is that in the "Foundry Set" of proofs, dated 26 September 1927, the dialogue from "You've got to realize" to "please stop talking" is exactly the same as it is in the final version published in *Men Without Women* (KL/EH 120; *CSS* 214). Hemingway was apparently satisfied with the dialogue, including his cutting the sentence "I know we could."

8. Without referring to the sense of urgency intensified by Hemingway's revision of the waitress's reference to time, Joseph DeFalco notes that "having the characters awaiting a train which will stop for only two minutes, provides an intense focus upon the decision to be reached by the two characters in the short span of time available" (170).

9. Hilary Justice poses the question, "Is she saying thank you again, and for more than your carrying the heavy bags?" (49). Or, one might ask, is she smiling at him for leaving her alone for another minute, or for a much longer time? Or is she leaving him guessing why she is smiling?

10. Although mostly agreeing with Robert Paul Lamb that in "Hills" Hemingway "foreswore any sort of narrative commentary or access to any character's consciousness," I would take mild issue with "any" ("Hemingway and Dialogue" 469). Lamb does allow for "the exception of one key symbol near the end," but it is not clear that he is referring to the man's reflection about the customers "waiting reasonably" in the bar. Although Hemingway cut most of the references to the inner thoughts of the American man, he left one simple sentence giving the reader access to his reflections. For another different reading of the man's reflection about the customers at the bar "waiting reasonably," see Justice 49–50.

11. While believing that Hemingway left the ending of the story in open-ended ambiguity, I am persuaded by Paul Smith's reading of the final scene. Smith posits that while the man is in the bar drinking anise, the girl might be having a last look at the landscape. About the ending, he asks: "could she not have smiled ironically at him and said, 'I feel fine. . . . There's *nothing* wrong with *me*,' leaving him with the last remark of hers that he has not the wit to understand" (*Guide* 211–12). I am also persuaded by those who, like Robert Paul Lamb, read the final paragraph as Hemingway's leaving the couple to "an ambiguous fate" (*Art Matters* 203).

8. REVISING "A WAY YOU'LL NEVER BE"

Between writing "Hills" and "A Way," of course, Hemingway wrote not only *A Farewell to Arms* but also *Death in the Afternoon,* begun in mid-March 1930 and published by Scribner's on 23 September 1932 (Chamberlin 102, 119).

1. In their introduction to *Reading Hemingway's* Winner Take Nothing, Mark Cirino and Susan Vandagriff describe the characters in the collection as "loners and losers and misfits and ne'er do wells . . . grotesqueries" (xi). The placement of "A Way" between "Sea Change" and "Mother of a Queen" that Hemingway proposed in his 13 July letter to Perkins is the order in which the stories appear in *Winner Take Nothing.*

2. For a discussion of Pound and Hemingway in the early 1930s, including the letter from Pound to Hemingway dated 7 August 1933, see my essay "Hemingway's Marlin and Pound's Canto 40."

3. See also Flora, "Nick Adams in Italy," as well as Florczyk; Quick; and Sempreora.

4. Compare the opening paragraphs of "A Way" with the paragraphs beginning "In the ground" and ending "countless pallors of barren lies" (Barbusse, *Under Fire* 226–27). The same passage in the original French, titled *Le Feu* and published in 1916, is on pages 215–16. The passage in Barbusse's novel also includes in its description of the battle scene, along with the corpses, religious images and pamphlets, postcards, leaflets, and "paper words." Not present in this passage from *Under Fire* are references to mustard gas, gas masks, postcards showing rape, or a field kitchen—elements in Hemingway's opening description as published in "A Way." In *A Farewell to Arms*, Barbusse's *Le Feu* is the first book Count Greffi cites when Frederic Henry asks him, "What is there written in wartime?" (225).

5. As was shown in the 2017 exhibition at the New York Historical Society, *World War One Beyond the Trenches,* the gas mask cans were yellow. Yellow is the dominant color in John Singer Sargent's painting *Gassed* (1919), also part of that exhibition. For an extensive discussion of Sargent's painting, but without a reference to Hemingway's story, see Lubin 151–63.

6. Hemingway's addition of a mobile kitchen to the battle debris may reflect his knowledge that the first American casualty on the Italian front was Edward McKey, when his roving kitchen was destroyed by an Austrian shell on 17 June 1918. For an account of McKey's death while working in such a mobile canteen, and the parallels to Hemingway's own wounding, see Steven Florczyk 62–66, 69, 72, 74. As Florczyk points out, Hemingway falsely claimed in a letter home to his parents that he was the first American wounded in Italy (79). Rather, as the editors of the first volume of Hemingway's *Letters* point out, he was the first American to survive his being wounded on the Italian front (*Letters* vol. 1, 118, 119n1).

7. Stephen Dedalus's and Leopold and Molly Bloom's interior monologues in *Ulysses* seem the clearest influence on Nick's interior monologues in "A Way." Hemingway would also have found interior monologues in Gertrude Stein's *Three Lives,* and he employed them in his earlier novels, such as *The Sun Also Rises* and *A Farewell to Arms,* as well as in later novels like *The Old Man and the Sea.* At around the time he was continuing to revise "A Way," Hemingway wrote in a letter on 3 April 1933 to Arnold Gingrich about Joyce's work: "no one can write better than him, technically. I learned much from him" (*Letters* vol. 5, 365). For a discussion of the influence of Joyce's *Ulysses* on Hemingway's fiction, see Gajdusek, *Hemingway and Joyce;* and my essay "Ernest Hemingway's Reading." For Stein's and Joyce's influence on Hemingway's "Cat in the Rain," see chapter 3 above on Hemingway's revisions of "Cat in the Rain."

8. The other occasions are the reference to the hysterical tears of Francis Macomber's wife after she shot him, the "hysteria" of patriotic celebration of soldiers' homecoming in "Soldier's Home," the "hysterical" woman in "The Butterfly and the Tank" (*CSS* 28, 111, 432), and Renata's insistence that she is "not an hysterical" in *Across the River and into the Trees* (254).

9. Relevant to the "Savoia" sequence in Nick's interior monologue is the following account of an attack reported in Thompson: "The countdown was excruciating; after fixing bayonets and draining the double tot of grappa, the men had to get through endless minutes before their officer shouted '*Avanti Savoia*' and led them into the smoking din. . . . The men knew an attack was imminent when the military police mounted their machine guns behind the trench, ready to shoot at soldiers who lingered when the cry of 'Savoy' went up" (*The White War* 226–27).

10. "bail," *Oxford English Dictionary Online,* Oxford UP.

11. Mark Cirino reads "his own" as a reference to Nick's watch "that he consulted before the attack." He allows that the phrase is "ambiguous enough" to refer to "his own platoon formation and even the center of his own psyche" ("A Way You'll Never Be" 113). While agreeing that the language is ambiguous and that there are multiple possible antecedents to "get it" and "his own," I believe that the references are to the liquor Nick says enabled him to go "stinking" in every other attack.

12. This reference to a cave-in reprises the story Hemingway apparently told to Ezra Pound that he was buried alive for four or five days. In a letter to John Quinn dated 10 August 1922, Pound wrote with apparent belief in the stories he must have heard: "Hemingway is a good chap. Was with Italian Arditi, buried alive or rather dead for five days, with no special reason for coming to" (*Letters to John Quinn* 217). Pound memorialized the apocryphal story in Canto XVI: "And Ernie Hemingway went to it . . . / And they buried him for four days" (*Cantos* 72). In the original version published in 1925 as part of *A Draft of XVI Cantos,* Pound used the pseudonym Cyril Hammerton instead of naming Hemingway. See chapter 1, note 3 above.

13. The article "The Teleferica" in the 20 July 1918 issue of *Scientific American* praises it as central to a "supreme classic of mountain warfare" (46). In a letter to his family dated 1 November 1918, Hemingway praised the "skilled Alpine climbers" who "fight and conquer" in the mountains that are almost "impassable" (*Letters* vol. 1, 149). In my original essay "Nick Adams's Interior Monologues in 'A Way You'll Never Be,'" readers can find a reproduction of the cover of that issue of *Scientific American,* with its drawing of soldiers and machine gun being carried up the mountain by the teleferica. Likewise, readers can find a reproduction of a second illustration inside the article of a wounded soldier who is being loaded onto a stretcher for transportation by the teleferica down the mountain.

14. Lest one read Nick's memories of Harry Pilcer and Gaby Deslys in Paris as an autobiographical reference, they were no longer performing their sensational hit "Laissez-les-Tomber!" when Hemingway was in Paris en route to the Italian front. They had been replaced by Mistinguett and Maurice Chevalier. Furthermore, in a letter to his parents on 3 June 1918, Hemingway reported that he went to the "Follies Bergert" [*sic*], not to the Casino de Paris, where "*Laissez*" was playing (Hemingway, *Letters* vol. 1, 110; Gardiner 152–56).

15. For a discussion of the allusions to Gaby Deslys, Harry Pilcer, and the lines from the 1916 song "A Broken Doll," see Flora, *Hemingway's Nick Adams* 130–31. For a discussion of Deslys, especially her performances and actions during World War I, see chapters 12–17 in Gardiner.

16. For a discussion of dream-vision in Hemingway's earlier story "Now I Lay Me," see chapter 6 above. Dante's *Inferno,* with its nightmarish dream-visions, seems even more present in "A Way You'll Never Be." As Paul Smith summarizes Josef Yokelson's argument in his essay published in 1969, "the bearded and red-eyed lieutenant" who confronts and threatens Nick "seems an analogue to Dante's Charon" (*Guide* 274).

17. Philip Young connects the change in the river's width by the yellow house with the swamp at the end of "Big Two-Hearted River." He apparently was the first scholar to discuss the yellow house and the river as forming in Nick's mind "the geography of the place where he was blown up" (53). Since Philip Young's analysis of the yellow house and the river, Joseph Flora and Ellen Andrews Knodt discuss that landscape in relation to Nick Adams. My reading of the yellow house is closer to Knodt's ("Towards a Better Understanding" 80–82) than to Flora's argument that the yellow house "suggests his father's cowardice, and thence all male weak-

ness, including Nick's own fears and uncertainties" ("Nick Adams in Italy" 196). In contrast, for Knodt the yellow house reflects Nick's "psychic trauma" after being shot in the head.

18. Portogrande (actually spelled Portegrandi) can be located on a map that includes Mestre, Zenzon, and San Dona, all four of which are included either in the dialogue between Paravicini and Nick or in Nick's interior monologues. It seems unlikely that the Austrians actually advanced to Portogrande/Portegrandi (on the Sile River well south of the Piave River); Nick's memory of watching Austrians try to wade across a river there is probably another fictional detail. On aspects of this allusion to Portogrande, I have benefited from communications with Michael Kim Roos.

19. See, for instance, the sequence of Brett's leaving with the Count and Jake's interior monologue about "The old grievance" of his war wound (*SAR-HLE* 25–26).

20. Nick's revisiting the scene where he was wounded recalls Hemingway's "A Veteran Visits the Old Front" (*DLT* 176–80). See also Alex Vernon's comment associating the yellow house with "that dreamlike, story-like way of happenings that never happened" ("The Old Front" 11–12).

21. Hemingway's portrait of Nick's recurring dreams and nightmares calls to mind Freud's discussion of "traumatic neurosis" approaching "hysteria" in *Beyond the Pleasure Principle* (29). Freud discusses how dreams can be a means of bringing one back to the "accident . . . from which he wakes in another fright" (30). Philip Young discusses Freud's concept of "repetition compulsion" in relation to the traumatic shock of wounded soldiers, such as portrayed in "A Way" (165–69). Mark Cirino cites a different text by Freud (*Psychopathology of Everyday Life*) to make a similar point about "screen memories" where the yellow house has displaced Nick's memory of the man shooting at him (Cirino, "A Way You'll Never Be" 120).

22. This image of the Rockwell illustration can be viewed on the Library of Congress website.

23. This exchange is similar to one between two sergeants and Frederic Henry in *A Farewell to Arms* (170). There the question about whether Frederic is North or South American is reported in free indirect discourse, not direct dialogue, as here in "A Way." Although the conversation does not escalate into hostility and a manic monologue, as occurs with Nick Adams and the Italians in the story, in the next chapter of *Farewell* Frederic shoots one of the sergeants for deserting instead of following his orders—among the most disturbing scenes in the novel (177).

24. Mark Cirino points out that the first edition of *Winner Take Nothing* reads "hit them with a hat" ("A Way You'll Never Be" 119). My reexamination of the typescript draft (KL/EH folder 815) showed the phrase as "hit them with a hat." The setting copy Hemingway used in reviewing and editing his stories for *Winner Take Nothing* also has "hat," not "bat" (KL/EH folder 222). Robert W. Trogdon makes a strong case for the aptness of "hat" as echoing Nick's reference in "Big Two-Hearted River" to the futility of trying to catch grasshoppers with a hat ("Hemingway and Textual Studies" 41–42; *CSS* 174). Either means of seeking to catch grasshoppers—with a bat or a hat—is absurd, and Nick's allusion to grasshopper-catching suggests his manic state of mind.

25. Issues of the *Scientific American* of 1918 are included in Michael Reynolds's inventory of Hemingway's reading (*Hemingway's Reading* 86). His entry indicates that Hemingway's father sent the issues to him while he was convalescing in the hospital in Milan. In his letters home during his period of surgeries and convalescence, Hemingway repeatedly requested reading material in the form of American newspapers and magazines. See, for instance, the letters dated 29 July, 4 August, 29 August, 11 September, and 14 November (*Letters* vol. 1, 121, 124, 136,

140, 156). For a discussion of Hemingway's reading of scientific journals during this period, see Roos, "The Doctor and the Doctor's Son."

26. An examination of the influence of Hemingway's fiction on the blend of absurdist humor and horrific trauma in war stories by such writers as Joseph Heller, J. D. Salinger, and Tim O'Brien is beyond the scope of this book. However, just to cite a few examples, Heller's Yossarian in *Catch 22*, Salinger's Seymour Glass in "For Esmé—with Love and Squalor," and O'Brien's *The Things They Carried* seem to bear the influence of Hemingway's Nick Adams stories set on the Italian front. At the 18th International Hemingway Conference in Paris, in a presentation titled "What's Funny in *A Farewell to Arms*," Verna Kale suggested that Frederic Henry's humor plays an important role in his healing. Here I am making a similar argument about Nick Adams's sense of humor in "A Way You'll Never Be."

27. The phrase "clublike impact" is similar to language Hemingway read about the head wound Prince Andrei received in the translation by Constance Garnett that he owned of Tolstoy's *War and Peace* (*CSS* 314; Tolstoy 313). In a letter to Jane Heap around 23 August 1925, Hemingway wrote that he had "just read . . . Constance Garnett's translation of War and Peace" (*Letters* vol. 2, 384). Together with Paravicini's reference to trepanning, and Nick's promise that the American soldiers to come "have never had their heads caved in," Nick's memory of a bearded man aiming his rifle at him and squeezing the trigger points to his being wounded in the head. On the other hand, as the late Peter L. Hays pointed out to me, his "choking, coughing it onto the rock" is not consistent with a head wound (e-mail, 25 June 2021). In an essay Hemingway published a couple of years after this story, he refers to both types of wounds: "Hit in the head you will die quickly. . . . But if you are not hit in the head you will be hit in the chest and choke in it" (*BL* 209–10). In the case of Nick's memory of being wounded, Hemingway leaves the precise, physical nature of the wound unclear, instead emphasizing its enduring psychological trauma.

28. Hemingway might have read of the "nodding plumes" on the helmets of the Bersaglieri bicyclists in combat, whose discipline was "the best in the Italian army," in G. M. Trevelyan's *Scenes from Italy's War* (83–84, 86). For a photograph of Italian cavalry on the road to Fossalta in 1918, see plate 17 in Baker. For a recent discussion of Hemingway's reading of Trevelyan in connection with *A Farewell to Arms*, see Roos, "I Fixed the Dates."

9. REVISING "THE GAMBLER, THE NUN, AND THE RADIO"

This chapter is a revision and expansion of a presentation I gave at the 19th Biennial Hemingway Society Conference at Sheridan, Wyoming, on July 18, 2022.

1. In her fine essay about "Gambler," Ann L. Putnam refers to the story's "comedy strangely mixed with darkness" ("Opiates, Laughter" 161).

2. For a full and informative discussion of these songs, see Nicole J. Camastra's commentary on "The Gambler, the Nun, and the Radio" (249–51).

3. I am indebted to Elizabeth Lloyd-Kimbrel for her guidance about films to watch in preparation for writing this chapter.

4. Hemingway based the character Pedro Romero in *The Sun Also Rises* on a real-life matador named Cayetano Ordóñez (or Niño de la Palma, his professional name), whom Hemingway had seen in 1925 in his first season as a matador (Stonebeck 248; Svoboda, *Hemingway's* The Sun Also Rises 5). Decades later he wrote *The Dangerous Summer* in part about his son, Antonio

Ordóñez. In naming his gambler Cayetano, Hemingway perhaps implies the connection Scott Donaldson makes between Romero and Cayetano.

5. For an excellent discussion of the "musicality of this passage," and the repetition in Hemingway's prose as "indicative of both fugue and variation," see Camastra 261–62.

6. In a letter to Pound dated 14 June 1933, Hemingway offered to approach Scribner's about publishing Pound's *ABC of Economics* (*Letters* vol. 5, 412–13, 413n1). In his letter to Pound dated 11 November 1933, Hemingway reacted to a nationally broadcast radio address by President Roosevelt: "Am damned disgusted with the whole show—Hope youse can save it with economics—it's funny as hell at home now" (*Letters* vol. 5, 537n3).

7. In her reading of "Gambler," Ann L. Putnam argues that the final ending "represents escape not involvement." She sees the story as shrinking "to a tiny pointed light in the image of a man turned toward a radio." Even the story's humor seems, in her reading, "silenced by the whispering hiss of the radio's sweet lies" (165). I read the story as ending on a more ambiguous, open-ended note—with the humor still audible, even if barely.

8. For a discussion of Cayetano and Frazer as "a *pair* of characters to tell what is essentially a single story," see Putnam, "Opiates, Laughter, and the Radio's Sweet Lies," 160–63. Especially intriguing is Putnam's argument that "Cayetano's professionalism and dedication to craft suggests parallels with a writer's life—and what this strange life does to one's human attachments" (163).

10. FROM "TOMB OF MY GRANDFATHER" TO "FATHERS AND SONS"

1. For a review of recent scholarship, see Donald A. Daiker's commentary on "Fathers and Sons" in *Reading Hemingway's* Winner Take Nothing, edited by Mark Cirino and Susan Vandergriff. The most extensive discussions of "Fathers and Sons" as a work of art are by Dudley; Flora, *Hemingway's Nick Adams;* and Smith, *Guide.* More often, as most skillfully in Reynolds's *Hemingway: The 1930s,* scholars focus on the biographical dimensions of the story.

2. Although Hemingway does not rename Prudy as Trudy until the typescript draft contained in folder 385a, I will refer to her as Trudy from this point of the chapter. Likewise, while Hemingway spelled her last name "Gilbey" in "Tomb of My Grandfather," I use the spelling of "Gilby" that he used in "Fathers and Sons" (*SS-HLE* 411; *CSS* 373).

3. For a fine reading of "Ten Indians," see Daiker, "'I Think Dad Probably Waited for Me.'"

4. "bugger, n. 1": "2. A person who penetrates the anus of someone during sexual intercourse; a person who performs any act classed as 'buggery' (see buggery n. 2). Chiefly as a term of abuse or contempt." *Oxford English Dictionary Online.*

5. "mash, v. 1": "To beat into a soft mass; to crush, pound, or smash to a pulp; to squash." "mash, v. 2": "*transitive.* To attract or excite amorous attention in (a person of the opposite sex)." *Oxford English Dictionary Online.*

6. As Ruth Bauerle argues about the arrest and trial of Caruso, "The event gained immortality when Joyce drew upon it for scenes in Bloom's trial in *Ulysses*" (125). Hemingway showed a substantial knowledge of Caruso by the time he wrote his parents from Toronto on 22 April 1920 (Hemingway, *Letters* vol. 1, 231nn3 and 4). See also my essay "Ernest Hemingway's Reading of James Joyce's *Ulysses.*"

7. Susan F. Beegel connects this stripping of the landscape with a "forestry holocaust enabled by new forms of transport, felling, and mill technology" ("Environment" 238).

8. As Carl Eby notes, "The threat is clearly ironic"; he further suggests a "fetishistic dimension" to Nick's threat (293). Nick's reaction is both violent and hysterical. Mark Kevin Dudley argues that in "Fathers and Sons," Hemingway "violently confronts the prospects of miscegenation" and depicts Nick's "quite violent defense of his own sister's maidenhood" (12). Amy Strong defends Hemingway's portrait of Trudy in "Fathers and Sons" as an example of Hemingway's "openly defying white anxieties over miscegenation" (326). Strong argues further that Hemingway "made a point of humanizing Indians through his writing" and "challenges the entrenched stereotypes of American Indians that had flourished in popular culture" (326–27). In his essay "Hemingway's Nick Adams and His Lost 'Indian Girl,'" Donald A. Daiker traces the disappearance of Trudy in several of Hemingway's Nick Adams stories, including the unfinished and posthumously published "The Last Good Country." Daiker connects her vanishing with the vanishing of Indians and their way of life in stories like "The Light of the World" and "Fathers and Sons"—and with the theme of loss pervasive in Hemingway's fiction.

9. As Nancy Comley and Robert Scholes argue, "Nick is trading one sign of manhood for another" (12). On Nick's struggle to assure himself of his masculinity, see McCann 271.

10. See Donald A. Daiker's discussion of this passage, along with his praise for Sheldon Grebstein's analysis, in his commentary on "Fathers and Sons" in *Reading Hemingway's* Winner Take Nothing 288–89.

11. See Joseph Flora's observation that in "Fathers and Sons" Hemingway swerves from the "clipped, staccato" sentences of *In Our Time* and "The Killers" and instead writes in "sentences tending to be long and even languid" (*Study of the Short Fiction* 46).

12. In his preface to his edition of Hemingway's letters, Carlos Baker quotes Hemingway's comment that "he had picked up from an actual old Indian: 'Long time ago good, now heap shit'" (*Selected Letters* xi–xii).

13. Anne Edwards Boutelle observes that "[t]here is no explicit mention of his father's suicide, but there are enough heavy hints for the reader to feel that it is the true subject of the story" (142). For discussions of the depression and suicide of Hemingway's father, see Reynolds, "Hemingway's Home," and Donaldson, "Hemingway and Suicide." Privately, Hemingway wrote rather bluntly about his own father's suicide (*Letters* vol. 4, 14, 86, 246, 261, 639).

14. Erik Nakjavani describes Hemingway's portrait of the father's remade face as a "still life," pointing to the irony that the French phrase for "still life" is "*nature morte*" (99). See also his discussion of the Oedipal triangles in the story, particularly his discussion of Nick's revulsion at the smell of his father's underwear.

15. Thomas Strychacz claims in his essay "Masculinity," that "[n]one of Hemingway's major male characters deals with children in any significant way" (281). However, "A Day's Wait" and "Fathers and Sons" are two stories in *Winner Take Nothing* with narrators as fathers whom Hemingway depicts as dealing with their children.

WORKS CITED

Alighieri, Dante. *The Divine Comedy of Dante Alighieri*. Translated by Henry Wadsworth Longfellow, Houghton, Mifflin, 1893.

———. *Paradiso*. Translated by Robert Hollander and Jean Hollander, Doubleday, 2007.

Anderson, Margaret, and Jane Heap. "Comments." *Little Review*, vol. 9, no. 3, May 1923, p. 25.

Bacigalupo, Massimo. *Grotta Byron: Luoghi e libri*. Campanotto, 2001.

Baker, Carlos. *Ernest Hemingway: A Life Story*. Charles Scribner's Sons, 1969.

Baldwin, James, and Randall Kenan. *The Cross of Redemption: Uncollected Writings*. Pantheon, 2010.

Banks, Arthur. *A Military Atlas of the First World War*. Pen and Sword Books, 2013.

Barbusse, Henri. *Le Feu*. FB Editions, 2018.

———. *Under Fire*. Wilder Publications, 2010.

Bauerle, Ruth. "Caruso's Sin in the Fiendish Park: 'The Possible Was the Improbable and the Improbable the Inevitable.'" *James Joyce Quarterly*, vol. 38, no. 1/2, fall 2000–winter 2001, pp. 125–42.

Beall, John. "Bugs and Sam: Nick Adams's Guides in 'The Battler' and 'The Killers.'" *Hemingway Review*, vol. 38, no. 2, spring 2019, pp. 42–58.

———. "Ernest Hemingway's Reading of James Joyce's *Ulysses*." *James Joyce Quarterly*, vol. 51, no. 4, summer 2014, pp. 661–72.

———. "Hemingway as Craftsman: Revising 'Big Two-Hearted River.'" *Hemingway Review*, vol. 36, no. 2, spring 2017, pp. 79–94.

———. "Hemingway as Craftsman: Revising 'Fathers and Sons.'" *MidAmerica*, vol. 43, 2016, pp. 118–43.

———. "Hemingway's and Perkins's Formation of *Men Without Women*." *Hemingway Review*, vol. 36, no. 1, fall 2016, pp. 94–102.

———. "Hemingway's 'Cat in the Rain': The Presence of Stein and Joyce." *MidAmerica*, vol. 42, 2015, pp. 54–78.

———. "Hemingway's Dark Humor: 'A Way You'll Never Be.'" *Midwestern Miscellany,* vol. 43, spring/fall 2019, pp. 99–111.

———. "Hemingway's Formation of *In Our Time.*" *Hemingway Review,* vol. 35, no. 1, fall 2015, pp. 63–77.

———. "Hemingway's Marlin and Pound's Canto 40." *Hemingway Review,* vol. 41, no. 2, spring 2022, pp. 120–29.

———. "Hemingway's 'Now I Lay Me': Rivers, Writing, and Prayers." *MidAmerica,* vol. 44, 2017, pp. 41–64.

———. "Nick Adams's Interior Monologues in 'A Way You'll Never Be.'" *Hemingway Review,* vol. 40, no. 2, spring 2021, pp. 94–115.

———. "Pound, Hemingway, and the Inquest Series." *Paideuma,* vol. 44, 2017, pp. 173–204.

———. "Pound's Composition of Canto 16." *Cross-Cultural Pound,* edited by John Gery et al., Clemson UP, 2021, pp. 79–90.

Beegel, Susan F. "Environment." *Ernest Hemingway in Context,* edited by Debra A. Moddelmog and Suzanne del Gizzo, Cambridge UP, 2015, pp. 237–46.

———. *Hemingway's Craft of Omission: Four Manuscript Examples.* UMI Research Press, 1988.

Bell, Millicent. "*A Farewell to Arms:* Pseudoautobiography and Personal Metaphor." *Ernest Hemingway: The Writer in Context,* edited by James Nagel, U of Wisconsin P, 1984, pp. 107–28.

Bennett, Warren. "The Poor Kitty and the Padrone and the Tortoise-shell Cat in 'Cat in the Rain.'" *New Critical Approaches to the Short Stories of Ernest Hemingway,* edited by Jackson J. Benson, Duke UP, 1990, pp. 245–56.

Benson, Jackson J. "Patterns of Connection and Their Development in Hemingway's *In Our Time.*" *Critical Essays on Ernest Hemingway's* In Our Time, edited by Michael S. Reynolds, G. K. Hall, 1983, pp. 103–19.

Bishop, Janet C., Cecile Debray, and Rebecca A. Rabinow. *The Steins Collect.* San Francisco Museum of Modern Art, 2011.

Bishop, John Peale. "Homage to Hemingway." *The Collected Essays of John Peale Bishop,* Scribner's, 1948.

Boutelle, Ann Edwards. "Hemingway and 'Papa': Killing of the Father in the Nick Adams Fiction." *Journal of Modern Literature,* vol. 9, no. 1, 1981–82, pp. 133–46.

Bovey, Seth. "The Western Code of Hemingway's Gambler." *North Dakota Quarterly,* vol. 48, no. 3, 1990, pp. 86–93.

Brasch, James D., and Joseph Sigman. *Hemingway's Library: A Composite Record.* Garland, 1981.

Brisbane, Arthur. *Editorials from the Hearst Newspapers.* Albertson, 1906.

Brogan, Jacqueline Vaught. "Hemingway's *In Our Time:* A Cubist Anatomy." *Hemingway Review,* vol. 17, no. 2, 1998, pp. 31–46.

Brooks, Cleanth, and Robert Penn Warren. "The Killers." *The Short Stories of Ernest*

Hemingway: Critical Essays, edited by Jackson J. Benson, Duke UP, 1975, pp. 187–96.

Bruccoli, Matthew J., editor. *F. Scott Fitzgerald: A Life in Letters.* Simon and Schuster, 1995.

Bruccoli, Matthew J., editor, with Robert W. Trogdon. *The Only Thing That Counts: The Ernest Hemingway–Maxwell Perkins Correspondence.* Scribner's, 1996.

Bush, Ronald. *The Genesis of Ezra Pound's Cantos.* Princeton UP, 1976.

Cabanne, Christy, director. *Martyrs of the Alamo.* D. W. Griffith, 1915.

Camastra, Nicole J. "The Gambler, The Nun, and the Radio." *Reading Hemingway's Winner Take Nothing: Glossary and Commentary,* edited by Mark Cirino and Susan Vandergriff. Kent State UP, 2021, pp. 237–68.

Chamberlin, Brewster. *The Hemingway Log: A Chronology of His Life and Times.* U of Kansas P, 2015.

Cirino, Mark. *Ernest Hemingway: Thought in Action.* U of Wisconsin P, 2012.

——. *Reading Hemingway's* Across the River and into the Trees: *Glossary and Commentary.* Kent State UP, 2016.

——. "A Way You'll Never Be." *Reading Hemingway's* Winner Take Nothing: *Glossary and Commentary.* Kent State UP, 2021, pp. 99–123.

Cirino, Mark, and Susan Vandagriff. Introduction. *Reading Hemingway's* Winner Take Nothing: *Glossary and Commentary.* Kent State UP, 2021, pp. xi–xvi.

Cohen, Milton A. *Hemingway's Laboratory: The Paris* in our time. U of Alabama P, 2005.

Comley, Nancy R., and Robert Scholes. *Hemingway's Genders: Rereading the Hemingway Text.* Yale UP, 1994.

Cowley, Malcolm. *A Second Flowering.* Viking, 1974.

Culver, Michael. "The Art of Henry Strater: An Examination of the Illustrations for Pound's *A Draft of XVI Cantos.*" *Paideuma,* vol. 12, no. 2 and 3, fall and winter 1983, pp. 446–78.

Curnutt, Kirk. *Reading Hemingway's* Across the River and into the Trees: *Glossary and Commentary.* Kent State UP, 2016.

Daiker, Donald A. "Defending Hemingway's Henry Adams: The Doctor, the Critics, and the Doctor's Son." *Middle West Review,* vol. 3, no. 2, spring 2017, pp. 45–65.

——. "Fathers and Sons." *Reading Hemingway's* Winner Take Nothing: *Glossary and Commentary.* Kent State UP, 2021, pp. 269–91.

——. "Hemingway's Nick Adams and His Lost 'Indian Girl.'" *Hemingway Review,* vol. 42, no. 2, 2023, pp. 8–24.

——. "'I Think Dad Probably Waited for Me': Biography, Intertextuality, and Hemingway's 'Ten Indians.'" *MidAmerica,* vol. 42, 2015, pp. 36–53.

——. "In Defense of Hemingway's Dr. Adams: The Case for 'Indian Camp.'" *Hemingway Review,* vol. 35, no. 2, spring 2016, pp. 55–69.

Dearborn, Mary V. *Ernest Hemingway: A Biography.* Knopf, 2017.

DeFalco, Joseph. *The Hero in Hemingway's Short Stories.* U of Pittsburgh P, 1963.

Derounian, Kathryn Zabelle. "An Examination of the Drafts of Hemingway's Chapters 'Nick sat against the wall of the church. . . .'" *Critical Essays on Ernest Hemingway's In Our Time*, edited by Michael S. Reynolds, G. K. Hall, 1983, pp. 61–75.

Donaldson, Scott. *By Force of Will: The Life and Art of Ernest Hemingway.* Authors Guild Backinprint.com, 2001.

———. *Fitzgerald and Hemingway: Works and Days.* Columbia UP, 2009.

———. "Hemingway and Suicide." *Sewanee Review,* vol. 103, no. 2, spring 1995, pp. 287–95.

———. *Hemingway vs. Fitzgerald: The Rise and Fall of a Literary Friendship.* Overlook Press, 1999.

———. "Preparing for the End of 'A Canary for One.'" *Fitzgerald and Hemingway: Works and Days,* Columbia UP, 2009, pp. 260–68.

Dudley, Marc Kevin. *Hemingway, Race, and Art: Bloodlines and the Color Line.* Kent State UP, 2011.

Eby, Carl P. *Hemingway's Fetishism: Psychoanalysis and the Mirror of Manhood.* State U of New York P, 1999.

———. *Reading Hemingway's* The Garden of Eden: *Glossary and Commentary.* Kent State UP, 2023.

Eliot, T. S. *The Waste Land: A Facsimile and Transcript of the Original Drafts Including the Annotations of Ezra Pound.* Harcourt Brace Jovanovich, 1971.

Ellis, Havelock. *Studies in the Psychology of Sex.* F. A. Davis, 1914.

Ellmann, Richard. *James Joyce.* New and rev. ed., Oxford UP, 1982.

Fenton, Charles A. "No Money for the Kingbird: Hemingway's Prizefight Stories." *The Short Stories of Ernest Hemingway: Critical Essays,* edited by Jackson J. Benson, Duke UP, 1975, pp. 53–63.

"Fifty Billion German Allies Already in the American Field." *Scientific American,* 20 July 1918, pp. 47–49.

Fleming, Robert E. "Hemingway's 'The Killers': The Map and the Territory." *New Critical Approaches to the Short Stories of Ernest Hemingway,* edited by Jackson J. Benson, Duke UP, 1990, pp. 309–13.

Fleming, Victor, director. *The Virginian.* Paramount Studios, 1929.

Flora, Joseph M. *Ernest Hemingway: A Study of the Short Fiction.* Twayne, 1989.

———. *Hemingway's Nick Adams.* Louisiana State UP, 1982.

———. "Nick Adams in Italy." *Hemingway's Italy: New Perspectives,* edited by Rena Sanderson, Louisiana State UP, 2006, pp. 185–200.

———. *Reading Hemingway's* Men Without Women: *Glossary and Commentary.* Kent State UP, 2008.

Florczyk, Steven. *Hemingway, the Red Cross, and the Great War.* Kent State UP, 2014.

Ford, Hugh D. *Published in Paris: American and British Writers, Printers, and Publishers in Paris, 1920–1939.* Pushcart, 1980.

Freud, Sigmund. *Beyond the Pleasure Principle.* Bantam, 1959.

Fruscione, Joseph. "Knowing and Recombining: Ellison's Ways of Understanding Hemingway." *Hemingway and the Black Renaissance,* edited by Gary Edward Holcomb and Charles Scruggs, Ohio State UP, 2012, pp. 78–119.

Gajdusek, Robert E. *Hemingway and Joyce: A Study in Debt and Repayment.* Square Circle Press, 1984.

——. *Hemingway in His Own Country.* U of Notre Dame P, 2002.

Gardiner, James. *Gaby Deslys: A Fatal Attraction.* Sidgwick and Jackson, 1986.

Gay, Margaret Cooper. *How to Live with a Cat.* Simon and Schuster, 1947.

Gilbert, Martin. *The First World War: A Complete History.* Rosetta Books, 2014.

Gillis, Colin. "James Joyce and the Masturbating Boy." *James Joyce Quarterly,* vol. 50, no. 3, 2013, pp. 611–34.

Grebstein, Sheldon Norman. *Hemingway's Craft.* Southern Illinois UP, 1973.

Griffin, Peter. "A Foul Mood, A Dirty Joke: Hemingway's 'Cat in the Rain.'" *Hemingway Review,* vol. 20, no. 2, 2001, pp. 99–102.

Hemingway, Ernest. *Across the River and into the Trees.* Scribner's, 1996.

——. *By-line, Ernest Hemingway: Selected Articles and Dispatches of Four Decades.* Edited by William White, Simon and Schuster, 1998.

——. *Complete Poems.* Edited, with an introduction and notes, by Nicholas Gerogiannis, rev. ed., U of Nebraska P, 1992.

——. *The Complete Short Stories of Ernest Hemingway: The Finca Vigía Edition.* Scribner's, 2003.

——. *Dateline, Toronto: The Complete* Toronto Star *Dispatches, 1920–1924.* Edited by William White, Scribner's, 1985.

——. *Death in the Afternoon.* Scribner's, 2003.

——. "Ernest Hemingway." Interview by George Plimpton. *Writers at Work: The Paris Review Interviews, Second Series,* edited by George Plimpton, Penguin, 1977, pp. 215–30.

——. *Ernest Hemingway: Selected Letters, 1917–1961.* Edited by Carlos Baker, Scribner's, 1981.

——. *Farewell to Arms: The Hemingway Library Edition.* Scribner's, 2014.

——. *The Garden of Eden.* Scribner's, 1986.

——. "Give Us a Prescription, Doctor." *Scribner's Magazine,* May 1933, pp. 272–78.

——. "Hills Like White Elephants." *transition,* August 1927, pp. 9–14.

——. "Homage to Ezra." *This Quarter,* vol. 1, no. 1, 1925, pp. 221–25.

——. *in our time.* Paris: Three Mountains Press, 1924.

——. *In Our Time: Stories by Ernest Hemingway.* Boni and Liveright, 1925.

——. *In Our Time.* Scribner's, 2003.

——. *In Our Time: A Norton Critical Edition.* Edited by J. Gerald Kennedy, W. W. Norton, 2022.

——. *The Letters of Ernest Hemingway.* Edited by Sandra Spanier et al., vol. 1, Cambridge UP, 2011.

———. *The Letters of Ernest Hemingway.* Edited by Sandra Spanier et al., vol. 2, Cambridge UP, 2011.

———. *The Letters of Ernest Hemingway.* Edited by Sandra Spanier et al., vol. 3, Cambridge UP, 2015.

———. *The Letters of Ernest Hemingway.* Edited by Sandra Spanier et al., vol. 4, Cambridge UP, 2018.

———. *The Letters of Ernest Hemingway.* Edited by Sandra Spanier et al., vol. 5, Cambridge UP, 2020.

———, editor. *Men at War.* Wings Books, 1991.

———. *A Moveable Feast.* Scribner's Books, 1964.

———. *I quarantanove racconti.* Translated by Vincenzo Mantovani, Einaudi, 2006.

———. *The Short Stories of Ernest Hemingway: The Hemingway Library Edition.* Scribner's, 2017.

———. *The Sun Also Rises: The Hemingway Library Edition.* Scribner's, 2014.

———. *Three Stories and Ten Poems.* Contact Editions, 1923.

Hemingway, Leicester. *My Brother, Ernest Hemingway.* World Publishing, 1961.

Holcomb, Gary Edward. "Race and Ethnicity: African Americans." *Ernest Hemingway in Context,* edited by Debra A. Moddlemog and Suzanne del Gizzo, Cambridge UP, 2015, pp. 307–14.

Holcomb, Gary Edward, and Charles Scruggs. *Hemingway and the Black Renaissance.* Ohio State UP, 2012.

Hollander, John. "Hemingway's Extraordinary Actuality." *Ernest Hemingway: Modern Critical Views,* edited by Harold Bloom, Chelsea House, 1985.

Hovey, Richard B. "Hemingway's 'Now I Lay Me': A Psychological Interpretation." *The Short Stories of Ernest Hemingway: Critical Essays,* edited by Jackson J. Benson, Duke UP, 1975, pp. 180–87.

Hurwitz, Harold M. "Hemingway's Tutor, Ezra Pound." *Modern Fiction Studies,* vol. 17, no. 4, winter 1971–72, pp. 469–82.

James, Will. *Smoky the Cowhorse.* Aladdin Paperbacks, 2008.

Joost, Nicholas. *Ernest Hemingway and the Little Magazines.* Barre Publishers, 1968.

Joyce, James, *Dubliners.* Edited by Robert Scholes and A. Walton Litz, Penguin, 1996.

———. *Letters.* Edited by Richard Ellmann, vol. 3, Viking, 1966.

———. *A Portrait of the Artist as a Young Man.* Edited by Seamus Deane, Penguin, 2003.

———. *Ulysses: The Corrected Text.* Edited by Hans Walter Gabler, Wolfhard Steppe, and Claus Melchoir, Vintage, 1986.

Justice, Hilary. *The Bones of the Others: The Hemingway Text from the Lost Manuscripts to the Posthumous Novels.* Kent State UP, 2006.

Kale, Verna. *Ernest Hemingway.* Reaktion Books, 2016.

———. "What's Funny in *A Farewell to Arms.*" *Blog//Los Angeles Review of Books,* 2 October 2018, blog.lareviewofbooks.org/essays/whats-funny-farewell-arms/.

Kennedy, J. Gerald. *Imagining Paris: Exile, Writing, and American Identity.* Yale UP, 1993.
———. Introduction. *The Letters of Ernest Hemingway,* vol. 2, edited by Sandra Spanier et al., Cambridge UP, 2011, pp. xlix–lix.
———. Introduction. *In Our Time: A Norton Critical Edition,* W. W. Norton, 2022, pp. ix–xx.
———. "What Hemingway Omitted from 'Cat in the Rain.'" *Les Cahiers de la Nouvelle: Journal of the Short Story in English,* vol. 1, 1983, pp. 75–81.
Kennedy, J. Gerald, and Kirk Curnutt. "Mrs. Krebs, Mother Stein, and 'Soldier's Home.'" *Hemingway Review,* vol. 12, no. 1, 1992, pp. 1–11.
Knodt, Ellen Andrews. "Getting Closer To 'It': Linking Hemingway's World War I Short Stories." *Midwestern Miscellany,* vol. 42, 2019, pp. 83–95.
———. "Towards a Better Understanding of Nicholas Adams in Hemingway's 'A Way You'll Never Be.'" *Hemingway Review,* vol. 35, no. 2, spring 2016, pp. 70–86.
Lamb, Robert Paul. *Art Matters: Hemingway, Craft, and the Creation of the Modern Short Story.* Louisiana State UP, 2010.
———. "Hemingway and the Creation of Twentieth-Century Dialogue." *Twentieth Century Literature,* vol. 42, no. 4, winter 1996, pp. 451–80.
———. *The Hemingway Short Story: A Study in Craft for Writers and Readers.* Louisiana State UP, 2013.
Lewis, Robert W., Jr. "Vivienne de Watteville, Hemingway's Companion on Kilimanjaro." *Texas Quarterly,* vol. 9, no. 4, winter 1966, pp. 75–88.
Lewis, Robert W., and Michael Kim Roos. *Reading Hemingway's A Farewell to Arms: Glossary and Commentary.* Kent State UP, 2019.
Lewis, Robert W., Jr., and Max Westbrook. "The Texas Manuscript of 'The Snows of Kilimanjaro.'" *Texas Quarterly,* vol. 9, no. 4, winter 1966, pp. 66–101.
———. "The 'Snows of Kilimanjaro' Collated and Annotated." *Texas Quarterly,* vol. 13, no. 2, summer 1970, pp. 67–143.
Lloyd-Kimbrel, Elizabeth. E-mail to the author. 2 February 2017.
Lodge, David. "Analysis and Interpretation of the Realist Text: A Pluralistic Approach to Ernest Hemingway's 'Cat in the Rain.'" *Poetics Today,* vol. 1, no. 4, 1980, pp. 5–22.
Longfellow, Henry Wadsworth, translator. *The Divine Comedy of Dante Alighieri.* Houghton Mifflin, 1893.
Lubin, David M. *Grand Illusions: American Art and the First World War.* Oxford UP, 2016.
Lynn, Kenneth Schuyler. *Hemingway.* Harvard UP, 1995.
Maclean, John N. "Foreword." *Ernest Hemingway's "Big Two-Hearted River,"* Mariner Classics, 2023.
Marcus, Norman. "Joe Gans and Ernest Hemingway." Pauldavisoncrime.com.
Marshall, Ian. "Rereading Hemingway: Rhetorics of Whiteness, Labor, and Identity." *Hemingway and the Black Renaissance,* edited by Gary Edward Holcomb and Charles Scruggs, Ohio State UP, 2012, pp. 177–213.

McAlmon, Robert, and Kay Boyle. *Being Geniuses Together, 1920–1930*. North Point, 1984.

McCann, Richard. "To Embrace or Kill: Fathers and Sons." *New Critical Approaches to the Short Stories of Ernest Hemingway,* edited by Jackson J. Benson, Duke UP, 1990, pp. 266–74.

McNeil, Everett. *In Texas with Davy Crockett: A Story of the Texas War of Independence.* Create Space Independent Publishing Platform, 2016.

Mellow, James. *Charmed Circle: Gertrude Stein and Company.* Praeger, 1974.

———. *Hemingway: A Life Without Consequences.* Houghton, 1992.

Meredith, George. "An Essay on Comedy." *Comedy,* edited, with an introduction and appendix, by Wylie Sypher, Johns Hopkins UP, 1994.

Mermin, Dorothy. "Speaker and Auditor in Browning's Dramatic Monologues." *University of Toronto Quarterly,* vol. 45, no. 2, 1976, pp. 139–58.

Méry, Fernand. *Her Majesty the Cat.* Criterion Books, 1957.

Meyers, Jeffrey. *Hemingway: A Biography.* Harper and Row, 1985.

Mix, Tom, director. *The Man from Texas.* Sinister Studio, 1915.

Moddelmog, Debra A. "The Unifying Consciousness of a Divided Conscience." *In Our Time: A Norton Critical Edition,* edited by J. Gerald Kennedy, W. W. Norton, 2022, pp. 209–25.

Moddelmog, Debra A., and Suzanne del Gizzo, editors. *Ernest Hemingway in Context.* Cambridge UP, 2015.

Monteiro, George. "'This Is My Pal Bugs': Ernest Hemingway's 'The Battler.'" *New Critical Approaches to the Short Stories of Ernest Hemingway,* edited by Jackson J. Benson, Duke UP, 1990, pp. 224–28.

Moody, Anthony David. *Ezra Pound: Poet—A Portrait of the Man and His Work: The Epic Years, 1921–1939.* Oxford UP, 2014.

Morrison, Toni. *Playing in the Dark: Whiteness and the Literary Imagination.* Vintage, 1993.

Nakjavani, Erik. "The Fantasies of Omnipotence and Powerlessness." *Hemingway: Up in Michigan,* edited by Frederic J. Svoboda, Michigan State UP, 1995, pp. 91–101.

Neel, Hildy Coleman. "The War Monument in 'Cat in the Rain': Then and Now." *Hemingway Review,* vol. 19, no. 2, 2000, pp. 102–4.

Ng, Lay Sion. "Toward a Politics of Cure: Jake Barnes's Embracing of Otherness in *The Sun Also Rises.*" *Hemingway Review,* vol. 41, no. 2, spring 2022, pp. 31–48.

Nickel, Matthew C. *Hemingway's Dark Night: Catholic Influences and Intertextualities in the Work of Ernest Hemingway.* New Street Communications, 2013.

O'Connor, Frank. *The Lonely Voice: A Study of the Short Story.* Melville House, 2004.

Oldsey, Bernard. "Hemingway's Beginnings and Endings." *College Literature,* vol. 7, no. 3, 1980, pp. 213–38.

Oxford English Dictionary Online. Oxford UP.

Paul, Steve. *Hemingway at Eighteen: The Pivotal Year That Launched an American Legend.* Chicago Review Press, 2017.

Perloff, Marjorie. "'Ninety-Percent Rotarian': Gertrude Stein's Hemingway." *American Literature*, vol. 62, no. 4, 1990, pp. 668–83.

Pondrom, Cyrena N. "An Introduction to the Achievement of Gertrude Stein." Introduction. *Geography and Plays*, by Gertrude Stein, U of Wisconsin P, 1993, pp. vii–lv.

Pottle, Russ, "Allegories of Travel and Tourism in 'Hills Like White Elephants.'" *Hemingway's Spain: Imagining the Spanish World*, edited by Carl P. Eby and Mark Cirino, Kent State UP, 2016.

Pound, Ezra, *The Cantos of Ezra Pound*. New Directions, 1993.

———. "Essay on Inquest." Ezra Pound Papers YCAL MSS 43, Box 107, folder 4528, Beinecke Rare Books and Manuscripts Library, Yale University, 1926.

———. *Indiscretions*. Three Mountains Press, 1923.

———. "Inquest Sketch." Ezra Pound Papers YCAL MSS 43, Box 107, folder 4527, Beinecke Rare Books and Manuscripts Library, Yale University, 1923–24.

———. *The Letters of Ezra Pound, 1907–1941*. Edited by D. D. Paige, Harcourt, Brace, 1950.

———. *Literary Essays of Ezra Pound*. New Directions, 1954.

———. *New Selected Poems and Translations*. Edited by Richard Sieburth, New Directions, 2010.

———. *Pavannes and Divagations*. New Directions, 1974.

Pound, Ezra, et al. *Ezra Pound and James Laughlin Selected Letters*. W. W. Norton, 1994.

———. *Ezra Pound to His Parents: Letters 1895–1929*. Oxford UP, 2010.

———. *Pound/*The Little Review: *The Letters of Ezra Pound to Margaret Anderson: The Little Review Correspondence*. New Directions, 1988.

———. *Pound/Ford, the Story of a Literary Friendship: The Correspondence between Ezra Pound and Ford Madox Ford and Their Writings about Each Other*. New Directions, 1982.

———. *Pound/Williams: Selected Letters of Ezra Pound and William Carlos Williams*. New Directions, 1996.

———. *The Selected Letters of Ezra Pound to John Quinn, 1915–1924*. Duke UP, 1991.

Pound, Ezra, and Forrest Read. *Pound/Joyce: The Letters of Ezra Pound to James Joyce, with Pound's Essays on Joyce*. New Directions, 1970.

Putnam, Ann L. "Opiates, Laughter, and the Radio's Sweet Lies: Community and Isolation in Hemingway's 'The Gambler, the Nun, and the Radio.'" *Hemingway Repossessed*, edited by Kenneth Rosen, Praeger Publishers, 1994, pp. 159–68.

———. "Waiting for the End in Hemingway's 'A Pursuit Race.'" *Hemingway's Neglected Short Fiction*, edited by Susan F. Beegel, U of Alabama P, 1992, pp. 185–94.

Quick, Paul S. "Hemingway's 'A Way You'll Never Be' and Nick Adams's Search for Identity." *Hemingway Review*, vol. 22, no. 2, spring 2003, pp. 30–44.

Read, Forrest. "Pound, Joyce, and Flaubert." *New Approaches to Ezra Pound*, edited by Eva Hesse, U of California P, 1969, pp. 125–44.

Reck, Michael. *Ezra Pound: A Close-Up*. McGraw-Hill, 1973.

Reynolds, Michael S. *Hemingway: The Homecoming*. W. W. Norton, 1999.

——. *Hemingway: The 1930s*. W. W. Norton, 1998.

——. *Hemingway: The Paris Years*. Blackwell, 1989.

——. "Hemingway's Home: Depression and Suicide." *American Literature*, vol. 57, no. 4, December 1985, pp. 600–610.

——. "Hemingway's *In Our Time:* Biography of a Book." *In Our Time: A Norton Critical Edition*, edited by J. Gerald Kennedy, W. W. Norton, 2022, pp. 194–209.

——. *Hemingway's Reading: An Inventory*. Princeton UP, 1981.

——. "Hemingway's Stein: Another Misplaced Review." *American Literature*, vol. 55, no. 3, 1983, pp. 431–34.

——. *The Young Hemingway*. W. W. Norton, 1998.

Roos, Michael Kim. "The Doctor and the Doctor's Son: Clarence Hemingway and the Conflict of Science and Faith." *Midwestern Miscellany*, vol. 43, spring/fall 2019, pp. 29–48.

——. "'I Fixed the Dates' and Other Details: The Logic and Illogic of Chronology and Topography in Frederic Henry's Caporetto Retreat." *Hemingway Review*, vol. 39, no. 2, spring 2020, pp. 9–23.

Rozen, Wayne. "Great White Hope: Not Great, No Hope." *New York Times*, 3 July 2010.

Ryan, Dennis. "Dating Hemingway's Early Style/Parsing Gertrude Stein's Modernism." *Journal of American Studies*, vol. 29, no. 2, 1995, pp. 229–40.

Sanford, Marcelline Hemingway. *At the Hemingways: With Fifty Years of Correspondence between Ernest and Marcelline Hemingway*. Centennial Ed., U of Idaho P, 1999.

Sempreora, Margot. "Nick at Night: Nocturnal Metafictions in Three Hemingway Stories." *Hemingway Review*, vol. 22, no. 1, fall 2002, pp. 19–33.

Shapiro, James. *A Year in the Life of William Shakespeare: 1599*. HarperCollins, 2005.

"Signor Caruso, Tenor, Arrested in Zoo." *New York Times*, 17 November 1906, p. 1.

Siodmark, Robert, director. *The Killers*. Universal Studios, 1946.

Smiley, Pamela. "Gender-Linked Miscommunication in 'Hills Like White Elephants.'" *New Critical Approaches to the Stories of Ernest Hemingway*, edited by Jackson J. Benson, Duke UP, 1990, pp. 288–99.

Smith, Paul. "Hemingway's Early Manuscripts: The Theory and Practice of Omission." *Journal of Modern Literature*, vol. 10, no. 2, 1983, pp. 268–88.

——. "Hemingway's Senses of an Ending: *In Our Time* and After." *Hemingway: Eight Decades of Criticism*, edited by Linda Wagner-Martin, Michigan State UP, 2009, pp. 231–40.

——. "1924: Hemingway's Luggage and the Miraculous Year." *The Cambridge Companion to Ernest Hemingway*, edited by Scott Donaldson, Cambridge UP, pp. 36–54.

——. *A Reader's Guide to the Short Stories of Ernest Hemingway*. G. K. Hall, 1989.

Stein, Gertrude. *Geography and Plays*. U of Wisconsin P, 1993.

——. *Writings, 1903–1932*. Library of America, 1998.

Stephens, Robert O., editor. *Ernest Hemingway: The Critical Reception*. Burt Franklin, 1977.

Stone, Edward. "Hemingway's Mr. Frazer: From Revolution to Radio." *Journal of Modern Literature,* vol. 1, no. 3, March 1971, pp. 375–88.

Stoneback, H. R. *Reading Hemingway's* The Sun Also Rises: *Glossary and Commentary.* Kent State UP, 2007.

Strong, Amy. "Race and Ethnicity: American Indian." *Ernest Hemingway in Context,* edited by Debra A. Moddelmog and Suzanne del Gizzo, Cambridge UP, 2015, pp. 323–31.

Strychacz, Thomas. "In Our Time, Out of Season." *The Cambridge Companion to Ernest Hemingway,* edited by Scott Donaldson, Cambridge UP, 1996, pp. 55–86.

———. "Masculinity." *Ernest Hemingway in Context,* edited by Debra A. Moddelmog and Suzanne del Gizzo, Cambridge UP, 2015, pp. 277–86.

Svoboda, Frederic J. "False Wilderness: Northern Michigan as Created in the Nick Adams Stories." *Hemingway: Up in Michigan Perspectives,* edited by Svoboda and Joseph J. Waldmeir, Michigan State UP, 1995.

———. *Hemingway's* The Sun Also Rises: *The Crafting of a Style.* Kansas UP, 1983.

Sylvester, Bickford, Larry Grimes, and Peter L. Hays. *Reading Hemingway's* The Old Man and the Sea: *Glossary and Commentary.* Kent State UP, 2018.

"The Teleferica." *Scientific American,* 20 July 1918, pp. 46, 58.

Tetlow, Wendolyn E. *Hemingway's* In Our Time: *Lyrical Dimensions.* Bucknell UP, 1992.

Thompson, Mark. *The White War: Life and Death on the Italian Front, 1915–1919.* Basic Books, 2010.

Thomson, Virgil. *Virgil Thomson.* E. P. Dutton, 1985.

Tóibín, Colm, editor. *One Hundred Years of James Joyce's* Ulysses. Pennsylvania State UP and the Morgan Library and Museum, 2022.

Tolstoy, Leo. *War and Peace.* Translated by Constance Garnett, Modern Library, Random House, 2002.

Trogdon, Robert W. "Hemingway and Textual Studies." *The New Hemingway Studies,* edited by Suzanne del Gizzo and Kirk Curnutt, Cambridge UP, 2020, pp. 33–46.

Trevelyan, G. M. *Scenes from Italy's War.* Houghton Mifflin, 1919.

Vaill, Amanda, *Everybody Was So Young: Gerald and Sara Murphy, a Lost Generation Love Story.* Broadway Books, 1999.

Vendler, Helen. *Our Secret Discipline: Yeats and Lyric Form.* Harvard UP, 2007.

Vernon, Alex. "The Old Front." *Hemingway Review,* vol. 38, no. 1, fall 2018, pp. 10–15.

———. "War, Gender, and Ernest Hemingway." *Hemingway: Eight Decades of Criticism,* edited by Linda Wagner-Martin, Michigan State UP, 2009, pp. 91–114.

Vila-Matas, Enrique. *Never Any End to Paris.* New Directions, 2011.

Wagner-Martin, Linda [published as Linda Wagner]. "Juxtaposition in Hemingway's *In Our Time.*" In Our Time: *A Norton Critical Edition,* edited by J. Gerald Kennedy, 2022, pp. 225–34.

Watts, Emily Stipes. *Ernest Hemingway and the Arts.* U of Illinois P, 1971.

West, Kevin R. "What He Says about 'the Cat': Enrique Vila-Matas on Hemingway's 'Cat in the Rain.'" *Hemingway Review*, vol. 34, no. 2, 2015, pp. 105–10.

Williams, Wirt. *The Tragic Art of Ernest Hemingway*. Louisiana State UP, 1981.

Wister, Owen. *The Virginian*. Digireads, 2017.

Wright-Cleveland, Margaret E. *"Cane* and *In Our Time." Hemingway and the Black Renaissance,* edited by Gary Edward Holcomb and Charles Scruggs, Ohio State UP, 2012, pp. 151–76.

Wyatt, David. *Hemingway, Style, and the Art of Emotion*. Cambridge UP, 2015.

Young, Philip. *Ernest Hemingway: A Reconsideration*. Rev. ed., Pennsylvania State UP, 1966.

INDEX

ABC of Economics (Pound), 267n6

Across the River and into the Trees (Hemingway), 225, 261n6, 263n8

"Ada" (Stein), 48–50, 57–58, 64

Adams, Nicholas, naming of, 159, 225

addition, revision by, 13; "The Battler," 97, 99–101, 104, 106, 108–10; "Cat in the Rain," 50–51, 54–55, 59–60; "Fathers and Sons," 217–18, 224, 225–30, 231–34, 235–37; "Gambler," 191–92, 198–99, 202–5, 207; "Hills," 140–43, 145–46, 149, 151; "Indian Camp," 26, 28–29, 37–39, 42–43; *in our time,* 15–16, 18–19; "Now I Lay Me," 117–29; "River," 68–85, 88–90; "The Sisters" (Joyce), 32, 40, 42; "Snows," 242–47; "A Way," 157–60, 163, 166–67, 174–75, 178, 184

adverbs, discussion of, 56–57, 123, 225, 251n5

African American characters, 95–104, 108–11

"After the Storm" (Hemingway), 154

Alighieri, Dante, 254n7, 260–61n6, 264n16

alliteration in "River," 79, 81

All Quiet on the Western Front (Remarque), 159

"Alpine Idyll, An" (Hemingway), 103, 113

ambiguity: "Cat in the Rain," 58, 60, 62, 256n23, 262n11; "Fathers and Sons," 226; "Hills," 147, 150–52

American idiom in "River," 69–72, 90, 209

"Among School Children" (Yeats), 2–3

Anderson, Margaret, 8, 23

Anderson, Sherwood, 9, 24

Antonia (ship), 23

"Araby" (Joyce), 24, 34

Architect's Table, The (Picasso), 46, 64, 254n3

Art Matters (Lamb), 32, 38, 49, 67, 144, 147, 155, 253n7, 254n6, 258nn11–12, 260n5, 262n11

authorial intrusion in "Indian Camp," 38–39

automatic writing, 248

automobile accident, Hemingway's, 188, 199

Bacigalupo, Massimo, 51, 255n17

"bail" in "A Way," 165

Baker, Carlos, 268n12

Baldridge, C. LeRoy, 111, 259nn17–18

Baldwin, James, 112

"Banal Story" (Hemingway), 17, 124, 126

Barbusse, Henri, 159, 263n4

battlefield. *See* war, references to

"Battler, The" (Hemingway), 95–104; addition, revision by, 97, 99–101, 104, 106, 108–10; campsites and homes not made in, 80; characters outside the dominant white culture, 95–96; deletions, revision by, 96, 101, 104, 106, 109, 258n10; dialogue, 101; dramatic monologue, 100–102; film of, 259n16; and "Indian Camp," 100–101; mist rising in "River," 71; narrative comments/

"Battler, The" (*continued*)
commentary, 100; narrative point of view, 100; placement of, 95; racial identities, 96–97; racist language, 96, 100, 104, 111, 258n6; replacement, revision by, 98, 100, 102, 104–6, 258n10; spoken words, 99; and "The Killers," 111–12

Bauerle, Ruth, 267n6

Beach, Sylvia, 9, 22–24, 46, 103, 253–54n2

Beegel, Susan F., 1, 3, 13, 267n7

Bennett, Warren, 256n24

Benson, Jackson J., 256n23

"Big Two-Hearted River" (Hemingway), 66–94, 256n1, 264n17; addition, revision by, 68–85, 88–90; alliteration, 79, 81; American idiom, 69–72, 90, 209; cutting wartime images, 75, 90; death scenes, 92–93; deletions, revision by, 70–71, 77, 86, 91; dialogue, 67; ending(s), 25, 67–70, 85–91, 96, 257n8, 257nn4–5; and "Fathers and Sons," 227–28, 235, 239; first-person narration, 256n2; framing chapters of Cardinella's execution and Maera's death, 92–93; grasshoppers, 67, 70, 154, 179–80, 265n24; handwritten revisions or drafts, 68–71, 73–74, 87, 91–92; interior monologues, 68, 70–71, 78, 80, 83–84, 88, 90; metafictional self-references, 119–20, 257n5; moving chapters 14 and 15, 92; narrative point of view, 70, 74–76; and "Now I Lay Me," 116, 122–23, 126, 130; part 1 of, 80, 87, 92–93; part 2 of, 80–81, 87, 90, 92; placement of, 91–94, 209; repetitions, 48, 71–73, 76–84; replacement, revision by, 68, 70–74, 77–78, 88; spoken words, 67, 71; and Stein, 47; third-person narration, 69–70, 78; three-page pencil insert, 68, 72–74, 77, 90, 227; as a two-part story, 25. *See also* "On Writing" (Hemingway)

Billings, MT, 188, 198–99

Bird, Bill, 9, 11, 66, 86

blend of languages in "Cat in the Rain," 52–54

"Boarding House, The" (Joyce), 56, 61

Boni and Liveright, 96, 103, 258n6

Boutelle, Anne Edwards, 268n13

Bovey, Seth, 196–97

boxing world, 96–104

Brisbane, Arthur, 124–26, 261n7

"Broken Doll, A" (Jolson), 169

bullfighting: "Cat in the Rain," 46–47, 61–65; critic in "The Undefeated," 124, 126; *in our time*, 9, 16–17; in Stein, 57–58, 64, 255n15

burning scenes in "Now I Lay Me," 115–21, 126–28, 260n2, 260n4

Cabanne, Christy, 193–94

Câblogramme Western Union paper, 61, 92, 256n21

Callaghan, Morley, 113

Camastra, Nicole J., 203, 266n2, 267n5

"Canary for One, A" (Hemingway), 1, 3, 113, 136

Caruso, Enrico, 218–19, 267n6

"Cat in the Rain" (Hemingway), 44–65, 255n14, 255n17, 256n19, 256n24; addition, revision by, 50–51, 54–55, 59–60; ambiguity, 58, 60, 62, 256n23; blend of languages, 52–54; bullfighting chapters, 46–47, 61–65; deletions, revision by, 51; dialogue, 45–46, 52–56; ending(s), 60; eroticism, 48–50, 52, 58–59; "False Start" draft, 44–47, 53–54, 133; "First Draft Original Manuscript," 44–48, 51; gender, 53–54, 58, 63; handwritten revisions or drafts, 61; intimacy, 54–55, 59, 64 marriage, 55–57, 60–65; narrative comments/commentary, 54; narrative point of view, 45, 53; repetitions, 48, 50–52, 57, 79; replacement, revision by, 46; shifts in gender in references to the cat, 53–54, 255n17; spoken words, 63; war monument, 45–46, 50–51, 255–56n18

cave-in in "A Way," 164–66, 264n12

Cayetano in "Gambler," 187, 192–99, 204–8, 267n4, 267n8

Chamberlin, Brewster, 23, 24, 46, 47, 66, 103, 134, 136, 153, 188, 261n2

changes in titles, 104, 187, 189, 206–7

character, distinction between narrator and, 201

Chevron, Andrew, 258n9

circular narration in "A Way," 162

Cirino, Mark, 108, 155, 173, 262n1, 264n11, 265n21, 265n24

Clarks Fork, WY, 188

"Clay" (Joyce), 61, 255n18

Cohen, George, 177

Cohen, Milton, 4, 9, 10–11, 13, 17, 19, 62, 251n5, 256n20, 256n23

collages, 64–65

color yellow, reference to in "A Way," 169–70, 263n5

combined sentences in "Hills," 137–38, 141

combined sentences in "Now I Lay Me," 127

comedy/humor: dialogue, 219; in "Fathers and Sons," 217–19; in "Gambler," 191, 194–97; in *in our time*, 13–14; slapstick comedy, 57, 62, 165, 191; in "A Way," 154–55, 160, 165, 176–82, 184, 186, 266n26

Comley, Nancy, 268n9

commas, 85, 121, 137, 141, 146, 150–51, 220, 243–44

Commedia (Alighieri), 260n6

"Composition as Explanation" (Stein), 74

composition of place, 50, 121–22

conjunctions, discussion of, 145, 170–72, 175

Consolidated Press Association, 9

Contact Press, 22

"Continuation of a Work in Progress" (Joyce), 136

continuous present, 74

copyright restrictions, 1–2, 242, 247

"Counterparts" (Joyce), 56–57, 61, 254–55n12

cover illustration of *Life Magazine*, 177

cover illustration of *Scientific American*, 166, 264n13

"Cross-Country Snow" (Hemingway), 61, 66, 87, 239

Curnutt, Kirk, 1, 47, 62, 254n6

"Cyclops" chapter of *Ulysses*, 58, 64

Daiker, Donald A., 118–19, 253n6, 257n1, 258n7, 260n4, 267n1, 267n3, 268n8, 268n10

Dangerous Summer, The (Hemingway), 266–67n4

Darantière, Maurice, 22

"Dark Night, The" (Nickel), 260n6

"Day's Wait, A" (Hemingway), 268n15

"Dead, The" (Joyce), 67–68, 78, 257n8

Death in the Afternoon (Hemingway), 255n15

dedication in "The Killers," 104

DeFalco, Joseph, 262n8

Delaware transcript of "Snows," 242–47

deletions, revision by, 10, 13; "The Battler," 96, 101, 104, 106, 109, 258n10; "Cat in the Rain," 51; "Fathers and Sons," 217, 219, 225, 228–29; "Gambler," 195, 199, 202, 206; "Hills," 134, 137, 143, 147–52, 262n7; "Indian Camp," 24, 25–27, 30, 36–37; *in our time*, 13–15; "Now I Lay Me," 117–18, 120–21; "River," 70–71, 77, 86, 91; "Snows," 243–45

Derounian, Kathryn, 1, 4, 7, 13–16, 251n4

Deslys, Gaby, 168, 264nn14–15

Dial, 10, 24

dialogue: "The Battler," 101; "Cat in the Rain," 45–46, 52–56; "Fathers and Sons," 219; "Gambler," 190, 201; "Hills," 135, 138–48, 261–62n7; "Indian Camp," 32, 41; *in our time*, 17; "The Killers," 105; "Now I Lay Me," 124, 262n7; "River," 67; "A Way," 178, 185, 265n18

division into shorter paragraphs, 83, 90

division into two sentences, 84, 141, 146

"Doctor and the Doctor's Wife, The" (Hemingway), 66, 80, 102, 119, 214, 230, 260n4

Donaldson, Scott, 1, 3, 155, 196, 260n2, 267n4

Dos Passos, John, 95, 188

Draft of XVI Cantos, A (Pound), 9, 11–12, 19–20, 251n3, 260n6, 264n12

dramatic monologue in "The Battler," 100–102

dream-visions in "A Way," 182–84, 260n6, 264n16

Dubliners (Joyce), 24–43, 52, 56–58, 61, 67, 253n5, 254n5

Dudley, Marc Kevin, 220, 223, 258n8, 258n12, 259n15, 267n1, 268n8

Eby, Carl, 1, 52, 254n10, 255n17, 268n8

echo, 142–43. *See also* repetitions

elegy in "Fathers and Sons," 227–29

Eliot, T. S., 8, 12, 44–47

Elmore, Brown, 97

ending(s): "Cat in the Rain," 60; "Fathers and Sons," 216; "Gambler," 187, 198–207, 241, 267n7; "Hills," 152; "Homage to Switzerland," 153; influences for, 57–58; "River," 25, 67–70, 85–91, 96, 257nn4–5, 257n8; stereotypical endings, Westerns, 200–201, 205–6; "A Way," 184–85

"End of Something, The" (Hemingway), 59, 60, 66, 68, 75, 228

eroticism: "Cat in the Rain," 48–50, 52, 58–59; "Fathers and Sons," 224, 225

Esquire, 242

"Essay on Comedy" (Meredith), 186

"Essay on Inquest" (Pound), 12, 251n2

"Exiles" issue of the *Little Review,* 8–13, 24

"experiment" in "Gambler," 192

"False Start" draft of "Cat the Rain," 44–47, 53–54, 133

Farewell to Arms, A (Hemingway), 116, 120, 153, 154, 159, 167, 187, 188, 255n14, 260n6, 263n4, 263n7, 265n23

"Fathers and Sons" (Hemingway), 156, 209–39, 240–41, 247–48, 249, 268n11, 268n15; addition, revision by, 217–18, 224, 225–30, 231–34, 235–37; ambiguity, 226; "broken descriptors" in, 220; comedy/humor, 217–19; deletions, revision by, 217, 219, 225, 228–29; ; elegy, 227–29; ending(s), 216; eroticism, 224, 225; first-person narration, 210, 212, 214, 216, 218–19, 224, 237; folder 382, earliest manuscript fragment, 210–13; folder 383, "Tomb of My Grandfather," 215–24; folder 384, next manuscript fragment, 213–15; future verb tenses, 237–38; handwritten revisions or drafts, 216, 224–30, 233, 235, 241; "heartbeat" speech, 213–14; imperfect, shift from past perfect to, 224; interior monologues, 210, 212–13, 224, 226, 228, 230, 236; manuscript frag-

ments, 210–24, 241, 248; marriage, 219; "mashing" anecdote, 218–19, 225; miscegenation, 268n8; naming of Nicholas Adams, 159, narrative comments/commentary, 223; narrative point of view, 223–24, 225; placement of, 209; racist language, 212, 221; repetitions, 222–23, 224, 227; setting copy with handwritten title, 230–39; sexual education, 211–12, 214–15, 217–18, 226, 235; smells, 212–13, 229, 231–33; spoken words, 234; third-person narration, 216, 219, 222–25; three-page pencil insert, folder 385a, 210, 224–30, 231; transitions, 229, 231; twenty-five-page manuscript, "Tomb of My Grandfather," 215–24; untitled fourteen-page typescript, 210, 224–30, 241; verb tenses, shifts in, 224, 237–38; vignettes of the narrator's father, 217–18, 228–30

female characters, 60, 222

Festival of San Fermin in Pamplona, 103, 133–34

"field kitchen" in "A Way," 159–60, 263n4, 263n6

"Fifty Billion German Allies Already in the American Field," 180

"Fifty Grand" (Hemingway), 103, 113

film, references to in *in our time,* 18–19

film noir adaptation of "The Killers," 110–11, 259n16

film of "The Battler," 259n16

Finnegans Wake (Joyce), 4, 47, 86, 136, 253n5

"First Draft Original Manuscript" of "Cat in the Rain," 44–48, 51

first-person narration: "Fathers and Sons," 210, 212, 214, 216, 218–19, 224, 237; first- to third-person narration shift, 69–70, 137, 156–57, 187, 189–92, 194–95, 198–202, 207, 222–25; "Gambler," 187, 189–92, 194–95, 198–202, 207; "Hills," 135, 137; "Now I Lay Me," 122; "River," 256n2; "A Way," 156–57

Fitzgerald, F. Scott, 103, 115, 133, 135

flashbacks, 115, 166–67, 210, 213, 217–18, 220, 227, 228, 231, 241, 243–44, 252n3

Flora, Joseph, 25, 27, 138, 140–41, 149, 151, 155, 176–77, 222, 257n3, 258n6, 258n12, 259n13, 259n14, 259n19, 261n7, 264–65n17, 268n11
Florczyk, Steve, 169, 263n6
Ford, Ford Madox, 4, 23–24
Forum, The, 126
For Whom the Bell Tolls (Hemingway), 60, 225
Fossalta, Italy, 95, 157, 170–74, 182, 260n3, 266n28
fourteen-page typescript of "Fathers and Sons," 210, 224–30, 241
France, 23, 95, 136
Frazer in "Gambler," 188, 190–92, 194–98, 200–208, 267n8
free indirect discourse, 211, 265n23
Freud, Sigmund, 265n21
Fruscione, Joseph, 109, 258n9

Gains, Lawrence, 252n1
Gajdusek, Robert, 24, 67, 255n18
"Gambler, the Nun, and the Radio, The" (Hemingway), 187–208, 239, 240–41; addition, revision by, 191–92, 198–99, 202–5, 207; characters, 187, 193, 197; comedy/humor, 191, 194–97; deletions, revision by, 195, 199, 202, 206; dialogue, 190, 201; ending(s), 187, 198–207, 241, 267n7; "experiment" in, 192; first-person narration, 187, 189–92, 194–95, 198–202, 207; "Give Us a Prescription, Doctor," 190, 192, 201–7; handwritten revisions or drafts, 190; interior monologues, 192, 200, 204–5; narrative point of view, 194–95, 201–2; narrator and character, 201; racist language, 193, 197; repetitions, 191; replacement, revision by, 190, 200, 207; shootout, twist on the Western, 197–98, 200–201; stereotypes of Mexicans, 192–97, 201, 207–8; stereotypical endings, Westerns, 200–201, 205–6; third-person narration, 189–92, 194–95, 201–2, 207
Garden of Eden, The (Hemingway), 4, 60, 256n19

Garnett, Constance, 266n27
gas masks in "A Way," 159–60, 170, 263nn4–5
Gassed (Sargent), 263n5
gender in "Cat in the Rain," 53–54, 58, 63, 255n17
Genoa Economic Conference, 9
"Gentle Lena, The" (Stein), 56–57
Geography and Plays (Stein), 46–49, 57–61, 95–96, 248, 254n5
"Get a Seeing-Eyed Dog" (Hemingway), 240
"Getting Closer to 'It'" (Knodt), 155
Gillis, Colin, 49
Gingrich, Arnold, 206–7, 263n7
"Give Us a Prescription, Doctor" (Hemingway). *See* "Gambler, the Nun, and the Radio, The" (Hemingway)
"God Rest You Merry, Gentlemen" (Hemingway), 153, 239
grasshoppers, 67, 70, 121, 154, 176, 178–81, 183, 185, 265n24. *See also* "locust" lecture in "A Way"
Grebstein, Sheldon, 155, 258n5, 258n6, 261n3, 268n10
Griffith, D. W., 193–94, 201

hallucinatory sequence in "A Way," 168–69
Hamlet (Shakespeare), 2, 185
handwritten revisions or drafts: "Cat in the Rain," 61; and copyright, 2; "Fathers and Sons," 216, 224–30, 233, 235, 241; "Gambler," 190; "Hills," 136–37, 139; "Indian Camp," 29, 35, 42–43; "The Killers," 105; "Now I Lay Me," 114, 116; "River," 68–71, 73–74, 87, 91–92; "Snows," 242, 244, 247; *Sun Also Rises,* 103; "A Way," 157–60, 163, 166–67, 174–75, 178, 184
handwritten titles, 114, 119, 158, 230–39
"Happy Ending, The" (Hemingway), 241–42
Harry Ransom Center, University of Texas, 242–46
Hays, Peter L., 266n27
Heap, Jane, 8, 23, 266n27
"heartbeat" speech in an early fragment draft of "Fathers and Sons," 213–14
Heller, Joseph, 180, 266n26

Hemingway, Hadley, 22–24, 44, 46, 52, 86, 87, 115, 133–40, 255n16, 261n1
Hemingway, Jack, 24, 188
Hemingway, Marceline, 260n4
Hemingway, Seán, 241, 247
Hemingway Library Edition, 87, 141–43, 145, 148, 157, 169, 176–77, 189–90, 194, 210, 215, 224, 240–42, 244, 247, 256n2, 261–62n7
Hemingway Short Story, The (Lamb), 38, 86, 253n7
"Hemingway's *In Our Time*" (Reynolds), 86
Hemingway's Laboratory (Cohen), 10. *See also* Cohen, Milton
Hemingway's Nick Adams (Flora), 155. *See also* Flora, Joseph
"Hemingway's Nick Adams and His Lost 'Indian Girl'" (Daiker), 268n8
Hemingway's The Sun Also Rises (Svoboda), 1
Hemingway: The 1930s (Reynolds), 188. *See also* Reynolds, Michael S.
Henry, Frederic, 265n23
"Hills Like White Elephants" (Hemingway), 115, 133–52, 249, 255n14; addition, revision by, 140–43, 145–46, 149, 151; ambiguity, 147, 150–52, 262n11; combined sentences, 137–38, 141; deletions, revision by, 134, 137, 143, 147–52, 262n7; dialogue, 135, 138–48, 261–62n7; ending(s), 152; female characters, 60, 222; first-person narration, 135, 137; handwritten revisions or drafts, 136–37, 139; "look" (verb), 140–41; narrative comments/commentary, 139, 141, 144, 262n10; 1925 draft, 133–43; 1927 manuscript, 137–52; repetitions, 138, 140–43, 145–46; replacement, revision by, 138, 141, 149–50; similes, 140–42; spoken words, 139–40, 142, 145, 150, 152; third-person narration, 137; waitress in, 139–40, 262n8
Holcomb, Gary Edward, 102, 258n12
Hollander, John, 261n6
"Homage to Ezra" (Hemingway), 20, 251n5
"Homage to Switzerland" (Hemingway), 153, 239
Horne, Bill, 22

Hotel Ambos Mundos stationery, 241
Hotel Brevoort, New York, stationery, 190, 200
Houston, Sam, 194
"How Marriage Began" (Brisbane's column), 126
"Hugh Selwyn Mauberley" (Pound), 15, 19
humor. *See* comedy/humor
hysteria in "A Way," 163, 186, 263n8

illustrations for "The Killers," 111, 259nn18–19
Imagism, 4, 11, 20. *See also* vignettes in the *Little Review*
"I Must Try to Write the History of Belmonte" (Stein), 57–58, 64, 255n15
"In Another Country" (Hemingway), 113–15, 119, 124, 126, 133, 136, 170
"In Another Country—Two" (Hemingway), 114, 118, 120, 123, 261n2
"Indian Camp" (Hemingway), 21, 23–43, 47, 66, 248–49, 252n1; addition, revision by, 26, 28–29, 37–39, 42–43; authorial intrusion, 38–39; and "The Battler," 100–101; deletions, revision by, 24, 25–27, 30, 36–37; dialogue, 32, 41; and "Fathers and Sons," 214, 220, 239; focalization, 253n7; handwritten revisions or drafts, 29, 35, 42–43; interior monologues, 42; and "The Killers," 108; narrative point of view, 27, 29–30, 32, 35–40, 253n7; repetitions, 28–29; replacement, revision by, 34–36, 38; and "River," 67, 70, 79–80; spoken questions, 30–32, 34, 40; spoken words, 26; and "A Way," 160
Indiscretions (Pound), 11–12
Inferno (Alighieri), 260–61n4, 264n16
in our time (Hemingway), 8–21, 22–23, 47, 61–62; addition, revision by, 15–16, 18–19; bullfighting, 9, 16–17, 61–62; comedy/humor, 13–14; deletions, revision by, 13–15; dialogue, 17; film references, 18–19; Maera, death of, 16–19; manuscript draft, 17–18; narrative point of view, 13, 17; "Nick sat against the wall" chapter, 13–16, 23, 95, 102, 187; repetitions, 17–18; replacement,

revision by, 15–18; spoken words, 16–18; war chapters, 19

In Our Time (Hemingway), 2, 24–25, 33, 37, 40, 47–48, 50, 52, 61–62, 65, 66–68, 73, 75, 79, 87–88, 91–94, 99, 102, 103, 160, 170, 209, 257n5, 268n11

"Inquest" series, 9–13, 19–20, 251n2

"Inquest Sketch" (Pound), 19, 251n2

insect warfare, 154, 180

interior monologues: "Fathers and Sons," 210, 212–13, 224, 226, 228, 230, 236; "Gambler," 192, 200, 202–3, 204–5; "Indian Camp," 42; "River," 68, 70–71, 78, 80, 83–84, 88, 90; "Snows," 243, 246; "A Way," 153–54, 158, 160, 162–77, 182–86, 263n7, 263n9

In Texas with Davy Crockett (McNeil), 192

irony, 62–65, 144–45, 158–60, 174, 191, 196–97, 203, 211, 220, 231, 248

it (pronoun), 147–48, 150, 165–66, 174–75, 236

Italian Arditi, 14–15, 264n12

Italian front, 169–70

James, Will, 189, 192–93

Jeffries, James J., 217, 225

Jolson, Al, 169

Joost, Nicholas, 8

Joyce, James, 3–4, 8, 11–12, 14, 24–43, 45–52, 56–61, 64, 66–68, 78, 86, 95–96, 136, 218–19, 248, 253n2, 253n5, 254–55n12, 254n5, 254n7, 255n17, 255n18, 257n8, 263n7, 267n6

Justice, Hilary, 1, 115, 136, 142, 144, 145–49, 151, 261n7, 262n9

Kale, Verna, 152, 266n26

Kennedy, J. Gerald, 47, 86, 255n17, 257n4

Kennedy Library, 18, 68, 87, 92, 174, 189, 225, 242–48

Key West typescript of "Prescription" (earlier title of "Gambler"), 202–4

"Killers, The" (Hemingway), 68, 103–12, 113–15, 133, 258n12, 259n15, 259n17, 259n19; and "The Battler," 111–12; dedication in,

104; dialogue, 105; *film noir* adaptation, 110–11, 259n16; handwritten revisions or drafts, 105; illustrations for, 111, 259nn18–19; Madrid draft, 104–10, 258n10; narrative point of view, 105–7; and "Now I Lay Me," 114–15; placement, 114; racist language, 102–5, 108, 111; staccato sentences, 268n11; third-person narration, 104–5

Knodt, Ellen Andrews, 155, 170, 264–65n17

Lamb, Robert Paul, 25, 30, 32, 36, 38, 49, 67, 72, 86, 144, 147, 151, 155, 252n4, 253n7, 256n3, 257n5, 262n10

landscapes, 45, 86, 133, 137–38, 142–45, 158, 170, 175, 187, 205–6, 209, 216, 220, 227–29, 232, 264n17, 267n7

"Last Good Country, The" (Hemingway), 129, 268n8

Laughlin, James, 19–20

Le Feu (Barbusse), 159, 263n4

"L'Envoi" (Hemingway), 91, 93–94

Lewis, Robert W., Jr., 163, 242–47

Liberty, 203

Life Magazine, 177–78

"Light of the World, The" (Hemingway), 230, 268n8

linked repetitions, 49–51

Little Review, 8–13, 23–24

Litz, A. Walton, 253n5

Liveright, Horace, 95. *See also* Boni and Liveright

Lloyd-Kimbrel, Elizabeth, 169, 257n1, 266n3

"locust" lecture in "A Way," 157, 174, 176–82, 185

Lodge, David, 60, 254n11, 255n17

Lubin, David, 177

Macfadden, Bernarr, 202–3

MacGregor, Robert M., 19

Maclean, John N., 77

MacLeish, Archibald, 106, 110, 188–89, 193, 197

Madrid draft of "The Killers," 104–10, 258n10

Making of Americans, The (Stein), 46–47, 66, 248

Malatesta cantos (Pound), 20, 252n8

Man from Texas, The (film), 193, 201

Mantovani, Vincenzo, 255n17

manuscript draft(s) and fragments, 1-4,
240-41; "The Battler," 104; "Cat in the
Rain," 47-48, 50-51, 54-56, 59; "Fathers
and Sons," 210-15; "Gambler," 190, 199-
200; "Hills," 133-34, 136-52, 261-62n7;
"Indian Camp," 26, 33, 35-37, 38-40,
252n1; *in our time*, 17-18; "The Killers,"
104-10; "Now I Lay Me," 115-20, 123,
126-27; "River," 69-91; "Snows," 246-47;
"A Way," 156-62, 169, 170, 174, 176-77, 181,
184. *See also* typescript draft(s)

Marcus, Norman, 97

marriage: "Cat in the Rain," 55-57, 60-65;
"Fathers and Sons," 213-15, 219

Marshall, Ian, 110, 258n6, 258n12

Martyrs of the Alamo (film), 193-94, 201

masculinity, 260n4, 268n9

"Masculinity" (Strychacz), 268n15

"mashing" anecdote in "Fathers and Sons,"
218-19, 225

"Matter of Colour, A" (Hemingway), 96-97,
99

McAlmon, Robert, 22

McCann, Richard, 230

McKey, Edward, 263n6

McNeil, Everett, 192

"Melanctha" (Stein), 52, 74, 95-96

Mellow, James, 116, 254n5, 257n5,
259-60n2

Men at War (Hemingway), 159, 176,
262n7

Men Without Women (Hemingway), 2; "A
Banal Story" in, 17; "Hills" in, 133-34, 138,
141-42, 145-48; "The Killers" in, 107-8;
"Now I Lay Me" in, 114, 124, 126-27, 209;
stories involving boxers, 103; writing in
popular culture, 124

Meredith, George, 186

Mestre, 185, 265n18

metafictional self-references, 119-20, 179,
257n5

metaphor, "drum tight," 79-80

metaphor, locusts, 178-80

metaphor, trout, 86

Meyers, Jeffrey, 235, 256n20, 258n12

Michigan stories, 102

"Miss Furr and Miss Skeene" (Stein), 64

Mix, Tom, 193

Mizener, Arthur, 47

Moddelmog, Debra A., 257n5

monologues. *See* "locust" lecture in "A Way"

Monroe, Harriet, 10, 12, 14

Moody, David, 252n8

Moorhead, Ethel, 66, 248

Morrison, Toni, 96, 102, 257n3

"Mother of a Queen, The" (Hemingway), 154,
262n1

Moveable Feast, A (Hemingway), 19-20

"Mr. and Mrs. Elliot" (Hemingway), 48, 60-
62, 64, 66

mustard gas in "A Way," 158-60, 169-70,
263n4

"My Old Man" (Hemingway), 22, 92

Nakjavani, Erik, 268n14

narrative comments/commentary: "The
Battler," 100; "Cat in the Rain," 54;
"Fathers and Sons," 223; "Hills," 139, 141,
144, 262n10

narrative markers, 106, 110, 162, 182-83

narrative point of view: "The Battler," 100;
"Cat in the Rain," 45, 53; "Fathers and
Sons," 223-24, 225; first- to third-person shift, 69-70, 137, 156-57, 187, 189-92,
194-95, 198-202, 207, 223-25; "Gambler,"
194-95, 201-2; "Indian Camp," 27, 29-30,
32, 35-40, 253n7; *in our time*, 13, 17; "The
Killers," 105-7; "River," 70, 74-76

"Natural History of the Dead, A" (Hemingway), 170

"Nausicaa" chapter of *Ulysses* (Joyce), 8,
58-59, 64

"New Slain Knight, The" (Hemingway),
259n15

Nick Adams stories. *See* "Battler, The"
(Hemingway); "Big Two-Hearted River"
(Hemingway); "Fathers and Sons" (Hem-

ingway); "Indian Camp" (Hemingway); "Killers, The" (Hemingway); "Now I Lay Me" (Hemingway); "Way You'll Never Be, A" (Hemingway)

Nickel, Matthew, 15, 120, 121, 128, 136, 260n6, 261n5

"Nick sat against the wall" chapter in *in our time*, 13–16, 23, 95, 102, 187

nocturnal meditations, 122, 129, 170–71, 176, 204

"Now I Lay Me" (Hemingway), 108, 113–32, 249, 261n2; addition, revision by, 117–29; appendix, drafts of, 129–32; burning scenes, 115–21, 126–28, 260n2, 260n4; deletions, revision by, 117–18, 120–21; dialogue, 124, 262n7; dream-visions, 260n6, 264n16; "experiment" in, 192; and "Fathers and Sons," 214, 235, 238; grasshoppers, 119, 121, 179; handwritten revisions or drafts, 114, 116; and "The Killers," 114–15; mustard gas, 170; nocturnal meditations, 176; out-of-body experiences, 120–21, 129; placement of, 136, 209; prayer, 127–30; repetitions, 118–20, 121–22; replacement, revision by, 116; and "River," 91; second draft, 127; similes, 120, 122; spoken words, 117; and "A Way," 161

Oak Park, IL, 95, 97, 116, 260n2

O'Brien, Tim, 180, 266n26

Ojibway people, 79–80, 209, 211–14, 216, 220, 222, 228–29, 231, 233–34, 237

Old Man and the Sea, The (Hemingway), 196, 263n7

"Old Newsman Writes: A Letter from Cuba" (Hemingway), 1

Oldsey, Bernard, 256n1

One Hundred Years of James Joyce's Ulysses (Tóibín), 4

"On Writing" (Hemingway), 68. *See also* "Big Two-Hearted River" (Hemingway); ending(s)

Ordóñez, Cayetano, 266n4. *See also* Cayetano in "Gambler"

Our Secret Discipline (Vendler), 2–3

out-of-body experiences in "Now I Lay Me," 120–21, 129

"Out of Season" (Hemingway), 22, 44, 60–61, 63–64, 255n13

"Over There" (Cohen), 177

"Painful Case, A" (Joyce), 56, 61

paratactic syntax, 129, 171, 175

Paris, France, 8–9, 66, 85, 115, 168–74, 243–45, 264n14

Paris Review, 47, 254n4

past tense, discussion of, 74, 88, 121, 224, 237

past-tense clauses, discussion of, 175

past-tense verbs, discussion of, 74, 80, 88

Paul, Steve, 257n2

pauses, 73, 84–85, 141, 168, 175, 228

Pavannes and Divagations (Pound), 12

PBS series on Hemingway (Novick and Burns), 2

pencil corrections. *See* handwritten revisions or drafts

Perkins, Maxwell, 103, 262n1; "Fathers and Sons," 209, 215, 230; "Gambler," 189, 206–7; "Hills," 136; "The Killers," 111, 259n17; "Now I Lay Me," 113–15; "A Way," 154, 155–56, 185; Western genre disclaimer, 193

Perloff, Marjorie, 49

Petoskey, MI, 102–4, 258n9

Pfeiffer, Pauline, 104, 115, 136, 188–89, 206

Piave River, 157, 170, 182

Picasso, Pablo, 46, 64, 254n3

Pilcer, Harry, 168–70, 264nn14–15

"Pilgrim on the Gila, A" (Wister), 192

placement of stories and chapters, 91–94, 95, 102, 133, 136, 154, 262n1

Plimpton, George, 47, 254n4

Poetry Magazine, 10, 14

point of view. *See* narrative point of view

"Porter, The" (Hemingway), 259n15

Portogrande, 172–73, 184, 185, 265n18

Portrait of the Artist as a Young Man, A (Joyce), 49–50, 52, 86, 122, 260n6

postcards in "A Way," 154, 156–57, 159, 177, 184, 263n4

Pottle, Russ, 133, 149, 261n1

Pound, Ezra, 8–21, 24, 44–47, 64, 86, 154, 200, 202–3, 248, 251n2, 251n3, 251n5, 252n2, 252n7, 252n8, 260n6, 264n12, 267n6
prayer in "Now I Lay Me," 127–30
present participles, discussion of, 74
print version(s). *See* published version(s)
published version(s): "The Battler," 97–99, 101, 258n6; "Cat in the Rain," 55; "Fathers and Sons," 212, 214, 216–17, 220–22, 229, 231–33, 235–36, 237–38; "Gambler," 194, 196, 198; "Hills," 135–37, 141, 144, 150, 262n7; "Indian Camp," 28–29, 33, 37; *in our time*, 16–18; "The Killers," 104, 105–7, 109; "Now I Lay Me," 118, 119, 121, 123–24; "River," 71, 73–75, 77, 78–79, 82, 87–91, 256n2; "Snows," 244; "A Way," 156–57, 159–61, 167, 184. *See also* manuscript draft(s) and fragments; typescript draft(s)
Putnam, Ann L., 130, 189, 201, 266n1, 267n7, 267n8

Quinn, John, 14, 251n2, 264n12

racial identities in "The Battler," 96–97
racist language: "The Battler," 96, 100, 104, 111, 258n6; "Fathers and Sons," 212, 221; "Gambler," 193, 197; "The Killers," 102–5, 108, 111
racist stereotypes. *See* stereotypes of Mexicans
Rapallo, Italy, 44–46, 52, 133, 252n8, 255n18
Reader's Guide (Smith), 7, 22, 24, 25, 44, 46, 53, 66, 87, 95, 103, 106, 114, 115, 116, 119, 120, 130, 131, 133, 134, 136, 153, 155, 156, 158, 190, 199, 200, 202, 204, 206, 209, 210, 213, 241, 242, 243, 247, 252n1, 253n2, 254n10, 255n13, 255n17, 259n1, 261n2, 262n11, 264n16, 267n1
Reading Hemingway's Across the River and into the Trees (Cirino), 1
Reading Hemingway's A Farewell to Arms (Lewis and Roos), 1
Reading Hemingway series, 1
Reading Hemingway's Men Without Women (Flora), 1
Reading Hemingway's The Garden of Eden (Eby), 1
Reading Hemingway's The Old Man and the Sea (Sylvester, Grimes, and Hays), 1
Reading Hemingway's The Sun Also Rises (Stoneback), 1
Reading Hemingway's To Have and Have Not (Curnutt), 1
Reading Hemingway's Winner Take Nothing (Cirino and Vandagriff), 262n1, 267n1, 268n10
repetitions: "Cat in the Rain," 48, 50–52, 57, 79; "Fathers and Sons," 222–23, 224, 227; "Gambler," 191; "Hills," 138, 140–43, 145–46; "Indian Camp," 28–29; *in our time*, 17–18; in Joyce, 41, 48–49, 51–52, 56; "Now I Lay Me," 118–20, 121–22; "River," 48, 71–73, 76–84; in Stein, 48–49, 51–52, 57; "A Way," 156–57, 163–68, 174
replacement, revision by, 3, 13; "The Battler," 98, 100, 102, 104–6, 258n10; "Cat in the Rain," 46; "Gambler," 190, 200, 207; "Hills," 138, 141, 149–50; "Indian Camp," 34–36, 38; *in our time*, 15–18; "Now I Lay Me," 116; "River," 68, 70–74, 77–78, 88; "The Sisters" (Joyce), 34; "Snows," 243–44; "A Way," 156, 158, 161
revision, Hemingway's art of: "The Battler," 95–103; "Big Two-Hearted River," 66–94; "Cat in the Rain," 44–65; change in titles, 104, 187, 189, 206–7; ending(s), 60, 67–70, 85–91, 184–85, 198–207, 257n8, 257nn4–5, 267n7; "Exiles" issue of the *Little Review*, 8–13, 24; "Fathers and Sons," 210–39; first-to third-person narration shift, 69–70, 137, 156–57, 187, 189–92, 194–95, 198–202, 207, 222–25; "The Gambler, the Nun, and the Radio," 187–208; "Hills Like White Elephants," 133–52; "Indian Camp," 23–43; *in our time*, 8–21; "The Killers," 103–12; "Now I Lay Me," 113–32; repetitions, 16–17, 29–30, 48, 57, 71–73, 76–84, 118–20, 121–22, 138, 140–43, 145–46, 156–57, 163–68, 174, 191, 222–23, 224, 227; "The Snows of Kilimanjaro," 242–47; "A Way You'll Never

Be," 153–86. *See also* addition, revision by; deletions, revision by; replacement, revision by

Reynolds, Michael S., 9–11, 14, 20, 23–24, 44, 52, 61, 67, 86, 96, 115, 120, 136, 188, 209, 252n8, 253n1, 254n3, 255n16, 256n1, 257n9, 258n6, 265n25, 267n1

rhythms/rhythmic repetitions, 46, 48, 49, 50, 51–52, 79, 224, 254n8, 254n11

"Riparto d'Assalto" (Hemingway), 14–15

Rockwell, Norman, 177–78

Romero of *The Sun Also Rises*, 196, 255n15, 266–67n4

Roos, Michael Kim, 1, 79, 163, 257n1, 265n18, 266n25, 266n28

Rosenfeld, Paul, 48

Sacré Coeur, 168–72, 182

Saintes-Maries-de-la-Mer, 136

Salinger, J. D., 180, 266n26

San Dona, 181–82, 265n18

Sargent, John Singer, 263n5

"Savoia" sequence in "A Way," 163–67, 184–85, 263n9

Scenes from Italy's War (Trevelyan), 266n28

Scholes, Robert, 253n5, 268n9

Scientific American, 166–67, 180, 264n13, 265–66n25

Scribner's and Sons, 19, 103, 153, 267n6

Scribner's Magazine, 111, 113, 115, 136, 153, 190, 192, 199, 201–2, 204, 206–7, 259n18

"Sea Change" (Hemingway), 60, 154, 262n1

Sempreora, Margot, 260n4, 261n7, 263n3

sequence of stories and chapters. *See* placement of stories and chapters

Shakespeare, Dorothy, 13, 44

Shakespeare, William, 2, 149, 185

Shakespeare and Company, 9, 22–24, 103

Shapiro, James, 2

Shipman, Evan, 159

similes, 120, 122, 140–42, 168–69, 225, 253n7

Siodmark, Robert, 111, 259n16

"Sirens" chapter of Joyce's *Ulysses*, 218–19

"Sisters, The" (Joyce), 24–43, 67, 253n5

slapstick comedy, 57, 62, 165, 191

smells in "Fathers and Sons," 212–13, 229, 231–33

smells in Joyce's "The Sisters," 33–34

Smiley, Pamela, 261n6

Smith, Paul, 1, 22, 24, 25, 44, 52, 53, 67, 76, 103, 114, 116, 119–20, 133–34, 155, 158, 162, 189, 199, 200, 206, 209, 210, 213, 224, 242–43, 247, 252n1, 256n1, 257n8, 258n12, 259n1, 261n2, 262n11, 264n16. See also *Reader's Guide* (Smith)

Smoky the Cowhorse (James), 189, 192–93

"Snows of Kilimanjaro, The" (Hemingway), 240–47; addition, revision by, 242–47; Delaware transcript, 242–47; deletions, revision by, 243–45; handwritten revisions or drafts, 244; interior monologues, 243, 246; Kennedy Library, manuscript fragments, 246–47; line break, 245–46; paragraph break, 247; penciled draft for the epigraph, 241; replacement, revision by, 243–44; Texas typescript, 242–45

"Soldier's Home" (Hemingway), 48, 66, 261n8, 263n8

Spain, 95

spoken English and Italian in "Cat in the Rain," 52–53

spoken monologues or lectures, 153–55, 158, 162, 174, 176, 185. *See also* "locust" lecture in "A Way"

spoken questions in "Indian Camp," 30–32, 34, 40

spoken words: "The Battler," 99; "Cat in the Rain," 63; "Fathers and Sons," 234; "Hills," 139–40, 142, 145, 150, 152; "Indian Camp," 26; *in our time*, 16–18; "Now I Lay Me," 117; "River," 67, 71; "A Way," 163–64

Stein, Gertrude, 23, 45–52, 56–61, 64, 66, 74, 86, 87, 90, 95–96, 123, 133–34, 137, 248, 252n2, 254n5, 255n15, 255n16, 257n8, 263n7

stereotypes of Mexicans, 192–97, 201, 207–8

stereotypical endings, Westerns, 200–201, 205–6

Stone, Edward, 207

Stoneback, H. R., 1, 255n15, 258n6

"Stories for Next Book" (Hemingway), 114
Strater, Henry, 9
stream-of-consciousness monologues, 154–55, 162–63. *See also* "locust" lecture in "A Way"
Strong, Amy, 268n8
Strychacz, Thomas, 254n3, 258n3, 268n15
"Summer People" (Hemingway), 59, 60, 92, 159, 212
Summit, IL, 104, 112, 258n9
Sun Also Rises, The (Hemingway), 59, 60–61, 90, 103, 108, 113, 134, 174, 196, 252n7, 255n15, 263n7, 266–67n4
Svoboda, Frederic J., 1, 102, 266n4

Tabula, 96–97
tear sheets, 204, 230
"teleferica," 166–68, 180, 264n13
"Ten Indians" (Hemingway), 108, 212, 261n2
Texas Quarterly, 242
Texas typescript of "Snows," 242–45
Thayer, Scofield, 10
third-person narration: "Fathers and Sons," 216, 219, 222–25; "Gambler," 189–92, 194–95, 201–2, 207; "Hills," 137; "River," 69–70, 78; "The Killers," 104–5; "A Way," 156–57
"Three Ambitions" (working title of "Gambler"), 189, 206, 241
"Three-Day Blow, The" (Hemingway), 66, 80, 95
Three Lives (Stein), 56–57, 254n5, 263n7
Three Mountains Press, 9–12, 19–20, 22, 66, 251n3
three-page pencil insert to "Fathers and Sons," 210, 224–30, 231
three-page pencil insert to "River," 68, 72–74, 77, 90, 227
Three Stories and Ten Poems (Hemingway), 22–23, 47
titles, 104, 114, 119, 158, 187, 189, 206–7, 230–39
Toklas, Alice B., 23, 48, 57, 64, 123, 242n2, 255n16
"Tomb of His Grandfather" (Hemingway), 156, 207, 215

"Tomb of My Grandfather" (working title of "Fathers and Sons"), 215–24, 237–39, 241
Toronto, Ontario, 23
Toronto Daily Star, 9–10, 23
Toronto Star, 10, 19, 252n1, 260n3
Torrents of Spring, The (Hemingway), 103
"Towards a Better Understanding" (Knodt), 155
Tower, The (Yeats), 3
Transatlantic Review, 4, 21, 23–24, 25, 37, 46–47, 66, 248, 252n2, 253n5
transition, 136, 141, 143, 145–46, 148–49
Trevelyan, G. M., 266n28
Trogdon, Robert W., 265n24
typescript draft(s), 2, 95, 240–42; "The Battler," 98, 100; "Fathers and Sons," 224–37; "Gambler," 190–207; "Indian Camp," 37; *in our time*, 14, 16–19; "The Killers," 106, 110; "Now I Lay Me," 117–25, 127–29; "River," 69–71, 87, 89–90; "Snows," 241–47; "A Way," 155–64, 167–68, 170–71, 174–80, 184–85, 265n24. *See also* manuscript draft(s) and fragments

Ulysses (Joyce), 4, 8, 11–12, 22, 24, 46, 47, 52, 57–58, 60–61, 64, 96, 172, 218–19, 253–54n2, 254n5, 255n17, 263n7, 267n6
"Undefeated, The" (Hemingway), 113–14, 124, 126, 133, 248
Under Fire (Barbusse), 159, 263n4
"Up in Michigan" (Hemingway), 22, 24, 48, 59, 95, 103, 114

Vandagriff, Susan, 262n1
"Vast Importance of Sleep, The" (Brisbane's column), 125
Vendler, Helen, 2–3
"Very Short Story, A" (Hemingway), 188
"Veteran Visits the Old Front, A" (Hemingway), 260n3, 265n20
vignettes in *Little Review*, 8–13, 24
Virginian, The (film), 197–98, 201
Virginian, The (Wister), 187–88, 190, 194, 200, 204, 205–6

Wagner-Martin, Linda, 64

Walsh, Ernest, 66, 248

war, references to, 266n26; cutting of wartime images in "River," 75, 90; Italian Arditi, 14–15; "Now I Lay Me," 114–20, 125,
127, 130, 260n3; war chapters of *in our
time,* 19; "A Way," 153–86, 266n27

"War in Italy" draft of "A Way," 156–57

war monument in "Cat in the Rain," 45–46,
50–51, 255–56n18

Waste Land, The (Eliot), 8, 12, 16, 44–46

"Way You'll Never Be, A" (Hemingway),
153–86, 206, 230, 239, 240, 249, 263n4,
265n21, 265n23; "bail" in, 165; cave-in,
164–66, 264n12; circular narration, 162;
comedy/humor, 154–55, 160, 165, 176–
82, 184, 186, 266n26; dialogue, 178, 185,
265n18; dream-visions, 182–84, 260n6,
264n16; ending(s), 184–85; "field kitchen"
in, 159–60, 263n4, 263n6; first-person
narration, 156–57; gas masks, 159–60, 170,
263nn4–5; grasshoppers, 154, 176, 178–81,
183, 185, 265n24; hallucinatory sequence,
168–69; handwritten revisions or drafts,
157–60, 163, 166–67, 175, 178, 184; hysteria, 163, 186, 263n8; interior monologues,
153–54, 158, 160, 162–77, 182–86, 263n7,
263n9; "locust" lecture, 157, 174, 176–82,
185; manuscript draft, 176–77; mustard
gas, 158–60, 169–70, 263n4; placement
of, 262n1; postcards, 154, 156–57, 159, 177,
184, 263n4; repetitions, 156–57, 163–68,
174; replacement, revision by, 156, 158, 161;
"Savoia" sequence, 163–67, 184–85, 263n9;
spoken words, 163–64; third-person narration, 156–57; transitions, 177; "War in

Italy" draft, 156–57; yellow house, 169–77,
182–84, 264–65n17, 265nn20–21

Weaver, Harriett, 253n2

West, Kevin R., 255n17, 256n24

Westbrook, Max, 242–47

Western fiction and film/art: stereotypes
of Mexicans, 192–97, 201, 207–8; stereotypical endings, 200–201, 205–6; twist on
the Western shootout, 197–98, 200–201.
See also "The Gambler, the Nun, and the
Radio"

Williams, William Carlos, 20

"Wine of Wyoming" (Hemingway), 187

Winner Take Nothing (Hemingway), 153–54,
156, 158, 166, 181, 190, 195, 198–99, 202–5,
207, 209, 211, 213, 230–39, 241, 248, 262n1,
265n24, 268n15; setting copy used in compiling, 166, 181, 265n24

Wister, Owen, 187–88, 190, 192, 194, 200,
204, 205–6

"Woppian Way, The" (Hemingway), 14

"Work in Progress" (Joyce), 66, 136

World War One Beyond the Trenches exhibition, 263n5

writing arm, Hemingway's, 188–89, 199

Year in the Life of William Shakespeare, A
(Shapiro), 2

Yeats, William Butler, 2–3

yellow house in "A Way," 169–77, 182–84,
264–65n17, 265nn20–21

Yokelson, Josef, 264n16

Young, Philip, 264n17, 265n21

Zenzon, 181–82, 265n18

www.ingramcontent.com/pod-product-compliance
Lightning Source LLC
Chambersburg PA
CBHW020444100426
42812CB00036B/3451/J